Sept. 30–Oct. 1, 2013
Greenville, NC, USA

**Association for
Computing Machinery**

Advancing Computing as a Science & Profession

SIGDOC'13

Proceedings of the 31st ACM International Conference on
Design of Communication

Sponsored by:
ACM SIGDOC

Supported by:
**East Carolina University, Adobe, Madcap Software, Pearson,
Extreme Networks, and Indiana University School
of Informatics & Computing**

**Association for
Computing Machinery**

Advancing Computing as a Science & Profession

The Association for Computing Machinery
2 Penn Plaza, Suite 701
New York, New York 10121-0701

Notice to Past Authors of ACM-Published Articles
ACM intends to create a complete electronic archive of all articles and/or other material previously published by ACM. If you have written a work that has been previously published by ACM in any journal or conference proceedings prior to 1978, or any SIG Newsletter at any time, and you do NOT want this work to appear in the ACM Digital Library, please inform permissions@acm.org, stating the title of the work, the author(s), and where and when published.

ISBN: 978-1-4503-2131-0 (Digital)

ISBN: 978-1-4503-2609-4 (Print)

Additional copies may be ordered prepaid from:

ACM Order Department
PO Box 30777
New York, NY 10087-0777, USA

Phone: 1-800-342-6626 (USA and Canada)
+1-212-626-0500 (Global)
Fax: +1-212-944-1318
E-mail: acmhelp@acm.org
Hours of Operation: 8:30 am – 4:30 pm ET

Printed in the USA

Welcome to the 31st International Conference on the Design of Communication!

Our conference this year provides a premiere opportunity to hear researchers and practitioners share the latest investigations and experiences in the design of communication. Over the two days of the conference, you will interact with an exciting, international group of academic and industry researchers as well as practitioners. Part of SIGDOC's appeal is its mix of researchers and practitioners and the synergy that interaction provides. We look forward to another high-energy conference that will increase the levels of that mixing.

Our program includes many different opportunities to engage with fellow design of communication thinkers, including workshops, papers, panels, experience reports, and posters. The conference program embraces a variety of perspectives, reflecting how the design of communication intersects with the related areas of user experience design, information architecture, interaction design, and documentation. From the many submissions made to the conference this year, we have put together a strong program, with exceptionally high quality work. The varied methods used in the studies discussed this year are intriguing, ranging from large-scale surveys to ethnographies, from deployment studies to discourse analyses. The diversity of perspectives is also mirrored by geographic diversity among contributors.

SIGDOC requires a significant amount of work on several fronts. A team of dedicated individuals has made the conference possible this year. Our success with SIGDOC 2013 is due to the tireless efforts of the chairs, paper reviewers, and student volunteers. Profound thanks to all those who have made this event possible. We also appreciate the financial support received from our generous supporters.

We hope that you will find this program interesting and thought-provoking and that the conference will provide you with a valuable opportunity to share ideas with other researchers and practitioners from around the world. Please enjoy SIGDOC 2013.

Michael J. Albers
SIGDOC '13 General Chair
East Carolina University, USA

Kathie Gossett
SIGDOC '13 Program Chair
Iowa State University, USA

Table of Contents

SIGDOC'13 Papers

SIGDOC'13 Posters

SIGDOC 2013 Conference Organization

General Chair: Michael J. Albers, *East Carolina University*

Program Chair: Katherine Gossett, *Iowa State University*

Webpage: Guiseppe Getto, *East Carolina University*

Workshop Chair: Stewart Whittemore, *Auburn University*

Treasurer: David Jones, *The Nerdery*

Program Committee:
Michael Albers, *East Carolina University*
Kathie Gossett, *Iowa State University*
Manuela Aparicio, *ISCTE*
Dave Clark, *University of Wisconsin-Milwaukee*
Carlos Costa, *ISCTE, IUL*
David Christensen, *Utah State University*
Renata Fortes, *University of Sao Paulo*
Kathy Haramundanis, *Hewlett-Packard*
William Hart-Davidson, *Michigan State University*
Maurice Hendrix, *Serious Games Institute*
Johndan Johnson-Eilola, *Clarkson University*
Dave Jones, *The Nerdery*
Fotis Liarokapis, *Coventry University*
Rudy McDaniel, *University of Central Florida*
Brian McNely, *University of Kentucky*
Brad Mehlenbacher, *North Carolina State University*
Ryan Moeller, *Utah State University*
Arthur Money, *Brunel University, London*
David Novick, *University of Texas-El Paso*
Robert Pierce, *IBM*
Liza Potts, *Michigan State University*
Stuart Selber, *Pennsylvania State University*
Clay Spinuzzi, *University of Texas at Austin*
John Stamey, *Coastal Carolina University*
Jason Swarts, *North Carolina State University*
Christa Teston, *University of Idaho*
Rebecca Walton, *Utah State University*
Stewart Whittemore, *Auburn University*
Marco Winckler, *University Paul Sabatier*

SIGDOC 2013 Sponsor & Supporters

Sponsor:

S I G D O C
Special Interest Group on
Design of Communication

Supporters:

East Carolina
UNIVERSITY

Adobe

madcap
software

PEARSON

extreme
networks™

SCHOOL OF INFORMATICS
AND COMPUTING
INDIANA UNIVERSITY
IUPUI

Contributors:

O'REILLY®

CRC PRESS
Taylor & Francis Group

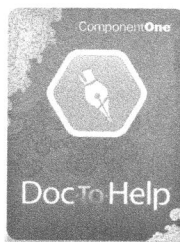

ComponentOne
DocToHelp

Use of 5E Models to Enhance User Experience

Michael J. Albers
Department of English
East Carolina University
Greenville, NC 27858

albersm@ecu.edu

ABSTRACT

Understanding the terminology used by different user groups as they interact with a system's information is a primary focus of information analysis. User terminology directly reflects audience groups' mental models, how they perceive the overall situation, and how their needs differ from other groups. The web of mappings of terminology between user groups and system interaction goals provides a path to developing a 5E model that can be carried forward into the design process. During the early information analysis, the designers and user experience people have to analyze multiple audiences, create personas, create a 5E model for each persona, and then resolve and merge the differences so that the final design works for all audiences. Building 5E models for multiple audiences provides a method to optimize across those audiences.

Categories and Subject Descriptors

H.0 Information Systems: General

Keywords

Information relationships, information design, human-centered design, technical communication,5E models

1. INTRODUCTION

Some years ago, HCI researcher Panu Korhonen of Nokia outlined to me how HCI is changing, as follows: In the early days the Nokia HCI people were told "Please evaluate our user interface, and make it easy to use." That gave way to "Please help us design this user interface so that it is easy to use." That, in turn, led to a request: "Please help us find what the users really need so that we know how to design this user interface." And now, the engineers are pleading with us: "Look at this area for the 21st century, centered on the exploration of new forms of living with and through technologies that give primacy to human actors, their values, and their activities [6, p. 50].

The underlying technology focus of this opening quote reveals what has always caused me trouble with many ideas and methods of information analysis. They tend to focus on "with and through technologies" rather than ways of comprehending and understanding information. The technology has privileged status rather than the technology being viewed as a means to enable comprehension. Privileged status should be given to methods of communicating information, with the technology only being a part of those methods. An important element that needs to be addressed for complex systems is that a straightforward view of technology serving information to a user fails to capture the full process. Instead, high quality communication depends on the information relationships.

> Defining the information needs in a complex system is about defining the communication required to communicate the information relationships, not individual information elements. It requires thinking about the complexity of the whole rather than the simplicity of the parts. It is about communicating the non-linear, dynamic relationships and not linear cause-effect relationships. It is about understanding how people interact with information. As such, it is about the cognitive and social psychology of people interacting with information and not about either the people or the texts in isolation [4].

The preceding quote brings up an interesting question that often does not seem to be explicitly mentioned (although it exists as an underlying assumption) in the literature about information analysis: "What should be communicated?" With usability testing, the question "Is the user gaining the proper information" is replaced with "Is the user gaining what we are giving them." With open-ended complex information systems, "Is the user gaining the proper information" becomes a deep and complex question that must be explicitly answered. Audience analysis focused on demographics doesn't help since it doesn't capture the information needs. Instead, the information analysis must define the information needs, the information relationships, and the audience terminology [2]. The importance of information needs and relationships are obvious, but the terminology is just as important since the correspondence of content terminology and audience knowledge (terminology) directly affects comprehension.

A complex information system's fundamental design goal is to provide content (and secondarily, create interfaces) that communicate the needed information in an efficient manner that reduces readers' uncertainty, maximizes comprehension, and minimizes cognitive load. These three factors are measured not in terms of the information applied to its current context, but to understanding the overall long-term situation development [3]. A goal of reducing people's uncertainty, maximizing comprehension, and reducing cognitive load must remain a focus throughout the entire content design and development process.

The 5E models (figure 1) [13] help because they give a clear visual that emphasizes relative user priorities about how they need to receive the information. Communication can be considered as occurring as part of a conversation [14]—actually multiple conversations with multiple audiences for any specific document. As part of the cyclical information analysis process, we can develop a 5E model that reflects each of the different audiences (personas) that have been identified. The 5E model helps shape the conversation: What does the reader expect, what information elements do they privilege, what relationships do they expect, and what terminology do they expect within the conversation.

A 5E model has five dimensions: effective, efficient, engaging, error tolerant, and easy to learn. The model must contain all five dimensions since, in reality, they are an integrated whole. However, by splitting them up, the relative sizes of the bubbles directly correlate with their relative importance. Thus, the design team gains a visual that displays all five dimensions balanced for the context. "This model provides a way of understanding the relationship between the content, and its presentation and use, that can guide the creation of the visual presentation, information design, and navigation structure as a unified product that meets user needs" [13, p.100]

Short definitions for each dimension are:

Effective: The completeness and accuracy with which users achieve their goals.

Efficient: The speed (with accuracy) with which users can obtain and comprehend information.

Engaging: The degree to which the tone and style makes the information satisfying to use.

Error tolerant: How well the design prevents errors, or helps with error recovery.

Easy to learn: How well the system supports both initial orientation and deepening understanding of its capabilities.

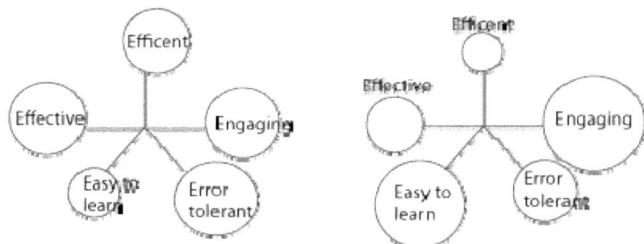

Figure 1. 5E model. The model divides the information analysis into five areas and then sets the relative size of those five areas. The two 5E models shown display the differences required for two different personas within a single project.

Each persona should have its own 5E model. The design team gains a representation that lets them visually compare the different bubble sizes and take them into account on design decisions. The 5E model helps focus design choices because it focuses the design discussions on each of the five bubbles and whether that specific design choice makes sense for this specific 5E model. For example, design changes that would increase the efficiency aspects of an interface may be deemed unnecessary (too time costly for the return on investment) if the efficiency bubble were small.

Within the information analysis process (figure 2), the 5E model is one of the outcomes of the analysis. After the information needs and requirements are collected, a 5E model can be developed for each persona.

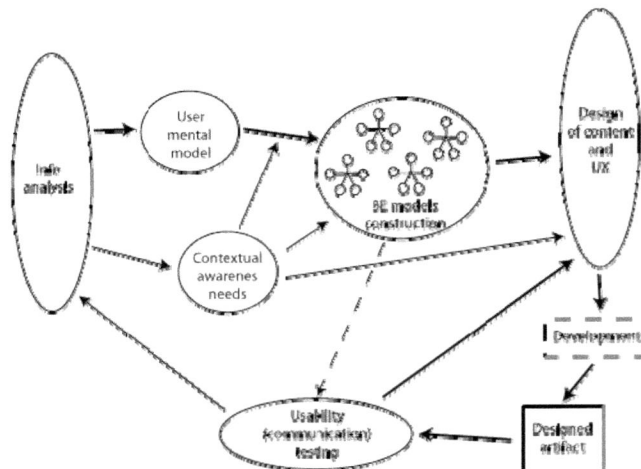

Figure 2. A cyclic information analysis and development process. The 5E model development assists in transforming the information analysis findings into a form that can be used by development and testing.

Clearly, any information analysis methodology strives to capture the needed information. However, the 5E model helps to make the priority differences between personas visually explicit. A strong visual representation of how the various personas differ can help emphasize those differences as they apply to the development process. The various stakeholders within an information development project inevitably have different concerns. The system developers focus on ensuring the system meets the specified requirements. The content developers focus on ensuring the information exists within the system. Management focuses on budget, organizational priorities, and regulatory compliance [7]. Reconciling these different concerns is not a simple task. The use of 5E models can help keep the needs of the different personas up-front in the design decision-making process and keep all of the stakeholders focused on all users.

2. IT'S ALL CONVERSATION

This section returns to the idea briefly introduced in the previous section that all communication can be considered as a conversation. The design and presentation of technical information needs to be thought of not as "providing the information" but as "engaging in a conversation." Written technical communication is an asynchronous conversation, but a conversation never the less. The goal of an information analysis is to predict what information people need and how to present it; in conversation terms, this means determining how a conversation must proceed so that a person gains and comprehends the proper information.

The information analysis should be shaped around how to engage in a conversation. Reshaping the analysis and design questions into conversation terms accentuates the difference between knowing what information a persona needs—a data dump can suffice—and how that information must be presented to maximize comprehension—how to engage in a meaningful conversation.

Technical documentation is written for other people to read. In the end, a conversation is all stories and terminology that have a purpose [14]. A meaningful conversation revolves around *purpose:* the goals, why, what, how. It requires the use of terms both parties understand. Thus, thinking of the communication situation as a conversation leads directly to thinking about the terminology requirements. Developing a good 5E model provides a means of capturing the important elements that address the purpose of the conversation.

3. (IR) RATIONAL VIEW OF INTERACTION

An unstated assumption deeply rooted into almost every information analysis is the base assumption that people operate in a situation in a rational manner. In this context, rational behavior means that people attempt to make choices aimed at an *optimal* level of benefit; that they always strive to make the *best* choice. Society values rational behavior and the analysis assumes a rational reading and interaction behavior.

Thus, people are expected to engage in the conversation by accepting the information and processing it rationally. There is the assumption that their thought processes will be internal consistent, clearly specified relationships will lead to achieving the overall goals, and the information will be properly connected to the environment. This creates an orderly and predictable train of thought that leads to an optimal answer. But this also leads to problems with system implementation.

- Groupthink can develop.

- Any innovation for trying to solve a problem can be suppressed and the problem solver is limited to the actions and knowledge that created the problem.

- People's decision making process is not rational. They are not internally consistent and may pursue side goals that are not within the main goal stream. For example: a manager making decisions that benefit their department but may cost the overall company more money.

- Fragmentation of goals across the organization cause rational action for one group to appear irrational for another.

The assumption of rational behavior forms the basis of many decision making studies [8]. But can design teams really operate from this view and assume rational human-information interaction (HII)? Unfortunately, people do not tend to operate in a fully rational manner, but engage in a naturalistic approach to decision making [11]. The psychology of decision making has long since dispelled the idea that people are rational decision makers; an approach that carries over to their interaction with any complex information situation. That is borne out by many post hoc analyses of accidents and other incidents that arise from poor decisions. The people had the information available and often acknowledge having known it, but they ignored it for a wide variety of reasons. Interestingly, most of the reasons make sense when viewed within the context of the situation at the time the interaction occurred. It is only with hindsight that the problems and irrationalness became apparent.

One element in the lack of rational decision-making behavior is that people self-define what information they consider important and how much information they are willing to consider. A view that typically is highly local to the situation, while the decision itself sets off ripples that extend beyond the sphere of information initially considered.

People have to draw the lines around the information to limit it to a manageable amount. However, the limits they define do not necessarily conform to the amount needed to fully comprehend the situation and build the contextual awareness. Limiting the boundary makes it easy to analyze, but harder to see the future ripple effects of any decision. The limits also make it easier to drift since the boundaries get redrawn with each decision, which leads to drift; in other words, the renormalization of the person's worldview so it always sits at the center of what is deemed important.

From an information analysis perspective, this leads to problems in determining the appropriate levels of abstraction to use when analyzing and describing complex informational systems or socio-technical systems [5]. Rather than using different terms to describe the same thing, though, here we are talking about people working within the same situation but using different levels of abstraction, often based on drawing the boundaries of the situation differently [7]. Of course, if different groups are using different terms and drawing boundaries differently, then the analysis is doubly difficult. Failing to fully study each of the personas can lead to an analysis that assumes one set of boundaries (one persona) applies to all personas.

4. FITTING 5E MODELS INTO THE DESIGN TEAM DECISION PROCESS

Use of 5E models can help to overcome the issues of irrational decision making and help to ensure that people receive the information they need in a manner that maximizes communication.

Figure 3 shows a loop where people search through all of the available information, pull out what they believe is relevant, build the relationships between that relevant information so they can understand the situation, and finally make a decision. That decision results in the situation changing and, consequently, the available information changing, which starts the decision cycle over.

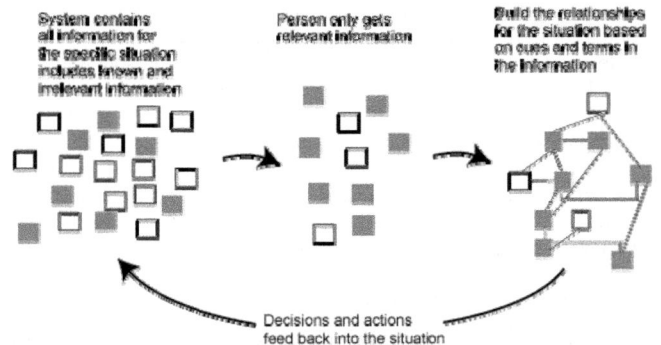

Figure 3. Extracting information and building relationships. After the system provides the relevant information, then the person must mentally process it and build the information relationships based on the cues and terminology within the information.

Figure 3 shows the decision-making process from the reader's viewpoint, but a design team works from a different viewpoint. They need to make decisions about what content goes into each of the small boxes (information elements) and what affordances and terminology within that information cue the relationships. A design team can easily succumb to time or other pressures and create a design for only one persona or attempt a generic one-size-fits-all. Being forced to address the designs issues raised by the 5E models can help keep the design team focused on the information needs of all personas and prevent tunnel vision.

The 5E model is part of the analysis process, not part of the user's decision making process. Figure 4 reveals how the 5E models assists a design team to make content decisions. Although a 5E model can't help eliminate a design team's external pressures, it can make explicit the needs of different personas within each of the small boxes. The proper terminology and the cues to form information relationships need to exist within each information element and need to be shaped for each persona.

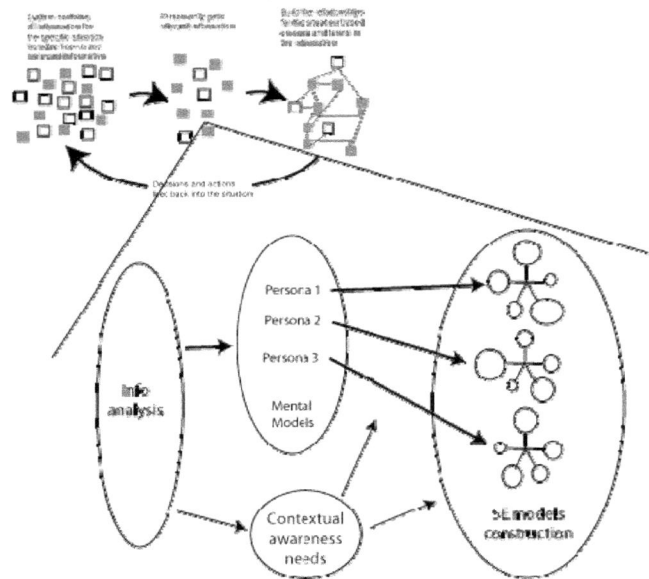

Figure 4. Fitting the 5E model into each information element. For each information element, the design team needs to consider how the 5E model fits into the persona needs so that the information will fit those needs.

The 5E models that result from the information analysis help content design and development to ensure that the user's decision cycle moves as smoothly as possible. When a person interacts with information, they can only extract information and build relationships if the information is presented in terms they understand; in other words, using their terminology. This statement is nothing new. For many years the technical communication literature has said content must be in user terms. However, it typically then only makes vague references to how to learn and incorporate those user terms within the information analysis. Developing terminology requirements as part of constructing a 5E model can help to pull aside that vague veil.

Many systems are under-utilized because they introduce ways of working that conflict with other aspects of a person's job. Either this can be a real conflict where procedures or information flow conflict with how the work must be done, or it can be a terminology conflict where poor design has introduced term changes that fail to be meaningful to the user. Or, worse, they may introduce a term for a concept where that term already has an explicit meaning for a different concept. One source of the problem of under-utilized systems arises because information analysis is a complex operation within the socio-technical issues that revolve around effectively communicating information. Unfortunately, it tends to be over-simplified.

For example, information analysis often assumes a few interviews with subject matter experts can provide all of the answers. However, experts often give their information needs at a data level (the individual values they look at). This fails to capture the implicit mental integration they perform with that data. On the other hand, it makes design and development easy since it only requires dumping data. However, information analysis interviews also need to probe how the data is used, why they need specific information, what key terms make it salient, how they build

relationships, and in what order it is needed. Designs that support building higher levels of contextual awareness depend on providing integrated information.

Interviewing the subject matter experts may provide the information needs but is not sufficient for designing a system that supports multiple personas. Even beyond the different experience/knowledge level and roles, different personas can have different terms for the same information needs and build different relationships. Mapping between the terminologies used by the different personas is an important element of information analysis. Comprehension will be higher and cognitive load lower if a reader doesn't have to mentally translate terms.

5. INFORMATION ANALYSIS AND 5E MODELS

Most technical communicators describe their job as providing proper information to fit the reader's information needs. This job description raises the question of what is meant by information. Drucker [9] argued that "Information is data imbued with relevance and purpose" (p. 5), a definition closely related to common data, information, and knowledge hierarchies [1]. Dissecting the final two terms of Drucker's statement, *relevance* means more than just being relevant to the situation, but also being relevant to the reader's current knowledge state. If a piece of information is already known, then it is not relevant. This does not mean that it is not important to know the information, but since it is already known, it is not relevant to provide it to the reader. Likewise for *purpose*; data that fails to help the reader build an appropriate view fails to fit the purpose [3]. Communication is a conversation; the conversation must consider the purpose.

Many design teams privilege a mantra of technical communication: "make the information as simple as possible." On the surface, this is good advice, but a significant problem is that many times "as simple as possible" is interpreted as meaning anybody can use it (write so anyone can understand it). However, many texts are not intended for "anyone" as readers. A government form must be understood by a random person, but a business report should not be written for a novice in marketing or finance. The terminology needed for "anyone" is not the terminology needed for the finance person. Or, in general terms, the terminology must be appropriate for the personas; it only needs to be appropriate for the general public if they *are* one of the personas.

Some of the blame for the "as simple as possible" mantra misunderstanding arises because technical communication too often assumes a Platonic ideal of an audience that describes individual behavior in one situation. At best, this assumption only applies to closed situations that can be fully defined. Although individual behavior in one situation makes the terminology decisions simple, this behavior does not exist in real-world situations. Non-trivial information interaction occurs within open-ended complex situations. In addition to rendering irrelevant the question "do we have all the information?" it also prevents fully diagramming a search or task path and brings the design team face to face with irrational decision making behavior.

> When an individual or an organization seeks to attain a goal within a completely closed system, it is possible in principle for a complete knowledge of the system and of its options and probabilities to be obtained, so that a completely rational pattern of response can be drawn up....In most real life situations, however, and particularly

in the face of the most important problems to which decision-makers are required to address themselves, the issue is much less simple; for, in such cases, they usually deal with open systems in which they are unable to gain a complete knowledge of the implications of one action as a set against those of another [15, p. 134].

Decisions and actions within complex situations are not repeatable since they depend on past situation history. Design teams cannot assume there is a single input and output—a valid assumption in a simple situation. Complex situations contain multiple audiences, multiple inputs and outputs, and the requirements of any one element may contradict or conflict with the requirements of other elements. Simple situations are easy to study (and fits most laboratory studies), but by not dealing with the multiple inputs and outputs and the interrelationships, miss the real critical issues in a communication situation. I will grant that this is a very messy process to study; technical communication needs some dedicated research projects into how to perform it and make sense of it.

Using a 5E model can help prevent information analysis from falling into an assumption that having information available or not available is sufficient. Besides being over-simplistic at many levels, an available/not-available binary fails to consider the HII issues that support comprehension. Even when the information is placed in the proper location within the text, there are many factors that can prevent a person from fully comprehending it. They may not realize its significance, they may be skimming and it lacks salience, they may not know they need that information, or it might conflict with prior knowledge. In addition, a design team needs to remember that all of these factors get multiplied by the number of personas. The proper design answer for each persona is different even if the base information remains the same.

6. USABILITY AND TESTING ISSUES

A difficulty in usability testing is how to replicate the proper stress and cognitive load levels of the actual situation. Hailey's [10] findings call into question how well even usability people can evaluate the contextual level of the information, primarily because the field lacks a clear model of how to do so. The effect here can be very profound with expert level testing. Through their experience and training, they know how to analyze the information. However, in a high cognitive load situation, they may forget or not attend to non-visible information. Also, non-information factors, such as corporate politics, will come into play in the real situation, but will be ignored in a testing situation. These problems are understood by any experienced usability tester, but addressing them is difficult.

Usability testing of complex information involves a more tightly woven interaction than of simple information. It is not a matter of clicks or knowing if a person can find individual information elements. Usability test design must confront the issue that, as people evaluate complex information to gain knowledge, they do not follow a clean linear path suitable for a procedural text. Rather than looking up single elements, a person needs to find and integrate several pieces of information [12]. The small squares in figure 3 are the individual information elements, but the usability needs to determine if people are building the web of relationships.

Using a 5E model helps to both develop a test that takes these issues into account and to interpret the results. For example, if the efficient bubble was different between personas, the importance of the time required to comprehend the information would differ. Likewise, different sized easy to learn bubbles would mean

different interpretations of interaction difficulties that arise from learning issues.

7. CONCLUSION

The most important job of a design team is to determine if the proper information, both content and quantity, has been provided with the proper presentation. The design team needs to answer the question "how to determine if a text has the proper amount of information?" In particular, they need to ensure the system is not including too much or too little information. There is a large gap between knowing a persona's information needs and defining the appropriate terminology and presentation to communicate that information.

The 5E model helps the design team fit the goals to the environment of the reader. "People never act in a vacuum: they must achieve their goals in the environments in which they find themselves, and their success or failure depends to a great extent upon the degree to which their environment is congenial to their goals" [15, p. 109]. Defining the relative size of the 5E bubbles requires consideration of both the situation and the persona. Unfortunately, both situation and personas are complex entities themselves, and the relative sizes of the bubbles vary in response to situations changes.

To paraphrase Norman, "if the user can't find the information or comprehend it, then it's not in the system." Many design teams fall back on variations of "The information is right here" or "The information is correct" followed by "we can't help it if the user can't understand it." Sorry, but it is the design team's fault for creating and displaying content that fails to support a person's needs. People do not need perfect or complete knowledge, all they need is information that is accurate enough for their current situation to enable them to move toward their goal. Design teams can never fully answer how much is enough until after the fact—typically after a major failure which leads to a postmortem study—but they have to make a good attempt at it.

Creating high quality 5E models as part of the information analysis will result in higher quality design, development, and testing. The user terminology will have been captured and the relative use and importance of that terminology will have been apportioned within the model. Creating individual models for each persona allows for comparison and ensuring all information elements are designed to communication with all relevant personas.

8. REFERENCES

[1] Albers, M. (2004). Communication of Complex Information: User Goals and Information Needs for Dynamic Web Information. Mahwah, NJ: Erlbaum.

[2] Albers, M. (2010). Usability and information relationships: Considering content relationships when testing complex information. In M. Albers & B. Still. (Eds). Usability of Complex Information Systems: Evaluation of User Interaction (109–132). Boca Ratan, Fl: CRC Press.

[3] Albers, M. (2012a). Communication as reducing uncertainty. 30th Annual International Conference on Design of Communication. Seattle, WA. October 4–5, 2012.

[4] Albers, M.(2012b). Information analysis: A complex socio-technical problem. Presented at Symposium on Communicating Complex Information. Greenville, NC. February 24-25, 2012.

[5]   Avgerou, C. (2001). The significance of context in information systems and organizational change. *Information Systems Journal 11*, 43–63

[6]   Bannon, L. (2011). Reimaging HCI: Toward a more human-centered perspective. Interactions 13.4, 50–57.

[7]   Baxter, G. & Sommerville, I. (2011). Socio-technical systems: From design methods to systems engineering. Interacting with Computers 23, 4–17

[8]   Dekker, S. (2011). Drift into Failure: From Hunting Broken Components to Understanding Complex Systems. Burlington, VT: Ashgate.

[9]   Drucker, P. (1998). The coming of the new organization. Harvard Business Review on Knowledge Management. (pp.1–19.). Boston: Harvard Business School Publishing.

[10] Hailey, D. (2010)   Combining rhetorical theory with usability theory to evaluate quality of writing in web-based texts. In M. Albers & B. Still. (Eds). Usability of Complex Information Systems: Evaluation of User Interaction (17–46). Boca Ratan, Fl: CRC Press.

[11] Klein, G. (1999). Sources of Power: How People Make Decisions. Cambridge, MA: MIT.

[12] Morrison, J., Pirolli, P., & Card, S. (2001). A taxonomic analysis of what world wide web activities significantly impact people's decisions and actions. Presented at the Association for Computing Machinery's Conference on Human Factors in Computing Systems, Seattle. March 31 - April 5, 2001.

[13] Quesenbery, W. (2002). Dimensions of usability. In Albers, M. & B. Mazur. (Eds). Content and Complexity: Information Design in Technical Communication (pp. 81–102). Mahwah, NJ: Erlbaum.

[14] Redish, J. (2013). Purposes, personas, conversations. Presented at the STC Technical Communication Summit. Atlanta GA. May 6–8, 2013.

[15] Turner, B. & Pigeon, N. (1997). Man Made Disasters. Oxford, UK: Butterworth-Heinemann.

A Customized Mobile Application for a Cerebral Palsy User

Luciana Correia
Lima de Faria
Borges
UFMT-IC–LAVI EP-USP
Av. Fernando Correa
Costa, 2.367, Cuiabá,
MT-Brasil, 55 065
81327452, 78.060-900
lucianafariaborges
@gmail.com

Lucia Vilela Leite
Filgueiras
EP- USP
Av. Prof. Luciano
Gualberto,158, São
Paulo, SP-Brasil, 05508-
900
lucia.filgueiras@poli.
usp.br

Cristiano Maciel
UFMT - IC –LAVI
Av. Fernando Correa da
Costa,2.367
Cuiabá, MT-Brasil
cmaciel@ufmt.br

Vinicius Carvalho
Pereira
UFMT – IL - LAVI
Av. Fernando Correa da
Costa,2.367
Cuiabá, MT-Brasil
vinicius.carpe@yahoo.fr

ABSTRACT

Mobile web has created several opportunities for the development of assistive technologies that can support disabled people in the performance of daily life activities. Mobile applications can be developed using participatory design methods which result in customized assistive solutions. In this paper, we describe the development of a mobile application to support M, a man with cerebral palsy in his communication and professional activities, highlighting the use of a participatory design method. We discuss the changes that mobile web can bring to disabled people´s lives, in the light of this experience. We conclude that mobile web applications can be configured as interesting solutions for assistive technologies.

Categories and Subject Descriptors

H5.m [Information Interfaces and Presentation]: miscellaneous; D.2.10 [Software Engineering]: Design - *Methodologies*

Keywords

Mobile Assistive Technology, Participatory Design, Cerebral Palsy User, Customization

1. INTRODUCTION

Assistive technologies are focused on assisting people with impairments in their limitations so as to provide them with greater autonomy and quality of life.

One can easily notice the large percentage of assistive technology which are proposed in academic papers that end up unused or abandoned, expressing the mismatch between the researchers´ ideas and real users needs. [11, 14]

The present scenario allows observing, however, that such technologies, especially computational ones, tend to be offered in a standardized way. However, when it comes to impaired users,

assistive computational technologies that aid one impaired user will rarely assist another.

Conceiving a solution in customized assistive technology for each impaired user seems to be a way of meeting target users' needs and expectations. This customization is aimed at overcoming barriers that prevent impaired users from using the technology, by expanding their abilities and minimizing their impairments.

In rehabilitation institutions, therapists have to make a series of hardware and software adjustments so that the available

On the other hand, the web is usually seen as an important aid for people with disabilities. Most studies focus on how to design more accessible web sites or tools that can help simplifying designers´ tasks. Researches on adaptations to integrate assistive technologies by web semantic [14,10,16] or improving web accessibility for people with disability [7] are examples of the efforts made by the scientific community to develop this field.

Mobile web has brought a new scenario in which applications can be developed to address disabled people´s needs when they are most needed– in their daily lives, anywhere at any time.

Due to the diversity which characterizes mobile applications, customization may enrich them, because users can pick any combination of applications that is suitable to their needs.

This paper discusses the results of a research that intended to develop a method for including disabled people on the design of their assistive technologies. In this research, besides its target (the participatory design method), we have developed a mobile application for one impaired user. This mobile application is part native, part web-based. We describe herein the participatory design process, emphasizing on how this solution impacted the impaired user´s life.

We chose the action research approach and used a participatory design method – PD4CAT (detailed in section 3) to develop a customized mobile application. This process involved a team composed of three therapists from a rehabilitation institute (an occupational therapist, a psycho-pedagogue and a social assistant), one of their patients, his caregiver, and three computer scientists.

We believe that our experience can influence other researchers in the use of participatory design methods to build inclusive mobile applications.

This paper is organized as follows: Section 2 presents some former developments of mobile applications for disabled users. Section 3 briefly presents aspects of participatory design and describes the adopted method, PD4CAT. Section 4 shows the resulting mobile application, emphasizing mobility requirements derived from the participatory design method. Finally, Section 5 reports changes in the impaired user´s life after the introduction of the mobile application.

2. MOBILE APPLICATIONS FOR DISABELD USERS

Mobility applications for people with special needs are not something new. The available devices and mobile applications are constantly being improved to meet their needs. We can take for instance electronic alternative communicators (e.g. Gotalk Express, Tango, Dyna Write, M³, Maestro) or the modern mobile phones, such as smartphones, which can make provide different applications to support some disabilities.

However, as aforesaid, a major issue is that such applications are mainly offered with little or no possibility of customization to each impaired user´s specific needs.

3. PARTICIPATORY DESIGN OF ASSISTIVE TECHNOLOGY

The characteristic of having the end-user actively involved as a co-designer in his solution design process [12] to reflect his own perspectives and needs [9] has made PD an adequate approach to developing assistive technologies.

In a software development process, participatory design helps to sensitize the development team to the social aspects of the technology under inception. This gives robustness and sustainability to the computational techniques throughout the process and product generated [4].

Our literature review has focused on PD as a mechanism for bridging the gap for people with disabilities. Our review [17] has shown that there is a lack of research in this field, and led our team to the decision to perform an action research in order to develop a participatory design method for developing customized assistive technologies. The studies identified in the review helped us to underpin some criteria for this action research study.

Frauenberger et al. [2] use participatory design to create improvements in a technological learning environment for children, especially those presenting autism and Asperger syndrome.

Garzotto and Bordogna [3] developed a tool for children with serious cognitive impairment, limited body movements and verbal communication.

Hirano et al. [6] and Hayes et al. [5] presented prototypes to aid children suffering from autism.

Prior [13] presented a participatory design experience for adults with communication, cognitive and motor impairment in the CHAMPION project design.

According to McGrenere et al. [8], a small number of aphasic individuals and other expert researchers were involved as stakeholders in a participatory design approach to create customizable software applications for people with aphasia.

Boyd-Graber et al. [1] described a participatory design approach in which proxies (speech language pathologists) assumed the role of stakeholders to develop a system to support people with aphasia.

Among these researches, Frauenberger et al. [2], Prior [13] and McGrenere et al. [8] directly involved end users in participatory design practices. The other ones relied on stakeholders who represented these impaired users, acting as people in charge and designers in these practices. These people in charge were either classmates or specialized professionals, such as neuroscientists, educators, assistive technology experts, therapists, and speech-language pathologists.

It should be stressed that impaired individuals usually count on close persons to act as people in charge, speaking or acting on their behalf.

It should also be emphasized that, in order to allow the inclusion of individuals with severe limitations in design practices, as found in Prior [13], some strategies were applied and some materials adapted. These strategies include creating opportunities for them to talk to the research team, respecting the impaired users´ pace, once they frequently present communication difficulties. Likewise, screen layouts were adapted to a magnet board to allow motor impaired participants in wheelchairs to directly act in user interface mock ups.

During these activities, we verified that in most participatory design processes ice-breaking strategies were preliminarily used to bring researchers, stakeholders and technology together, as well as focal team discussion techniques, interviews and observations.

Advancing in the design process, different techniques were adopted from the requirement gathering stage to rapid prototyping cycles, such as scenarios, brainstorming, low-fidelity prototyping (creating material with paper, drawing, painting, labeling, mock ups with concrete objects and storyboards), and high-fidelity prototypes (generation of links and video animation and software-based prototypes).

These studies show that including people with disabilities in participatory design, especially those whose condition is aggravated by more severe limitations, is still a research challenge. This inclusion effort focusing on a particular disability case is thus discussed herein.

Based on these studies, we have proposed a participatory design method, which we have named PD4CAT – Participatory Design for Customized Assistive Technology.

This method enables to include impaired stakeholders in participatory design practices to conceive their customized assistive technology.

PD4CAT comprises five phases (Figure 1): 1. Team composition; 2. Solution inception; 3. Solution detailed specification; 4. Solution design and Participatory evaluation. There is also the phase of production for participatory design, which does not affect directly the solution product, but supports the other phases in the process, by means of adjusting strategies and necessary artifacts to PD activities Phase 1, Team composition, consists in the initial contacts among computer researchers, health professionals, patients and caregivers. As a result of this phase, a patient and key stakeholders for the PD team are selected to be engaged in the research with PD4CAT, so as to customize the assistive technology to the impaired user needs.

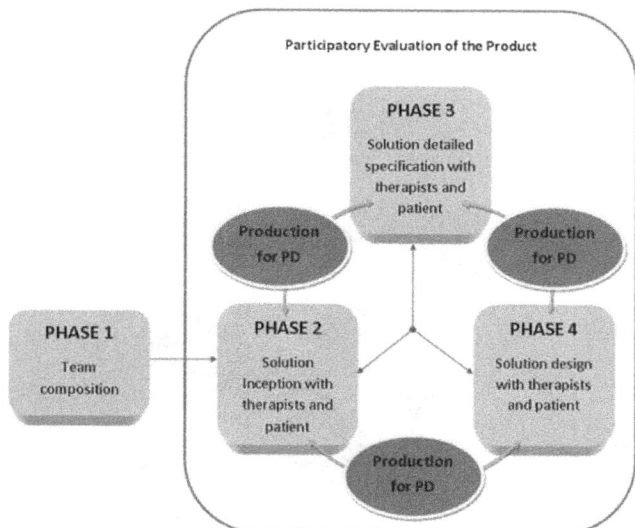

Figure 1. Flowchart of PD4CAT stages

Phase 2, Solution inception, is the product preconception phase, in which the impaired user's context is investigated and his therapeutic and daily needs are detected, in order to identify specific computational solutions for them. As a result of this phase, a high level solution to benefit the impaired user is indicated.

Phase 3, Solution detailed specification, aims to define the details of the solution indicated in phase 2, by means of PD practices with all the stakeholders to meet the end user's needs. By the end of this phase, thee software requirements and the necessary physical adaptations for the solution must be established.

In phase 4, Solution design, the graphic project is defined to conceive a good usability for the interface, by means of PD practices with the stakeholders. By the end of this phase, the interface graphics proposed by the stakeholders in PD practices are produced.

The participatory evaluation phase focuses on assessing the process and the product, and takes place throughout all the aforementioned phases.

The greatest benefit we can derive from PD4CAT is the possibility that an impaired person acts as a co-designer of his/her customized computational solution. To do so, this method adapts PD techniques and combines them with some conventional techniques for software development. In action research cycles, the necessary strategies are discovered for each case, considering the case under study and the involved group.

4. INCEPTING M'S MOBILE APPLICATION WITH PD4CAT

According to the process mentioned in the previous section, a cycle of research-action practices with participatory design was conducted for/with M to discover his customized computational solution.

4.1 Preliminary Perceptions of M by the Therapists

M is 46 years old, presents cerebral palsy sequel, spasticity in the upper and lower limbs, and has a certain handling capacity in his left hand. His oral communication is difficult to understand, being only usually understood by people who have lived with him for a longer period. He presents preserved understanding. He is literate and completed his secondary education.

M's parents are both dead and he lives alone. He manages to eat by himself. He depends on others to bathe, brush his teeth and lie down. He has a caregiver who helps him to lie down at night and, in the morning, she helps him to have a shower and moves him from the bed to the wheelchair. The impaired user has used a motor wheelchair for ten years, moves independently about the city with its aid, takes buses, and works with direct sale products.

M presents great creative potential. Some of the improvisations he made to minimize his limitations were: a PVC tube he carries in his wheelchair and uses to urinate in non-adapted washrooms in town; a bell to warn the bus driver when he needs to get off the bus; an adequately twisted spoon for him to eat by himself.

In addition to that, M has a cell phone permanently connected to an earphone, which he wears the whole day long. The phone call is automatically answered after the second ring, so that M can talk to the person who called him. M is able to pronounce in a clearer fashion pretty short utterances, such as "hello", "bye" and "ok". So, he is able to communicate on the phone with brief answers.

Moreover, he is the active leader of a community that fights for the disabled individuals' cause. He is usually aided by close friends and his caregiver when he needs to communicate with the other members of that community.

M seldom uses two non-mobile computers: one in the rehabilitation institute, and the other in a friend's house. He needs help to do so, for example when he must type or adjust the position of the screen or the keyboard, in order to access them. This is due to his motor impairment, which requires some specific adjustments.

During the therapy, M was found not to know the communication board with the alphabet, and was interested in it. He thus had the opportunity of meeting another patient at the institution who used it. After the meeting, he was surprised to see that such colleague, who is very spastic, could communicate. M then asked the therapists if he could use a resource like that, and expressed satisfaction when one of the therapists answered positively.

In a visit to M's home, it was verified that he could not adapt to the paper board made by the therapists for his case. M reported that he could not carry it all the time in his wheelchair, so as to use it when necessary.

4.2 Listening to M and to his Caregiver

A team of three therapists (an occupational therapist, a psycho-pedagogue, a social assistant) and three computer scientists visited M's home.

In an informal talk with M, only possible to understand due to the caregiver's translation, it was clearly observed that the impaired user needs a device to aid his communication wherever he is.

M says he needs people to understand what he says, as some are very prejudiced and think he is just roaming about, and look down on him. The caregiver confirms this need, telling that one day a man tried to help M on the street, but he pushed the motor wheelchair in a wrong direction, and M could not get rid of the man for being unable to communicate. At that moment, M was in a hurry and needed to catch a bus in the opposite direction; as the man could not understand what he wanted, he hindered M in his activities.

M also talks about the difficulties he faces to move in the city looking for an unknown address, when he needs to take a different bus, for example, get off the bus in the adequate stop and seek an address.

Another fact reported by the caregiver concerning the barriers that M had to face was his water bill, which was only partially paid by him, as the bill came in two installments. In the second month, his water was cut off, and he received a bill charging a much higher value besides the water reconnection fee. M feels limited to claim his rights due to the difficulty in communicating in environments where other people can communicate easily.

The caregiver says there are several other cases in which M has his independence harmed for not being able to communicate anywhere he has to go.

M works with direct sales and says he has about sixteen monthly clients. He makes appointed visits to them. One of the therapists suggests a mock sale. She says "Make believe I'm a client" and asks him how he would conduct the sale with her.

M says he shows a DVD which advertisement and presents the products he sells. Clients, after choosing the product, fill in an order in the company order pad, which he carries along. M demonstrates how he calculates the order price in his calculator (Figure 2) and receives the amount from the client. A friend helps him to order the products by the Internet. M explains that the payment can only be made in cash, and also that he is trying to acquire a credit card terminal.

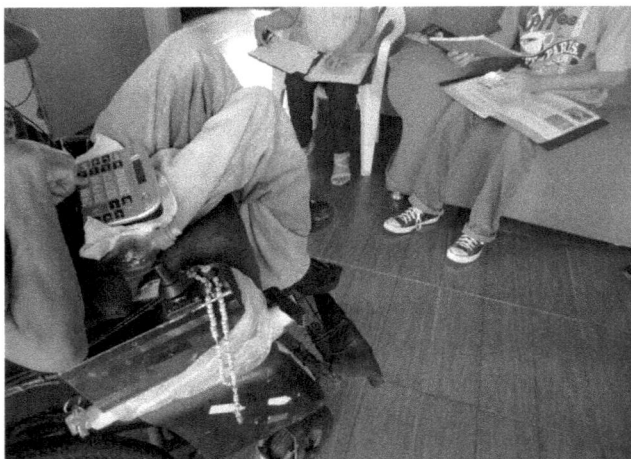

Figure 2: M using his calculator when demonstrating how he conducts a sale.

4.3 Therapeutic Assessments and Simulations with M

Demonstrating how he interacts daily with the objects around him, M shows how he communicates using his cell phone (Figure 3).

The caregiver says he communicates much clearer when talking on the cell phone than in person. Even so, his speech is difficult to understand. M also manages to send cell phone messages, yet he takes a long time, and says he finds it hard to see the letters on the screen. He shows how he uses a magnifying glass to expand the image.

When we show him a touch screen cell phone with a larger screen, M praises the possibility of touching the screen, and says this is easier for him than pressing his cell phone keys.

After that, a test is conducted on a notebook, to check the access possibility on that computer. M prefers to use the mouse, yet he finds it difficult to see the screen. After the developers expand the images on the screen, the difficulty is reduced. M uses a text editor in the notebook, and after adjusting it with the team in a position that allows reading and accessing the keyboard, M types the sentence "I love life a lot", as in Figure 4.

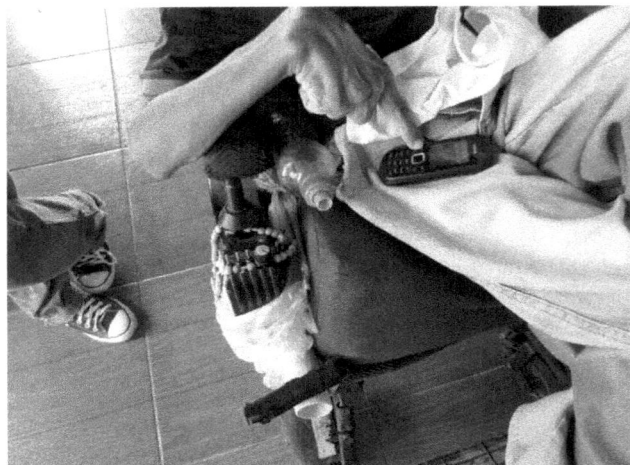

Figure 3. M using his cell phone

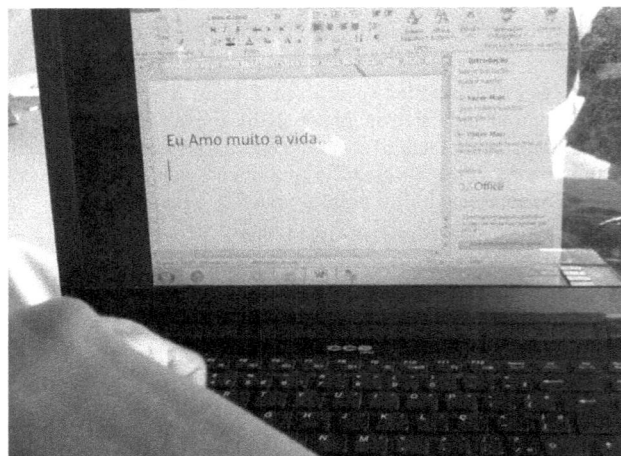

Figure 4. M typing with the notebook text editor

When asked about his experience with the notebook, M expresses the need of having a table on his wheelchair to support his elbow so that he can write or type. M demonstrates with his folder the most adequate position for a possible support table, as in Figure 6.

The impaired user says he needs a notebook as the one he has used, including web access, so that he can go to university.

M access his emails and websites aided by the therapists, a friend or the caregiver. These people help him type and select different resources in personal computers that are not adapted to his motor impairment. He is also helped to read information on the screen if the letters are too small, due to his visual impairment. The therapists and the caregiver comment he wants to go to university very much and an adapted mobile technology accessing web everywhere he goes would be an interesting assistive technology for him.

M adds: "I want an adaptation to help me at the university. I think of studying Law or Business Administration".

M says he needs a table on his wheelchair to help with the arm support and typing with the left hand. But it has to be laterally adjusted so that he can see it from the right angle and it does not interfere with the position of his leg. Again, it must be possible to fold this table when M is not using it.

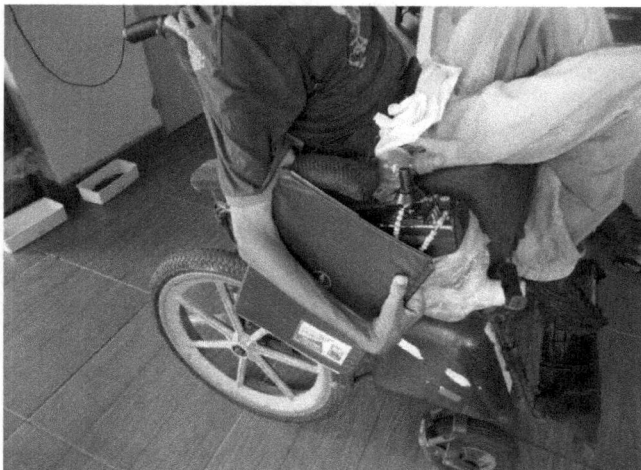

Figure 6. M demonstrating the table mobility on his wheelchair and the ideal height

4.4 Building Materials with the Therapists for PD Practices with M

By means of discussions with the focus group concerning the observations and contacts with M and his caregiver, the therapist team and two of the computer scientists presented the following solution propositions for a set of mobile applications to aid M´s daily life:

1. Communication app: by means of typed messages, the device should aid M's communication, speaking what M types. Messages can be organized as:
   a) Routine messages (the mostly used) – readymade, for daily predictable contexts;
   b) Spokesperson messages - made at home to convey a more detailed message for a specific case, when M is alone on the street. This message will generally have to be composed with the aid of the caregiver, for being more complex for M;
   c) Occasional messages – independently made by M.
2. Sales app: the device should support his salesman work, including:
   a) Mobile web access to show the products advertisement to clients, replacing the DVD which was formerly used;
   b) Mobile web form for ordering products using the internet; Integrated calculator; Cloud-based database with clients' data related to their preferences, and reminders of possible dates for new product purchases;
3. Contact message for setting up the next visit, based on the estimated consumption;
4. Budget control of M's revenues and expenses;
5. Appointment control integrated to a calendar;
6. Daily schedule with sound warnings (reminders);
7. Weekly planning;

Once again, the stakeholders suggested that these resources should be available on a mobile device that could access the web, no matter where M is.

Besides, as M has limited eyesight, some items on the screen have to be read by the software so that he can interact with the resources provided. Thus, the selected items on the screen have to be read aloud by the device screen.

After this idea creation process (idealizing), part of the PD4CAT phase of solution detailed specification, a proposal was made to elicit M's ideas concerning the functionalities of his device, with the aid of the caregiver interpretation. Besides, post-its, blank paper, pens and glue were provided to the whole team, including M and the caregiver, so that they could make some interface prototypes.

4.5 Idealizing and Prototyping with M

A team composed of three therapists (a psycho-pedagogue, a speech therapist, an occupational therapist) and three computer scientists, including a designer, paid a new visit to M.

During the visit, M was given a tablet to assess the possibility of having this mobile computational device available on his wheelchair. A plywood board was also taken to demonstrate how it could be adjusted to the wheelchair, so that the resource did not run the risk of falling down or being out of M's reach.

M oriented the ideal positioning of the table, the board and the tablet again, to warrant his visual and hearing access, besides his interaction with the device. (Figure 7)

The designer made a sketch indicating M's requests as to the proposal of a table adapted to his wheelchair, as in Figure 8.

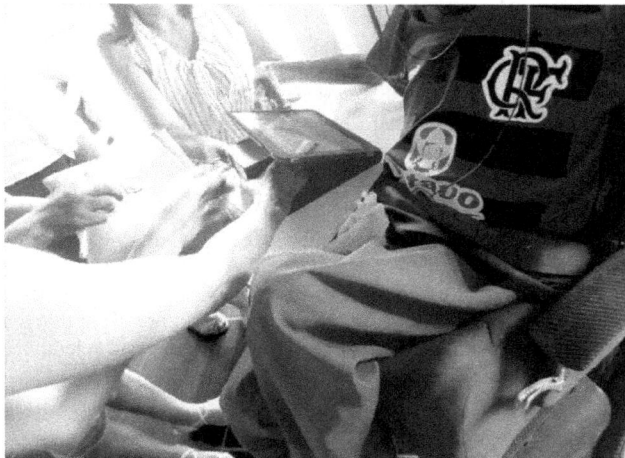

Figure 7. M guiding the tablet and plywood board positioning on his wheelchair

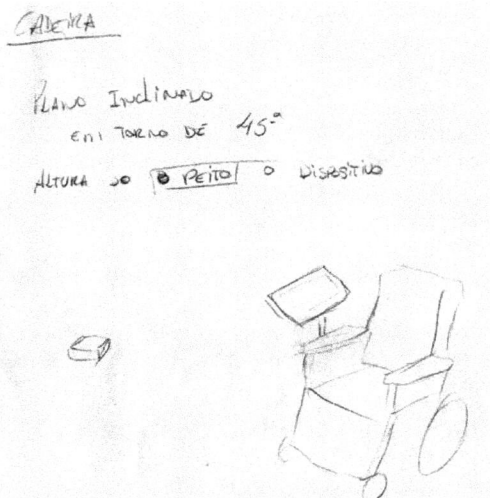

Figure 8. Designer's sketch for the proposed table on M's wheelchair

After different simulated positioning with the device on the plywood board and on the wheelchair, M was asked about what he would like the device to do, and which buttons it should have.

The first thing he suggested was that the device allowed him to show the video for selling his products anywhere close to a potential customer. He also wanted to use the device to receive e-mails from the company he represents, and to talk to clients by means of direct on-line messages. This web access should be available out of his house as well.

M tried to type on the virtual keyboard of a tablet offered by the team, but he found it hard to see the letters he typed, as they were much smaller than the letters on the virtual keyboard of the device. Therefore, the researcher started to read aloud each letter typed by M on the virtual keyboard. M nimbly corrected each typing mistake. In the end, M presented everyone with the complete sentence he typed: "Merry Christmas". Everybody rejoiced and wished one another a merry Christmas.

After this experience, the researcher asked M whether it would be more interesting if the device read aloud each letter typed, to facilitate his visual perception, and he agreed. It was also verified that, due to M's visual impairment, it would be interesting that the device read aloud the screen, at each touch on keys and selections, for M to be guided in his access and interaction.

Then, M asked if the device could also read everything he typed, to help him communicate with people.

The team asked M about his interest on the device automatically showing the most commonly used sentences. He answered positively and exemplified that he often uses "thank you" and "hello".

Furthermore, he said that sometimes he has to ask his caregiver to write down messages for him, which he carries when he goes to his clients' houses. He said this happens when he goes somewhere for the first time. M also showed that he would like these messages to be recorded in the device and that it spoke them on his behalf when activated.

M also revealed he needs a calculator for adding up the products sold. He said he uses the calculator to add his day-to-day expenses as well. He asked someone to write down the numbers, which he added up. "I sometimes learn the values by heart", M said.

M revealed he has a savings account, and that the caregiver types the password into the impaired user's cell phone. M usually goes to the bank by himself and asks a clerk he trusts to conduct the operation he needs. At this point, M suggests that the device could retrieve this password for him, as his cell phone does, but without producing any sound concerning the password.

M would also like a schedule to organize his weekly and daily appointments, with a calendar and an alarm clock.

Besides, he showed to be very excited about the possibility of listening to music. When asked about watching films, he said he does it, but only on TV and sometimes at the movie theater.

As M enlisted his wishes for the solution and assessed the possibilities presented, the team designer, together with one of the researchers, generated interface proposals with the indicated functionalities. In parallel, M indicated where each of the buttons should be, how they should be called and which images they should be represented by.

After some questions to M about his ideas on buttons that expressed the required functions, (e.g. communicating with another person), the designer sketched some drawings the size of a blank piece of paper, so that M could criticize and suggest changes. M also said how he would like the device to read the buttons aloud. For example, the voice synthesizer button should be called "I want to talk to you". Some of the sketches made by the designer, resulting from the PD interactions and M's ideas, are shown in Figures 9 and 10, which improved the solution usability.

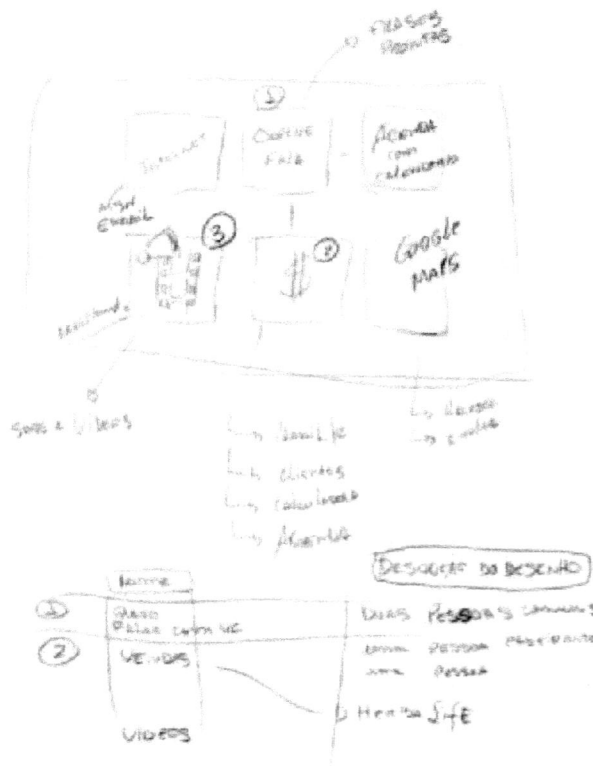

Figure 9. Sketch of the solution requirements on the interface

Figure 10. Sketch of the "I want to talk to you" icon

4.6 M's mobile solution

As a result from the process herein described, which was integrated by the impaired target user, a computational solution was developed to warrant M mobile access to the web and to help him in work and daily situations, which include mobility, communication, positioning and entertainment aspects. After the design process to conceive the solution, the computer scientists implemented it. In a cycle of participatory assessment, the stakeholders presented suggestions for improvement, so as to meet M's needs, which led back to the implementation process.

Figure 11 depicts the main interface of the solution proposed for M.

Figure 11. Main interface of the solution for a tablet

Some of these solution functionalities are presented hereafter.

To support the communication of the verbally impaired user, the button "I want to talk to you" (Figure 11) can reproduce by synthesized voice any typed text (Figure 12).

The option Save (Figure 12) enables the impaired user or a caregiver to save longer messages for later use, when the user needs to engage in real-time communication.

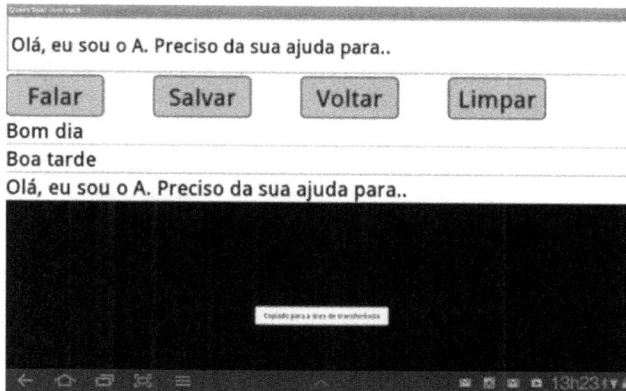

Figure 12: Functionality "I want to talk to you".

The designed solution permits direct and fast access to an automatic map positioning application on the web (Figure 13), so that the user can find any address he needs.

Figure 13: Accessing the location aid of the solution

The user can also access the advertising videos for his products on the web, so as to show them to any person, no matter where he is (Figure 14).

Figure 14: Accessing advertising videos with the solution.

The solution also enables the impaired user to schedule on the web his daily and professional appointments (Figure 15), being reminded of them by sound alarms, in the set date and time. Such resources are available on the cloud.

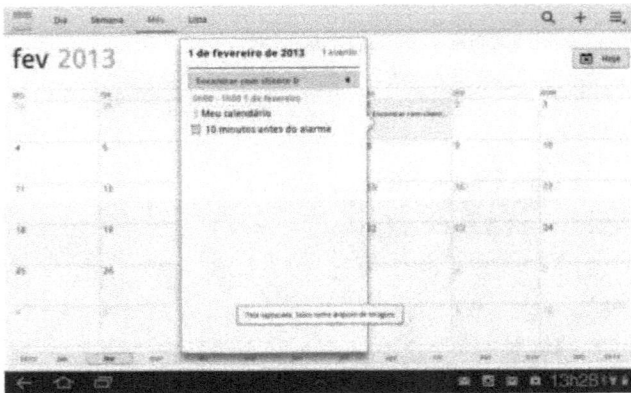
Figure 15: Appointments schedule.

Besides, the solution enables, by means of cloud computing, the control and updating of Ms clients' data, anywhere at any time (Figure 16). In this functionality, the user is also aided to calculate the values of each sale, by accessing the icon "Calculator" on Figure 16.

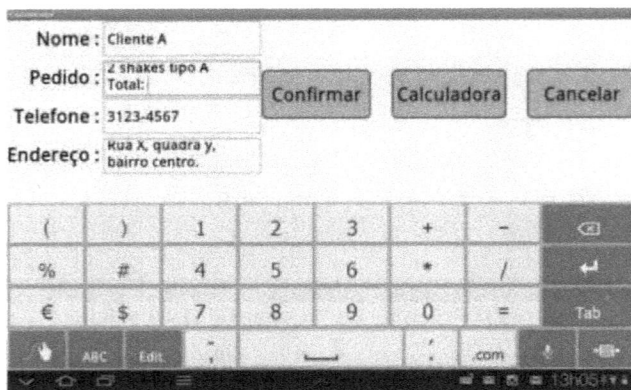
Figure 16: Controlling clients' data with the solution.

5. ADAPTING THE ASSISTIVE TECHNOLOGY TO OVERCOME USERS' BARRIERS

The hardware and the software were adapted to overcome some of the user's barriers, in order to allow him to access the resources of the mobile solution in his day by day and work contexts.

The barrier of his low sight was overcome by implementing a screen reader in the solution. Besides, with the aid of the impaired user as a designer, we designed interfaces accessible to his sight, by exploring shapes, sizes and colors that best fitted his needs.

The barrier of his low hearing was overcome by providing a device that enabled volume adjustments to the tone the target user needed, whether indoors or outdoors.

The barrier of his functional limbs motor limitations was overcome by providing the user with a good-sized virtual keyboard. A touch screen was chosen for demanding less effort to type. A word predictor was adapted to all textboxes in the solution, in order to help the user type correctly.

In addition to that, we added a resource to save longer messages M has typed, so that he can reuse them later on, instead of typing them all again.

Finally, the communication barrier was overcome by means of the functionality "I want to talk to you", which allows the user to express himself with typed texts, as mentioned before.

Nowadays, using the designed mobile solution, M can talk to strangers anywhere, at any time, not depending on his caregiver to do so. Therefore, he is more independent in his sales work and in general social interactions. The device permits him to type what he needs to say, speaking on his behalf in a way all people can understand.

It is important to notice that, before using the device, M´s communication was very precarious, so that he could only be understood by people who knew him very well or with the aid of his caregiver. This limited his independence and autonomy in daily and work activities.

Now, with the designed solution, M is helped to find any address he is looking for, no matter where he is. This functionality is especially important when he needs to take a bus or visit new clients, which is a must in his job. This technology permits M to do these things safely, independently and fast.

Besides, when he gets to a client´s house, he doesn´t need any more to use the client´s DVD player or VCR to show his advertisement videos. Instead, he can now show these videos or any advertising material in his tablet, irrespective of where he is, which enhances his sale chances.

In the past, if a client got interested in one of the products sold by M, the client himself had to fill in a form with his personal data and those of the desired product. Then, M went to a friend´s house, where she typed the order for him in the firm website. Now, M can do it all on his own, at the moment of the sale, no matter where he and the client are.

The after-sales support and the contact with the clients used to be guided by the notes taken by M´s caregiver. This included the estimated dates for the next sales (based on the amount of product bought by each client), and the control of payments to receive and bills to pay.

Now, M masters his own schedule independently, and it has sound alarms to remind him of his appointments, income, bills and invoices.

6. DISCUSSIONS AND RECOMMENDATIONS FOR THE PROCESS WITH PD4CAT

From the observation and engagement in the PD experiences with the stakeholders' group, at each of the process phases presented by Figure 1, reflections and recommendations for this process are listed as follows.

In the initial contact phase, it was verified that the impaired user and the caregiver trust easier in the proposal presented by the computer scientists if it is introduced by the therapists.

Still in the preliminary phases, ethnographic based observations have shown to be fundamental to bring computer scientists closer to the impaired user's universe. It allows these professionals to adapt to his or her context, ensuring a more consistent exploration of the PD practices with the stakeholders.

In later phases, it is important that observations, interviews and other activities reveal as many patients' characteristics and possibilities as possible, such as: what his environment is like, his needs, desires, abilities, limitations, experiences, how he relates with the people around him, what resources he would like, what rehabilitation perspectives he has. The more information revealed, the closer the approach to the impaired user's universe, which favors the emergence of adequate solutions, both for the prototypes idealized by impaired user, and for the activities and resources proposed in the PD practices.

The therapists and the caregiver were fundamental members in the team to favor the impaired user's inclusion, once they minimized M's communication and mobility constraints, and showed ways to understand his manifestations, also allowing his participation in the conception and the building of materials. It is also worth stressing that the ideas proposed by the therapists, before the practices with the impaired user, were very close to the ideas proposed by M. From our view, this expresses a therapist-patient state of empathy attained along the coexistence time in the therapy, which should be valued in the process.

Hence, at each phase, it shows to be adequate and recommended to first conduct practices with the therapist team, aiming at the conception of PD practices to be used with the impaired user, once the team is knowledgeable about the patient's abilities and constraints. This will certainly boost his engagement in the activities.

After the practice(s) with the therapy team for building artifacts, the therapy team and the caregiver should be included in the practices with the patient, so that the computer professional can learn faster how to communicate with the patient, despite his constraints. It is recommendable for a computer professional, even as a process moderator, to adopt an observer-learner attitude as to the therapist-patient-caregiver relationship.

The collection of requirements for the impaired user's solution should not be explored in a fragmented way, that is, focusing solely on software or hardware functionalities, or on mechanical issues. Practices allowing the freedom of expression of each member of the multidisciplinary team should be provided, in an attitude that values and respects divergence, at the same time as it seeks a consensus. Providing such freedom of expression, associated to metaphors related to the impaired user's context and focusing on a practical solution for his case, shows to be very fruitful.

As from a preliminary planning concerning the strategies to be adopted with the impaired user focused on the PD practices, the therapists have the potential to aid in the choice and necessary adjustments. However, only through practice and direct contact with the impaired user can the success of the choice and adjustments be verified. At each practice with the impaired user, strategy alternatives have to be taken into account, so that the time with the impaired user can be used to the most, in case the previously chosen strategies fail to work.

The more time the group spends with the impaired user, the greater the team's experience is, and the greater the success chances are in terms of proposals for more adequate and refined activities for the impaired user. Yet, at each session, it is of the utmost importance to respect the impaired user's need to rest as well as that of the team, so that work flows in a relaxed and pleasurable way.

Once a relaxing, pleasurable and free atmosphere manages to be developed, the team's empathy and availability is naturally expanded. This happened to the herein presented stakeholder team, who, even away from the meetings, kept seeking ideas and solutions to the issues investigated during the practices.

Documenting each session in a field journal, reports, and video recordings was fundamental for the useful information not to be lost in the process or over time. At each subsequent practice, an initial activity for recapitulating what was surveyed and chosen at the previous session proved to be worthwhile.

At each participation opportunity for the team members, especially the computer scientists, their commitment and involvement with the project were noticed to increase.

The video recordings or just bits of them have been very useful to be presented to team members that were absent in a certain practice and needed to have a better understanding of what had been explored. This resource also proved useful to stimulate stakeholders who were absent at one of the PD practices.

7. CONCLUSIONS

From the experience we got from this field research, we can realize an urgent want for customized assistive technologies for impaired people. Such need was met in M´s case.

Customizing the technology was crucial to enable the target user to use it according to his needs. The differentiator of this work was the fact that we focused on participatory design to engage the impaired user as a co-designer, so as to warrant the necessary customization.

As a result from this process, we got to an assistive technology solution that allowed the necessary adaptations to web and cloud access, also considering functional needs posed by the target user and the other stakeholders.

We can see that the web-based ubiquitous resources of the solution help M in his daily and work activities, at any time, wherever he is. Examples of such adapted web resources include map location aid, cloud-based control of clients' database and appointments. Such resources increased M's independence.

M states that he is very satisfied with the support he is getting from the mobile solution to overcome his needs. He now says that he would like the solution to help him communicate in English, which would allow him to give lectures abroad, representing the company he works for.

The continuous assessment of the customized mobile solution in M´s day by day leads to future works of this research, such as investigating the medium and long-term effects of the customization process promoted within PD4CAT. Another future work will consist of an attempt to generalize the computational effort of customizing mobile solutions for impaired users. This is intended to meet the needs of a wider group of users, respecting their individual needs and specificities.

Besides, although the application of this research is for one single individual, it is a first step to develop customized solutions for impaired people. In future researches, we intend to study the use of PD4CAT for other patients, so as to refine the method and generalize it. Therefore, such researches would focus on a software development structure based on componentization.

Regarding the process experienced with PD4CAT, successful results concerning the inclusion of M in participatory design were perceptible.

His body and sound expressions were determinant to express his desires, needs and likes, such as: enthusiasm, little interest, great interest, no interest, pause to conceive an idea, attempt and effort to find a possibility for accessing the resource. He paid great attention and made a great effort to actively participate in the design process.

The success of this inclusion work was also expressed by the therapist team, the designer and the developers. These members showed to be constantly motivated, interested, thankful; they felt they were listened to, respected and stimulated to create ideas, innovations, and additionally cooperated in the solution of problems that emerged along the work.

The assessment process was implicit at each meeting throughout this cycle, once the ideas kept being refined. The therapists, the impaired user, the caregivers and the computer scientists, at different moments of every new meeting, naturally shared reflections that occurred at extra-meeting moments about new ideas, interesting possibilities, needs and solution desires.

We concluded that the inclusion of the impaired user and other PD participants was beneficial, especially concerning the obtained results, which met the target user´s needs. Besides, there was a great acceptance of the whole team towards the solution: whenever they had to talk to other people about the solution, they showed satisfaction and excitement regarding the possibilities of the device.

8. ACKNOWLEDGMENTS

Our thanks to the rehabilitation institution which enabled this research.

9. REFERENCES

[1] Boyd-Graber, J. L., S. S. Nikolova, et al. (2006). *Participatory Design with Proxies: Developing a Desktop-PDA System to Support People with Aphasia*. Proceedings of the SIGCHI conference on Human Factors in computing systems. Montreal, Quebec, Canada.

[2] Frauenberger, C., J. Good, et al. (2010). *Phenomenology, a Framework for Participatory Design*. Proceedings of the 11th Biennial Participatory Design Conference. Sydney, Australia, ACM: 187-190.

[3] Garzotto, F. and M. Bordogna (2010). *Paper-Based Multimedia Interaction as Learning Tool for Disabled Children*. Proceedings of the 9th International Conference on Interaction Design and Children %@ 978-1-60558-951-0. Barcelona, Spain, ACM: 79-88.

[4] Hakken, D., M. Teli, et al. (2010). *Intercalating the Social and the Technical: Socially Robust and Enduring Computing*. Proceedings of the 11th Biennial Participatory Design Conference. Sydney, Australia, ACM: 231-234.

[5] Hayes, G. R., S. G. M. Hirano, et al. (2010). *Interactive Visual Supports for Children with Autism*, Personal and Ubiquitous Computing.

[6] Hirano, S. H., M. T. Yeganyan, et al. (2010). Vsked: Evaluation of a System to Support Classroom Activities for Children with Autism, Atlanta, GA.

[7] Matthew Tylee, A., J. B. Matthew & H. C. M. Colin. 2012. Towards ubiquitous accessibility: capability-based profiles and adaptations, delivered via the semantic web. In *Proceedings of the International Cross-Disciplinary Conference on Web Accessibility*. Lyon, France: ACM.

[8] McGrenere, J., R. Davies, et al. (2002). Insights from the Aphasia Project: Designing Technology for and with People who Have Aphasia. SIGCAPH Comput. Phys. Handicap.(73-74): 112-118.

[9] Muller, M. (1997). *Participatory Practices in the Software Lifecycle* In:Handbook of Human-Computer Interaction. M.G.Helander, T.K.Landauer, P.V.Prabhu (eds.). Elsevier Science, pp. 255-297.

[10] Philip, A., A. V. Carlos & P. Christopher. 2012. Developing a semantic user and device modeling framework that supports UI adaptability of web 2.0 applications for people with special needs. In *Proceedings of the International Cross-Disciplinary Conference on Web Accessibility*. Lyon, France: ACM.

[11] Phillips, B. and Zhao, H. 1993. Predictors of assistive technology abandonment. *Assistive Technology*. Taylor & Francis. 5(1): 36-45.

[12] Preece, J., Y. Rogers, et al. (2005). *Design de Interação: Além da Interação Homem Computador*. Porto Alegre, Bookman.

[13] Prior, S. (2010). HCI Methods for Including Adults with Disabilities in the Design Of CHAMPION, Atlanta, GA.

[14] Rehema, B. & T. L. Jude. 2008. A web design framework for improved accessibility for people with disabilities (WDFAD). Proceedings of the 2008 international cross-disciplinary conference on Web accessibility (W4A). Beijing, China: ACM.

[15] Scherer, M.J. 1996. Outcomes of assistive technology use on quality of life. Disability & Rehabilitation. *Informa Healthcare*. 18(9): 439-448.

[16] Yevgen, B., P. B. Jeffrey, D. Glenn & I. V. Ramakrishnan. 2010. More than meets the eye: a survey of screen-reader browsing strategies. In *Proceedings of the 2010 International Cross Disciplinary Conference on Web Accessibility (W4A)*. Raleigh, North Carolina: ACM.

[17] Borges, L. C. L.. F.; Filgueiras, L. V. L.; Maciel, C. (2011). *Towards a participatory development technique of assistive technology for mobility and speech impaired patients*. Proceedings of the X Symposium on Human Factors in Computing Systems. Porto de Galinhas, Pernambuco, Brazil, ACM.

Design Research Methods to Understand User Needs for an eTextile Knee Sleeve

Ceara Byrne
Georgia Institute of Technology
North Avenue
Atlanta, GA 30332
ceara.byrne@gatech.edu

Claudia B. Rebola
Georgia Institute of Technology
North Avenue
Atlanta, GA 30332
crw@gatech.edu

Clint Zeagler
Georgia Institute of Technology
North Avenue
Atlanta, GA 30332
clintzeagler@gatech.edu

ABSTRACT

Knee replacement surgery is dramatically increasing in the United States for people over the age of 45 and rehabilitation after surgery is a necessary step for the success of the replacement. Rehabilitation requires regular access to a wide variety of resources and personnel. Currently, there are no self-care tools to enable tracking a patient's rehabilitative progress at home. As such, there is an opportunity to design and develop sensing technology tools to help alleviate the healthcare system and empower people in the knee rehabilitation process. The purpose of this paper is to describe the design process for a wearable, home rehabilitation device for knee replacement: an eTextile Knee Sleeve. More specifically, it describes the design research methods undertaken to understand user needs, including expert interviews, rehabilitation observation, and a participatory design workshop, to leverage advancements in technology and the field of eTextiles.

Categories and Subject Descriptors

H.5.2 [**Information Systems**]: User Interfaces – *evaluation/methodology, input devices and strategies, prototyping, theory and methods, user-centered design.*

General Terms

Human Factors, Documentation, Design, Reliability, and Experimentation.

Keywords

Rehabilitation, Older Adults, Human Centered Design methods, user research, observation, expert interviews, and participatory design workshop.

1. INTRODUCTION

Knee replacement surgery is dramatically increasing in the United States for people over the age of 45 (1, 2). One of the main reasons for the rise in surgeries is because it is an inexpensive and effective method for treating degenerative joint diseases (3-5). Knee replacement surgery is a method for

treating diseases, such as Osteoarthritis, Rheumatoid Arthritis, and Post-Traumatic Arthritis. After surgery, rehabilitation requires regular access to a large variety of resources and personnel, such as isokinetic devices, physical therapists, and primary physicians (6). As the demand for post-operative, rehabilitative care increases, the ability to marginally relieve the healthcare system by offloading resources to the patient is necessary.

Advancements in technology have introduced electronics into wearable products, and within the past 20 years, have engendered the new field of smart textiles, or eTextiles (7, 8). eTextiles enable digital components and electronics to be embedded into the fabric, providing additional functionality to wearable products. eTextile research into the medical fields have focused on the monitoring of motor functions, patterns, ambient sensing, and the integration into orthotics, prostheses, and mobility assistive devices. However, few studies have been done to understand the wearability of technologies within the medical field and their feasibility as a consumable product (9, 10). Furthermore, research has not approached the problem from a fully integrative perspective, encompassing healthcare professionals and patients as feedback mechanisms in the iterative design processes.

The purpose of this paper is to describe the design process for a wearable, home rehabilitation device for knee replacement. More specifically, it describes the design research methods undertaken to understand user needs. This project utilized design ethnography tools such as expert interviews, rehabilitation observation, and a participatory design workshop, to leverage advancements in technology and the field of eTextiles. It investigated the product feasibility and acceptance of discreet on-body sensors to provide a product that enables patients to better perform rehabilitation on their own, but also to allow for a feedback loop for physicians and therapists to view patient progress.

2. RELATED WORK

Within the past 20 years, the medical industry has popularized sensing technologies as a feedback mechanism for physiology, motion, and mobility. In relation to tracking knee movement, a variety of methods have been used, but without full product success. As an example, Gibbs and Asada (11) used an array of single conductive fibers around the knee and hip joints on a pair of spandex pants to detect expansion and contraction of said joints. While successfully detecting flexion, as the sensor warmed up, their results provided less accurate results each time the pants were worn. In the same realm of biofeedback devices,

Munro et al (12), developed a knee sleeve with a fabric sensor placed over the kneecap in order to track the degree of knee flexion for athletic training improvement. Functional testing however, showed that consistent feedback was not found due to sensor instability.

Additionally, current research looks at more complicated methods to track movement, in which, bulky goniometers in stabilizer braces help track flexion and extension or use the Kinect to estimate angles based on bodily protuberances. However, using new sensors on the body can provide more accurate data. While placing sensors on the body produces a lot of noise in the data collected, the closer a sensor is to the information being sensed, the easier it is for the information to be accurate. This accuracy is integral to biofeedback systems – users will not tolerate inaccuracy. Rhodes (13) and Starner (14) have a "two-second rule" for devices. If a device consistently takes longer than two seconds to activate, users will ultimately stop using the device. The same can be translated to user information. If the information users receive is consistently inaccurate or inaccessible to them, they will find a more suitable device to meet their needs.

Even though the aforementioned methods are necessary to develop sensing technology tools, they fail to incorporate user needs. These methods focus on involving users later on in the development process as they do user testing. There exists an opportunity to involve key product stakeholders early on in the process to provide real-time user feedback during design and development (15). The next sections describe in detail the different methods used in order to understand user needs for designing a wearable home rehabilitation device for knee replacement.

3. USER RESEARCH
This project utilized three main methods as part of a design ethnography approach. These methods included: 1-expert interviews; 2- observations; and 3- participatory design workshops. Together, the three methods contributed to the understanding of user needs to leverage advancements in technology and the field of eTextiles.

3.1 Expert Interviews
Semi-structured expert interviews were conducted with three Physical Therapists, an Applied Physiologist, and two Total Knee Replacement patients. A total of 6 expert interviews were conducted to discover the sentiments that surrounded rehabilitation and potential opportunities that existed. Each interview lasted approximately 30 minutes to an hour and addressed questions such as, "Tell me more about the rehabilitation process," "How does rehabilitation change from person to person?," and "What do you think would help encourage rehabilitation in the home?" Major findings for the expert interviews were compiled with the observational analyses. The goals of the interviews were to learn more about the process of rehabilitation, how it has changed throughout the years, and to understand what the stakeholders envisioned for the future.

3.1.1 Expert Interview 1
An Applied Physiology Professor at the Georgia Institute of Technology was interviewed. The expert provided an overview of physical therapy before offering insightful directions for the project.

Resistance training and balance exercises are the two main parts of knee rehabilitation. The earlier you start rehabilitation after surgery, the more extensive your range of motion will be in the future. There are different types of knee rehabilitation devices, but the better ones provide feedback on your range of motion, such as Isokinetic devices.

Isokinetic devices, such as the ones produced by Kin-Com and Cybex, are typically used during rehabilitation because they quantify and validate the amount of movement by measuring knee motion and the forces your knee can manage. They also bend the knee to the degree specified by the physical therapist, therefore ensuring proper rehabilitation results.

Following, she provided a few areas for further research.

3.1.1.1 Compression stockings
The expert suggested the integration of the sensors into compression hose. Older adults typically use compression hose to alleviate swelling in their legs, but doctors also recommend them because they are known to prevent blood clotting.

3.1.1.2 Hip and Knee Alignment
The expert also talked about the high instance of hip surgeries and potential areas of concern, such as the importance of hip and knee alignments. The possibility of integrating a means to detect ankle alignment in respect to the knee is important for the older generation because it ensures that other surgeries have been done properly.

3.1.1.3 Stimulation
It was also suggested integrating a stimulation device to enhance physical therapy. It isn't just about the quantity, but also about the quality of rehabilitation. Stimulation provides better rehabilitation by inciting a muscle to activate. The expert particularly suggested stimulating the Vastis Medialis, the muscle next to the patella that helps control bending, because it might be beneficial.

3.1.1.4 Temperature
Finally, the expert directed attention towards whether warmth provided a knitted structure would provide a better-perceived rehabilitation experience, as opposed to the traditional one. The expert postulated whether this allowed the user to do more movement, and asked how a device such as this would this affect the pain scale?

3.1.2 Expert Interview 2 – Physical Therapist Coordinator
A licensed physical therapist and the coordinator for the physical therapists in a local rehabilitation center was also interviewed. After providing a rundown of the facilities and the timeline of the process, the expert talked about the importance of range of motion within therapy and patient accountability during rehabilitation. Physical therapists often know when patients do not perform their rehabilitation at home and often get frustrated when the patient does not perform it properly. When the patient gets to the facility, their range of motion is approximately 90 degrees and, typically, their goal is to get the person to bend to 110 degrees. In the beginning of rehabilitation, they use the other knee as a baseline for the range of motion.

3.1.3 Expert Interviews 3 & 4 – Physical Therapists
Interviews were also conducted with two additional physical therapists. They stated that the majority of patients are arthritic

patients or ones who have pain, but Patella femoral syndrome is another big reason people have surgery. Furthermore, the two biggest problems people face after knee surgery are to have to go back to the hospital for a manipulation or an infection. A manipulation is when scar tissue build-up starts to limit the range of motion and a patient has to go back into surgery to get it removed. Rehabilitation is painful for many reasons, however, it's primarily painful because the scar runs right over where you're stretching. Initially after surgery, patients will receive a brace, but both patients and physical therapists discard them because they are not useful and because they limit the range of motion.

Potential opportunities for device features were discussed, such as vibratory feedback. They said it might help to activate the Vastis Medialis, but they hadn't seen any studies on it. Because the brace limits range of motion, physical therapists are wary of anything that goes over the knee and suggest using two Velcro straps above and below the knee. They offer that using Velcro straps allows the technology to be passed from one patient to the next, while the Velcro can be disposed of. All three therapists confirmed that placement of the sensors is incredibly important and, if accelerometers were going to be used, they would have to dissect the leg in order to get a proper reading of the degree.

3.1.4 Expert Interviews 5 & 6
Interviews using directed storytelling techniques were also conducted with patients at the facility to better understand their experiences and their needs. Directed storytelling is a method used to easily gather rich stories of lived experiences from participants. It is rooted in the social science method of narrative inquiry. Directed storytelling was leveraged for two reasons. The first was to trigger conversations between the researcher, the user, and their Physical Therapist for analysis and feedback on the overall rehabilitation process (16, 17). Secondly, it was used to understand product and service opportunities that were lacking or needing improvement (18-20). When coupled with shadowing techniques, as used during observation, researchers have the ability to gain a true sense of the user's actions, decision patterns, and routines.

3.1.5 Patient 1
P1 had undergone surgery 4 months prior. P1 recently (1 month ago) had to have a manipulation done to the previous surgery because they had accumulated scar tissue buildup in the knee and it had to be removed. The primary cause of this was due to failing to perform rehab after surgery. P1 said that it was scary to go through surgery and rehabilitation, and that it was easier to go through it the second time because P1 knew what to expect. During the rehab, P1 spoke about how hard it is to go through rehab, how they cheat at rehab when they are at home. P1 also spoke about physical therapists as being very encouraging when going through the whole process. "It's really painful, but they motivate you to push you further."

3.1.6 Patient 2
P2 had the surgery done on Dec. 31, 2012 and was hopefully in the last month of therapy. P2 had the left knee done 4 years prior and knew what to expect when going through it this time. P2 was impressed at how much better the technology had gotten and appreciated the shorter time both the operation and rehabilitation took. For the first knee replacement, P2 had gone to a class at the hospital that walked future patients through all the steps. The process for P2 was a stay in the hospital for 3 days after the surgery and then P2 went straight to the aforementioned rehabilitation clinic. After being there for a few weeks, P2 went home and a therapist came to see P2 2-3x a week for about 10-12 sessions. P2 said that the CPM machine was really beneficial, except that it left their knee very bruised afterwards.

When asked about what P2 thought the tool might use to motivate P2, P2 responded with "When you see you're making progress, that's motivation. It would be good, though, to know how far away you are from the end goal."

In terms of a user interface for patients, write everything down on a 5th grade level, not too simple, but simple enough. Use photos of exercises and provide information on what the different exercises will get you. ("This exercise would help me achieve three degrees" or "this exercise will make the hamstring stronger") The goal is to walk you through the exercises like a therapist would.

3.2 Observation
Not only is there a difference between what people say and what they do, but Carrillo (21) found that dialogues across different fields and, more importantly, within the same field, are more robust when engaged as a group, and shift the dialogues from assumption to reflection, and from individuals to the collective. Observation was also conducted to see how patients and Physical Therapists interacted. Five individuals were recruited for this phase, 3 Physical Therapists and 2 patients. The study was conducted in two-hour blocks for each patient, where the patient underwent 1 hour to 1.5-hours of physical therapy sessions. The major findings that came out of the observation were:

1. Rehab is slow. Not only is it an arduous process to go through, but the physical act of movement is slow and spasmodic.

2. Rehab is hard. Without the physical therapist present, users have a tendency to forego their rehab at home.

3. There is a disconnection between Health Professionals and Patients. Not only is there a lack of communication between them, but also there is a lack of tools and rehabilitation aids for patients.

3.3 Analysis
Affinity maps were created during the analysis of the observations and interviews. Affinity mapping is a tool used to group data and information by their natural relationships.

3.3.1 Affinity Map - Baseline
Using Affinity Maps, two chief directions emerged from the observational studies. First, the Affinity Map was organized based upon consistent themes that arose during the observation. These themes can be found in Figure 1 and are:

1. Physical therapy is difficult to properly be performed at home, is typically neglected, and often leads to surgical manipulations or infection in the future.

2. The role of the Physical Therapist is both an educator and a motivator.

3. The various tools used in the rehabilitation center, such as heating pads during initial stretching, home exercise sheets, and resistance training.

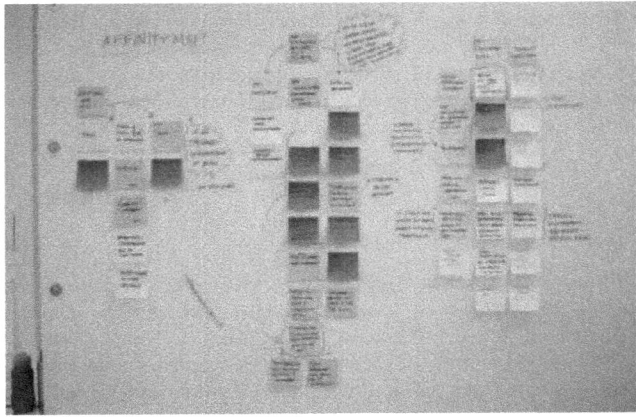

Figure 1. Observational Analysis.

Key observations using Figure 1 concluded that, despite understanding that they were being held fully accountable for their rehabilitation, the patients felt it was "too hard" to perform proper rehabilitation, which was performed 3 times daily for 15 to 30 minutes in the home and often led to regression in their rehabilitation at home. Despite patient problems, physical therapists often responded in direct correlation to the amount of effort the patient wanted to put in – e.g. the more a patient pushed themselves, the more the physical therapist pushed the patient. Attitude about rehabilitation was very important.

The process of rehabilitation typically started with a heating pad being used during stretching. In order to make up for the regression, physical therapists would slowly build up the exercises during their sessions to push the patient to their limit, which often led to the patients closing their eyes throughout and bracing themselves while the physical therapist worked on their knee. Additionally, simple language, analogies, and metaphors were frequently used to encourage patients. A patient's progress was determined using a goniometer to measure the degree of flexion and extension of the knee. The placement of the goniometer was crucial to determining the angle, as it bisected the leg.

3.3.2 *Affinity Map – Patient & PT Disconnection*

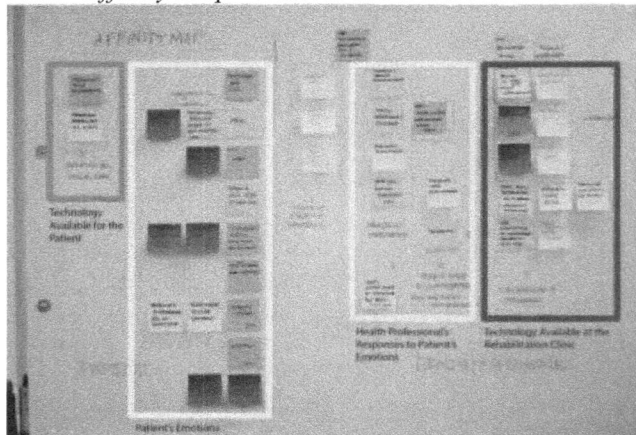

Figure 2. Observational Analysis: Patient / Physical Therapist Disconnection.

Additionally, rehab is very emotional. The Affinity Map was re-arranged to show the disconnection between the technology-centric Physical Therapist and the emotion-centric patient. The darker orange (see Figure 2) corresponds to the amount of technology available for the patient to use in the home, while the dark blue outlines the technology provided at the rehabilitation clinic. Additionally, the light orange refers to the emotions that the patients consistently brought up during the rehabilitation session, while the light blue outlines the tools used by the physical therapists to mediate those emotions. Figure 2 clearly shows the difference in technology between patient and physical therapist and shows how under-prepared physical therapists are to handle the patient emotionally and physically.

4. PRODUCT IDEATION WORKSHOP

Participatory design is a rising research method for product development and human computer interaction (22). Its value stems from examining the "third space", or region of overlap between researchers and product end-users. By engaging both end-users and designers, this method blends their collective knowledge into new insights and plans for action (23). A variety of techniques to encourage the "third space" are available, such as workshops, and were utilized within this study.

Two well-known formats for these workshops are the Future Workshop (24, 25), where participants "critique the present, envision the future, and develop their ideas" as a group, and Sander's conceptual "say-do-make", where participants use "generative tools" to explore past experiences and what they envision for the future (20, 26) . Leveraging these two frameworks, this study used four tools to explore the present and future for a better rehabilitation product. First, a "mind map" technique was used. It is a word association tool that was used both as a primer, to engage participants in the workshop, and used to understand how different stakeholders perceived the current state of rehabilitation by using central themes identified from ethnographic research. Secondly, a creative matrix was used to promote divergent thinking. By juxtaposing categories related to stakeholders with categories related to possible, future solutions, a large number of ideas are created that are related to different product aspects. This creative matrix was coupled with a technique called the Kano Analysis, whereby the participants are asked to categorize the concepts and attributes as either a required, desired, exciting, neutral, or an anti-feature. The Kano Analysis was done to understand the positive and negative features of the future product. Lastly, the workshop ended with a design and build activity using physical materials as a way for participants to explore features that would enhance the rehabilitation experience using eTextiles.

4.1 Workshop Analysis

The goal of the participatory design workshop was to understand the needs of the users through the evaluation and design of an ideal feedback device. Six people familiar with rehabilitation were recruited for the participatory design workshop, three females and three males, from a variety of different backgrounds. Table 1 showcases the demographics of the participants involved.

	Gender	Occupation	Age	Injury
1	M	Product Designer	>40	MCL Tear and Rehab, Both Knees
2	F	Architecture Student	<40	Broken Wrist, Rehab
3	F	Architecture Student	<40	ACL, MCL Patellar Tear and Rehab
4	F	Homemaker	>40	Knee Pain
5	M	Architect	>40	Knee, Ankle - Currently in Rehab
6	M	Senior Research Engineer	>40	MCL Injury, Rehab

Table 1. Workshop Participant Demographics

Key findings from the workshop provided a glimpse into product features people valued, focused around invisibility, and moved the product away from appearing as a technology product. Results from the mind map showed that people view rehabilitation as an arduous, uncomfortable, expensive, yet required process. In contrast, wearable products were supposed to be comfortable, light, and breathable, but they had to be careful as to not be itchy, heavy, or difficult to put on or take off. Moreover, technology was perceived as confusing, modern, bionic, advanced, complicated, and even expensive. Participants pushed for a tool that would provide feedback, but would not appear to use technology.

While the mind map was slightly abstract, the KANO analysis provided a clear set of features for the product. Users ranked features such as invisibility and reliability as required, while comfort and colors were ranked lower, only being considered desirable features. On the other hand, audible feedback and reminders to perform rehabilitation were considered anti-features (see Table 2). Interestingly, one participant wrote down habit-forming as a desired feature, yet two others ranked it as an anti-feature.

Required Features	Invisible, Reliable, Tracking, Customizable, and Easy to Use
Desired Features	Fits under Clothes, USB Capable, Tracking, Variety of Colors, Neutral Colors, Modern, and Not Geeky
Exciter / Delighter	Comfortable, Washable, Have a Long Battery Life, and FUN
Neutral Features	None
Anti-Features	Noise, No Immediate Feedback and Tracking, and Reminders to Perform Rehab

Table 2: Product Ideation Workshop: KANO Analysis

During the design and build phase of the workshop, participants had a chance to propose new ideas. Most participants developed products that were hidden in everyday wearable products, such as belt loops, socks, jean seams, and kinesthetic tape. The participants additionally provided a wide range of technologies to be considered, such as multiple accelerometers, microwaves, sonar, IR, and stretch sensors.

5. CONCLUSION

This paper described the design research methods undertaken for understanding user needs in the design and development of a wearable e-textile rehabilitation knee sleeve. It provided insight into the development of a socially acceptable and wearable knee rehabilitation device. Interviews, observation and participatory workshops were utilized to delve into understanding knee replacement rehabilitation. Interviews highlighted issues within the process of rehabilitation, such as the amount of information, or lack thereof, about the user's experience throughout the process. More research needs to be conducted on how to alleviate the user's struggle and encourage proper rehabilitation in the home. The observations provided an in depth understanding of the problem area and directions for improvement. While the physical therapists are well-prepared to tackle rehabilitation, from both emotional and physical standpoints, the users are not provided with the tools they need. Lastly, the Participatory Ideation Workshop provided novel and unique insight into hierarchal design criteria for a knee rehabilitation device. While the required features were straightforward, the Anti-Features were insightful and helped to provide a clearer design direction. Overall, the aforementioned process provided a solid basis for understanding user perceptions of what wearable technologies for knee rehabilitation should be and what should ultimately be communicated to the user. However, a longer, more comprehensive study into how the product would be used in situ over the course of a few months is necessary. A study, as such, would allow for validating user needs and to understand how the tracking of rehabilitation in the home would influence the overall experience of rehabilitation and allow for more substantial data and insight into the user's experience.

6. ACKNOWLEDGMENTS
Special thanks are given to Dr. Millard-Stafford for her expertise in the field of rehabilitation. In addition, the Interactive Product Design Laboratory at the School of ID and GVU Center at Georgia Tech for allowing access and expertise in the technology development.

7. REFERENCES
[1] Henderson MD R. Average age of partial and total knee replacement dropping

[2] Slover J ZJD. Increasing use of total knee replacement and revision surgery. JAMA. 2012;308(12):1266-8.

[3] Losina E, Walensky RP, Kessler CL, Emrani PS, Reichmann WM, Wright EA, et al. Cost-effectiveness of total knee arthroplasty in the United States: patient risk and hospital volume. Archives of internal medicine. 2009;169(12):1113.

[4] Ethgen O, Bruyere O, Richy F, Dardennes C, Reginster J-Y. Health-related quality of life in total hip and total knee arthroplastyA qualitative and systematic review of the literature. The Journal of Bone & Joint Surgery. 2004;86(5):963-74.

[5] Lavernia CJ, Guzman JF, Gachupin-Garcia A. Cost effectiveness and quality of life in knee arthroplasty. Clinical orthopaedics and related research. 1997;345:134-9.

[6] Westby MD, Backman CL. Patient and health professional views on rehabilitation practices and outcomes following total hip and knee arthroplasty for osteoarthritis:a focus group study. BMC Health Serv Res. 2010;10:119. Epub 2010/05/13.

[7] Bonfiglio A. Wearable monitoring systems: Springer; 2011.

[8] 8. Seymour S. Fashionable Technology: The Intersection of Design, Fashion, Science, and Technology: Springer London, Limited; 2008.

[9] Bonato P. Advances in wearable technology and applications in physical medicine and rehabilitation. Journal of NeuroEngineering and Rehabilitation. 2005;2(1):2.

[10] Patel S, Park H, Bonato P, Chan L, Rodgers M. A review of wearable sensors and systems with application in rehabilitation. Journal of neuroengineering and rehabilitation. 2012;9(12):1-17.

[11] Gibbs PT, Asada HH. Wearable Conductive Fiber Sensors for Multi-Axis Human Joint Angle Measurements. Journal of NeuroEngineering and Rehabilitation. 2005;2(7). Epub 02 March 2005.

[12] Munro BJ, Campbell TE, Wallace GG, Steele JR. The intelligent knee sleeve: A wearable biofeedback device. Sensors and Actuators B: Chemical. 2008;131(2):541-7.

[13] Rhodes BJ. Just-in-time information retrieval: Massachusetts Institute of Technology; 2000.

[14] Starner T. Project Glass: An Extension of the Self. Pervasive Computing, IEEE. 2013;12(2):14-6.

[15] Hanington B. Universal Methods of Design: 100 Ways to Research Complex Problems, Develop Innovative Ideas, and Design Effective Solutions: Rockport Publishers; 2012.

[16] Salvador T, Howells K. Focus troupe: using drama to create common context for new product concept end-user evaluations. CHI 98 Cconference Summary on Human Factors in Computing Systems; Los Angeles, California, USA. 286734: ACM; 1998. p. 251-2.

[17] Sato S, Salvador T. Methods & tools: Playacting and focus troupes:: theater techniques for creating quick, intense, immersive, and engaging focus group sessions. interactions. 1999;6(5):35-41.

[18] Brandt E, Grunnet C, editors. Evoking the future: Drama and props in user centered design. Participatory Design Conference 2000; 2000; New York: CPSR.

[19] Lafreniere D. CUTA: a simple, practical, low-cost approach to task analysis. interactions. 1996;3(5):35-9.

[20] Sanders EBN. Generative tools for co-designing. Collaborative design. 2000;1(2):3-12.

[21] Carrillo R. Intersections of official script and learners' script in Third Space: A case study on Latino families in an afterschool computer program. In Proceedings of Fourth International Conference of the Learning Sciences; Mahwab, NJ: Lawrence Erlbaum Associates.; 2000.

[22] Rebola CB, Sanford J, Milchus K, Quesenbery W, Castro D. Designing New Technologies within a Participatory Approach. Design for All. 2012;7(7):143-64.

[23] Muller MJ. Participatory design: the third space in HCI. In: Julie AJ, Andrew S, editors. The human-computer interaction handbook: L. Erlbaum Associates Inc.; 2003. p. 1051-68.

[24] Bødker K, Kensing F, Simonsen J. Participatory IT Design: Designing for business and workplace realitites. Cambridge, MA, USA: MIT Press; 2004.

[25] Kensing F, Madsen KH. Generating visions: future workshops and metaphorical design. Design at work: L. Erlbaum Associates Inc.; 1992. p. 155-68.

[26] Sanders EN. Design for effective communications: Creating contexts for clarity and meaning. In: Frascara J, editor. New York: Allworth Press; 2006.

The Pragmatic Web: Addressing Complex Communication in Public Administration using Tailored Delivery

Nathalie Colineau & Cécile Paris
CSIRO – ICT Centre
cnr. Vimiera and Pembroke Roads
Marsfield, NSW 2122, Australia
(+61) 2 9372 4222
{nathalie.colineau,cecile.paris}@csiro.au

Keith VanderLinden
Department of Computer Science
Calvin College
Grand Rapids, MI, 49546, USA
(+1) 616 526 7111
kvlinden@calvin.edu

ABSTRACT

Public administrations must communicate with a diverse citizenry concerning complex programs and initiatives. Because producing individual communications for a large citizenry is expensive, the communications are written generically, carefully discussing all possible contingencies and details. Because the programs are complex, these generic communications are difficult to understand. One way to communicate more effectively in this complex environment is to automatically tailor each communication based on the context of each individual citizen. This paper presents a prototype system that produces web presentations describing the programs offered by a public administration agency to the citizenry it serves. The work is presented as an example of work on the pragmatic web. Particular attention is focused on the system's authoring tool, which allows authors to produce and configure the resources required to drive the tailoring mechanism.

Categories and Subject Descriptors

H.5 [**Information Interfaces and Presentation**]: General; I.2.7; [**Natural Language Processing**]: Language Generation.

Keywords

Tailored Information Delivery, Natural Language Generation, Public Administration.

1. INTRODUCTION

The communication that takes place between a Public Administration (PA), i.e. a local, state or federal government, and the citizenry it serves is complex. The administrative tasks are themselves complex, which inevitably leads to imposing bureaucracy, and the citizenry is both large and diverse, which makes effective, personalized communication challenging. The resulting communication is largely generic, impersonal and difficult to understand.

Consider the task of a citizen who is a student looking for educational support programs for which they may be eligible. In Australia, these programs are administered by the Department of Human Services (DHS), which currently provides the following

summary description of its four student programs: ABSTUDY, Assistance for Isolated Children, Austudy and Youth Allowance.

ABSTUDY provides help with costs for Aboriginal and/or Torres Strait Islander Australians who are studying or undertaking an Australian Apprenticeship. The Assistance for Isolated Children Scheme helps parents and carers with the extra costs of educating their children. Austudy provides financial help to full-time students and Australian Apprentices aged 25 or more. Youth Allowance provides financial help for young people who are studying and training full-time, undertaking a full-time Australian Apprenticeship, or looking for work or sick. [1]

This summary is clear enough. Indigenous students can get ABSTUDY, isolated students, the Isolated Children's Scheme, older students, Austudy and traditional students, Youth Allowance. However, there are complexities in the eligibility requirements for each of these programs, the details of which are shown in Figure 1 (a). The text in this figure, generated by the tailoring system discussed in this paper, gives a short description of each program and lists the three or four eligibility requirements associated with each. Austudy students, for example, must be 25 years of age or over, a citizen or resident and taking an approved course, full-time. Clearly the question of eligibility is not that simple.

The text quoted above and the text in Figure 1(a) are written for generic audiences. Any citizen ought to be able to read either text and determine whether or not he or she is eligible for a student program. This makes the texts complex because they are filled with complicated conditions, many or most of which are irrelevant to any particular citizen.

As an alternative, consider the situation in which we know the citizen is a 52-year-old Australian resident pursuing an approved, full-time course of study. In this context, most of the material included in Figure 1(a) can be removed as irrelevant. There is no need to mention the ABSTUDY, Isolated Children or any of the other programs because the user is not eligible for them, nor is there need to mention the detailed eligibility requirements for the Austudy program because the citizen is known to satisfy them. The result is the much simpler statement shown in Figure 1(b), which was also produced by DHS-Myriad.

This approach to addressing complexity in communications takes context into account. That is, it supports *pragmatic reasoning*. This paper starts by discussing the background of the complexity inherent to public administration and of pragmatic approaches used to addressing it. It then details the Myriad-based tailored information delivery application with particular emphasis on the authoring tool. It closes by comparing and contrasting this work with related work and concluding that pragmatic tailoring shows promise in addressing complexity in PA communication.

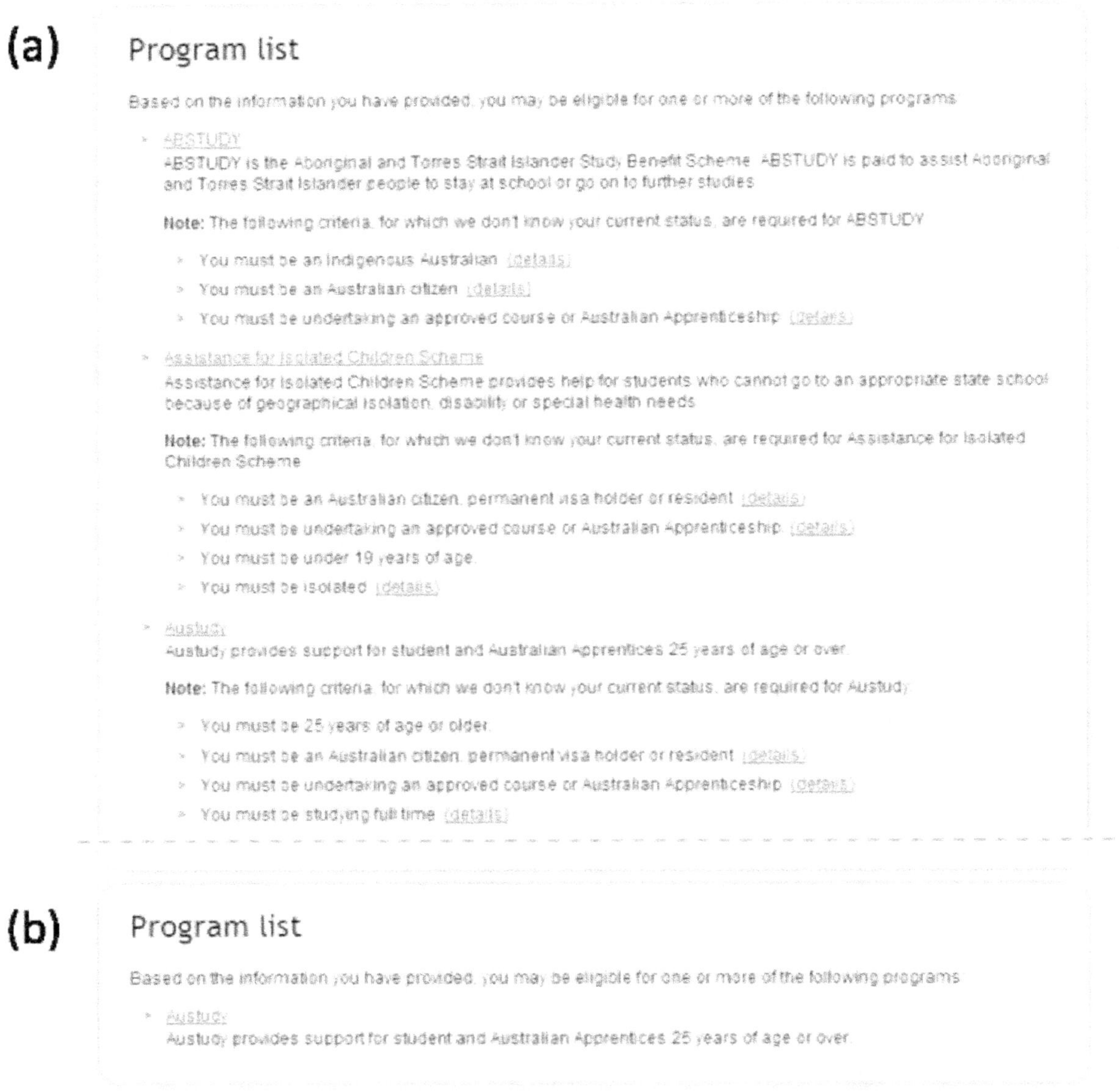

(a) Program list

Based on the information you have provided, you may be eligible for one or more of the following programs

> ABSTUDY
> ABSTUDY is the Aboriginal and Torres Strait Islander Study Benefit Scheme. ABSTUDY is paid to assist Aboriginal and Torres Strait Islander people to stay at school or go on to further studies
>
> **Note:** The following criteria, for which we don't know your current status, are required for ABSTUDY
>
>> You must be an Indigenous Australian (details)
>> You must be an Australian citizen (details)
>> You must be undertaking an approved course or Australian Apprenticeship (details)

> Assistance for Isolated Children Scheme
> Assistance for Isolated Children Scheme provides help for students who cannot go to an appropriate state school because of geographical isolation, disability or special health needs
>
> **Note:** The following criteria, for which we don't know your current status, are required for Assistance for Isolated Children Scheme
>
>> You must be an Australian citizen, permanent visa holder or resident (details)
>> You must be undertaking an approved course or Australian Apprenticeship (details)
>> You must be under 19 years of age
>> You must be isolated (details)

> Austudy
> Austudy provides support for student and Australian Apprentices 25 years of age or over
>
> **Note:** The following criteria, for which we don't know your current status, are required for Austudy
>
>> You must be 25 years of age or older
>> You must be an Australian citizen, permanent visa holder or resident (details)
>> You must be undertaking an approved course or Australian Apprenticeship (details)
>> You must be studying full time (details)

(b) Program list

Based on the information you have provided, you may be eligible for one or more of the following programs

> Austudy
> Austudy provides support for student and Australian Apprentices 25 years of age or over

Figure 1. (a) Extract of generic eligibility requirements for ABSTUDY, Isolated Children and Austudy; (b) a tailored version

2. BACKGROUND

This section discusses the background related first to the complexity of communication in PA and second to the potential use of pragmatic web tools to help address this complexity.

2.1 Public Administration

PA refers to the process of administering government policy and is well known to be a complex function. While one might wish to simplify government administrations and attempting to do so can be useful, such simplifying efforts will ultimately run up against the irreducible complexity of large-scale bureaucracy. The larger and more diverse the citizenry, the larger and more complex the bureaucracy.

Max Weber [2] characterized PAs as being:

- *Hierarchical* – Government bureaucracies are built as layers upon layers of administration. DHS, for example, is certainly hierarchical.
- *Rule-based* – The bureaucracies are based on carefully codified rules. DHS enforces carefully specified laws.
- *Specialized* – Bureaucracies require specially trained bureaucrats who are promoted based on competence. DHS includes many specialized departments.
- *Impersonal* – Bureaucratic decisions are intended to be made by-the-book, in an even-handed manner. DHS tries to treat Australians even-handedly.
- *Inward and/or upward focused* – Bureaucracies serve either the organization that created them (upward) or themselves (inward). DHS is established and maintained by the Australian government, so it is naturally upward-focused, but works hard to be outward-focused.

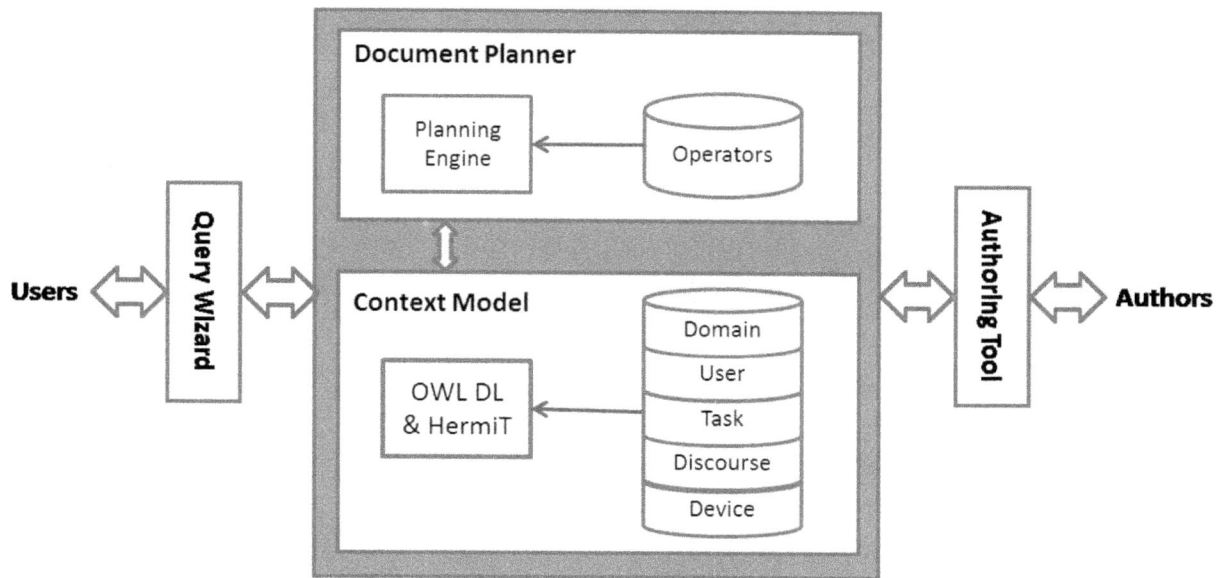

Figure 3. System Architecture

The complexity clearly comes from the hierarchical nature of the system and the complex and specialized rules that must be implemented. These rules are not like scientific laws, which one expects to be based on common, underlying principles, but rather are the work of *ad hoc* political processes playing out over time.

The complexity of structure and rules makes communication in PA challenging. This is particularly true given the impersonal and in/up-ward-focused nature of the organization, which does not lend itself to personal contact or to clear communication. Communication between PAs and their citizenry is famously stilted and frustrating, and the texts produced by PAs famously difficult to understand.

Note that the bureaucratic features of government administration can apply equally well to larger private organizations such as corporations and universities. Thus, the approach described in this paper can be applied to other bureaucratic domains outside the realm of PA.

2.2 The Pragmatic Web

Communicating effectively in a bureaucratic environment is a challenge for communicators. One technology that has helped is the World-Wide-Web. The Web allows PAs to publish and collect information for a variety of purposes and is central to so-called open-government initiatives[1]. However, the Web is a general-purpose tool that can be used in many ways, some effective and some ineffective. Thus, it makes sense to carefully consider the nature of the use of the Web for communication.

At a fundamental level, the Web is a semiotic system, that is, a symbolic system encoding communication [3]. Following the work of Charles Morris [4], semiotic systems are commonly viewed at three levels:

- *Syntax* specifies the structure of how symbols relate to each other.

- *Semantics* specifies how symbols relate to the real objects they signify, i.e., their meaning.
- *Pragmatics* specifies how symbols relate to people in context.

At its syntactic level, the Web is constructed from URLs, HTML and its communication mediated by HTTP. This syntactic view of the Web was originally specified by Berners-Lee in the early 1990s [5]. The simple syntactic rules have proven valuable and have allowed the Web to scale from humble beginnings to its current massive and growing size. Still, effective communication via the Web remains a challenge.

In the early 2000s, Berners-Lee began advocating the establishment of a semantic level for the Web [6]. At this level, syntactic web pages are coded with semantic features that are intended to more clearly specify the meaning of the syntactic elements. Considerable work has been done on technologies supporting this so-called *semantic web*. One such technology, the OWL description logic [7], is deployed by the system described in this paper and is described below.

As might be expected based on the development of the syntactic and then semantic web, recent calls have been made to continue the progression to the third semiotic level and establish features in support of a *pragmatic web* [8] [9]. This so-called pragmatic view of the Web extends the semantic features by adding the ability to represent and reason about the context of communication. A wide variety of context-based features have been deployed, either explicitly or implicitly, by web-based communication systems, including the use of dynamic web pages, web-browsing history and models of the characteristics of the users. The system described in this paper falls under this view of the pragmatic web. Ultimately, work on the pragmatic web seeks to implement tools that support collaborative work in specific contexts [10].

---

[1] See, e.g., http://www.whitehouse.gov/open.

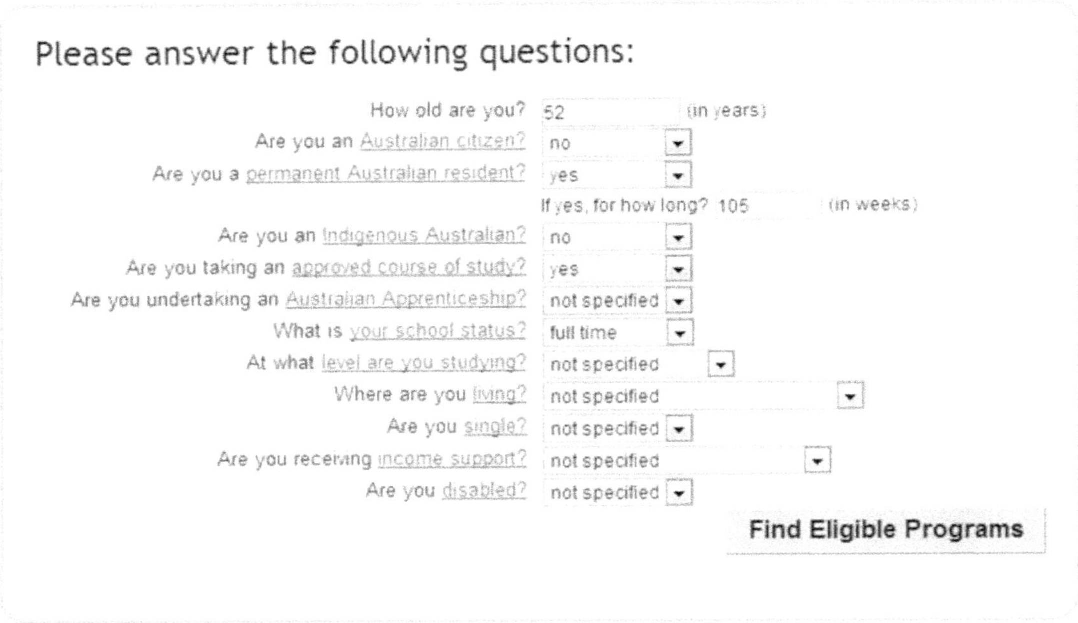

Please answer the following questions:

How old are you?	52	(in years)
Are you an Australian citizen?	no ▼	
Are you a permanent Australian resident?	yes ▼	
	If yes, for how long? 105	(in weeks)
Are you an Indigenous Australian?	no ▼	
Are you taking an approved course of study?	yes ▼	
Are you undertaking an Australian Apprenticeship?	not specified ▼	
What is your school status?	full time ▼	
At what level are you studying?	not specified ▼	
Where are you living?	not specified ▼	
Are you single?	not specified ▼	
Are you receiving income support?	not specified ▼	
Are you disabled?	not specified ▼	

Find Eligible Programs

Figure 4. Query Wizard

3. SYSTEM ARCHITECTURE

The architecture of the DHS-Myriad system is shown in Figure 2. The basic components include the query wizard, document planner, context models and authoring tool. The output of the system is a dynamic website tailored for a particular user. This section discusses each in turn, with particular attention paid to the authoring tool.

3.1 Query Wizard

The query wizard, shown on the left of Figure 2, uses an HTML-forms-based questionnaire to collect demographic information from the reader, including their age, citizenship, school status, and all the other contextual information required to make eligibility and tailoring decisions throughout the website. Figure 4 shows the wizard in use by a 52-year-old, non-indigenous, Australian resident of 105 weeks pursuing an approved course, full time.

When the user presses the "Find Eligible Programs" button, the wizard stores the user information in the user context model and then asks the Document Planner to present a list of programs for which the reader is potentially eligible. If the user provides no information, then the system returns the full list of all possible programs as partially shown in Figure 1 (a). If the user provides the information shown in Figure 4, the system returns the drastically reduced list of potential programs shown in Figure 1 (b). The more contextual information the reader provides, the more tailoring the system performs.

The query wizard mechanism has the ability to automatically plan and produce wizard questions using Ontology Verbalization (OV) techniques [11]. Details on this and other features of the query wizard can be found elsewhere [12].

3.2 Document Planner

The Document Planner, shown in the upper-middle of Figure 2, uses a text planning engine and declarative plan operators [13] to produce a discourse tree structured with rhetorical relations coded in Rhetorical Structure Theory [14] and populated with information

content. These are well-known technologies in the Natural Language Generation (NLG) community [15], and they are built into the Myriad platform on which the DHS-Myriad system is built. Information on the general nature of the Myriad architecture can be found elsewhere [16].

The DHS-Myriad system exhibits one key departure from traditional approaches to building NLG applications in that it allows the author to write coarse-grained information units. Traditional NLG applications have tended to include tactical generation components that work with units at the lexical and sentence levels. While the Myriad platform supports this traditional mode, it also supports units at the level of paragraphs and sections. This hybrid approach to generation allows the automatic generation of sentences when possible but also enables the assembly of more coarse-grained units when needed.

The main disadvantage of coarse-grained NLG is the stylistic infelicities that can occur when structuring the units in different orders. The relative scarcity of these infelicities in citizen-focused PA documents has been detailed elsewhere, but in those cases where they do occur, the authoring tool discussed below allows the author to hand-author text segments as needed.

The advantages of the coarse-grained approach to generation are that: (1) it is more efficient, both in terms of computation and representation; (2) it is more easily used by authors with limited technical training; and (3) it allows the application to rely on text units carefully written by professional authors to satisfy the legal and political requirements placed on the content.

The plan operators for the DHS-Myriad system were hand-built to be used to generate the sorts of user-oriented texts required to present government programs to citizens. For example, if the user selects the "Austudy" link in Figure 1 (b), they get the following summary of the Austudy program.

This web material has been produced for you on 29/May/2013 12:47PM based on the information you have provided

Austudy provides support for student and Australian Apprentices 25 years of age or over. Austudy can help students by providing money for living expenses, accommodation expenses, education expenses, fares, prescription medicines or personal loans.

Am I Eligible?
What are the rules about income and assets?
How much Austudy can I get?
How do I make a claim?
What are my rights and responsibilities?
How can I contact DHS?

This generic structure is specified by a single plan operator that can be used to summarize all programs. It starts with a personalized template filled with the current date and time and includes canned titles for standard program elements. These are more coarse-grained information units.

If the user selects "Am I Eligible?", they get the following.

You've told us that you meet the following criteria:
- *You are 25 years of age or older.*
- *You are an Australian citizen, permanent visa holder or resident. (details)*
- *You are undertaking an approved course or Australian Apprenticeship. (details)*
- *You are studying full time. (details)*

so you should be eligible for this program.

This paragraph summarizes the information provided by the user, see Figure 4, in the context of the Austudy eligibility requirements. Note that the system uses OWL-DL-based reasoning to determine that a user who is 52 satisfies the conditions of being 25 years and older. The age feedback (i.e., "You are 25 years of age...") is generated directly from the user model knowledgebase using fine-grained generation; the residence feedback (i.e., "You are an Australian...") is a more coarse-grained information unit that was hand-written by the author because the automatically generated text does not handle the "or"-aggregation in a fluent manner. Aggregation is a challenging problem in NLG [17]. Had the user not given their age, residency and study status, this page would have detailed each of the requirements.

If the user selects "How much Austudy can I get?", see the original Austudy text above, they get, among other things, the following:

Rates of Austudy

The rates listed here are fortnightly maximum payment rates and serve as a guide only. They are effective from 1 January 2011.

- *single: $388.70*
- *single, on long-term income support: $472.10*

This text selects the appropriate payment rates for the user based on the information they gave to the query wizard. Note that because the user did not specify whether they are on long-term income support or not (see Figure 4) the tailoring mechanism includes both values.

3.3 Context Model

The Context Model, shown on the lower-middle of Figure 2, represents the elements of the context of communication. It is implemented using OWL-DL [7].

The context model represents the full context of communication, including concepts and individuals from the domain, user, tasks, discourse history and computation device (e.g., desktop, smartphone, etc.). The primary requirements for this project focus on: (1) the user model, which represents the contextual information provided by the user; and (2) the domain model, which represents the content fragments, domain individuals and eligibility constraints. The Context Model also supports the representation of a device context, the discourse history and the task context [16], but these are not deployed in this application. Taken together, these models form the basis for the pragmatic reasoning required by the tailoring application.

The user and domain models represent concepts, individuals and properties. The concepts and relationships are fixed and represented in an OWL ontology. The user model contains only one concept, User, and a range of properties, such as hasAge, hasRace, etc. As discussed above, when the query wizard runs, it asserts a new individual of type User, and associates the specified properties. The domain model includes the concepts, such as Program and Condition, and properties, such as hasCondition. As will be discussed in the next section, the author can add new domain individuals as needed for new programs, conditions, etc.

The domain model also includes the author-specified texts that are included in the tailored output. This will also be discussed in the next section.

The prototype supports the eligibility reasoning required for tailoring decisions using categorical reasoning as implemented by HermiT [18], a reasoner for OWL ontologies. For each user, the prototype asserts an individual of class Person and sets the properties for that individual as appropriate, e.g., race, age, etc. It then uses HermiT's classification to determine if the individual's properties satisfy the properties required for any of the programs or other content elements. The results of this reasoning are provided to the Document Planner for use in content planning and structuring.

More details can be found elsewhere regarding the general structure and reusability of the context model [19] and on the precise representation of the eligibility conditions [12].

3.4 Authoring Tool

The context model described in the previous section is based on OWL-DL and can be built and configured using the Protégé-OWL ontology editor[2], but this tool is only useful to properly trained knowledge engineers. Technical authors would find it too complex to use productively. As an alternative, DHS-Myriad offers an authoring tool, shown on the right of Figure 2, which is intended to be used by technical authors to specify the elements of the context model that are required to drive the system. The authoring tool interface is shown in Figure 5.

The authoring tool shows the concept hierarchy built into the context model, individual instances of those concepts and the relationships between the individuals. This section covers each of these in turn.

---

[2] See http://protege.stanford.edu.

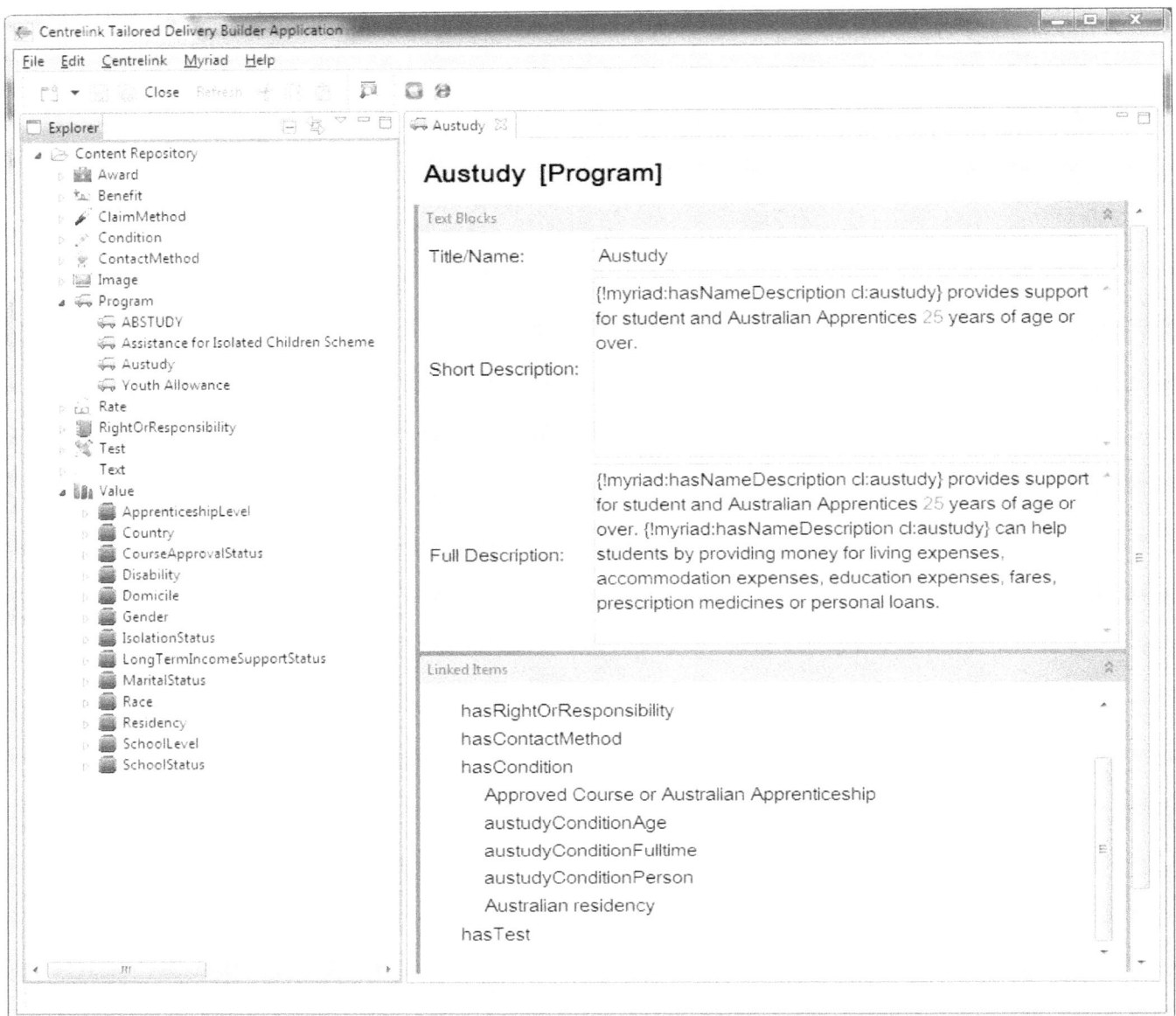

Figure 5. The web authoring tool presenting the Austudy program

3.4.1 Concepts

The authoring tool lists the domain concepts contained in the context model (see the "Explorer" panel on the left of Figure 5). These concepts include awards, benefits, claim methods, and other basic classes of objects required by the PA domain. It doesn't list the other context sub-models shown in Figure 2: the user model only contains one concept, User, and is built by the query wizard as described above, not by the author; the task, discourse and device sub-models are not deployed in this system.

These concepts are fixed in the system; the author cannot modify them using the authoring tool. The expectation is that they don't change very often. For example, PAs will always offer benefits, programs, payment rates and will always specify eligibility requirements in terms of "Values" such as gender, race and marital status.

Allowing authors or groups of authors to augment and maintain this ontology of shared concepts would be an interesting idea and would follow much current work on the pragmatic web.

3.4.2 Individuals

In addition to concepts, the context model also represents individuals, or instances of those concepts. For example, the explorer pane on the left of Figure 5 lists the four student support programs offered by DHS, all under the Program concept: ABSTUDY, Assistance for Isolated Children, Austudy and Youth Allowance. These programs are represented as OWL individuals.

The authoring tool allows authors to add new individuals using an entry form. The entry form for the Austudy individual is shown in the panel on the right side of Figure 5. The author uses this panel to specify the formal name of the program, a short description and a longer description.. These are hand-authored texts fragments that are used by the document planner in appropriate places in the tailored documents. The short description is shown in Figure 1 (b);

the long description is shown in the program text quoted in the document planner section above. These discourse plans are also fixed in the system.

Note that the text fragments include codes referencing features of other individuals in the context model. For example, both codes start with the reference:

{!myriad:hasNameDescription cl:austudy}

This reference gets the value of the name the Austudy instance, which allows the author to use the official name of the program consistently throughout the text.

3.4.3 Relationships

The context model also supports relationships between individuals. For example, the Austudy individual shown in Figure 5 has a set of five eligibility requirements listed in the "Linked Items" panel under the hasCondition property (see the bottom right panel of the figure). These are represented as separate individuals and are related to the Austudy individual using OWL-DL properties. They represent the conditions that the Austudy recipient must: be taking an approved course; have an appropriate age; be pursing full-time study; be a person; and be an Australian citizen or resident. They can be configured by the author using the authoring tool.

Interestingly, Austudy recipients must be people, as opposed to schools or organizations. This condition is included in the knowledge base for reasoning purposes but is never expressed in the tailored output. While it would be syntactically and semantically correct to say "You must be a person.", pragmatics dictate that such an expression is neither needed nor wanted.

If the author selects the "Australian Residency" condition in the authoring tool, the editor opens a new panel for the residency condition individual. This panel includes the following logical condition, specified using Manchester OWL syntax.

(gc:hasCitizenship value gc:australia) or
((gc:hasResidency value gc:permanentAustralianResident) and
(gc:hasResidencyPeriod some xsd:integer[>= 104]))

This indicates that to satisfy the Australian residency condition, the user individual must either have Australian citizenship or have been an Australian resident for at least two years. Because conditions like this can be difficult to express automatically, the tool allows the author to enter a hand-written fragment expressing the condition in a clear way. The following text fragment is currently used for this condition.

You must

- *be an Australian permanent resident*
- *be in Australia on the day you claim, and*
- *have been in Australia as an Australian resident for at least 104 weeks (there are some exceptions).*

Note: information from Australia's immigration department may be used in assessing claims and can be used to assess ongoing entitlements.

Simpler conditions specified in OWL-DL can be generated automatically based on the logic and lexical items associated with each individual and each property. For example, the age condition

individual linked to the Austudy individual specifies the following condition:

(gc:hasAge some xsd:integer[>= 25])

This condition is automatically expressed as:

You must be 25 years of age or older.

This is an example of OV (discussed above). No hand-authored text fragment is specified for this condition individual.

To add a new program like the "Assistance for Isolated Children Scheme", the author would create new individuals for the program, conditions, benefits, tests, etc. and link them together using properties.

The technical authors from DHS reviewed this tool and managed to use it successfully in an informal test. No formal usability testing has yet been conducted on this tool. In is not yet clear whether they would be able to specify the logical conditions using Manchester OWL syntax as described above.

4. ASSESSEMENT AND RELATED WORK

In a series of formal usability tests, the tailored documentation generated by the DHS-Myriad system has proved itself to be easier to read and more quickly understood than the original static webpages that DHS was using originally. More details on these tests can be found elsewhere [20]. Since the completion of the study, DHS has upgraded their website to a more dynamic system that incorporates many of the ideas explored in this demonstrator.[3]

This section now compares and contrasts the work presented in this paper with other approaches that generally address issues related to tailored information delivery.

4.1 Tailoring in Document Automation tools

The work presented in this paper can be seen as part of the broader, commercial field of Document Automation (DA). DA systems (e.g., HotDocs[4], Exari[5], LogicNets[6] and Arbortext[7]) have been used in the legal profession to automate the production of custom-built legal documents (e.g., deeds of sale, standardized agreements, etc.) and in the technical documentation field to produce model-specific product documentation and decision support systems. These tools provide mail-merge-like features extended with conditional inclusion/exclusion of coarse-grained text units generally on the order of sections, paragraphs or perhaps sentences. DA systems generally provide tools for two tasks:

- **Template construction** – In this task, trained authors construct reusable templates, often from existing documents. This function matches the function performed by the authoring tool described in this paper.

- **Document assembly** – In this task, an application uses an interview system to collect relevant characteristics from the user and then automatically constructs a personalized document for that user based on an appropriate template. This function matches the fnction performed by the query wizard described in this paper.

Such tools support the elision of text units that are not appropriate for given readers. For example, they could elide the Austudy program for users known to be under 25. DA tools implement

---

[3] See the "Payment Finder" here: http://www.humanservices. gov.au/customer/themes/students-and-trainees

[4] See http://www.hotdocs.com/.

[5] See http://www.exari.com/.

[6] See http://www.logicnets.com/.

[7] See http://www.ptc.com/products/arbortext/.

tailoring-by-elision by allowing authors to add logical conditions to content units, roughly at the sentence level and above. The document assembly tool then acquires information about the reader's individual context and builds a brochure that includes only the content units whose conditions match those of the reader.

While this tailoring-by-elision approach is useful, it does not support the hybrid approach that mixes hand-authored texts with OV. Neither does it easily support more complex tailoring such as the condition feedback discussed the Document Planner section.

DA tools do have useful authoring support. HotDocs provides a tool for specifying complex logical conditions, which would be helpful in allowing authors to specify the OWL-DL logical conditions described above. LogicNets provides an authoring tool that configures a decision network that is used to drive the user interaction with the system. This decision-net approach is interesting, but it is not clear what benefit it would offer in PA eligibility tasks.

4.2 Tailoring in Language Generation

This work presented in this paper is based on the theory and techniques developed in Natural Language Generation (NLG) for tailored delivery [15]. Relevant systems include STOP, which produced tailored smoking cessation letters [21], and HealthDoc, which generated tailored health-education documents [22]. Though in a different domain, these systems are similar in scope and orientation to the current work. The work reported here tends to manage a greater volume of more coarsely-grained text units and is thus more limited in its ability to address detailed issues in sentence-level generation, e.g., referring expressions [22], aggregation [17], and variation in expressional form [23].

Historically, NLG systems have relied on carefully specified knowledge bases, built by the NLG researchers themselves, to drive the generation process (see work on WYSIWYM for a notable exception [24]). It has been a challenge to allow authors who are untrained in knowledge specification to load and configure the knowledge base themselves. DHS-Myriad offers the authoring tool described in the previous section to address this issue.

The domain concept ontology included in the context model performs a similar function that performed by the Generalized upper model [25]. However, the upper model was designed to support general sentence generation whereas the context model described here is designed to support document generation in the PA domain.

4.3 Tailoring in Medical Informatics

Work on tailoring has been a common theme in eHealth applications [26]. In a meta-study of tailored health documents [27], Hawkins *et al.* report that tailoring in eHealth has generally proven to be effective, particularly when there is a relatively large variation in the readers. The PA domain serves a similarly diverse constituency that varies on a number of scales, including age, race, domicile, family status, etc.

Hawkins *et al.* identified the following three forms of tailoring as being commonly effective in eHealth applications:

- **Personalization** – A document should identify itself to its reader as a tailored document, for example, by saying things like "this document has been produced for you…"

- **Feedback** – A document should refer to information provided by the reader, for example, by saying things like "You've told us that …".

- **Content matching** – A document should include the most appropriate content for a particular reader, for example, by choosing information units based on the reader's personal information. This comprises a variety of content selection techniques.

These three forms of tailoring are demonstrated by the three sample texts discussed in the document planner section.

One relevant health-informatics system is the Michigan Tailoring System (MTS).[8] This system includes an authoring tool, the MTS Workbench, which focuses on health informatics, and a tailored delivery tool, the MTS Engine, which provides tailoring-by-elision features common to DA tools. The author uses the MTS Workbench to specify document content and then adds logical conditions for the inclusion/elision of different portions of the text. The MTS Engine then queries the conditions from a user and produces the appropriate tailored message. The system pays care attention to the design of effective survey questions. While this approach is interesting, it's largely focused on health informatics and doesn't allow the easy reuse of text fragments across multiple documents, which commonly required in PA texts.

4.4 Tailoring in Adaptive Hypermedia

A variety of techniques, including those from DA and NLG, have been applied to the adaptive presentation of hypermedia content. Using the terms and categories defined by Kobsa *et al.* (2001) in their survey of Adaptive Hypermedia (AH) [28], the application described here collects user-supplied demographic data using an on-line questionnaire, which is commonly done in fielded systems, and then tailors the bulk of its content using a fragment-variant approach, which selects and assembles pre-authored fragments of text. This approach works well for the carefully-worded, legal content commonly found in citizen-focused PA texts where generating sentences on-the-fly from first principles is not possible given that all material has to be legally approved before release.

The application represents and reasons about its users and its content using a knowledge base implemented with semantic web technologies [7], which can be seen as what Bunt *et al.* would categorize as domain-dependent, abstract information [29]. Of particular concern in citizen-focused PA texts is the notion of eligibility. The application uses OWL-DL [18] to represent and reason about eligibility conditions in order to determine both whether a user is eligible for a particular program and what content to include.

One relevant AH system is AHA! [30], which focuses on general-purpose, educational web materials. This system includes web-based authoring tools that support the conditional adaptation of objects, link adaptation and layout tools common to AH applications [31]. The platform includes reasoning, but not full OWL-DL-based reasoning. It focusses on adapting paths through a knowledge structure, as is commonly done in educational systems, but provides less support for the hybrid approach to generation used in the Myriad platform.

---

[8] See http://chcr.umich.edu/mts/.

5. CONCLUSIONS

This paper has presented DHS-Myriad, an information delivery tool that produces websites for PA programs that are tailored to individual users. This work can be seen as an application of the pragmatic web. The system includes a knowledge base with reasoning capabilities, a document planner and an authoring tool. The output of the system has proven itself to be understandable and useful in formal tests, which indicates that the approach to tailoring shows promise in the domain of PA.

Future work on the system will include further work on the authoring tool in preparation for more formal tests of its usability.

6. ACKNOWLEDGMENTS

This research has been funded by the CSIRO-DHS Human Services Delivery Research Alliance (HSDRA) and by Calvin College. It is based on work done with Adam Strickland at the CSIRO ICT Centre. The author would also like to thank Carol Taylor, Liz Mclachlan, Matt Barden, Suzie Hardy and Rowena Alder from DHS, Australia's Department of Human Services and the students who participated in the usability studies. This work was conducted using the Protégé resource, which is supported by grant GM10331601 from the National Institute of General Medical Sciences of the United States National Institutes of Health.

7. REFERENCES

[1] DHS, May 2013. [Online]. Available: http://www.humanservices.gov.au/customer/subjects/payments-for-students-and-trainees.

[2] M. Weber, Economy and Society, University of California Press, 1978.

[3] M. P. Singh, "The Pragmatic Web: Preliminary Thoughts," in *Proceedings of the NSF-OntoWeb Workshop on Database and Information Systems Research for Semantic Web and Enterprises*, 2002.

[4] C. Morris, Signs, Language and Behavior, New York: Prentice Hall, 1946.

[5] T. Berners-Lee, Weaving the Web, SanFrancisco: Harper, 1999.

[6] T. Berners-Lee, J. Hendler and O. Lassila, "The Semantic Web," *Scientific American*, 2001.

[7] M. K. Smith, C. Welty and D. L. McGuinness, "OWL Web Ontology Language Guide," 2004. [Online]. Available: http://www.w3.org/TR/owl-guide/.

[8] M. Schoop, A. deMoor and J. L. Dietz, "The Pragmatic Web: A Manifesto," *Communications of the ACM*, vol. 49, no. 5, pp. 75-76, 2006.

[9] P. DiMaio, "The Missing Pragmatic Link in the Semantic Web," *Business Intelligence Advisory Service*, vol. 8, no. 7, 2008.

[10] P. Pohjola, "The Pragmatic Web: Some Key Issues," in *Processing iSemantics*, Graz, 2010.

[11] A. Third, S. Williams and R. Power, "OWL to English: a tool for generating organised easily-navigated hypertexts from ontologies," in *Proceedings of the 10th International Semantic Web Conference*, Bonn, Germany, 2011.

[12] N. Colineau, C. Paris and K. Vander Linden, "Expressing Conditions in Tailored Brochures for Public Administration," in *Proceedings of the 11th ACM Symposium on Document Engineering*, Mountain View, CA, 2011.

[13] J. D. Moore and C. L. Paris, "Planning text for advisory dialogues: Capturing intentional and rhetorical information," *Computational Linguistics*, vol. 19, no. 4, pp. 651-694, 1993.

[14] W. C. Mann and S. A. Thompson, "Rhetorical structure theory: Toward a functional theory of text organization," *Text*, vol. 8, no. 3, pp. 243-281, 1988.

[15] E. Reiter and R. Dale, Building Natural Language Generation Systems, Cambridge University Press, 2000.

[16] C. L. Paris, N. Colineau, A. Lampert and K. Vander Linden, "Discourse Planning for Information Composition and Delivery: A Reusable Platform," *Natural Language Engineering*, vol. 16, no. 1, pp. 61-98, 2010.

[17] H. Dalianis, "Aggregation in Natural Language Generation," *Journal of Computational Intelligence*, vol. 15, no. 4, pp. 384-414, 1999.

[18] B. Motik, R. Shearer and I. Horrocks, "Hypertableau Reasoning for Description Logics," *Journal of Artificial Intelligence Research*, vol. 36, pp. 165-228, 2009.

[19] N. Colineau, C. Paris and K. VanderLinden, "From Generic to Tailored Documents in Public Administration," *Information Polity*, vol. 17, no. 2, pp. 177-193, 2012.

[20] N. Colineau, C. Paris and K. VanderLinden, "Automatically Producing Tailored Web Materials for Public Administration," *New Review of HyperMedia*, vol. 19, no. 2, pp. 158-181, 2013.

[21] E. Reiter, R. Robertson and L. M. Osman, "Lessons from a Failure: Generating Tailored Smoking Cessation Letters," *Artificial Intelligence*, vol. 144, no. 1, pp. 41-58, 2003.

[22] C. DiMarco, P. Bray, H. D. Covvey, D. Cowan, V. DiCuccio, E. Hovy, J. Lipa and C. Yang, "Authoring and Generation of Individualised Patient Education Materials," *Journal on Information Technology in Healthcare*, vol. 6, no. 1, pp. 63-71, 2008.

[23] J. A. Bateman and C. Paris, "Phrasing text in terms the user can understand," in *Proceedings of the 11th International Joint Conference on Artificial Intelligence*, 1989.

[24] C. Hallett, R. Power and D. Scott, "Composing Questions through Conceptual Authoring," *Computational Linguistics*, vol. 33, no. 1, pp. 105-133, 2007.

[25] J. Bateman, R. Henschel and F. Rinaldi, "Generalized Upper Model 2.0," GMD/Institut für Integrierte Publikations- und Informationssysteme, Darmstadt, 1995.

[26] A. Cawsey, F. Grasso and C. Paris, "Adaptive Information for Consumers of Healthcare," in *The Adaptive Web:*

Methods and Strategies of Web Personalization, Berlin, Springer-Verlag, 2007, pp. 465-484.

[27] R. P. Hawkins, M. Kreuter, K. Resnicow, M. Fishbein and A. Dijkstra, "Understanding tailoring in communicating about health," *Health Education Research,* vol. 23, no. 3, pp. 454-466, 2008.

[28] A. Kobsa, J. Koenemann and W. Pohl, "Personalised hypermedia presentation techniques for improving online customer relationships," *Knowledge Engineering Review,* vol. 16, no. 2, pp. 111-155, 2001.

[29] A. Bunt, G. Carenini and C. Conati, "Adaptive Content Presentation for the Web," in *The Adaptive Web: Methods and Strategies of Web Personalization*, Berlin, Springer-Verlag, 2007, pp. 409-432.

[30] P. De Bra, D. Smits and N. Stash, "The Design of AHA!," May 2013. [Online]. Available: http://aha.win.tue.nl:18080/aha/ahadesign/.

[31] P. Brusilovsky, "Developing adaptive educational hypermedia systems: From design models to authoring tools," in *Authoring Tools for Advanced Technology Learning Environment*, T. Murray, S. Blessing and S. Ainsworth, Eds., Dordrecht, Kluwer Academic Publishers, 2003, pp. 377-409.

Simplifying Business Complexity with Frameworks

Clare Cotugno, PhD
ccotugno@electronicink.com

Shannon L. Fitzhugh, PhD
sfitzhugh@electronicink.com

Raegan M. Hoeft, PhD
rhoeft@electronicink.com

Electronic Ink
1 South Broad St. 19th Floor
Philadelphia, PA 19107

ABSTRACT
How does an interdisciplinary team with professional training in different disciplines document and redesign a complex business process in just a few weeks? How can they persuade a global client that change is understandable and possible? By using a macroergonomic framework to parse and analyze data and educate and empower stakeholders, this team of user experience researchers and designers simplified complexity within their own process and for their client as well.

Categories and Subject Descriptors
K.6.1

Keywords
Business Processes, Human Factors, Usability, Ergonomics, Macroergonomics, User Experience Design, Content Strategy, Content Management, Publishing Processes

1. INTRODUCTION
We work for a design consultancy called Electronic Ink. Electronic Ink deploys interdisciplinary teams to help all kinds of companies improve their business systems and processes. Our company is an eclectic mix of human factors experts, cognitive psychologists, business strategists, interaction designers, writers, content strategists and developers. Clients often come to us with a specific problem and goal; other times, they just come with the feeling that business ought to be going better, faster, smoother, or more profitably. Depending on the client's industry and challenge, our company pulls together a team to investigate and design a solution. One of our distinguishing factors in the marketplace is our commitment to considering first and foremost what we call the "human context" in any business. As we analyze and develop better systems, our solutions must take into account the physical, psychological and social realities of the workplace.

Our design solutions often consist of streamlining processes within a business. This could include eliminating unnecessary and duplicate steps, integrating disparate systems, eliminating excess data that clogs workflow, and standardizing processes. Each of these is a different way of reducing complexities in a business system or process.

When we talk about complexity within our work, there are really two different kinds of complexity that we must pay attention to: (a) the business complexity of the client and the client's problem space, and (b) the project complexity in terms of how the client's project will be planned and executed.

To be honest, though, we rarely have the opportunity to sit back and think calmly about the complexities of individual projects. After the fact, when there's time and hindsight, we're usually on to the next big challenge. In working on this paper, we ended up doing a kind of meta-analysis of the project's complexities and what we've learned.

1.1 Business Complexity
As we approached this project report, we began by defining our terms. We all "know" what complexity is, but would we be able to explain it if someone asked us? How often do we really think about how many different types of complexity there are?

There are actually multiple ways of defining complexity within a business organization, and we found two especially useful models. By "useful" we mean that these terms helped us understand and explain to ourselves and our clients some business challenges.

From a macroergonomic perspective, business or organizational complexity is defined by the extent of the existence of structural differentiation and structural integration. [2] Structural differentiation denotes the extent to which the business is segmented into unique pieces, be it horizontally, vertically, spatially, or some combination of these. Think here in terms of departments, locations, or lines of business that operate in relatively siloed fashion. Hospitals, banks, publishing houses, city governments – these are some examples of businesses that are characterized by a high degree of structural differentiation. The more differentiated the structure, the more likely that an organization will need a complex system to achieve "structural integration" – the ability to facilitate interaction between and among the different parts. Think here about the many technologies, roles, and processes that complex businesses put in place to ensure communication, coordination and control over the unique parts. Poor or complicated structural integration can lead to costly errors and employee frustration. If your local bank, hospital or utility has ever been acquired by a larger corporation, you've probably had firsthand experience with a sad discrepancy between structural differentiation and structural integration. While you might "belong" to a new bank, it can take quite some time for the larger entity to recognize your existence and communicate smoothly with you.

These perspectives are meaningful to us because they help us parse a complicated organization into different elements as we try to explain the current state of a business and propose and prioritize design solutions.

Other perspectives of business complexity focus on the differences between internal and external complexity. [4] Internal complexity includes the above mentioned differentiation, plus other internal factors, such as products or services produced, technology used, and the employees themselves. In contrast, external complexities are the environmental characteristics that constitute the context in which a business operates. Laws, language, culture, utilities and services available can be external complexities. They may be stable but they may also be highly unpredictable and dynamic, depending on the type of business organization. This differentiation is useful to us as we think about what situations our customers can change (internal factors, like head count, technology platform, office location) and what they can't change (external factors like legal constraints, inclement weather, the national language, or civil unrest).

1.2 Project Complexity

In addition to the complexity of most large, modern businesses, as a consultancy we are also faced with complexity specific to the project for which are hired. There are varying factors that contribute to the complexity of a specific project. Perhaps the most profound complexity is determined by the project's scope.

If a client asks us to look into one function, one department or one discrete area of their business, the project feels relatively simple – or at least reasonably contained. However, sometimes we're asked to investigate and solve for problems or processes that cross departments or divisions or that involve multiple, flawed communication systems. We consider these projects with their wide and deep scope to be complex. To recur to our definitions of complexity, we're dealing with a high degree of structural differentiation and usually very messy or nonexistent structural integration.

Scope dictates the size and makeup of our project team. Our research teams consist of a researcher and either a designer, business strategist or content strategist. The two-person team can only do so much research in a given project period, so a wider scope might require multiple research teams that work concurrently. The more teams on the project, the more difficult the data analysis becomes. Sometimes there is only one team, but it can still get complicated if individuals are rotated on and off the team because of limited availability. This creates the same problem of bringing the data together for a holistic analysis.

Finally, the timeline of the project can add varying levels of complexity. Short timelines may make in-depth analysis of the problem difficult and can jeopardize our ability to uncover the root of a problem. Long timelines may offer additional hours for analysis and synthesis, but may also weaken focus. Many times a complex process, large amounts of data, and a long time in which to analyze, can tempt us toward a needlessly elaborate explanation of a process.

2. PROJECT REPORT OVERVIEW

The following project report describes two different ways we simplified complexity in a recent project. We had to (a) simplify our internal process for tackling a complex problem and (b) simplify the presentation of that complex problem to the client. Specifically, this report focuses on the methods and outcomes used by our interdisciplinary team to solve a complex problem with a pharmaceutical client's aggregate reporting process. We also added a third element (c) a kind of meta-analysis of the project complexity afforded us by writing this paper.

2.1 The Project

Electronic Ink set out to understand the process of aggregate report writing for a small pharmaceutical company. The client's business goals were: (a) improve the efficiency of the report writing process, (b) improve the quality and consistency of the final published products, and (c) reduce the cost of producing the reports. In addition to the business goals, there were personnel goals: (a) alleviate the stress and create a process that allowed for greater employee satisfaction, and (b) determine the skill sets needed for the tasks that had to be completed for the reporting process to be successful. The stakes were high for our client, as they were poised to double their product line in the next few years. They had to achieve scalable ways of communicating better across distinct entities within the business if they were going to thrive.

2.2 The Team

Our company drew from our interdisciplinary professionals to create the appropriate team for this project. The team comprised a researcher with robust experience in corporate settings (cognitive psychologist), a designer with special strengths in dashboarding and the challenges of global companies (interaction designer), and a content strategist with experience analyzing and improving internal authoring and publishing processes (Ph.D. in English). A third researcher with additional experience in highly-regulated, elaborate corporate structures supplemented our efforts during collaborative sessions in our office (human factors psychologist).

2.3 The Research Activities

We conducted a combination of individual employee field observations (17) and group interviews (5). The field observations consisted of 2-hour sessions with individuals in their natural working environment, observing the day-to-day methods for completing their jobs. This included observations of the technologies used, analog work-arounds, process flows, etc. The discovery team asked questions where needed.

The team shared findings and insights daily, via emails, ad hoc conversations and some scheduled check-ins. Under the direction of the lead researcher, the team worked together to pool observations and notes from the research activities. The team parsed our findings, diagrammed the client's current reporting process and identified pain points where personnel, technology, or an unhappy combination of both were compromising the process or product.

2.4 The Solution

We delivered a "current-state" process map that identified the steps in the process and the technology, personnel, and documents involved in each step in the process. We also identified the difficulties or gaps in the process and made high-level recommendations for redress – such as recommending a change in tools, in timeline, in meeting procedures, and knowledge transfer.

3. COMPLEXITY

3.1 Complexity of Client Process

The client process of aggregate reporting was fraught with complexity from beginning to end. The level of structural differentiation in the company was great. There existed several different departments responsible for different arms of the business, and within each of these arms, the structure was varied. For example, in the reporting group, there were dedicated product teams that were responsible for knowing the history of one particular product. However, in the clinical department, different people were responsible for different uses of a given product. Two people could work virtually side-by-side, spend their days dealing with exactly the same drug, but know nothing about each other's work, because each dealt with the product in a different context. To complicate the structural differentiation even further, the company operated in the global market and thus had departments and personnel worldwide.

Integration between the global departments was vital to the success of the organization; however the level of structural integration was fair at best. The communication was fragmented and was not monitored by anyone at the management level. In addition, the methods used for information exchange, another vital aspect for the aggregate reporting group, were inefficient and insecure, putting the company at risk.

The levels of internal and external complexity were also very great. Recent regulatory changes were causing confusion and stress among the reporting team. Teams were responsible for three different reports for each product; each report duplicated some but not all of the information in other reports. Finally reporting periods and deadlines overlapped in many instances, exponentially complicating and intensifying workflow.

Internally, many of the personnel were given tasks and responsibilities outside of their expertise and training. This led to a culture of fear and insecurity both within the reporting department and across the various departments that provided information for the aggregate reports. The global nature of the company also hindered communication with non-US-based personnel.

3.2 Complexity of Project

The scope of the project was to streamline the aggregate reporting process and through this, improve the quality of the reports generated. Thus our focus seemed to be relatively small – "just" the one group. Once we began interviews, it soon became clear that the single group had to interact with people across several other groups. Thus our primary focus on the aggregate reporting group quickly gained a secondary focus on the interactions with other departments. To understand these interactions, we had to investigate at least the basic workings of each department. In other words, as we realized we needed to understand the structural integration of the company, we were slipping into the dreaded "scope creep."

While there was only one team assigned to the project, three individuals from three different backgrounds were conducting field observations. With three people participating in the observations there were three sets of notes from three different perspectives that needed to be reconciled. These notes,

handwritten and taken on the fly, contained both overlapping and unique information. Sorting out the wheat from the chaff was a complex problem in and of itself. The scope creep added research inquiries leaving only one week for data analysis, explanation and high-level recommendations for the client.

3.3 Simplification!

3.3.1 Simplification of our process

The macroeconomic framework pictured in Figure 1 lent itself well to the challenge of bringing three sets of notes together for analysis. [1] The framework defined the business context – from external complexities down to internal tools. The levels in the framework equated roughly to the elements involved in our client's process.

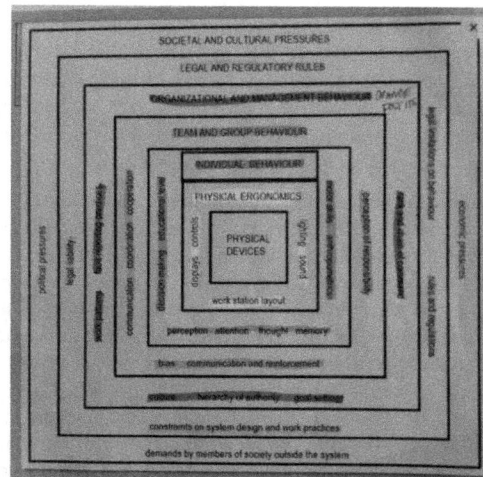

Figure 1. Macroergonomic Framework

Our client's aggregate reporting process had complexities from the outermost level (societal and cultural pressures) down to the level of the physical setting and devices in which individual employees involved in the process worked. Each category in the diagram above could correlate to a contextual element that posed constraints on the aggregate reporting system.

By explaining the levels described in the diagram and assigning each one a color, our lead researcher was able to have each member of the CI team parse his or her notes onto a colored "post it."

On the walls of the project room, she placed posters representing the key internal elements that made up the aggregate reporting workflow (the individual reports involved, the various software systems, and the departments). Team members placed each observation on the appropriate poster to create an affinity diagram that took up all four walls of the project room (See Figure 2).

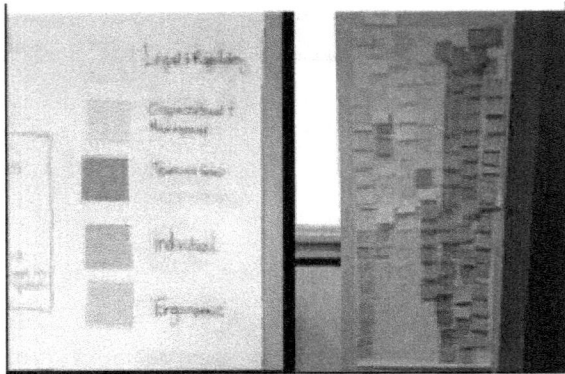

Figure 2. Affinity Diagramming

Note in the photo above that colored (and therefore conceptual) patterns began emerging as the colored post-its were used in affinity diagramming. A huge amount of data was parsed in just one afternoon as each team member dropped by to participate in the diagramming (another simplification—no need for rigid scheduling – our project manager was delighted).

As we completed our affinity diagramming, we also took breaks to create what we called the "real" workflow (See Figure 3), a diagram that reflected the inputs and sequence of events behind the client's aggregate reporting process. We called it the "real" one because the way things got done deviated in ways small and large from the official workflow that the client management had described to us before we observed the process itself. It took the entire team's observations to construct the workflow diagram – but when we finally deemed it complete, we had an excellent point of reference. We referred to it frequently during analysis as a means of pointing out problem areas and suggesting workflow adjustments.

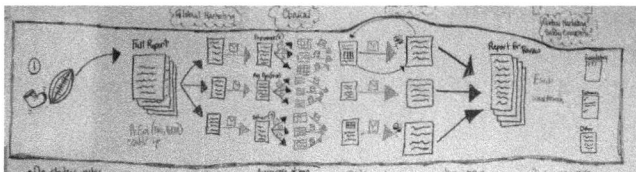

Figure 3. "Real" Workflow Diagram

These seemingly small and decidedly non-technical methods both simplified and deepened our process. This method not only allowed all team members to put their data into the mix, it also gave the designer and content strategist an unusual level of involvement in the act of analysis along with the researcher.

It was a natural, even organic progression from slapping up post-it notes to discussing categories, identifying overlaps or more nuanced observations, to discussing the meaning and implications of the emerging structure. When the project moved on to design phases and to further discussions with the client, all team members were nearly equally able to explain our findings and recommendations.

3.3.2 Simplify a complex message
As a business, our own success depends upon simple and clear presentation of our findings and recommendations. Usually, we are delivering our work to a subset of people who will have to

"sell" our findings to their colleagues and management. A win with our immediate client contacts does not necessarily mean further business or a phase two project. It behooves us then, to think carefully about how we'll share our findings. Part of our job, then, is to deliver our advice in a way that the client, a non-specialist, can then use as a teaching tool within his or her organization. The stakes are doubled, in other words, as we find ways to share our findings and recommendations

While we managed to simplify the complexities within our team and methodology to provide a quick, insightful and robust set of findings for ourselves, we still needed to find a way to deliver this material simply.

Years ago, our business was likely to create detailed written reports to communicate findings to our clients. Over the past few years, however, we have found the appetite for reports has been supplanted by the desire for quick, easy to digest visuals. Thus, we put as much of our design expertise into the way we present solutions as we put into the solutions themselves.

3.3.2.1 Clarity supports simplicity
Because our macroergonomic framework used laymen's terms, we were able to share both the Figure 1 and Figure 3 activities with our client. Moreover, we arranged to have them visit our project room periodically, a practice our company embraces, so clients can see what we're doing. Did the client understand absolutely everything we were up to? No. But they got the idea, they got to ask questions, and they saw firsthand the sophisticated thinking that was going in to our seemingly simple design solutions.

3.3.2.2 Visual artifacts spread insight easily
Rather than delivering a simple as-is workflow diagram showing sequential steps and the tools used, we layered on icons indicating at a glance the level of frustration or conflict involved in each step. The deliverable (which we cannot provide here due to confidentiality agreements) gave the audience "the whole story" of the process – not just the "what" but the "how" and the "so what" of the process. They were able to follow the timeline and understand:

- Roles involved
- Data inputs
- Data outputs
- Technology used
- Emotional climate at each step

This "as-is" workflow served as a potent foil to the "future-state," redesigned workflow that we offered later in the project. Our client was able to compare and contrast the redesign to the current state. Most important, the client was able to use both versions of the workflow to advance their strategic plan throughout the company. By offering a simple, intuitive artifact, we helped them advance toward company acceptance of the redesign.

We supplemented these findings with other tools that would help the client see and understand our solutions. By rearranging work groups and providing accurate, industry standard description of qualifications and roles, we were able to show how with just a few new hires, the workflow could be improved.

3.3.3 Simplifying choices by predicting outcomes
Before we could create a finalized, future-state vision for the client, we had to hear their concerns and help them envision how

any number of smaller decisions about timing training, headcount and technology might affect outcome.

We created a simplified macroergonomic framework to help the client see what kind of impact different decisions might make (see Figure 4). The pyramid below proved to be an excellent way of showing the client that an organizational change (top of pyramid) while difficult to implement, could affect the entire company structure and culture. A change at the individual or team level would help locally, but would not advance company-wide change. Put another way, structural integration would not be improved directly by local change within a single department or location.

Figure 4 Decision Impact Pyramid

3.3.4 Client outcome

Redesign is only the first step of implementing change in a business. Currently, our client is in the early phases of implementing our redesigned workflow. The gratification of seeing our research and recommendations played out in the real world is tempered by how long it takes a complex business to change course. Nonetheless, not every client manages to begin making changes mere weeks after we deliver our findings, as this client did. We believe that the many ways we simplified complexity gave our client the confidence and energy to begin changing right away.

4. LESSONS LEARNED

4.1.1 Revisit your approach basics

Our company ideal is always to engage all the disciplines in the work – from sales through delivery and scoping further work with a client. Using frameworks, as we have shown, brought us much closer to this in reality. We thought of ourselves as seasoned collaborators, nonetheless, approaching the work this way introduced some growing pains. We'd like to share them here in hopes that anyone tempted to follow our example will enjoy smoother sailing.

Communication must grow to keep up with growing collaboration.

When designers participate in research and analysis; when researchers scrutinize design deliverables; when designers weigh in on a written findings and recommendations report, it can be hard to maintain a single thread of communication. Throughout the project, we found ourselves stumbling and backtracking in lots of little ways because we were not all clear on who was done with what.

Projects that embrace this method of collaboration should reinforce the need for a unified communication channel. Create an email circulation list and **stick to it**, so everybody sees everything. Commit to clear and succinct subject lines on those emails, so team members can respond efficiently and appropriately. Schedule regular short meetings (15 minutes per day) as well as a longer weekly meeting that allows sufficient time to make sure everybody is up to speed and knows what to do next. It's tough to figure out when a casual conversation between two team members arrives at a point that should be shared with the whole team. Use these regular meetings to help strike the balance between formal and informal communication.

Don't throw out clear definitions of roles and responsibilities.

It is very difficult to enable such collaboration, yet make sure that the person with the appropriate expertise and experience is still making the decisions that matter. Fortunately, we avoided turf wars – everyone was pretty excited to have a chance to be more involved in all phases of the work, and that good spirit prevailed. Nonetheless, we were surprised at how muddy some decisions became. We considered ourselves veterans of collaborative work at the company, yet we were surprised at how this method launched us into some very muddy decision-making waters. Although we were a pretty confident bunch (in ourselves and in each other) we'd be lying if we didn't acknowledge that we each felt a pang of "Hey, back off, you novice!" at one or another point in the project. We recommend that at the internal project kickoff, the project manager clearly establishes who has the last word on which decisions and deliverables. This will help everyone be more flexible and open in the work leading up to decision points.

Summon your best project manager.

If you have worked in industry, you already know how vital the project manager is for any project. Using the framework added significantly to the challenges of the project manager. As the last vestiges of serial workflow crumbled ("handing off" research to design, for example,) the PM found himself with more people in more meetings; more review threads to track, and, let's face it, more personalities bouncing off each other more often, week after week. This is not for the faint of heart. The PM has to be willing and able to keep the team on track and working within the established roles and responsibilities, even as he or she faces complaints when somebody feels suddenly 'left out' of this new collaborative extravaganza. Put your strongest PM on the job and empower him or her. As he or she gains experience, promote knowledge sharing and mentoring to bring less experienced PMs up to the task. And remind everybody at the outset that this is a new challenge and as such, the PM needs clear, constructive feedback.

4.1.2 Take what you've learned and think big
Mine what's out there and adapt it to your needs.

After this project, we were further convinced that applying frameworks to data gathered by interdisciplinary teams was an efficient way to make the most of the abilities and insights of the team. As a result, our research group has an ongoing practice of surveying and gathering what we call "flexible frameworks" and sharing them across the company. We chose our name deliberately: in a company full of designers and researchers, anything smacking of mass production or proscription is bound to meet with resistance. Our goal is always to give people enough structure to facilitate collaboration and kick start analysis, not to shortchange the analysis or its outcomes.

Encourage reuse.

We found that certain aspects of working with the framework could apply to other clients within the same industry. For example, once we had articulated basic aspects and challenges of the safety and regulatory context for our pharmaceutical client, we had language and elements that would be applicable, with some tweaking, to other clients in that industry. We'd also created a cross-disciplinary team that knew more than any of us ever thought possible about reporting and compliance within the drug industry. Similarly, the work helped us build some basic language and thinking around tiers of management and business strategy. What's significant here is not just that some of the material can be reused – it's also the fact that we've now got a team that includes designers in thinking about how companies imagine and deploy business strategies and tactics. This isn't always something our people learn within their disciplinary training.

This is just the beginning of what we believe we'll do with frameworks. The method is helping to develop expertise within the company while delivering holistic, impressive solutions to the client.

5. Conclusion

By working together on this paper, we have enjoyed the rare opportunity to look back at a project from a brief respite and understand its implications. Writing solidified certain ideas and bolstered them with expert research. We now share a common vocabulary with which to analyze business structures and processes. Structural differentiation, structural integration, internal complexity, and external complexity are just a few. Sharing a common vocabulary is crucial and rare within interdisciplinary teams and these more clearly articulated concepts are even more compelling when we think about presenting to clients. As we bring this to a close, we can also appreciate that the project described and the paper you have just read have given us valuable insights into making our own processes more efficient and we can truly say we're actually using our expertise on our internal organization.

6. ACKNOWLEDGMENTS

The authors would like to thank SIGDOC for presenting such an inspiring conference theme for 2013. We would also like to thank Electronic Ink for supporting our efforts here.

7. REFERENCES

[1] Brown, C. and Legg, S. 2011. Human factors and ergonomics for business sustainability. In *Critical Studies on Corporate Responsibility*, G. Eweje and M. Perry, Eds. Emerald Group Publishing Limited, Bingley UK, 59-79.

[2] Hendrick, H. and Kleiner, B. 2002. *Macroergonomics: Theories, Methods, and Applications*. Lawrence Erlbaum Associates, Mahwah, NJ.

[3] Jakupovic, A., Pavlic, M., and Candrlic, S. 2010. Application of analytic hierarchy process (AHP) to measure the complexity of the business sector and business software. *Proceedings of the Third C* Conf. on Comp Sci. and Software Eng* (May 2010), 35-42.

[4] Vicari, S. 1998. La creatività dell'impresa. Tra caso e necessità, ETAS, Milano, Italy.

An Approach to Improve the Accessibility and Usability of Existing Web System

Ana Luiza Dias, Renata Pontin de Mattos Fortes, Paulo Cesar Masiero,
Willian Massami Watanabe, Matheus Edson Ramos
Computer Science Department, Institute of Mathematics and Computer Sciences
University of São Paulo – USP, São Carlos, Brazil
{anadias, renata, masiero}@icmc.usp.br; watanabe_willian@yahoo.com; matheuser@usp.br

ABSTRACT

The Web is currently the main way of providing computing services, reaching a larger number of users with different characteristics. As the complexity and interactivity of systems is increased, users become more demanding towards all the requirements associated to their distinct needs. Implementing the interaction requirements in the Web has become the main focus of accessibility and usability studies, describing essential design features which provide users with quality, assured systems. The focus on the users reinforced that as the number of users grows and the system became available to a wide variety of users, accessibility and usability features become even more critical to a Web application's success. In this paper, we present ACCESSA, a practical approach to rapidly improve the accessibility of existing Web systems, acting mainly in the interface design with no changes to the functional requirements of systems. The ACCESSA is based on the WCAG 2.0 guidelines and other patterns, choosing the guidelines that present lower implementation costs and represent higher severity accessibility issues.

Categories and Subject Descriptors

H.5.2 User Interfaces [User-centered design]

General Terms

Design, Human Factors, Standardization, Languages.

Keywords

Web systems, Web Usability and Accessibility, User requirements.

1. INTRODUCTION

The continuous changing of the use perspective of the Web applications is an irreversible fact. Contents that were simple to navigate are becoming more and more complex due to updates of many dynamic components included in those systems [17]. One of the perceived reasons for these changes is the concern of the adequacy of the contents to the characteristics, diversity and needs of users, and the way they interact with information and services available on the Web [16].

With the technological advances and increased popularity of the Web, several technologies have been developed to extend the possibilities of HTML. However most of the companies and developers that create Web systems do not follow the standards that ensure the universality of the Web, such as: matching the possibilities of use, flexibility in use, simple and intuitive use, capture of information, fault tolerance, small physical effort, size and space to use interaction patterns [10]. This breaking with the standards and principles to create Web systems brought several consequences to their evolution, since the use of the Web by users with little experience and even for use on mobile devices is hampered by the lack of standardization [11].

Thus, even with advanced technology to promote various forms of Web interactivity, researches on digital inclusion for people with disabilities have shown not only the lack of accessible solutions in universities, business and government environment, but also the lack of usability in Web systems, since the interface is the communication part mainly for the user perform their tasks [11][13].

This paper presents an approach, named ACCESSA, focused on users to improve the accessibility and usability of existing Web systems. A viability study was realized for the evolution of the process and the users and specialist were essential to have a product that met all the requirements of users. We used the AgendAloca system (a Group Calendar system that aims to fill the gap between information for use by students and teachers at a specific University) as a viability study to perceive how user participation is fundamental to insert the attributes of accessibility and usability into Web applications, validating the Approach presented here. The development of two versions of AgendAloca system will be described, showing the evolution of the interface.

The main goal of ACCESSA is to use the triangulation of methods, which some designers already perform, focusing on their real results based on case study. Consequently, the approach proposed in this paper is practicable and may be useful for reengineering processes. Additionally, this paper presents some attractive ideas by combining the various aspects of usability and accessibility evaluation in one approach to rapidly improve the accessibility of a Web system, acting mainly in interface design without changing the functionality.

This paper is organized as follows: in Section 2 the Accessibility and Usability of Web System is presented; Section 3 presents the proposal Approach. The Viability Study and AgendAloca System can be found in Sections 4. In Section 5 the results of the applied approach are presented, followed the results that compare two versions of the AgendAloca System in Section 6. Finally, in Section 7, final remarks are presented.

2. ACCESSIBILITY AND USABILITY OF WEB SYSTEM

A concept that is misunderstood in relation to accessibility is that to developing systems thinking about accessibility implies limitations in usability. Many developers argue that accessibility guidelines limit the use of technologies such as JavaScript, animations, applets and other technologies that can be used to improve the usability of a system. The recommendations do not preclude the use of these technologies, but only indicate that they should be used following certain principles and guidelines so that they do not become barriers [1][21].

Accessibility means unlimited use of Web systems for all people, independent of individual disabilities [11][25] and should be inserted early in the development process of systems, whether conventional or Web-based [18]. Despite the limitations of the Web Content Accessibility Guidelines (WCAG), such as the difficulty to understand the language that describes the guidelines [3], they are the dominant approach to support developers building accessible systems [11].

Although accessibility is an essential quality attribute for people with disabilities, it has not gained due recognition as a fundamental non-functional requirement in a software project, such as security, performance, accuracy and usability [1] [14]. Even though most of the systems available do not show good accessibility [11], some studies have been concerned about how to incorporate accessibility in existing systems [19] to meet the needs of a diverse population and support the awareness of how the fact of considering accessibility helps developing more usable systems for all people [34].

The current version of WCAG (2.0) was elaborated to be technologically neutral, being applicable to technologies available now and in the future. The guidelines also provide objective testable criteria that can be evaluated with a combination of automatic testing and human evaluation [35].

Many authors [8][15][22][32][33][35] argue that accessibility evaluation processes of Web interfaces, restricted to revisions with automatic accessibility evaluation tools, are sufficient. However, one of the problems with evaluations based only on automatic accessibility verification is that not all checkpoints can be automatically verified [31]. Another problem, mentioned by Brajnik [5], is that guidelines such as the WCAG do not enable the evaluator to distinguish serious problems from trivial ones, regardless of the existence of well-defined priority levels.

For instance, in the guideline checkpoint 1.1, in WCAG 1.0, it is recommended that every image that is presented on a Web page must have an alternative text, being a priority 1 checkpoint. However, according to Brajnik [5], most Web images have an "emotional" purpose, and do not aggregate content to the document. Thus, there is no need to effectively include an alternative text for every image. It is important to highlight that people with sensorial and/or cognitive limitations develop specific abilities, such as the preference for, and the use of keyboard key combinations, not usual to people who has not the referred limitations. Thus, Web accessibility evaluation should include, apart from automatic verification tools, user tasks verifications focused on difficulties encountered in performing daily work. These tasks can guide user's mental models to overcome the difficulties, and contribute to making satisfactory the interaction of impaired users with a Web-based application of their interest.

Therefore, many authors have performed tests with the participation of real users to check the Web accessibility [22][26], since those tests simulate conditions of use from the final user's perspective, by prioritizing, for instance, the analysis of the navigation easiness between screens of the user interface, and clarity of their texts and messages. This way, difficulties and problems faced by users during use sessions can be identified, enabling evaluators to formulate a more realistic diagnostic evaluation, and propose better corrective measures to designers. Based in these references, we created ACCESSA that can be used to improve the accessibility with some WCAG 2.0 guidelines.

3. THE PROPOSAL APPROACH

We present ACCESSA that is an approach focused on users to improve the accessibility of a Web System. The main idea is to rapidly improve the accessibility of existing Web systems, introducing practices to be included in interface the design phase of the development process, with no changes to the functionalities of systems. ACCESSA approach is based on the implementation of selected WCAG 2.0 guidelines and other patterns, which consist of accessibility features that present lower implementation costs and represent higher severity accessibility issues.

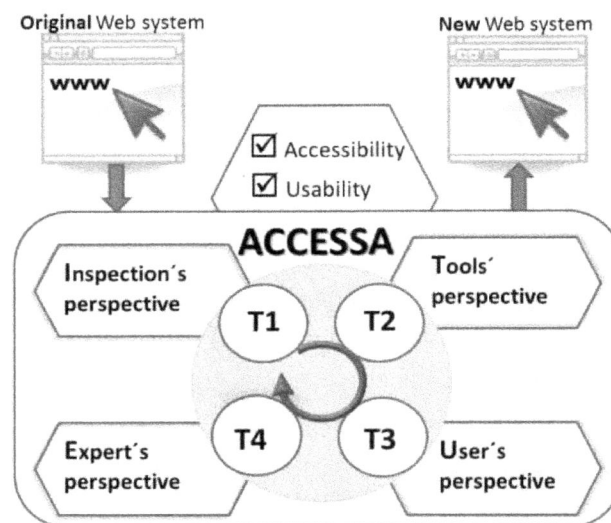

Figure 1. Overview of the ACCESSA

Figure 1 shows an overview of the ACCESSA approach, which makes use of four evaluation perspectives:

T1) **Inspection's perspective** is a conformance evaluation [5] given by an expert to determine if a Web site meets accessibility standards in accordance with WCAG 2.0[1] principles, which are Perceivable, Operable, Understandable and Robust;

T2) **Tools' perspective** is given by accessibility automatic evaluation tools, because the guidelines provide objective testable criteria, that can be evaluated with a combination of automatic testing (using automatic evaluation tools, like Hera[2] and daSilva[3]);

---

[1] http://www.w3.org/TR/WCAG/
[2] http://www.sidar.org/hera/index.php.en
[3] http://www.dasilva.org.br/

T3) **User's perspective**, expressed by the user's view of the interactivity of the system. It is represented by the retrieval of satisfaction data via three methods: 1) Pre-Section **questionnaires** (to collect the user profile) and Post-Section **questionnaires** (to collect user's opinion about the Web system under evaluation); 2) **informal think aloud** method [23] (which lead subjects into saying out loud what they are thinking about when navigating in Web system) and 3) **interview** (to know the opinion of the users on the system).

T4) **Expert's perspective**, provided by the analysis of the user performance during the execution of tasks [20][23], generating a set of change requirements.

In order to validate ACCESSA, we developed a viability study using the AgendAloca System, showing that rapidly achieves good improvement of accessibility in an existing system.

4. VIABILITY STUDY

According to Shull [29], the first study that should be made to evaluate a new approach is a viability study, which aims to verify whether this new technology is feasible and if the time spent is well used. These studies are typically performed in the academy, since they allow that new technologies be tested before being transferred to the industry to use them on a day-by-day basis.

4.1 AgendAloca System

Group Calendar Systems (GCS) consist of systems that integrate information for personal use or for use in a particular group. GCS are calendars that can be shared on a network like the Internet, for example. These systems allow concurrent user interactions, which enhances user awareness of commitment schedules made by others and might impact in their planned activities [26].

In the University of São Paulo (USP), the presentation of final year undergraduate projects (*Trabalho de Conclusão de Curso - TCC -* in Portuguese) is an essential step towards any student graduation, in which students present their work to a panel of lecturers. GCS present an important role of reconciling the multiple presentations of works of all students in the university. The need for providing communication between students and lectures to retrieve information related to the works that were developed (TCC) and dates that are convenient and available to both groups, were the main motivations behind the implementation of the AgendAloca system.

Before the development of the AgendAloca first version, the management of the schedule for presentations of the TCCs was performed manually; each student was asked to inform their preferred time and date for the presentation of TCC within a predetermined time. Thus, the version 1 of the online system on the Web was developed to manage the schedule and was used primarily to advertise the scheduled presentations online. It has been used for nearly six years by those involved (students and lectures). However, this initial version of the system was in disuse for no longer meeting the new requirements that came with new demands, such as the need of a feature that allow the participation of students and teachers while interacting in the choice of working hours through the system.

Over time the interaction with the system was intensified as the number of new users who had to access the system increased. Thus, accessibility and usability requirements became even more evident and had to be re-prioritized, and this led the development of AgendAloca version 2.

The AgendAloca version 1 was developed with CMS (Content Management Systems) Drupal version 6. The CMS Drupal was chosen due to the potential to reuse existing features and also for being an extensible modular framework, which allows adding features by means of the integration of modules (Figure 2).

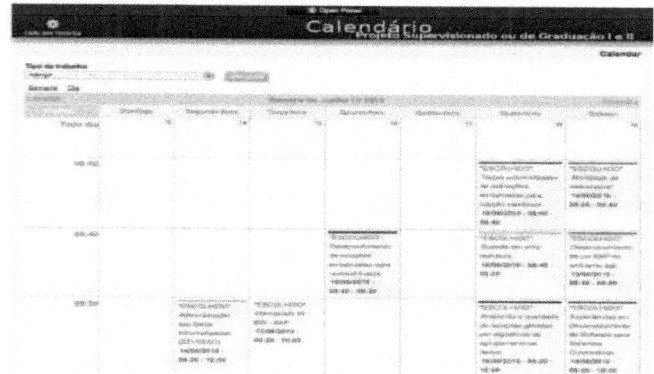

Figure 2. AgendAloca – version 1

While developing this version of AgendAloca (v1), it was necessary to elicit requirements with the teachers. After the elicitation of the requirements, the use cases of the system were separated into two groups: (a) use by students and (b) use by teachers.

In the first group of use cases (a. use by students), students could choose the time of their presentation, and enter information related to the work they developed (TCC). In the second group of use cases (b. use by teachers), teachers choose the work's presentation they would like to participate.

Despite the major benefits provided by the first version of the system, the accessibility and usability issues were not considered because of the urgency to provide the initial functionalities. Therefore, we decided to develop a second version of the system, but this time considering accessibility requirements to allow that new types of users benefit of AgendAloca's features. A summary of requirements and technologies addressed in the two versions are presented in Table 1.

Table 1. Summary of AgendAloca versions

AgendAloca versions	Technologies used	Main requirements were met
Version 1[4] (v.1)	CMS Drupal	- Manage the hours available for students to present TCC - Manage the participation of teachers in presentations scheduled by students
Version 2[5] (v.2)	API JSF API JAX-rs API JAXB	- Manage the hours available for students to present TCC - Manage the participation of teachers in presentations scheduled by students - Insert accessibility and usability

---

[4] http://agua.intermidia.icmc.usp.br/agendamento

[5] http://garapa.intermidia.icmc.usp.br:3000/agendaloca

To develop version 2, it was necessary to conduct a viability study that is explained in the next subsections.

4.2 Planning

The viability study[6] was conducted to evaluate the accessibility and usability of the AgendAloca System. The main hypothesis of this paper is to verify if the implementation of features associated to accessibility requirements also contribute to improve the general usability of the system.

In order to test our hypothesis we used ACCESSA (Section 3), to improve the accessibility of the AgendAloca system. And, then, we compared accessibility and usability metrics of the previous version of the system (v1) and the new generated version (v2). If the accessibility and usability metrics are both increased from the previous to the newer version of the system, then our hypothesis is supported by the viability study. If the accessibility and usability present different tendency in the metrics, then our hypothesis is rejected by the study.

As accessibility evaluation criteria, one quantitative metric was considered: the number of guidelines that did not have their Success Criteria met, according to a WCAG conformance evaluation.

As usability evaluation criteria, two quantitative metric groups were defined: the primary group consists of the metrics of time taken to perform a set of proposed tasks and the amount of errors obtained during an interaction session. The secondary group consists of metrics of amount of tasks completed successfully and the number of clicks performed during each task.

It is worth noticing that the ACCESSA approach includes four evaluation phases. And two of these phases have the objective of tracking the accessibility and usability metrics that are used in the viability study (considering the Inspection's perspective and the User's perspective). Thus we used the approach's accessibility and usability reports to verify our hypothesis validity.

4.3 Using the Approach

The ACCESSA was defined in order to raise the accessibility issues of the system and identify possible design solutions for these issues. In this context, we tested the first version of AgendAloca system with the four perspectives: the inspection's perspective; the industrial's perspective; the user's perspective and the expert's perspective.

4.3.1 Inspection's perspective

The Inspection's perspective consists of a WCAG 2.0 conformance evaluation to the system. The result was reported on a percentage scale of how many success criteria were not designed in the system for each WCAG 2.0 guideline. The results were generated by an accessibility specialist and are presented in Table 2.

AgendAloca v.1 does not support a great number of accessibility features. This is justifiable since the goal of the development was to deliver new functionalities with no understanding or knowledge about the accessibility guidelines. The few accessibility features that can be perceived are the result of CMS native modules, which were already implemented considering accessibility requirements. For instance, the mandatory use of alternative text on images.

---

6 To realize this study an approval of the ethics committee was obtained. CAAE 05700912.5.0000.5390.

Table 2. Evaluation of AgendAloca v.1 under inspection's perspective

Principles	Guidelines	Average
Perceivable	1.1 Text alternatives	100%
	1.2 Time-based Media[7]	0
	1.3 Adaptable	63%
	1.4 Distinguishable	72%
Final Average - Perceivable:		**78,5%**
Operable	2.1 Keyboard Accessible	100%
	2.2 Enough Time	75%
	2.3 Seizures	100%
	2.4 Navigable	38%
Final Average - Operable:		**75,7%**
Understandable	3.1 Readable	21%
	3.2 Predictable	92%
	3.3 Input Assistance	53%
Final Average - Understandable:		**55,6%**
Robust	4.1 Compatible	45%
Final Average - Robust:		**45%**

4.3.2 Tools' perspective

As Accessibility Evaluation and Repair tools in the Tools' perspective evaluation phase, we used daSilva tool and aDesigner tool [30]. The daSilva tool reported the system presented 16 errors and that 11 errors were classified as priority 1, 4 errors were classified as priority 2 and 1 error, priority 3. daSilva also reported 116 warning messages, which indicate checkpoints (considering that the Accessibility Evaluation and Report tools used in the study classify the accessibility issues identified according to the WCAG 1.0) that need to be evaluated manually and could be harmful to the navigation of the website. We also tested the AgendAloca version 1 with the aDesigner tool to verify the accessibility of Web systems for blind users using colors and gradation. A single problem on the menu of the website was reported by the tool.

4.3.3 User's perspective

The User's perspective evaluation scenario was conducted with two students from the University of São Paulo. This target audience was recruited for convenience according to the main motivation of the developed Web system, which is to support students at the end of their graduation courses to schedule and organize end-of-course monographs and presentations.

The students were asked to complete a number of tasks on the AgendAloca system. While these tasks were realized by the participants, we tracked the usability evaluation criteria described in Section 5.1. The metrics were collected by means of real-time monitoring of the user's activities using the Morae[8] tool, as presented in Figure 3.

The tasks that the participants were asked to execute were:

1. To do log in;
2. To show their own data;
3. To see the Group Calendar;
4. To register two accounts of students and
5. To do log off.

---

7 Guideline 1.2 received 0 because the AgendAloca system does not use audio/video contents anywhere.

8 http://www.techsmith.com/morae.html

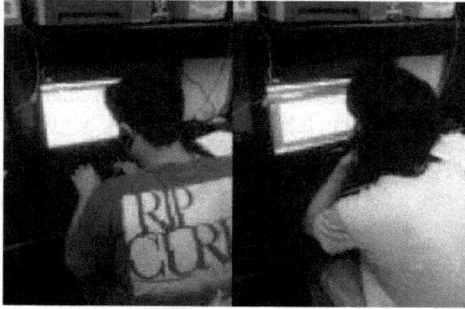

Figure 3. Users during the Viability Study

Both users are male and are 18 and 19 years old. They do not present any deficiency and present an Internet user profile of browsing the Web more than 24 hours per week in desktop, notebook and cell phone. They said that they like to learn new things and do not have fear or insecurity using the Web, but are not comfortable navigating through menus and going back to previous actions.

Some accessibility issues were collected as statements by the participants, as the following: *"the login button is hidden under a flap that exists only to confuse those who use the system for the first time"*, *"the system layout is confusing, making it harder to find the information"*, *"system functions are allocated in a few fields, i.e., there are few options for many options"*, and *"some fields were confused"*.

The users suggested that a simple field on the home page to login directly would ease the task accomplishment and some ambiguous options should be adjusted.

4.3.4 Expert's perspective

To realize the expert's perspective, we used indirect feedback, that is gathered by observing users as they interact with Web systems. According to Rocha and Baranauskas [23], the observation method is the most valuable form of collecting feedback about the user interaction, because it may involve valuable discoveries about the users of the system. The ways in which they use the functions of the system is fitted and aspects of the system that can be optimized to make the most effective and efficient use, making users more satisfied, become more evident. Additionally, we analyzed the video collected during the interaction with the users in order to complement the record of observation, as suggested by Nielsen [20].

The issues that were identified during the observation were all related to understanding (or a set of change requirements):

- The screens due to the large number of information.

- The functionality of some menu items because their names were not representative, and a mix of Portuguese and English words.

- The features because of the names and distribution of the menus (not distributed in an intuitive manner).

- What to do when certain features are activated.

These evidences that were observed and related the accessibility issues identified during the interaction with AgendAloca (v1) can discourage its use as a system.

4.4 Threat to the validity of the study

In all experimental studies there are threats that might affect the validity of the results. The threats related to this study were classified into four categories: internal validity, external validity, conclusion validity and construct validity [35].

4.4.1 Internal validity

In this study, we considered two main threats posed a risk of improper interpretation of results: (1) effects of training and (2) user experience. Regarding the first threat, there could be an effect caused by training, if the training of the participants involved in the evaluation of user's perspective for the first version of AgendAloca had lower quality than the training of participants of the evaluation of version 2. The risk was minimized because both received the same training (AgendAloca version 1 and 2). Regarding the user experience, it was also minimized because both did not know the AgendAloca system.

4.4.2 External validity

The population of participants is not statistically representative, because it is a homogeneous group of undergraduate students. The conduction of the experiment was done in a controlled environment. For these reasons the external validity of this experiment is compromised and the results and conclusions cannot be generalized. Although it is believed that the indicia found in this study is of high validity for the area and the research itself.

4.4.3 Conclusion validity

The amount and homogeneity of the sample are problems for the validity of this experiment, because the amount of subject is not ideal from the statistical point of view and all participants are students of the same institution. Reduced samples represent frequent problems in the field of HCI (Human Computer Interaction) and SE (Software Engineering) [4] [6]. Due to these factors, there is clear limitations in the results, which are considered as evidence of our hypothesis correctness, however are not conclusive.

4.4.4 Construct validity

Participants' and experiment drivers' expectations may influence the results. The participants may be influenced by drivers. In this experiment, the participants did not know which of the hypotheses for this risk was mitigated.

5. RESULTS OF THE APPLIED APPROACH

With the problems perceived during the viability study, we listed some accessibility and usability features that were inserted in version 2 of AgendAloca.

5.1 Accessibility features

According to a study conducted by Santos et al. [26] with middle aged people, the learning curve, success rate for doing certain tasks and user satisfaction towards the menu, used in the AgendAloca v1. was ranked with medium score. For this reason, the superfish dropdown menu was chosen as an accessible menu, since it has some aspects that make it more accessible and usable, such as: Indication that there are submenus available with small arrow images. The link corresponds to the whole box area, not just the text. There is visual indication when one item is selected; and the submenus have fade-in and fade-out animation effects when appearing and disappearing and it also has a small shadow around it. Furthermore, the superfish submenu keeps open briefly even if the mouse pointer moves out of it; this behavior assists users that have trouble pointing the mouse to one exact place inside a limited space. The superfish menu was evaluated with the best learning curve and received the second best rank according to users [26].

The menu was located in top of the system (Figure 2). However, when the system was tested in aDesigner tool a problem was found: a user that used the keyboard to navigate the system would take too long to make it to the search field. To solve this problem, the menu was placed on the left side of the system (Figure 4), and then to use the keyboard to navigate the system, the search field will be accessed first.

Figure 4. AgendAloca – version 2

To improve the accessibility of AgendAloca, we focused in solving the issues identified on the four perspective evaluation phases realized on the first version of the system. The issues raised during the evaluations and the accessible design solutions that were implemented in AgendAloca version 2 are presented in the next sections, classified according to the four principles of WCAG 2.0.

5.1.1 Perceivable
In the Perceivable Principle, the guidelines 1.3 Adaptable (1.3.1 Info and Relationships and 1.3.2 Meaningful Sequence) and 1.4 Distinguishable (1.4.4 Resize text and 1.4.6 Contrast) were addressed, as showed in Table 4.

5.1.2 Operable
In the Principle Operable, the guidelines 2.4 Navigable (2.4.1 Bypass Blocks, 2.4.2 Page Titled, 2.4.3 Focus Order, 2.4.4 Link Purpose, 2.4.5 Multiple Ways, 2.4.6 Headings and Labels, 2.4.7 Focus Visible and 2.4.9 Link Purpose) were addressed, as showed in Table 5.

Table 4. Improving the principle Perceivable

Guidelines/ Success Criteria		Accessibility problems in the first version	Improvements in the new version
1.3	1.3.1	Errors were presented in red without explanation of the meaning to the text.	All colored information has an equivalent in text form, errors are presented in red, and the word "error" will be available in the beginning of the error messages.

Guidelines/ Success Criteria		Accessibility problems in the first version	Improvements in the new version
	1.3.2	Using a screen reader or even tab key to navigate, the calendar navigation flows starting from the beginning of a line to the end, it is not instinctive because it travels by all the first presentations of each day of the week and then jump to the second line, the next day.	The navigation starts from the top of the column, pass by all presentation of that day until reach the end of the column and then jump to the top of the next column, the next day.
1.4	1.4.4	Nonexistent.	Except for captions and images of text, text can be resized without assistive technology up to 200 percent without loss of content or functionality
	1.4.6	Nonexistent.	Added a button to activate high contrast.

Table 5. Improving the principle Operable

Guidelines/ Success Criteria		Accessibility problems in the first version	Improvements in the new version
2.4	2.4.1	Nonexistent.	Added a link "Jump to content" that helps the screen reader users to jump directly to the main content area of the page.
	2.4.2	Nonexistent. The system just shows the system name on the title.	The system name and the purpose of the page are presented in each page.
	2.4.3	When the administrative tab is opened the focus starts from the search box, otherwise it starts from the user menu. Additionally the calendar does not have an instinctive focus order as explained in the item 1.3.2 of Table 4.	The focus starts from the top, and visits all elements from left to right in the pages, when the focus is on the calendar, it travels from beginning to the end of a column before moving to the next column.
	2.4.4	The text of some links, for example, to access the user information, is just the user name. In the calendar, to register a presentation it necessary to click in the title of the presentation box.	All links have a clear purpose according to the descriptive text, for instance, the users access their information in the "My account" link and to register a presentation they need to click the link "Register my presentation".

	2.4.5	There is only one difficult path to execute some tasks, for example for administrators add new users: they need to access 3 different pages, then, in the last one, select a tab to access the register form.	All this tasks are available in the main menu or using the search bar.
	2.4.6	Use of labels to explain all form inputs but it does not uses headings to explain page/section purposes.	Also uses label in all form inputs and uses headings in all main sections/pages to summarize the content.
	2.4.7	Nonexistent.	All elements show a border when are focused except form inputs that uses the cursor as an indicator of focus.
	2.4.9	As commented on the item 2.4.4, that is a Level AA criterion, the first system does not accomplish to it. In consequence, it does not accomplish to this requirement that is Level AAA, which is a refinement of the item 2.4.4.	In the development, that was a care to make all links self-explanatory, the links' text does not need the context to make sense.

5.1.3 Understandable

In the Principle Understandable, the guidelines 3.1 Readable (3.1.2 Language of Parts), 3.2 Predictable (3.2.4 Consistent Identification) and 3.3 Input Assistance (3.3.6 Error Prevention) were addressed, as showed in Table 6.

Table 6. Improving the principle Understandable

Guidelines/ Success Criteria		Accessibility problems in the first version	Improvements in the new version
3.1	3.1.2	The standard translation of the CMS does not cover 100% of the content, thus there are some parts of the system where the user can find the content partially in Portuguese, partially in English.	It was created internationalization buttons to change all system content to Portuguese or English.

3.2	3.2.4	In different pages, some buttons have the same functionality, but they have different labels. For instance, in the calendar page to filter the type of project the word used is "Apply". However, in the user page to filter the label is "Filter".	In all system, mainly to create, read, update and delete (CRUD) pages, all buttons and labels have the same terminology to not confuse the user.
3.3	3.3.6	In both systems it is possible to review input errors after submission.	A high score was added to the new system because it is possible review the information after a successful submission. It makes possible recheck and possibly updates the information.

5.1.4 Robust

In the Principle Robust, the guideline 4.1 Compatible (4.1.1 Parsing and 4.1.2 Name, Role, Value) was addressed, as showed in Table 7.

Table 7. Improving the principle Understandable

Guidelines/ Success Criteria		Accessibility problems in the first version	Improvements in the new version
4.1	4.1.1	After submit the system in the W3C HTML Validator[9] it was noted that the automatic code generation of the CMS generated several elements with the same id.	In the new version due to the little amount of generated code, the majority of the system code was written manually, it makes easy to avoid duplicated ids and to accomplish other specifications of this criterion.
	4.1.2	The login and search forms appear in a panel that slides from the top of the page after the use click the button open panel. This different approach is not identifiable by screen readers, so when the user navigates using the tab key this part of the system is unreachable. The system does not give information to the screen reader deal with this difference.	Standard HTML that works well with screen readers was used in the new system.

---

[9] http://validator.w3.org

Some characteristics about usability were also improved.

5.2   Usability features

The key to success of any Web system is based on the usability features and improvements done for making them comfortable to users. Therefore, besides the accessibility requirements, usability requirements to mainstream users were also taken into account [8]:

- Initial bar presenting the name of the system to the users identify rapidly the system;
- Searching area of the system, where the user can navigate and search what he/ she wishes;
- Information area about the system should be always available (breadcrumb) and
- Applying combination of colors according to motivational patterns suggested by Dias *et al.* [8].

It is important to highlight that the accessibility and usability requirements were inserted based on the requirements raised with the support of the ACCESSA approach presented in this work.

The same users, who conducted the study in version 1, also did it in version 2. Some user comments on version 2: "*I do not think the system has difficulties*", "*The registration process and viewing registrations is simple and well explained*", "*The system has easy access with a login screen accessible and all fields are clear*" and "*The system is very simple to use, has no ambiguous links and is easily used by inexperienced users, and also for people with disabilities*". The comparisons between the two versions of the system can be seen in the next section.

6.   DISCUSSION COMPARING V1 vs V2

We can perceive that even if users do not report many problems presented in the questionnaires, during interaction with the system many problems are found, according to the quantitative metric analysis. Also, WCAG 2.0 guidelines were not considered while developing the first version of the system, generating some problems during navigation of the users.

To demonstrate the evolution of accessibility of the AgendAloca, the interfaces of the two versions of the system were evaluated following the same principles explained in section 5.2. The inspection's perspective can be seen in Figure 5.

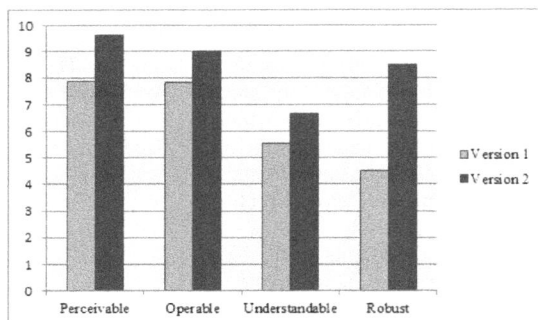

Figure 5. Evaluation of both versions of AgendAloca according to the WCAG 2.0 guidelines

According to Figure 5, inserting only the accessibility and usability features presented in section 6 in AgendAloca version 2.0 was enough to improve the accessibility and consequently the navigation for the users.

Starting the quantitative metrics analysis (the time taken to perform the proposed tasks, the amount of errors obtained with the interaction of the users, the amount of tasks completed successfully and the number of clicks performed during each task) we can see the comparison between AgendAloca version 1 and version 2.

Figure 6 shows that the time necessary to complete most tasks in version 2 was lower than in version 1. The users saved a long time on tasks, considering the log in functionality, which was significantly reduced in version 2, showing the own data and registering two accounts of students.

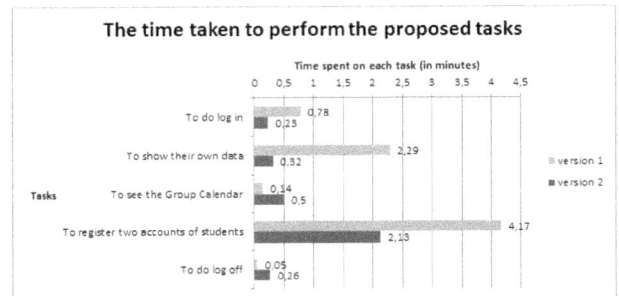

Figure 6. The time taken to perform the proposed tasks

Figure 7 shows the number of errors during the evaluation sessions. Task 2 presents the higher rates in this metric (Task – Showing their own data). It occurred because version 1 did not implement a way to visualize the data without showing the data in the form of editing. This behavior misled users while achieving this task.

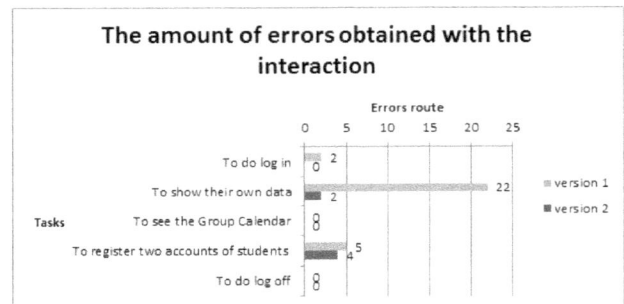

Figure 7. The amount of errors obtained with the interaction

Figure 8 shows the amount of tasks completed successfully. It is important to acknowledge that, in version 1, only the tasks seeing the group calendar and doing log off were easily completed. The others tasks presented many problems. On the other hand, version 2 presented one hundred percent success rate. This may be a reflection of a well-designed interface and functions becoming more visible.

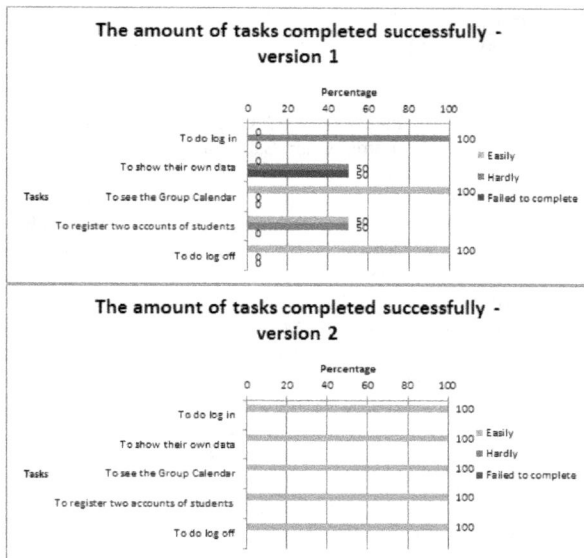

Figure 8. The amount of tasks completed successfully

Figure 9 shows that when the users realized all tasks easily and with a shorter time, then the number of clicks was also reduced. This is a very important outcome because the path to be memorized by the users becomes easier and this will raise their satisfaction with the system.

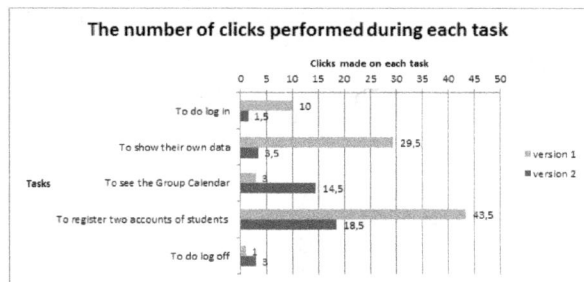

Figure 9. The number of clicks performed during each task

It is worth noticing that all results presented in the article give us evidence that the new interface is more accessible and usable than the first version. However, due to the limited number of participants, it is not possible to consider these results conclusive, being necessary to repeat this study with a larger sample size and more heterogeneous users, such as people with disabilities. Still on the participants, the reviewers observed that the time taken and errors performed may also depend on experience with technology and the system, alongside connection speed, interaction with assistive devices, etc. But, each user used both Web Systems, thus we do not think the difference in experience could bias the case study.

According to the quantitative metrics, version 2 accessibility features significantly improved the usability metrics. This can be understood as a result of AgendAloca system being developed considering accessibility requirements from the beginning of the development process. The results collected in our paper, support the hypothesis suggested by Petrie and Kheir [21] that present how usability metrics might be increased as the accessibility metrics are enhanced.

All results presented here give us evidence that the new interface is more accessible and more usable than the first version. Although, due to the small sample, it is not possible to consider these results conclusive, we intend to repeat this study with a larger sample and more heterogeneous users, such as people with disabilities. As a result, so far, ACCESSA is practicable and may be useful for the reengineering.

7. FINAL REMARKS

The paper presented an approach (ACCESSA) to rapidly improve the accessibility of existing Web system, acting mainly in interface design without changing the functionality. This is done based on the WCAG 2.0 guidelines and other patterns, choosing the guidelines that are easier to implement and cause more impact on accessibility.

Due the results presents in this paper about two versions of the AgendAloca system, it is possible to assert that the proposal presented in this paper supports the hypothesis that the ACCESSA assists in developing Web applications more accessible. ACCESSA use the methods, which some designers already perform, being practicable and may be useful for reengineering processes.

We intend to continue with the evolution of the AgendAloca system through evaluations with end users, including users with disabilities, through studies on the rate of success and failure in certain tasks, beyond the satisfaction of system utilization. As a consequence of the work presented in this paper, the authors intend to formalize a Web systems developing process. This process will include accessibility in all phases of development (considering the initial phases [8]), when the change costs are lower, may contribute to the development of new accessible Web systems.

8. REFERENCES

[1] Alexander, D. Usability and Accessibility: Best friends or Worst enemies? VALA, 2006.

[2] Baguma, R.; Stone, R. G.; Lubega, J. T.; Weide, T. P. Integrating Accessibility and Functional Requirements. In Proceedings of the 5th International Conference on Universal Access in Human-Computer Interaction. Part III: Applications and Services (UAHCI '09), Const. Stephanidis (Ed.). Springer-Verlag, Berlin, Heidelberg, 635-644.

[3] Bailey, C.; Pearson, E. Development and trial of an educational tool to support the accessibility evaluation process. In Proceedings of the International Cross-Disciplinary Conference on Web Accessibility (W4A '11). ACM, New York, NY, USA, Article 2, 10 pages.

[4] Bonifácio, B., Fernandes, P., Oliveira, H. A. B. F., Conte, T. UBICUA: A customizable usability inspection approach for Web mobile applications. In Proceedings o the IADIS Internacional Conference on WWW/Internet, 2011.

[5] Brajnik, G. Beyond Conformance: The Role of Accessibility Evaluation Methods, Proceedings of the 2008 international workshops on Web Information Systems Engineering. Auckland. New Zealand. 2008.

[6] Conte, T., Massolar, J., Mendes, E., et al. Usability Evaluation based on Web Design Perspectives. In Proceedings of the First Int. Symposium on Empirical Software Engineering and Measurement, 2007, 146 – 155.

[7] Dias, A. L., Fortes, R. P. M.; Masiero, P.C. Increasing the Quality of Web Systems: By Inserting Requirements of Accessibility and Usability. In *Proceedings of the 2012 Eighth International Conference on the Quality of Information and*

Communications Technology (QUATIC '12). IEEE Comp. Society, Washington, DC, USA, 224-229.

[8] Dias, A. L.; Anacleto, J. C.; Silveira, L. M.; Penteado, R. A. D.; Silva, M.A.R.; Buzatto, D.; Villena, J. M. R. Web collaboration motivated by colors emotionally based on common sense. In *Proceedings of the 2009 IEEE international conference on Systems, Man and Cybernetics* (SMC'09). IEEE Press, Piscataway, NJ, USA, 801-806.

[9] Fernandes, N.; Carriço, L. A macroscopic Web accessibility evaluation at different processing phases. In: W4A2012 - Communication, 2012, Lyon, France.

[10] Ferreira, S. B. L.; Nunes, R. R. e-Usabilidade. Rio de Janeiro: Ed. LTC, 179 p., 2008 (in Portuguese).

[11] Freire, A. P.; Goularte, R.; Fortes, R. P. M. Techniques for developing more accessible Web applications: a survey towards a process classification. In: SIGDOC '07: 25th annual ACM international conference on Design of communication, NY, USA: ACM, pp. 162–169, 2007.

[12] Jeschke, S.; Pfeiffer, O.; Vieritz, H. Using Web accessibility patterns for Web application development. In Proceedings of the 2009 ACM symposium on Applied Computing (SAC '09). ACM, New York, NY, USA, 129-135.

[13] Lazar, J.; Olalere, A. Investigation of best practices for maintaining section 508 Compliance in U.S. federal Web sites. In Proceedings of the 6th international conference on Universal access in human-computer interaction: design for all and eInclusion - Volume Part I (UAHCI'11), Constantine Stephanidis (Ed.). Springer, Berlin, Heidelberg, 498-506.

[14] Lew, P.; Olsina, L.; Zhang, L. Quality, quality in use, actual usability and user experience as key drivers for Web application evaluation. In Proceedings of the 10th international conference on Web engineering (ICWE'10), Boualem Benatallah, Fabio Casati, Gerti Kappel, and Gustavo Rossi (Eds.). Springer, Berlin, Heidelberg, 218-232.

[15] López, J. M.; Pascual, A.; Menduiña, C.; Granollers, T. Methodology for identifying and solving accessibility related issues in Web Content Management System environments. In: W4A2012 Tech. Paper, April 16-17, 2012.Lyon, France.

[16] Luna, E. R.; Garrigós, I.; Grigera, J.; Winckler, M. Capture and evolution of Web requirements using Webspec. In Proceedings of the 10th Int. Conference on Web engineering (ICWE'10). Springer, Berlin, Heidelberg, 173-188.

[17] Lunn, D.; Harper, S. Improving the accessibility of dynamic Web content for older users. In Proceedings of the International Cross-Disciplinary Conference on Web Accessibility (W4A '11). ACM, New York, NY, USA, Article 16, 2 pages.

[18] Martín, A.; Cechich, A; Rossi, G. Accessibility at early stages: insights from the designer perspective. In Proceedings of the Int. Cross-Disciplinary Conf. on Web Accessibility (W4A '11). ACM, NY, USA, Article 9, 9 pages.

[19] Mirri, S.; Salomoni, P.; Prandi, C. Augment browsing and standard profiling for enhancing Web accessibility. In Proceedings of the International Cross-Disciplinary Conference on Web Accessibility (W4A '11). ACM, New York, NY, USA, Article 5, 10 pages.

[20] Nielsen, J. Usability engineering. Boston, MA: Academic Press, 1993. 362p.

[21] Petrie, H.; Kheir, O. 2007. The relationship between accessibility and usability of websites. In *Proceedings of the SIGCHI Conference on Human Factors in Computing Systems* (CHI '07). ACM, New York, NY, USA, 397-406.

[22] Power, C.; Freire, A. P.; Petrie, H. e Swallow, D. Guidelines are Only Half of the Story: Accessibility Problems Encountered by Blind Users on the Web. In: CHI'12, May 5–10, 2012, Austin, Texas, USA.

[23] Rocha, H. V.; Baranauskas, M. C. C. Design e avaliação de interfaces humano-computador. São Paulo: IMW-USP, 2000. 242p. (in Portuguese).

[24] Romen, D.; Svanaes, D. Evaluating Web site accessibility: validating the WAI guidelines through usability testing with disabled users. In: NordiCHI '08: Proceedings of the 5th Nordic conference on Human-computer interaction, New York, NY, USA: ACM, 2008, p. 535.

[25] Sakamoto, S.G.; Silva, L. F.; Miranda, L. C. Identificando barreiras de acessibilidade web em dispositivos móveis: resultados de um estudo de caso orientado pela engenharia de requisitos. In *Proceedings of the 11th Brazilian Symposium on Human Factors in Computing Systems* (IHC '12). Brazilian Comp. Soc., POA, Brazil, 23-32 (in Portuguese).

[26] Santos, E. P. B.; Fortes, R. P.M. CMS instance of a tool to support the scheduling of undergraduate s final year project on the Web. In: Simpósio Brasileiro de Sistemas Multimídia e Web - WebMedia, 2010, BH-MG. SBC, 2010, 127-129.

[27] Santos, E. P. B.; Lara, S. M. A.; Watanabe, W. M.; A. Filho, M. C.; Fortes, R. P. M. Usability evaluation of horizontal navigation bar with drop-down menus by middle aged adults. In Proceedings of the 29th ACM Int. Conf. on Design of communication (SIGDOC '11). ACM, NY, USA, 145-150.

[28] Shelly, C. e Barta, M. Application of Traditional Software Testing Methodologies to Web Accessibility. In: proceedings of the 2010 international cross disciplinary conference on Web accessibility, W4A '10, New York, NY, USA, 2010.

[29] Shull, F., Carver, J., Travassos, G. H. An empirical methodology for introducing software processes. In 9th ACM SIGSOFT international symposium on Foundations of software engineering (2001), 288-296.

[30] Takagi, H.; Asakawa, C.; Fukuda, K.; Maeda, J. Accessibility designer: visualizing usability for the blind. SIGACCESS Access. Comput. 77-78 (Sept 2003), 177-184.

[31] Tanaka, E. H. Método Baseado em Heurísticas para avaliação da acessibilidade em sistemas de informação, Doctor Thesis, UNICAMP, Brazil, 2010 (in Portuguese).

[32] Tanaka, E.H. e Rocha, H.V. Evaluation of Web Accessibility Tools. In Proc. IHC&CLIHC'11, ACM (2011), 272-279.

[33] Vigo, M. and Brajnik, G. Automatic Web accessibility metrics: Where we are and where we can go. Interacting with Computers 23(2), 137-155. Elsevier. 2011. http://dx.doi.org/10.1016/j.intcom.2011.01.001

[34] Waller, A.; Hanson, V. L.; Sloan, D. Including accessibility within and beyond undergraduate computing courses. In Proceedings of the 11th international ACM SIGACCESS conference on Computers and accessibility (Assets '09). ACM, New York, NY, USA, 155-162.

[35] Watanabe, W. M.; Fortes, R. P. M.; Dias, A. L. 2012. Using acceptance tests to validate accessibility requirements in RIA. In Proceedings of the International Cross-Disciplinary Conference on Web Accessibility (W4A '12). ACM, New York, NY, USA, Article 15, 10 pages.

[36] Wöhlin, C., Runeson, P., Höst, M., Ohlsson, M. C., Regnell, B., Wessl, A. Experimentation in software engineering: an introduction. (2000) Kluwer Academic Publishers.

Analytics as Heuristics:
Technical Considerations for DOC

Brenton Faber
Worcester Polytechnic Institute
Salisbury Labs 19
100 Institute Rd, Worcester MA 01609
508-831-4390
bdfaber@wpi.edu

Keith Gagnon
Worcester Polytechnic Institute
Box 435
100 Institute Road, Worcester, MA 06109
kagagnon@wpi.edu

ABSTRACT

Abstract: This paper is an initial effort to articulate the rhetorical work of analytics for technical writers and designers of technical information. We situate analytics as a heuristic process, the intentional creation of forms and events for aggregating and assessing data within and across systems. Using examples from healthcare and library science we highlight: (1) The opportunities and complications of working with comprehensive data sets (100% of population) rather than representative samples; (2) The importance of outliers, and (3) The social dynamics associated with inventing concepts. We suggest that analytics is equally a social, technical, and rhetorical activity. Meaningful queries will invent and aggregate concepts that enable description, assessment, and change throughout a social system. We stress the contextual and social dynamics of analytics noting that like any rhetorical activity, analytics simultaneously construct, reflect, and impose value and meaning on systems under scrutiny.

Categories and Subject Descriptors

H.2.8 [**Information Systems**]: Database Management, Database applications, Data mining

Keywords

Keywords: Analytics, data, healthcare, heuristics rhetoric

1. Analytics, Heuristics & The Design of Communication

This paper situates analytics within heuristics suggesting that the availability of extensive digital data, both archived and real-time (streaming), has led to new opportunities and problems for writers and designers tasked with interpreting what is loosely called "big data".

Heuristics are a component of the Rhetorical cannon "invention." Formally, heuristics are strategies for generating content. Such strategies connect forms and actions, enabling writers and designers to generate content regularized processes. For example, heuristics provide (in)formal structures for brainstorming; research strategies and tools (who, where, why, what, when; Kenneth Burke's "pentad"); categories for

argument debate (ethos, logos, pathos), and structured processes for problem solving.

Analytics is primarily concerned with transforming raw and unstructured data into quantitative forms that can be mined, interpreted and validated. Advocates of analytics claim that such empirical data should be produced to inform and drive robust understandings of complex systems and ultimately enable better evidence-based decisions. As an emerging field, analytics requires strong quantitative skills for statistical analysis and model building, insightful social knowledge for building concepts and forms for analysis, and exceptional narrative abilities for designing meaningful and persuasive accounts.

Definitions of analytics can be field-dependent but most accounts ground the field in the tools of logistics and business intelligence [5, p.7]. Other accounts have extended the promise of analytics and big data to epidemiology, bio-statistics, and medical decision-making; film and game design; sports; and other entertainment industries. Analytics as both method and interpretive practice is realized more as an aggregation of tools and rhetorical approaches. As Davenport and Harris write, analytics is "the extensive use of data, statistical and quantitative analysis, explanatory and predictive models, and fact-based management to drive decisions and actions" [5, p.7].

Writers and rhetoric scholars may recognize and situate analytics within rhetorical heuristics, activities involved in the formal and informal generation of ideas and content for documents. We would like to use the term "electronic heuristics" to refer to software-based structured data mining tools. These are digital systems that have made the extraction, reporting, and quick interpretation of large data sets relatively simple and widely available. Electronic heuristics have made large domains of information transparent and easily accessible but like any rhetorical process have also created new problems and complications for writers and designers.

Recent and well-publicized examples of analytics include case studies from retail stores, sports, and politics. For example, retail giant Target has used customer data mining to predict if women customers were newly pregnant. Targeted customers were sent coupon books with pregnancy and baby specific products [7].[1] Professional sports has probably done more to popularize analytics than any other industry, specifically Major League Baseball and Oakland Athletics manager Billy Beane. Beane's analytics-based coaching methods led to a full reassessment of baseball strategy, recruiting, and the metrics used to interpret the game. Beane's approach, which has become known as Sabermetrics, has been the subject of numerous profiles, including the book and movie *Moneyball* [10]. MIT has a yearly conference investigating analytics and athletics [13] and *ESPN The Magazine* now produces an analytics issue [8]. In politics, data analysts have taken notice of the 2012 Democratic Presidential campaign for their successful demographic data segmentation and predictive modeling [11]. Campaign data analysts were able to predict inclination to donate to the campaign, likelihood to vote, and the ability of specific advertisements to generate action within very specific and precise demographic subsets.[2]

The above accounts have stressed and assumed the integrative aspects of analytical tools emphasizing, for example, statistical validity necessary for predictive models and robust data sets for appropriate population sampling. Researchers have also accurately shown pitfalls associated with false correlations and the random association of variables easily attained through unstructured data mining [2]. Such reports have shown that alongside the popularity of analytics, there exist important and serious limitations to data analysis when it is operated outside the formal structures of statistical practices. When not careful, practitioners and researchers may be led to misleading correlations or spurious associations when data mining or other analytics packages find generic relationships within their data sets.[3]

This paper emerged for somewhat different reasons. Over the course of several analytics projects and inquiries conducted for both research and professional practice [9, for e.g.], we discovered situational issues that required a reassessment of some more taken-for-granted heuristic methods. In what follows we offer preliminary insights for technical documentation from several large-scale data mining and analytics projects. Given the fairly recent emergence of analytics and its still rather nascent role as a heuristic for technical and scientific writers, there remain key issues about methodology, documentation, and data interpretation for our disciplinary community to still address. We hope that this paper can be an initial contribution to this conversation.

2. Heuristic Queries & Data Sets

While analytics tools seem to bracket issues related to population sampling, writers must still be cautious about the validity of a query, the contexts that inform the data, and the utility of the information generated.

In early 2013 we began working on a 66,000 patient data set provided to us by Dimensional Insight, a data analytics firm known internationally for its "Diver" data mining and business intelligence software [6]. As we began working with Diver and the healthcare dataset we realized our initial assumptions and anticipated efforts to create representative sampling and appropriately sized cohorts were disrupted by the ready ability to examine 100% of the health system's data.

As simple a claim as this may be, the ability to study events and characteristics in an entire population (to the level of each individual patient) with a few mouse clicks presents methodological issues for heuristics and reporting. For example, database tools quickly partition the 66,000 patients by diagnosis group, gender, age group, and ethnicity in 3 mouse clicks. Here, we do not require a representative sample to study patients' utilization by disease type because the analysis works with 100% of the data. We do not need to extrapolate from a sample. We know exactly how many patients fit our search criteria[4].

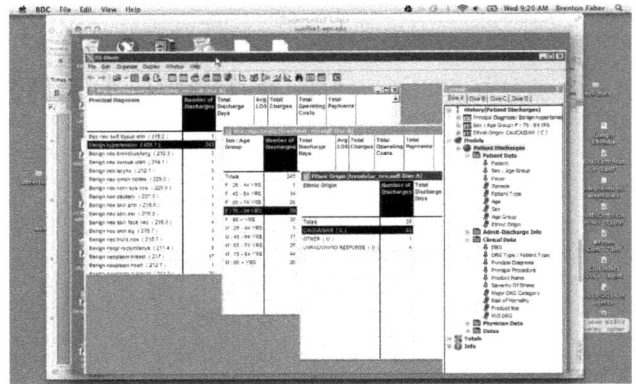

Figure 1. Caucasian Women Age 75-84 w/ Benign Hypertension

For example, the query in Figure 1 tells us that from 66,000 patients in the years under study, 53 Caucasian women aged 75-84 were seen with benign hypertension. These findings would seem to forestall questions regarding the appropriate size of a representative patient population group. However, the elimination of a sample group does not entirely negate sampling questions because results need to be subjected to significance issues and relevance testing at the reporting end of the query. We may know that 53 women were treated for a specific disease but external from any other information, context, or comparative data, the findings may not be that useful.

Similarly Figure 2 shows 3 women from a specific zip code aged +85 years with coagulation defects. Like the query from Figure 1, this information can be attained almost instantly from the data warehouse. As these examples show, data mining tools attached to a company's data warehouse or data repository enable analysts to reach such granularity quickly, simply, and without excessive training. However such findings still need to be assessed for accuracy in addition to significance, and meaning.

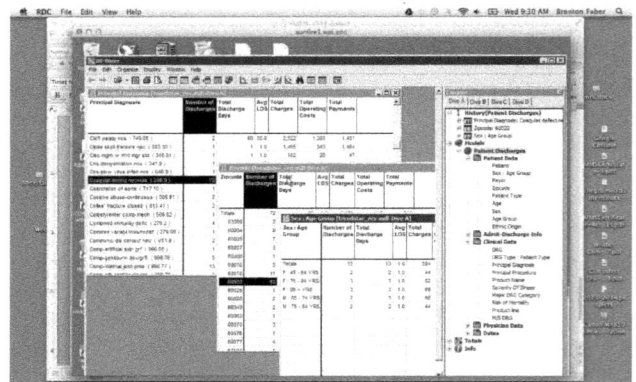

Figure 2. Women with coagulation defects by zip code

From a statistics standpoint, a population sized set of data greatly complicates the matter. With such a large set of data, statistical significance loses its effectiveness. When looking at several thousand to million data points, it is highly likely that a large number of relationships will be considered "statistically significant", as the power of statistical tests (their ability to detect an effect between treatment groups) increases with increasing sample size. This means that even minimal changes will be detected as statistically significant.

Appropriately designed queries will emerge from a relational understanding of the underlying database and the hierarchical structure of the data. Contextual issues can be crucial here as simple numbers apart from larger contextual cues (size of population for example) can quickly become misleading. It is common in healthcare to report patient visits but not individual patients. A clinic reporting 30 visits per day could be productive unless 20 of those visits are returning patients with unresolved complications from yesterday's visits. Without robust contextual understanding of the dynamics of the population in question, data analytics can be turned into a form of backward validation in which queries are used to support assumed or desired results (management bias, favoritism).

Heuristic queries can be descriptive – intending to show the characteristics of entire populations or subsets within the full population. These heuristics are relatively simple and informative but can be disconnected from actionable information. While it is informative to know how many patients have any particular disease turning this information into actionable strategy can be difficult.

More complicated queries are designed to solve specific problems, answer questions, and inform corporate strategy. These can be called intentional queries as they progressively attempt to answer "why" [1]. For example, Figure 3 arranges diagnosis by profit/loss showing the least profitable diagnoses, length of stay, and total discharge days. The query shows a $153,597 loss from patients with osteoarthritis in the lower leg.

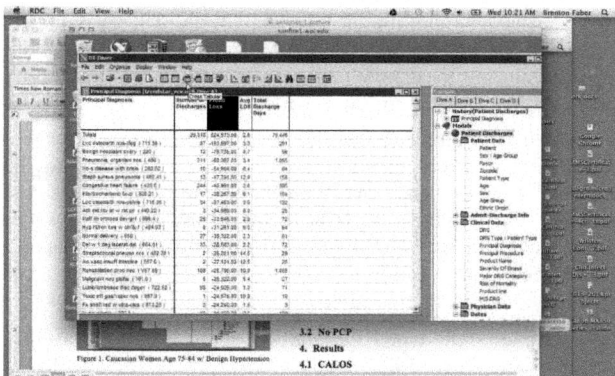

Figure 3. Least profitable diagnosis

Here, contextual information provides an important guide for assessing the "whys" to the simplistic query "where are we losing money?" Figure 4 examines the same patient population (osteoarthritis) by insurance subgroups and loss per patient. The resulting query shows that financial performance for this diagnosis is more dependent on insurance payor. In this group HMO insurances actually return a profit while Medicare shows a loss, disrupting the initial findings that this diagnosis was not profitable.

Due to the multivariate nature and the complex interplay of these variables, simple descriptive statistics breaks down at a population analysis level. More high-level techniques and modeling are required at this level of data. For example, dimensionality reduction as well as clustering methods have shown much utility in such a highly-dimensional space.

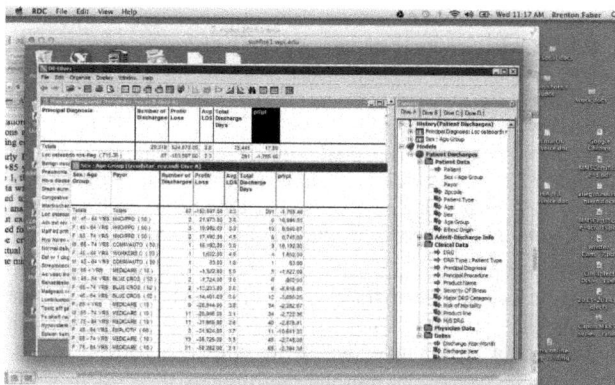

Figure 4. Profit/loss by payor and patient

The ability to examine and characterize 100% of the population provides a more detailed and comprehensive picture than population sampling. However the rhetorical heuristics that create these queries still need to be attentive to subject-area granularities and context to be useful. A subsequent query of the same patients can assess profit/loss by physician and show that Dr. *A* loses $4,081 per patient with osteoarthritis while Dr. *B* loses only $800 per patient. This information is only relevant however when we see that 90% of Dr. *A*'s patients are Medicare while 57% of Dr. *B*'s patients are Medicare and 1 patient (out of 14) turned a $9,000 profit altering Dr. *B*'s average.

3. Outliers

How do we treat the information that 1 of Dr. *B*'s patients inflated his average payment per patient turning an average loss of $7,000 to an average loss of $800? Statistically, this patient is an outlier and typically is removed from the data set or adjusted to better fit the statistical norm. Outliers push averages within data sets creating distorted descriptive accounts and make it impossible to attain accurate predictive models. Dr. *B* may have seen a $9,000 profit once but if every other patient over several years falls within a tight distribution a good financial model should not rely on another $9,000 windfall to break even.

Yet, outliers occur and can have real, actual implications for organizations. Process improvement efforts look to outliers as examples of flawed processes and deviations from standardized procedures. Here, outliers, both positive (a $9,000 profit) and negative (a $17,000 loss) suggest problems that can be further explored.

For example, health policy research has focused on examining hospital readmissions as a way to measure the quality of inpatient medical care. A readmission occurs when a discharged patient is admitted again to a hospital for the same reason that patient was initially admitted. In short, if a patient has been assessed to be healthy enough to go home the patient should not need to immediately come back for the same condition. Quality experts argue that if appropriate discharge protocols are followed, patients should not need the level of care provided by a hospital in-patient event, but rather that which can be received at a physician office or other out-patient services.

A readmission can be seen as an outlier, an event that happens relatively infrequently. But rather than ignore these outliers quality advocates claim that they can be used as a proxy for overall health system effectiveness.

Rather than discount outliers, analysts can use outliers as heuristic tools. For example, we recently designed several models to determine the implications of new payment structures on a hospital's revenue. One particular model examined what has come to be known as "bundled payments." Under this financing structure, the hospital would receive one payment for 90 days of care, regardless of how much or how little care a patient uses during those 90 days. The amount of each payment will depend on the specific diagnosis of the first visit.

The bundled payment initiative incentivizes the health system to manage excessive cost since each individual utilization that exceeds the payment bundle is a loss to the health system. Outliers are a key component of the model as patients whose costs greatly exceed the normal distribution point to medical, financial, and quality problems. On the other hand, some patients will be outliers in the profitable direction, needing significantly less procedures and care to improve. It is on these patients that the hospital will profit. Documenting outliers and the increase and decrease of outliers will be essential to managing such a system. The heuristics for this query therefore need to be designed to specifically locate outliers and even predict which patients may become outliers.

Outliers can be problematic for population studies as they distort the average creating an exaggerated representation of the group. However, as a heuristic device, outliers can provide useful insight into a system. Outliers (both positive and negative) can point to system disruptions, over allocation of resources, or other systemic issues.

4. Temporary concepts

As heuristic practice, analytics provides a time-dependent and therefore relatively temporary system assessment. Such analysis places various fields (social, economic, material, technological) in temporary alignment to investigate potential relationships and correlative meanings. Such allocations are neither permanent nor fixed but instead are designed to evoke a situated meaning.

Any particular aggregation of fields may produce a meaningful concept that can then be defined, quantified, compared, and tested throughout its own system and potentially across different systems. But any particular aggregation is not designed to indefinitely hold from one system to another or even from one moment within the particular system to another. That certain concepts retain meaning and value (readmission, cost, diagnosis) does not mean that they will always remain legitimate or valuable or that other concepts cannot be given temporary presence or status to explain a particular activity or form. Over time and practice, certain concepts may displace retained meanings, providing new ways to evaluate and describe a system. These new analytical tools will both reflect and constitute value by projecting what aggregations reviewers find valuable and by their status as a category of assessment.

As an example, our team recently worked with a library to examine book circulation patterns within its collection. Our first challenge was to determine which analytics (aggregation of concepts) would be appropriate to use to measure activity within the library collection. Simple use and activity could measure which books were popular (checked out most often) assigning a market value to the collection. Other approaches included comparing books to various lists of "books great libraries should own," assessing how often books in the collection have been cited by scholarly work, comparing the library's collection to readings used in local high school, community college, and university courses, or comparing the collection to books held by neighboring libraries.

Each aggregation ascribes a set of values and an ontological meaning to a library book collection and onto the actual collection put in place by this particular library. Was the collection designed to be a repository and archive of rare and unique work, an expression of popular reading choices, a thematic center for particular interest groups? A repository of what is accepted to be the best work ever written? The concepts we chose to examine the collection would necessarily create value-based aggregations, displace other aggregations, and establish a temporary set of expectations for the library's activities. Obviously, such work is highly social and must be collaborative and subject to several rounds of tests, evaluation, and feedback.

Returning to our work in healthcare, we can see tension among the legacy concepts used to measure medical systems and new concepts being promoted to change these systems. The metric "RVU" or "relative value units" count and weigh the engagements physicians have with patients. More severe patients take more time and therefore can generate a higher RVU. In a fee for service structure, physicians are reimbursed by meeting specific RVU goals. Here, systems are incentivized to see as many severely sick patients as quickly as possible. Under a different system (bundled payments for e.g.), a different set of analytical concepts will need to displace the hierarchy of time and money with concepts that better aggregate what we hope the new system will achieve (quality, prevention, and cost reduction).

5. Analytics as Rhetoric

As an emerging field, the electronic analysis of large data sets (analytics) offers technical writers and designers important opportunities but these new forms and activities are not without complications that require careful attention.

We conclude by emphasizing that however meaning is ascribed, quantitatively to the statistical effect size; qualitatively to the nuances of the social environment; or to other measures, analytics (like any other heuristic) requires the researcher/writer to understand the research-in-context. In other words, meaning can be seen as a dynamic combination of social context, actor intention, and quantitative findings.

For example, Beth Israel Deaconess medical center currently houses a sophisticated data analysis and mining package based on a data warehouse containing millions of data points regarding the diagnoses, lab results and treatment regimens given to each patient for each visit [4]. Mining such a large database almost guarantees that the researcher would be able to discover several statistically significant relationships amongst treatment regimens and disease progressions. However, the practical significance of many of these findings is minimal. For example, a certain drug may decrease LDL levels by 0.1 mg/dL and be considered a statistically significant finding over the people not using the drug. However, the effect size here is minimal, as such as decrease is not likely to impact the field of medicine (not "clinically" relevant). Yet, a medicine that could lower LDL levels by 30-40 mg/dL would have a much larger impact of the field of medicine.

Thus, it is important to understand the working context from which the data emerge. Interpreting the *practical significance* of the *statistically significant* findings that are intrinsic to large data is perhaps a more difficult rhetorical task. In such a large set of data, it is highly probable that any person capable of navigating the database and versed in statistical analysis could find significant results. The true importance is in determining which of these relations is relevant.

We encourage other studies of analytics projects to document and advance technical competency but also to help develop a better understanding of their social purpose and activity. Our field can benefit from robust case studies of analytics in workplaces and detailed accounts of how various designers create and mine databases for research and problem solving.

6. Notes

1. Target's data miners found that pregnancy and baby-specific coupons needed to be presented among other non-related products or customers would find the marketing package too invasive.

2. We also note the recent Netflix challenge. Netflix offered $1 million to any group that could, based on movies the customer had watched and rated, improve the algorithm that recommends and predicts what movies viewers might like.

3. A related concept is the relationships that are often found in large data sets (including texts) that are due to the large size of the sample and random variation. For example, secret codes found in large texts or messages seemingly hidden in documents like the complete works of Shakespeare. Such codes may be due to the random distribution of letters and large amounts of data that will necessarily generate random aggregations of characters.

4. The case examples referenced here do not include discussions of the prior work required to design the database or structure data being queried in ways that will result in the intended information when searched. While these are key rhetorical issues of heuristics that necessitate examination, they are outside the limits of this initial paper. We anticipate writing a "prequel" to elaborate the rhetorical exigencies of preparing large data sets for data mining in a following paper.

7. ACKNOWLEDGMENTS

We are grateful to Dimensional Insight for the use of their Diver data mining solution and healthcare data.

8. REFERENCES

[1] Anscome, G.E.M. 2000 [1957]. *Intention*. Cambridge: Harvard UP.

[2] Austin, P., M. Muhammad, D Juurlink and J. Hux. 2006. "Testing multiple statistical hypotheses resulted in spurious associations: a study of astrological signs and health. *Journal of Clinical Epidemiology 59*: 964-969.

[3] Baker, S. 2008. *The Numerati*. Boston and New York: Mariner Books, Houghton Mifflin Harcourt.

[4] Cerrato, P. "Beth Israel Deaconess Medical Center Embraces Analytics." *Informationweek - Online* (2012).

[5] Davenport, T. and Harris, J. 2007. *Competing on Analytics: The New Science of Winning*. Cambridge MA: Harvard Business Press.

[6] Dimensional Insight Corporate information at: Dimins.com

[7] Duhigg, D. 2012. "How companies learn your secrets." *New York Times* (16 Feb). http://www.nytimes.com/2012/02/19/magazine/shopping-habits.html?pagewanted=all.

[8] http://espnmediazone.com/us/press-releases/2013/02/espn-the-magazine-analytics-issue-on-newsstands-friday/

[9] Faber, B. 2012. "A visual metric for quality, finance, & capacity reporting." Society for Healthcare Systems Process Improvement. Proceedings. Institute of Industrial Engineers. March 1-4. New Orleans LA.

[10] Lewis, M. 2004. *MoneyBall: The art of winning an unfair game*. New York: W.W. Norton.

[11] Scherer, M. 2012. "Inside the secret world of the data crunchers who helped Obama win." *Time* (7 November). http://swampland.time.com/2012/11/07/inside-the-secret-world-of-quants-and-data-crunchers-who-helped-obama-win/?hpt=hp_t2

[12] Silver, N. 2012. *The signal and the noise: Why so many predictions fail – but some don't*. New York: Penguin Press.

[13] http://www.sloansportsconference.com/

Simplifying the Development of Cross-Platform Web User Interfaces by Collaborative Model-based Design

Vivian Genaro Motti[1], Dave Raggett[2], Sascha Van Cauwelaert[1], Jean Vanderdonckt[1]

[1]Université catholique de Louvain, Louvain School of Management,
Place des Doyens, 1 - B-1348 Louvain-la-Neuve, Belgium – +32 10 47{8349, 9013, 8525}
{vivian.genaromotti, sascha.vancauwelaert, jean.vanderdonckt}@uclouvain.be
[2]World Wide Web Consortium – dsr@w3.org

ABSTRACT

Ensuring responsive design of web applications requires their user interfaces to be able to adapt according to different contexts of use, which subsume the end users, the devices and platforms used to carry out the interactive tasks, and also the environment in which they occur. To address the challenges posed by responsive design, aiming to simplify their development by factoring out the common parts from the specific ones, this paper presents Quill, a web-based development environment that enables various stakeholders of a web application to collaboratively adopt a model-based design of the user interface for cross-platform deployment. The paper establishes a series of requirements for collaborative model-based design of cross-platform web user interfaces motivated by the literature, observational and situational design. It then elaborates on potential solutions that satisfy these requirements and explains the solution selected for Quill. A user survey has been conducted to determine how stakeholders appreciate model-based design user interface and how they estimate the importance of the requirements that lead to Quill.

Categories and Subject Descriptors

D.2.2 [**Software Engineering**]: Design Tools and Techniques – *Modules and interfaces; user interfaces.* D2.m [**Software Engineering**]: Miscellaneous – *Rapid Prototyping; reusable software.* H.5.2 [**Information Interfaces and Presentation**]: User Interfaces – *Graphical user interfaces.* I.3.6 [**Computer Graphics**]: Methodology and Techniques – *Interaction techniques.*

Keywords

Collaborative development; cross-platform design; model-based design of user interfaces; user interface description language.

1. INTRODUCTION

Developing the user interface (UI) of an interactive system is notoriously recognized as a complex and powerful [24], yet open, iterative, and incomplete process [22], namely because various stakeholders (end users, developers, designers, analysts, project leaders, marketing people) are involved with different background and inputs [6]. These stakeholders currently face many challenges when dealing with various *contexts of use* [7] in which end users are carrying out their interactive task with the system. Contexts of use vary mainly in terms of [3]: *users' profile* (disabilities, user preferences, and cognitive styles), *platforms* (device types, screen sizes, resolutions and interaction techniques), and *environmental* settings (mobile vs. stationary location, light, noise, and stability).

Application domains (e.g., e-Health, automotive industry) could also influence these contexts. Thus, the mobility, pervasiveness, and ubiquity of current computing trends also pose challenges when developing UIs with responsive design and with cross-device consistency, high usability, and great user experiences.

Given that it is neither scalable nor feasible to implement several UI versions considering specific characteristics of all contexts of use, developers must rely on approaches that are both: sufficiently generic to simplify the software development lifecycle, and flexible enough to properly accommodate requirements and constraints coming from these different contexts of use.

Model-Based Design of User Interfaces (MBUI) has maintained some attraction due to its main benefits [1,3,5,8,10,14,21]: it permits incremental development for a wide variety of technologies, it enables a common understanding of the UI specification through models by the exchange of common vocabulary, it reduces the cost of targeting multiple platforms, it facilitates changes to be applied at all points in the lifecycle, it enables developers to work top-down, bottom-up or middle-out. These benefits spring from a separation of concerns enabling designers to focus on important aspects of the development process while avoiding distractions with details that are best delegated to specialists in specific platforms. MBUI allows this to happen without incurring the high communication costs normally associated with collaboration between people with different skill sets. Many powerful tools exist today for developing Web UIs [13], the most typical being the interface builder with a visual editor for each corresponding operating system or environment. On the one hand, interface builders do not fully support adaptation to the context of use; on the other hand, there is a lack of tools (e.g., editors, design assistants and development environments) to facilitate MBUI adoption.

To tackle the aforementioned shortcomings, this paper presents Quill, a web-based development environment that enables various stakeholders of a web application to collaboratively adopt a model-based design of the user interface for cross-platform deployment, by defining and editing UI models addressing contexts. A *Systematic Literature Review* (SLR) helped to identify relevant requirements for creating and managing MBUI projects. These requirements lead to design decisions for the implementation of Quill that enables stakeholders to create and manage MBUI projects, and that designers and developers collaborate in the definition of UI models by dragging-and-dropping their components, specifying adaptation rules, and setting specific contexts of use (e.g., concerning the target delivery device).

This paper is organized as follows: Section 2 summarizes the motivations of Quill based on related work, Section 3 presents a set of requirements and their respective design decisions, Section 4 describes the tool and its main features that address these requirements, Section 5 validates the decisions with a case study, Section 6 reports on the results on an experimental study, and Section 6 concludes this paper with final remarks and future works.

2. RELATED WORK

The Cameleon Reference Framework (CRF) [3] defines the structure of UI models in four levels (Figure 1): Task and Domain, Abstract User Interface (AUI - that is independent of any interaction modality and implementation), Concrete User Interface (CUI - that is independent of any implementation for a given modality) and Final User Interface (FUI). Mappings between such levels are also specified (e.g., abstraction, reification and reflexion) and they vary according to specific contexts of use, leading consequently to specific transformations [9]. To support the development of MBUI, interaction modeling has been introduced in software engineering with three pillars: *models* that capture various UI-related aspects (e.g., task, domain, user, platform, environment) along with a *language* [10] that expresses these models, a step-wise *approach* that manipulates these models throughout the development life cycle, and *software* that supports applying the steps of this approach based on the models.

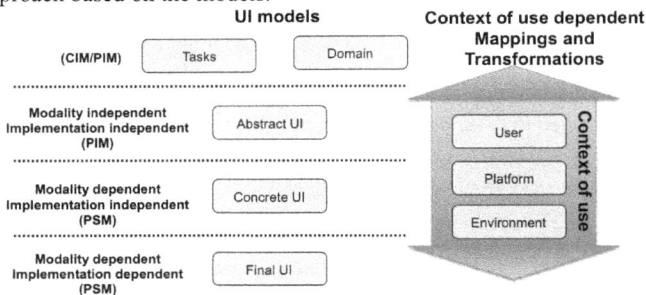

Figure 1. The Cameleon Reference Framework (CRF) [3].

Several MBUI environments have been introduced [1,2,5,8,9, 10,14,18], in particular for cross-platform [14,21], some of them being reported in the W3C MBUI Incubator group report [4]. For instance, Hera [23] provides transformations to generate web applications by relying on a 3-tier framework, integrating semantics, application and presentation aspects to generate UIs. Adaptation is also considered, but mainly focused on the users' characteristics. Mappings are defined and RDF was used to specify data transformations. Roam [5] exploits a task model for automatically generate an UI for different devices equipped with different resolutions. Gummy [14] adopts MBUI for supporting the development of cross-platform UIs in a coordinated way. Although most of these works are dedicated to tackle specific MBUI shortcomings, it is considered hard for them to follow recent advances, such as new technological standards (e.g., languages, approaches, devices, interaction modalities) that could induce a significant change in the contexts of use, regarding mobility, pervasiveness, ubiquity and context-awareness per se.

The first column of Table 1 lists other UI editors currently available for modeling and diagraming the UI of interactive systems. In the first column are listed software products for model creation, editing, and exploitation, but these tools do not support UI models. The second column of Figure 1 lists UI prototyping and sketching tools, but they do not support UI modeling neither. Concerning the UI design, sketching, and prototyping, there are several tools available in the market. Among them is MAQETTA [12], a visual authoring tool for designing HTML5-based UIs adopting an approach where UI elements are dragged from a palette and dropped onto a working area. Because MAQETTA [12] is itself a web-based application, no plug-ins, no add-ons, no download of any piece of software (e.g., a Java application) are required. Although it permits the design of UI mockups, the model-based approach is not integrated [12].

Table 1. Graphical Editors for Modeling, Diagraming, Sketching and Prototyping UIs [Source: Wiki (http://en.wikipedia.org/wiki/List_of_UML_tools) and Tools (http://c2.com/cgi/wiki?GuiPrototypingTools)]

Models and Diagrams	UI Sketching and Prototyping
ArgoUML: supports UML modeling runs as a Java platform being distributed under Eclipse license (http://argouml.tigris.org/)	**Balsamiq:** for sketching interfaces rapidly, and communicate design ideas (www.balsamiq.com)
Dia: for drawing diagrams for generic purposes, under GPL license (https://live.gnome.org/Dia)	**JustInMind:** a platform for defining prototypes for web and mobile applications (www.justinmind.com)
Visio: commercial editor of Microsoft for creating and sharing diagrams, enables collaborative features (http://visio.microsoft.com/)	**MAQETTA:** a visual authoring tool of HTML5 user interfaces in the browser, open source, WYSIWYG (maqetta.org)
Visual Paradigm: graphical tool for UML modeling (free for non-commercial use) (http://www.visual-paradigm.com/)	**SketchFlow:** a UI prototyping tool to create interactive prototypes (http://www.microsoft.com/ expression/products/ SketchFlow_Overview.aspx)

Besides MAQETTA, a series of alternative graphical editors have been issued to support activities for sketching and prototyping UIs with various levels of fidelity [6], some representative examples are briefly described in the second column of Table 1. Further relevant references and literature analysis can be retrieved from [4].

Although several environments have been developed to support UI specifications, most of them do not support the heterogeneity of contexts of use, e.g. regarding the fragmented device market that results from the quick and continuous technological evolution. To tackle this issue, tools like screenqueri.es, emulate the rendering in a set of pre-defined devices based on screen resolution mainly. Although an analysis of the (lack of) adaptation of UI can be achieved, users must manually submit the URLs of web pages, select the target delivery device(s), and then analyze potential adaptations required by these devices. Such tools are relevant, but do not simplify the ever increasing development complexity. These tools are rarely integrated within an Integrated Development Environment (IDE), which further delays the development.

It could be concluded from Table 1 that modeling tools are appropriate to capture one or many conceptual models of an interactive system in general, or a web application in general, but they do not cope with UI models specifically. When they do, they are restricted to one context of use, without taking into account the multiple contexts. UI sketching and prototyping tools are more fine grained to capture UI variations depending on the context of use, but it is the responsibility of designers and developers to properly address the peculiarities of these contexts through designs that are adapted, while considering the various viewpoints expressed by the stakeholders involved in a development lifecycle.

Therefore, a need arises for a collaborative web-based editor for creating UIs to web applications adopting a MBUI approach covering task, domain, abstract UI, concrete UI, and adaptation explicitly, which is Quill made for.

3. DEVELOPMENT OF QUILL

As previously discussed, an authoring tool needs to manage models for each level of abstraction as the user works on the application. Users must be able to select UI controls (e.g., edit fields, radio buttons, check boxes, list boxes, push buttons), drag them onto a canvas, adjust their properties, and link them for obtaining their behavior. In a persistent approach, when the user adds a group of radio buttons at the concrete level, an interaction unit of type "selection" must also be added in the abstract UI level, and automatically connected up to the application domain model [18], thus synchronizing the different levels. Further adjustments can be manually executed later, if necessary.

Authoring tools must be flexible, i.e. allowing users to choose their preferred work approach: top-down (e.g., starting from a selection that gives rise to a list box), bottom-up (e.g., vice-versa) or middle-out (e.g., an interaction unit of type "selection" is mapped onto a corresponding task in the task model and to a list box at the concrete level). Since transformations between these levels are not always transitive, the synchronization across levels remains a challenge. This feature can be ensured through a combination of techniques including direct manipulation of graphs, property lists, and browsing mechanisms. An agenda is also useful to guide developers on outstanding design tasks [18].

The next section describes the main shortcomings identified in the literature review that motivated the development of Quill. The presentation of the shortcomings is followed by their respective requirements, i.e. what Quill is expected to address. These requirements are consequently followed by the description of their respective design decisions, i.e. how Quill addresses these development challenges.

3.1 Shortcomings

The main MBUI shortcoming is still the lack of design environments and interactive systems that support all development stages (in a powerful, robust, and complete manner). By the analysis of the related works and tools, as presented and described in the previous section, a set of specific shortcomings could be identified:

S1. Inflexible Approaches. Stakeholders play different roles in the UI development life cycle (e.g., creating, editing, updating, validating a model), and have also different preferences, expertise levels and domains for ensuring these roles [4]. Although these roles may imply several levels at once, stakeholders are forced to work at one level at a time. The same applies for UI design, when starting from only one level of fidelity [6] is usually considered.

S2. Device's Incompatibilities. The outcomes generated with several tools are often not interoperable with different operating systems and/or devices [14]. Java-based applications, for instance, often require a set of libraries, pre-installation of plugins, or extensions and run just in specific environments (e.g., Eclipse [2]).

S3. Partial Consideration of Contexts of Use. Most tools address one specific contextual dimension at a time [21] (i.e., either the user or the platform or the environment, but not all at once), usually the platform constraints (e.g., screen resolutions, interaction techniques). Characteristics from users' profile, interaction modalities, or specific environmental constraints are often ignored. Because context-aware adaptation rules are not supported, a third-party simulation must be used for analyzing UI rendering.

S4. Little Design Guidance. There is a wide body of design usability knowledge (e.g., usability guidelines, style guides, UI patterns, design rules) that must be applied for each context [7], particularly a platform, but it is only partially incorporated in tools.

S5. Limited scalability. Since the CRF (Fig. 1) involves several levels of abstraction [3], either individually or concurrently, mod-

els located at these levels should be synchronized, thus affecting performance depending on model complexity [21].

S6. Inconsistencies. Current tools were not designed to run and perform equally in distinct platforms. This may lead to inconsistent [20] rendering or behaviors of the editors when they are used from different platforms [14,15].

S7. Limited Persistency. The transformations between the various CRF levels or fidelity levels [6] are rarely available in current editors [13]. Because the transformation across levels is not considered, they are either badly synchronized or not synchronized at all. As such, users must manually define and apply them, what can lead to inconsistent approaches and results, and also requires extra efforts of the end user to achieve persistency.

S8. Limited Scope. Current editors support either only modeling or prototyping activities [6,12], thus forcing users to use different software for modeling and designing activities [21]. Since such activities are tightly connected, MBUI design would benefit from a single integrated environment [18].

S9. Centralized and Local Development. Although UIs and their models are created and edited by stakeholders that are distributed in time and space [22], centralized and local development imposed by editors prevent them from collaborating, synchronously or asynchronously, remotely or together, in the same project.

S10. Accessibility Concerns. The usage of multiple modalities is absent or often just partially covered, causing accessibility issues [2] and incompatibility among the resulting models or UIs [20].

The 10 aforementioned shortcomings, identified during a systematic literature review, summarize critical factors for the success of the MBUI design. Editors currently available only partially support several features that are quite relevant for implementing MBUI. The CRF's 4 abstraction levels are usually not integrated and considered in the design process, thus making it difficult for stakeholders to appropriately implement UIs for different contexts of use. Therefore, specific context of use constraints are not considered and often a *one-size-fits-all* approach is adopted.

3.2 Requirements Elicitation for Quill

Based on the 10 shortcomings discussed in the previous section, corresponding requirements were elicited. They guided the definition of the design decisions and the consequent implementation of features that are available in Quill. These generic requirements cover both functional and non-functional aspects. Requirements were then analyzed, prioritized and associated with appropriate validation criteria to enable Quill's assessment. While the priorities were set as "must have", "should have" or "could have" (according to the MoSCoW method), the validation criteria were labeled as implemented, partially implemented or not (yet) implemented (Table 2).

R1. Flexibility. The development of MBUIs requires a flexible approach, in which stakeholders, depending on their profiles, preferences, interests or needs, must be able to follow top-to-bottom, bottom-to-top or middle-out approach, starting from the level of interest, and then being able to decide which level to tackle next. *Top-down* approach starts from a more abstract model and then specializes it (e.g. from a common AUI, one or several CUIs can be derived, according to contexts of use). *Bottom-up* approach bases in a concrete definition, generate a more abstracted one (e.g., from a CUI model specific for a context, by reverse engineering or retargeting [11], a common AUI can be achieved. In a *middle-out* approach, both directions can be followed.

Table 2. Association between functional and non-functional requirements and respective Design Decisions taken.

Req's	Design Decisions
R1: Flexibility	DD1 (must have): To offer choices for different users with different preferences or needs, Quill provides top-to-bottom, bottom-to-top or middle-out approaches as starting point for implementation
R2: Portability	DD2 (must have): HTML5, web-based application, no pre-installation of plugins or add-ons required
R3: Context-awareness	DD3 (must have): Browser-based, option to select specific platforms (or other contexts of use) for defining the CUI models (e.g. phone, tablet, vocal)
R4: Usability	DD4 (should have): GUI, automatic layout changes, animation to represent forced directed layout of graphs, design patterns and adaptation rules combined, manual transformations suggested and triggered by the system (organized in an agenda), HTML5 elements, such as canvas, facilitate the user interaction enabling also features like drag-and-drop items to the model
R5: Scalability	DD5.1 (must have): Voronoï diagrams, properties for the concepts handled (e.g. tasks) are presented in pop-ups dialog, overview+detail paradigm DD5.2 (must have): Regarding the rule engines, to provide inference and reasoning, first JavaScript tests will be run, and then file Node.js accordingly updated
R6: Consistency	DD6 (must have): The tool must perform consistently across different devices, besides being portable
R7: Persistence	DD7 (should have): To assure persistence across models of different abstraction levels, all transformations between them must be implemented (since not always the definitions are straightforward, a semi-automatic approach is adopted)
R8: Functionality	DD8 (must have): the application covers both model editing and UI design in a joint approach
R9: Collaboration	DD9 (must have): browser-based approach, models are stored in the cloud, users have associated roles and corresponding permissions, the editing is distributed and conflicts are solved with control system and conflict resolution mechanisms
R10: Efficiency	DD10 (could have): Varied complexity levels must be supported for users with different expertise levels, and also multi-formats and modalities must be considered to assure also interoperability

R2. Portability. Traditional UI development only enables reusability at the code level, while MBUI itself facilitates this consideration, because one single task model for instance, can derive several FUI models according to various contexts of use. Portability is then ensured by partially or fully reusing the models involved.

R3. Context-Awareness. Since the interaction nowadays takes place from different contexts of use, thus imposing constraints from the user (e.g. the user profile), the platform (e.g., interaction modality), and environment (e.g., location, light), MBUI should support context-awareness in the UI development life cycle.

R4. Usability. To ensure UI usability, relevant knowledge should be explicitly incorporated in the IDE to exploit it whenever needed, and not afterwards. For instance, a catalog of design patterns by means of associated adaptation rules orient the UI development towards good usability levels. Given that not all stakeholders are experts in quality domains, an editor should provide them with guidance on *how to* and *when* apply this usability knowledge, e.g., by selecting, retrieving, applying a pattern [21].

R5. Scalability. When a large set of model elements must be handled, it may be not scalable to visualize them, and also to manipulate them. Aiming to support tasks in this complex scenario, the editor must handle large-scale models without significantly degrading the performance and responsiveness of the application.

R6. Consistency. The application must also assure that its rendering (appearance) and behavior across devices, is consistent [20].

R7. Persistence. Any model creation or update must be reflected in the other levels by a set of transformations in order to consistently synchronize models of different abstraction levels.

R8. Scope. Both UI design and MBUI design must be covered in a joint approach.

R9. Collaboration. Stakeholders must be able to collaboratively interact while working for a common project.

R10. Efficiency. Models concerning interactive systems of varied complexity levels, i.e. ranging from simple to largely complex applications, must be supported by the editor, without significant performance decay, visualization or interaction problems. Moreover, the formats adopted should consider interoperability and exchange across different standards.

3.3 Quill Design Decisions

To address the requirements elicited in the previous sub-section, a set of solutions and possible implementations were analyzed and lead to the definitions of the corresponding design decisions, which were organized in a 2-layered architectural approach for both external and internal aspects, i.e. in a client-server approach.

DD1. Flexibility of interaction for creating the models. Given that the relationships between models follow a logical association, e.g. for an AUI Select the corresponding element can be the CUI Radio Group, the corresponding transformations are bi-directional holding the transformation from any levels and for both directions. Once the changes can be synchronized across different abstraction levels, i.e. the models are transformed according to editing made ensuring persistence, it is feasible that users can start their editing from any level, and then follow the work as needed.

DD2. Capability to render in different platforms. By using HTML5, AJAX and WebSockets, Quill is able to be executed in multi-platform environments and presents a consistent behavior, performing equally across devices. Because HTML5 is a standard technology, and platform-independent, in principle, any operating system must be supported in an attempt to assure portability.

DD3. Context-Awareness Support. Design Preferences Rules are considered and applied to fill gaps that are caused due to missing information. This process is analogous to W3C's Cascading Style Sheets (CSS), in which the conditions, when fulfilled, lead to changes in properties of elements. The rules indicate the actions for each given context of use, i.e. the contexts of use, once identified, are taken into account to adjust the UI model.

DD4. Usability Guidance. Rules as critics allow known problems to be detected, e.g. the use of specific color contrasts for users with color blindness. Such rules are relevant for assessing compliance with corporate guidelines. To provide such guidance in Quill a tab of Design Patterns provides relevant information from this domain of knowledge. Design patterns guide developers in implementing them. As such, the design assistant could note that the current design could present problems for people who are color blind, however, it would then be up to the designer to introduce additional color palettes and associate their use with different contexts of use.

DD5.1. Scalable Model Visualization. To provide a scalable visualization that performs consistently regardless of complexity levels, adequate rendering and manipulation mechanisms must be correctly implemented. By adopting Voronoï diagrams [16], large and complex UI models can still be visualized in a more scalable and accessible fashion, i.e. a large project can be completely accessible by navigating among the links and nodes of the diagrams, in an overview+detail paradigm that enables the view of the complete model (zoomed out) or a partial visualization of the model in more details (zoomed in). Graphical representations of models make it easier to view and interact with models compared with purely textual representations. A force-directed layout algorithm works for graphs, but fails to separate sub-branches of trees.

DD5.2. Scalable Rule Engine. From the server side perspective, complex models require powerful inference mechanisms. In Quill, a Forward Chaining Rule (FCR) engine permits dealing with the rules in a structure that connects events, conditions and actions. In principle, a change in model could be able to fire events, however this approach turned out to not be feasible due to scalability issues (the amount of rules can become exponential), and as such the abduction approach was proposed. For Complex Inferences and Reasoning: the current focus of Quill concerns the rule engines, while the prototyping occurs in a client application running JavaScript, a Pratt parser is used for high-level text syntax (facilitating to transform high level rule syntax into JavaScript objects) and a RETE algorithm [9] combined with the Abduction engine can be used for performing inferences for the models. The rule engines are then executed on the server via node.js.

DD6. The application must be compatible with and consistent in different systems. To perform equally in any platform, and to reach a large number of users, avoiding familiarity issues, the development in a web-based approach was chosen. This approach enables it to be used in any browser and online, which assures not only compatibility, but also a more "lightweight", simpler and faster interaction (since no previous installation, or specific plugins are initially required).

DD7. Persistence across different abstraction levels. The Abduction (ability to infer an explanation, given an observation and its corresponding theory) is applied in MBUI for relating AUI and CUI. An extension of relational table joins is considered, in which models can be represented as relational tables, which hold undefined values, and infer missing models. Conditions permit to perform inference and reasoning considering and acting upon several contexts of use and adaptation techniques to generate CUIs.

DD8. Large scope (concerning features available). In one single graphical editor, users have both features available: the model editing and the UI design integrated. Users are able to drag and drop components available in the menu, link them, specify their properties, having a complete and unified view of the UI design models.

DD9. Collaborative Interaction. The collaborative features, in regards to the revision control mechanism, permit several stakeholders to be concurrently involved participating in a common work project with live updates. Designers, developers, programmers, software architects and engineers can design, access and edit UI models for interactive systems within a single project, in a distributed fashion. Each user has a specific role associated (e.g., junior or senior), which provides also access to specific features of the application. One of the clients is appointed as a senior editor with the responsibility for committing changes to the models. The changes provided by other (junior) clients are passed to the senior editor for review. While a senior editor can review and accept changes, a regular editor specifies and proposes changes of the models for the senior editor. To solve conflicts resulting from concurrent editing, a nearly real time revision control system is adopted, with a 4-way conflict resolution mechanism. This hap-

pens automatically, based upon algorithms for serializing changes, and for rolling back and rolling forward sequences of changes. Each client keeps its own local undo history which is automatically updated to reflect changes committed by the senior client.

DD10. Efficiency. The graphic modality summed with a WYSIWYG approach intends at a didactic and intuitive interaction manner. Quill aims at covering different expertise levels of users to facilitate the interaction and although the visualization and editing is graphically performed, it can also be exported in an interchange format for other purposes of use, aiming a good accessibility. Moreover, by applying adaptation rules targeted at constrained contexts, users can identify good design decisions and adaptation techniques that are applicable in a given context.

3.4 Design Knowledge

The **Rich Domain Model** defines the data interfaces between the user interface and the application back-end. Besides basic data types, Quill supports default values, examples, constraints and embedded documentation. Constraints as regular expressions, constrain the value of string properties; indicate that a given interface, method or property is relevant based upon the values of other properties, is optional or must be provided by the user, and is persistent, i.e. that the values provided by a user are preserved in between invocations of the user interface.

Task models describe user interaction at an abstract level, e.g. which tasks can be carried out concurrently, which tasks pass information enabling other tasks, and which tasks represent a choice. Some tasks are performed by the user whilst others by the system. The task model can be used to determine what parts of the user interface to present in parallel or sequentially. On a small display, it may be appropriate to break the user interface into a sequence of simple dialogues, while on a larger display, these could be presented jointly or split across separate panes in a tab control.

Layout expertise is needed to generate candidate designs for the concrete user interface. This involves platform specific knowledge, e.g. the difference for touch based controls on a smart phone from those driven by a mouse pointer on a laptop. The design is influenced by rough estimates of the size of each control, based upon information in the domain model, including examples of expected user input. Quill deliberately uses a simple model of layout, e.g. vertical, horizontal and grid layout managers. This is enriched and mapped into CSS when skinning the final user interface generated from the concrete user interface models.

The **design rules** express knowledge for the design assistant. For instance: (i) Rules that propose designs, and which embody design preferences for particular platforms; (ii) Rules that determine which relationships hold in a given context of use; (iii) Rules that propose changes in response to events signaling changes in the context; (iv) Rules that critique designs, e.g., searching color contrasts that would create problems for color blind people.

Propagating changes across a design with event condition action rules requires every change to be matched with a rule, resulting in various rules that are hard to maintain. Another solution is to express logical relationships across different abstraction levels. If certain facts and certain relationships hold true, then it is possible to infer additional facts that must be true if the relationship is to hold. This is referred to as **abductive reasoning**. For simple conjunctive relationships, this can be cast as an extension of relational table joins, using logical variables for values shared across tables. A proof of concept is available as an interactive web page [9], it uses a 2-pass algorithm for the logical joins and abducing facts and allows enabling and disabling abduction to see the results.

4. A RUNNING EXAMPLE ON QUILL

Quill's architecture (Fig. 2) is organized in a client-server approach. The client application is implemented in HTML5 and provides the features as previously mentioned. The back-end of Quill is a cloud provisioned authoring server that implements an asynchronous messaging system, generating responses according to the changes made by the user and streamed to the server. The server, besides also streaming changes back to the UI (in HTML5), persists the UI models across the four CRF levels. This server is deployed as a Tomcat web application. In order to propagate changes across levels, a rule engine is adopted, simulating the effects of the changes according to specific contexts of use.

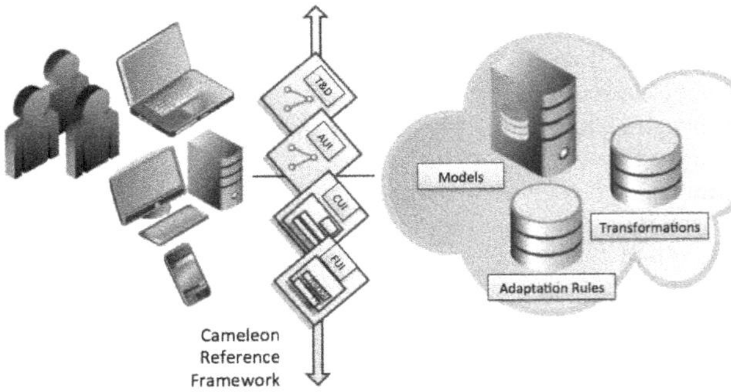

Figure 2. Architectural organization of Quill.

We exemplify Quill's functionalities and features, illustrating them with an actual application scenario as a proof-of-concept. This case study defined consists in a car rental application example in which users are able to rent a car (this is the official case study considered in the W3C MBUI group: http://www.w3.org/wiki/Model-Based_User_Interfaces). Thus, by interacting with the application, they can select the car of interest to rent, set the period for the rental (begin and end dates, in hour, day, month, and year), specify details about the car (preferences, requirements, constraints, etc.). For this application, a common domain model (Fig. 3) and a task model (Fig. 4) were defined, serving as a ground for generating the models for the other levels: abstract UI (Fig. 5), concrete UI (Fig. 6), and final UIs (Fig. 7).

For this case study, specific scenarios for contexts of use, mainly concerning the platform type, were selected, namely: a Desktop PC, a Tablet PC and a Smartphone. Their specifications guided the definitions of the models and also their transformations by means of appropriate adaptation rules. For further examples of various contexts of use, a *model voyager* enables the user to navigate within various levels of abstraction for the same case study and see the transformations (http://sites.uclouvain.be/mbui/). Fig. 8 reproduces the tree browsing of the car rental study that reaches to a context of use in which smartphones are used.

Fig. 4 shows the *task model* of the application, visualized as a Voronoï diagram, in which each (sub-)task has its properties specified or modified by the end user, the tasks can be also accessed and visualized in details. The task format is compatible with the CTT (Concur Task Trees) following its formal specification [17]. Fig. 5 illustrates an example of the *Abstract UI model* (AUI), while Fig. 6 reproduces an example of the *Concrete UI (CUI) model* for the car rental example. It shows possible fields that compose an entry form for the end users. In this phase, no layout specification is set. Selected adaptation rules appropriate to the target context will be responsible for defining specificities of the layout according to the context of use. In the example the UI model is being specified for a tablet device (delivery target).

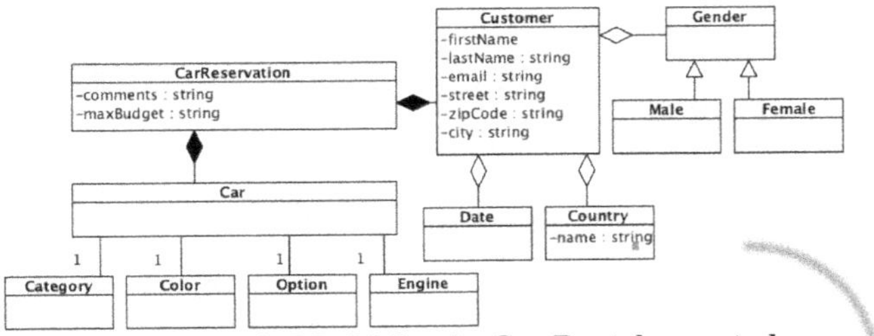

Figure 3. Domain Model for the Car Rental case study.

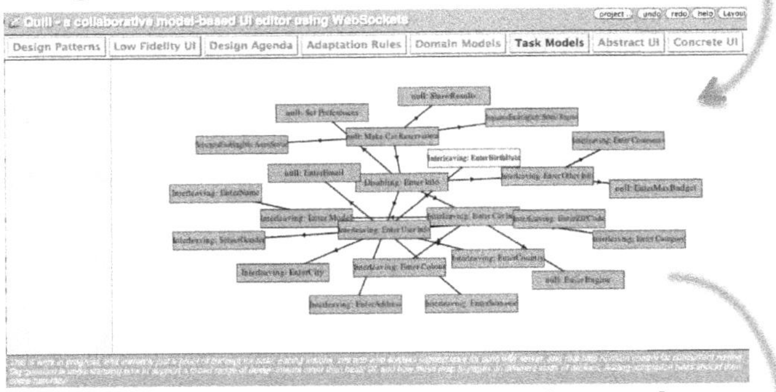

Figure 4. Task Model for the Car Rental case study.

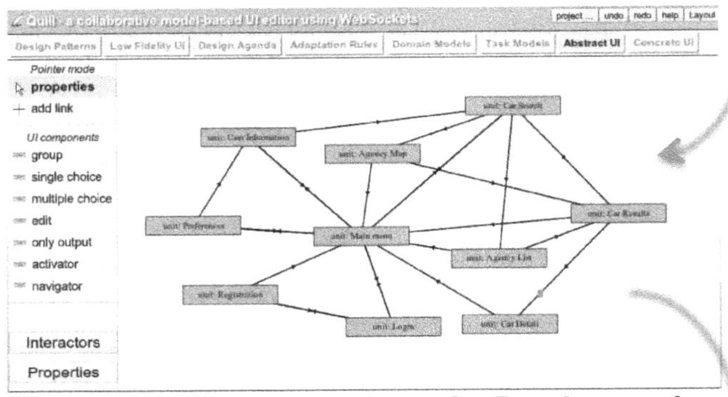

Figure 5. Abstract UI Model for the Car Rental case study.

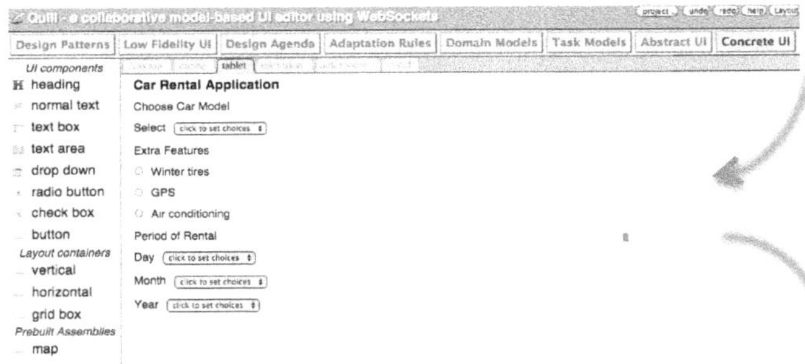

Figure 6. Concrete UI Model for the Car Rental case study.

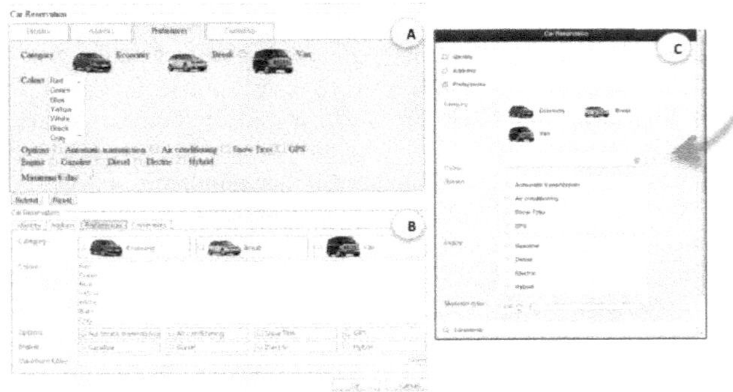

Figure 7. Final UIs for the Car Rental case study.

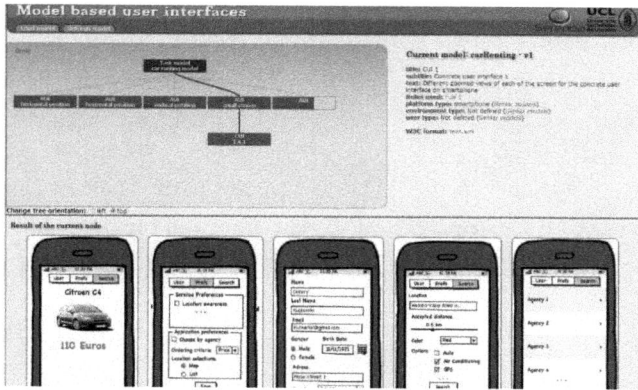

Figure 8. Model Voyager for the Car Rental case study.

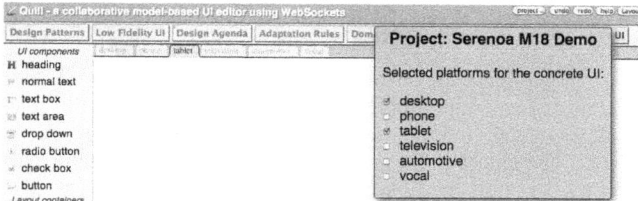

Figure 9. Quill Main Interface.

Quill supports features that are both inherent to the project management options (i.e. defining project, undo/re-do actions, help, layout specification – right side of Fig. 9) and related to the editing functions, that are organized in horizontal menus with selectable components (buttons and tabs), and a vertical menu with draggable components (buttons and icons). The tabs items support switching to different modes in the following tabs.

The *Design Patterns* tab (Fig. 9) provides a catalog of design patterns that guide users in the development of their applications. In low fidelity UI users can depict the UI enabling end user evaluation in the early stages of the development process. The *Design Agenda* tab enables users and system to collaboratively define and control tasks and milestones that "have already been" or "must still be" achieved. The tasks of this agenda are either triggered by the application or defined by the user. The *Adaptation Rules* tab gathers the transformations and actions triggered given specific conditions fulfilled by the context of use. Rules consider context belonging to the user, platform and environments, and application resources including navigation, presentation and contents (regardless of their given format). The *Domain Model* tab permits users to describe application domain properties, actions and notifications for the domain (Fig. 3). The *Task Model* tab enables users to access and edit task models that were previously created and that are associated with a given project, or to create new models for new projects. For the task models, properties like temporal relationship (e.g., order, sequences, and associations), name, task type. The *Abstract User Interface model tab* considers several containers and components that can be included, edited and specified. For the *Concrete User Interface model* tab, either FUIs suffer reverse engineering processes to be abstracted or AUI models are transformed (reified) into CUIs. User can also create their own CUI models, by selecting and organizing their components.

Quill enables prototyping of UIs in various levels of fidelity and abstraction by dragging components from the left menu and by dropping and arranging them in the central canvas. Their properties can be then refined. The components of the left menu vary according to the tab selected by the user. When the AUI choice is selected, two pointer modes are available: properties or add link.

Seven UI components can be selected (group, single or multiple choice, edit, only output, activator and navigator). When the CUI choice is selected, users can choose among: 8 UI components (heading, normal text, text box, text area, drop down, radio button, check box, and button), 3 Layout Containers (vertical, horizontal, and grid box), or 1 Prebuilt Assembly (map).

The CUI level also enables users to choose the platform of interest among the delivery targets available, i.e. a Desktop PC, Mobile Phone, Tablet PC, Television, Automotive, or Vocal. The central canvas is associated with the respective constraints imposed by such devices, providing users only features that are available in these specific cases. CUIs for the other targets are (semi) automatically synchronized and updated according to any model change.

Fig. 7 illustrates three Final UIs implemented, the selected tab shows the preferences of cars that are available for the end user, for instance regarding categories of cars, colors, options, engine and maximum cost can be specified. This UI is illustrative, since one specific device type (i.e. tablet PC) was considered, however other platforms, like a Desktop PC, or mobile ones, like a smartphone can also be selected as target delivery device. Fig. 10 demonstrates that the HTML5 code generated exhibits adaptation capabilities to the platform: the UI layout changes according to the screen resolution by, for instance, repositioning labels justified to the left or positioned on top of related edit fields.

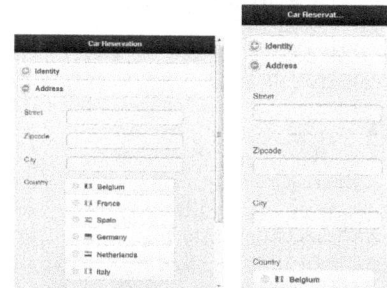

Figure 10. Final UI with adaptation capability.

Concerning the technical perspective, the technology adopted to implement Quill is HTML5, in a portable and lightweight client application. The main page is coded in 126 lines of code, and accommodates 8 specific functions implemented in JavaScript. The style sheets were specified using CSS (Cascade Style Sheet).

The first JavaScript function called WebSocket is responsible for connecting the application with the server. Then vector is a function that computes the graphical layout of the models. Force directed is also responsible for calculating the layout of the models, i.e. re-arranging nodes and links in a force directed graph layout approach, in this sense damping, repulsion and field are set, and an animation is applied to illustrate the movement transition. Quill launches the main UI, including the menus and canvas and it also connects to the server to access and load current projects on user demand. Abstract loads features that correspond to the respective UI level, composing the appropriate menu and rendering the model in the canvas if previously selected by the user. Concrete composes the horizontal sub-menu, with device options, load the workspace and respective features.

ASFE-DL [17] consists of a specific adaptation language that generates the AUI model. Appropriate interactors are charged and loaded and their respective properties are presented for editing. The Task function loads the workspace with the current task model, if available and previously selected and calls the functions that calculate the behavior, re-arrangement and animation of the task tree model diagram. Quill adopts an Apache2 open source license.

5. USER SURVEY

5.1 Method

While for the scientific community there are clear benefits of using model-based approaches and context-aware adaptation, for the industry, it may be no so evident whether the benefits actually compensate for the costs involved. To investigate this, a survey based on two main hypotheses has been defined:

H1) Stakeholders are aware of the importance and the benefits of: context-sensitivity, model-based approaches and adaptation.

H2) Stakeholders do not fully incorporate into their daily work practices: context-sensitivity, model-based approaches and adaptation.

The target respondents of this survey are practitioners working for Information Technology companies, with different expertise, background and roles (e.g. software engineers and architects, developers and designers). They live in different countries, (e.g. Belgium, Brazil, France, Germany, U.K., Spain) and work for different companies (e.g. Yahoo, Sony, BNP Paribas – Fortis). The questions focus on: (i) practitioner profile (years of experience, main role, company size); (ii) context (dimensions and information considered, perceived relevance, methods employed, and usage); (iii) adaptation (how techniques are identified, applied and presented); and (iv) MBUI approach and its perceived relevance (pros and cons). The survey has been defined and published online using Google docs, a message sent via email, invited participants to voluntarily collaborate.

5.2 Results

30 practitioners working for I.T. companies or as independent consultants replied to the survey. Concerning their *profile*, and their years of experience, 43% of the participants work from 5 to 10 years in the I.T. domain, 40% have been working for more than 10 years and only 17% for less than 5 years (Fig. 11 left). Concerning the company size, 46% of the participants work for large companies, 20% for small companies, 17% for medium-sized companies, 10% for micro-entities and 7% work independently (Fig. 11 right). Concerning their main roles, 40% of the participants are developers, 27% software engineers, 20% project managers, 7% software architects, 3% system analysts, and 3% support team leader (Fig. 12).

Concerning the *context*, in absolute numbers, out of the 30 participants, 25 stated to consider the users, 24 the platform, 12 the application domain and 9 the environment. Concerning the perceived relevance of context and its actual usage (Fig. 13) the user is classified as the most relevant dimension for most of the participants, followed by the platform and the application domain, while the environment is considered as the least relevant dimension. These results concern the participants' perception of the context relevance. When compared with the actual usage, again the user and platform are considered as the most relevant dimensions, while in practice also the application domain and environment are the least considered dimensions. However, although users are perceived as the most relevant dimension of context, in practice their information is not always used. The platform is more considered in practice than perceived as relevant. The environment is perceived as relevant and considered in practice, and the application domain is more considered as relevant as actually used in practice. Fig. 14 illustrates how many participants consider context by relevance level (left) versus actual usage (right). These graphics show that users are perceived as the most relevant dimension (by almost half of the participants), followed by the platform, application

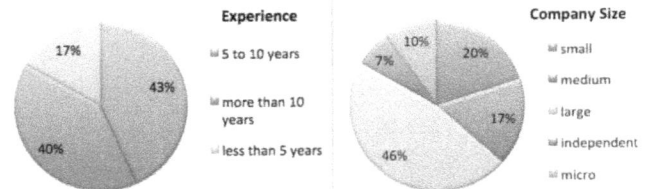

Figure 11. Participants profile: experience and company size.

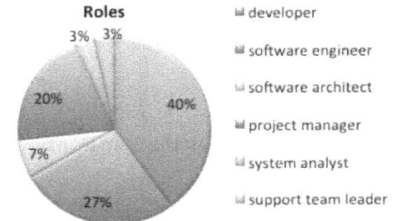

Figure 12. Participants profile: main roles.

domain and environment. The same trend is observed for the practical use of the dimensions (although with less significant differences). The environment was the dimension considered the least relevant by more participants and the least frequently used in practice. In practice, all participants consider to some extent: platform, application domain, and user. Fig. 13 shows the context dimensions that the participants use while developing systems, out of 30 participants, 25 consider the user, 24 the platform, 14 the application domain and 9 the environment. Only 4 out of 30 participants actually use all 4 dimensions together (user, platform, environment and application domain), also 8 use 3 dimensions. Most of them (18 out of 30) use just 2 (14) or 1 dimension (4).

Concerning the *user* and its information considered: most of the participants consider user preferences (20 out of 30), followed by demographics (14 out of 30) and interests (15 out of 30). 10 out of 30 participants though consider only impairments. Usually a combination of 2 dimensions is used (13 out of 30 participants), e.g. impairments and preferences (4), or interests and demographics (3 out of 30). Only 3 participants consider simultaneously all 4 dimensions. Regarding the methods for gathering user information: while 17 out of 30 participants rely on observation, 14 on guidelines, 12 on interviews, 5 on surveys and 6 just try to guess information. Two participants collect and monitor real usage data. Ten

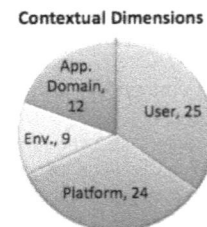

Figure 13. Context information: absolute numbers.

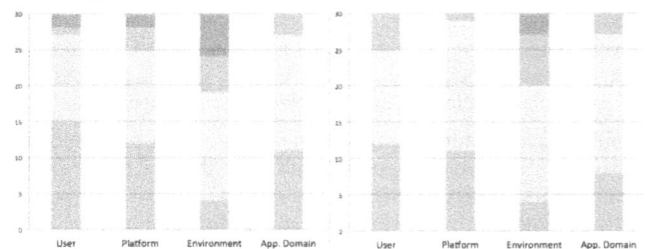

Figure 14. Context: perceived relevance and adoption.

participants use just one method, while 11 adopt 2, 6 use 3 methods and only 1 combine all 4 methods (guidelines, interviews, observations and surveys).

Concerning the *platform*, most of the participants (25 out of 30) consider the device and 23 out of 30 consider the technology, 23 consider the connections, and just 4 take the accessories into account. Just 5 out of 30 participants do not consider the device per se, but they (2 participants) consider the connections or (3 participants) the connections and the technologies available. To gather information about the platform, 16 out of 30 participants use a default specification; among which 6 also perform automatic tests, of which 2 also observe the context of use and 1 also tracks the user interaction. Two participants perform automatic tests, 4 observe users and just 1 participant interviews users. Just 1 participant tracks the user interaction (but combined with 3 other methods). Regarding the amount of methods, while the majority (16) employs just 1 technique at a time, the remaining participants (14) combine more than one technique. Three participants combine 3 methods and 11 combine 2 of them.

Concerning the *environment*, most of the participants (17 out of 30) do not consider any information. Among the remaining participants (13), 8 consider the light level, 5 the stability level, 4 the noise level, and 4 considered other information, as the user location (via GPS), temperature, and the 3G coverage. Concerning the methods adopted, observation sessions, user interviews, and surveys are applied. Just 1 participant informed to use sensors.

To search for *adaptation*, the participants use: pattern libraries (11 of 30), public guidelines (9 out 30), embedded features (8 out of 30), online repositories (7 out of 30). However, approximately half of the participants (16 out 30 participants) do not provide adaptation. Only 1 participant combines 4 information sources, while 5 combine 3, 9 combine 2, and 15 use only 1 or no source. For *adaptation strategies*, 6 out of 30 participants use UI graceful degradation [8], 10 use progressive enhancement, and 4 combine both strategies. Most of the stakeholders though (17 out of 30) do not use any of these, and just 1 participant uses animation to smoothly present to users the transition between original and adapted UIs.

Concerning the adoption of *models*, almost half of the participants (16 out of 30) informed to not use them, 6 participants use MDE, 11 use UML diagrams among which 3 use them combined with MDE. The participants of the survey remarked four main *benefits* of adopting models during the development process: (i) provide a common language and standards; (ii) facilitate reuse; (iii) generate systems that are more complete and have more qualities and (iv) aid communication, discussion and analysis. As *disadvantages* of adopting models, four remarks were noted, models: (i) are hard to customize, to adapt, and to maintain; (ii) lack support (or have incomplete support); (iii) are hard or slow to synchronize changes and (iv) require more expertise, efforts and time.

One aspect has been classified as both positive and negative for different participants: the optimization of the development phases. While some participants believe that fewer efforts are needed, others stated that more efforts are required, e.g. for expertise and time. Another aspect of disagreement is achieving a working prototype, while some participants consider it easier to do with models, others think it is actually harder. The same applies for the complexity of the projects, while one participant stated that models are not suitable for simple projects, other participants stated that models are not suitable for highly complex projects.

5.3 Discussion

The survey reached a variety of stakeholders with different roles, experience, and from different companies and countries.

Regarding the *context*, it is clear that mainly the user and platform are considered, while application domain and environment are not always so used. Actually it is possible that stakeholders were confused with such definitions, as some participants commented after replying the survey. Sometimes the concept of environment was misunderstood, being interpreted as the editor per se, and not the situation where the interaction takes place and its circumstances. The term application domain also raised some discussion, being misunderstood with cultural aspects of the user. Even by providing a short description about these concepts and some examples, not all participants could successfully comprehend such definitions. It may be that the user and the platform are more considered because when ignored or omitted the user interaction may be prevented. However, to complement such results, it is necessary to investigate to which extent the contextual information is actually covered. Concerning the H1, which states that stakeholders are aware of the importance of the concepts, it holds for context aspects, at least regarding user, platform and application domain. Environmental aspects are not considered as so important, or maybe it may be not clear for stakeholders what environment states for and how it can be effectively useful. Concerning H2, most of the participants stated to use context, at least to some extent, for their projects.

Adaptation is not used by most of the participants, since 16 out of 30 stated to not provide adaptation and to consider instead a standard scenario. This may be a result of previous work practices in software development, in which a conventional context of use was common (i.e. an able-bodied user, a Desktop PC, and a stable environment). Besides this, it is possible that stakeholders are not aware of which information to consider and how to do it. The participants are aware of the importance of adaptation, since they stated to consider context-awareness while developing their applications, which validates to some extent H1. However, concerning H2, it is remarkable that adaptation is not largely employed, which may result in static applications that are not suitable for dynamic and varied contexts of use.

The perspective of the participants about *models* shows that while they can perceive many benefits, they are still skeptical about their adoption; mainly because of the lack of support to adopt models or incomplete solutions. Without more complete frameworks, the use of models may be limited to academia or to specific activities. Concerning H1, it is clear that most participants are able to recognize the importance of models, however, concerning H2, we note that models are not widely used. Being useful to support certain activities, but not fully adopted. By analyzing the commentaries provided we believe that only by having more mature support, frameworks, standards and tools, stakeholders could see more benefits in using models, less costs, and then actually incorporate them into their daily work practices. The lack of consensus regarding the advantages and disadvantages of models may be justified by the fact that these assumptions are project-dependent, so while in certain cases more resources are indeed needed, in other ones the development is automatically optimized. Regarding complexity issues, there is a range in which models are suitable, however further investigations are needed to precise, identify criteria and to measure the complexity levels of projects, and also the costs of applying models, so that to effectively identify when it is suitable to actually adopt model-based approaches.

6. FINAL REMARKS AND CONCLUSION

This paper presented Quill, a web-based development environment that enables various stakeholders of a web application to collaboratively adopt a model-based design of the user interface for cross-platform deployment. Based on shortcomings identified in the literature and by observation, a set of 10 requirements was elicited that gave rise to design decisions on which the Quill development has been motivated and decided.

There are still many open questions to be discussed in MBUI, such as, but not limited to: the compatibility among heterogeneous contexts of use, the accessibility issues due to usage of a graphical representation in comparison with a textual description, the interoperability of applications regarding a technology and decisions that are both platform and technology independent, the consideration of context-awareness and all its consequent specificities, the decision of a web-based application concerning its drawback of online usage only and (un)availability problems, the definition of synchronous vs. asynchronous collaboration and consequent need of managing conflicts and defining user roles (permissions). Now, in Quill users can collaborate within the same project, however both asynchronous and concurrent editing must be supported, the usage of HTML5 which requires browser that are (really) HTML5-compliant. Not all the browsers available are actually HTML-5 compliant, which may cause differences of rendering and features supported. There are still many challenges that must be discussed, decided, and overcome to consolidate and release the proposed editor, among which we can highlight, for instance the definition and application of transformations between models across different abstraction levels, not always is straightforward, requiring also manual interference, in this sense a design agenda was adopted to remind users about the manual changes that must be done to appropriately synchronize models. Other solutions could be also thought, the design agenda can be enhanced in future efforts to accommodate also agile decisions, or user-centered design activities. Quill does not fix completely all the issues encountered in MBUI as discussed. However, it aims at pointing and addressing the most challenging issues.

Quill's main benefits are: it is a browser-based application, whose models are hosted on the cloud, it enables users to adopt flexible approaches, concerning the level from which they start to work, it enables collaboration among stakeholders of different expertise levels and domains, it supports also specific roles with corresponding permissions, MBUI is compliant with CRF, it is more straightforward to extend its functionalities with additional plugins and add-ons, (e.g., to calculate specific metrics), web services could augment Quill's functionalities. So far, a design pattern tab provides information concerning this specific domain, usability guidelines, adaptation techniques could also be incorporated for users that are not experts in these fields.

Quill will be extended with: (i) an adaptation rules editor that enables stakeholders to express adaptation rules in a controlled subset of natural language that can be easily mapped into any specific standard rule format for further processing, (ii) a Final UI emulator in which users visualize in a separate browser window the UI design, (iii) syntax coloring features.

Acknowledgments

The authors gratefully acknowledge the support of the FP7 Serenoa project, funded by the European Union through under reference FP7-ICT-258030. The authors also thank Raphaël Schramme for implementing the model voyager, and the various anonymous participants to the user survey.

7. REFERENCES

[1] Aquino, N., Vanderdonckt, J., Panach, I., and Pastor, O. Conceptual Modelling of Interaction. In *Handbook of Conceptual Modelling: Theory, Practice, and Research Challenges*, Embley, D. Thalheim, B. (eds.), Chapter 3. Springer-Verlag, Berlin (2011), 335–358.

[2] Assisi, R. V4all GUI designer for eclipse manual v.1.0. 2004. http://v4all.sourceforge.net/index_start.html.

[3] Calvary, G., Coutaz, J., Thevenin, D., Limbourg, Q., Bouillon, L., and Vanderdonckt, J. A Unifying Reference Framework for Multi-Target User Interfaces. *Inter. with Comp.* 15, 3 (2003), 289–308.

[4] Cantera Fonseca, J.M., González Calleros, J.M., Meixner, G., Paternò, F., Pullmann, J., Raggett, D., Schwabe, D., and Vanderdonckt, J. Model-Based User Interface Incubator Group, 4 May 2010. http://www.w3.org/2005/ Incubator/model-based-ui/XGR-mbui/.

[5] Chu, H.-H., Song, H., Wong, C., Kurakake, S., and Katagiri, M. Roam, a seamless application framework. *Journal of Systems and Software* 69, 3 (2004), 209–226.

[6] Coyette, A., Kieffer, S., and Vanderdonckt, J. Multi-Fidelity Prototyping of User Interfaces. In *Proc. of IFIP INTERACT'2007*. LNCS, Vol. 4662, Springer-Verlag, Berlin (2007), 149–162.

[7] Coutaz, J., Crowley, J.L., Dobson, S., and Garlan, D. Context is key. *Communications of the ACM* 48, 3 (March 2005), 49–53.

[8] Florins, M., Montero, F., Vanderdonckt, J., and Michotte, B. Splitting Rules for Graceful Degradation of User Interfaces. In *Proc. of AVI'2006*. ACM Press, New York (2006), 59–66.

[9] Heinrich, M., Lehmann, F., Springer, T., and Gaedke, M. Exploiting single-user web applications for shared editing: a generic transformation approach. In *Proc. of WWW'12*. ACM Press, New York, 1057–1066.

[10] Helms, J., Schaefer, R., Luyten, K., Vermeulen, J., Abrams, M., Coyette, A., and Vanderdonckt, J. Human-Centered Engineering with the User Interface Markup Language. In *Human-Centered Software Engineering*, Springer, London (2009), 141–173.

[11] Kumar, R., Talton, J.O., Ahmad, S., and Klemmer, S.R. Bricolage: Example-Based Retargeting for Web Design. In *Proc. of CHI'2011*. ACM Press, New York (2011), 2197–2206.

[12] Maqetta, Visual Authoring of HTML5 User Interfaces in the browser. Dojo Foundation. http://dojofoundation.org/projects/ maqetta.

[13] McKirdy, J. Choosing the UI tool which best suits your needs. In *Proc. of 7th IFIP Int. Conf. on Human-Computer Interaction Interact'99*. IOS Press (1999).

[14] Meskens, J., Vermeulen, J., Luyten, K., and Coninx, K. Gummy for Multi-Platform User Interface Designs: Shape me, Multiply me, Fix me, Use me. In *Proc. of AVI'2008*. ACM Press, NY (2008), 233-240.

[15] Mourouzis, A., Leonidis, A., Foukarakis, M., Antona, M., and Maglaveras, N. A novel design approach for multi-device adaptable user interfaces: concepts, methods and examples. In *Proc. of UAHCHI'2011*. Vol. 1. Springer, Berlin (2011), 400–409.

[16] Nocaj, A. and Brandes, U. Computing Voronoi Treemaps Faster, Simpler, and Resolution-independent. In Proc. of *Eurographics Conf. on Visualization EuroVis'2012*. S. Bruckner, S. Miksch, and H. Pfister (eds.). *Computer Graphics Forum* 31, 3 (2012).

[17] Paterno, F., Santoro, C., and Spano, L.D. Deliverable D3.2.2. ASFE-DL: Semantics, Syntaxes and Stylistics (R2). http://www.serenoafp7.eu/wp-content/uploads/2012/10/SERENOA_D3.2.2.pdf

[18] Raggett, D. The web of things: Extending the web into the real world. In *Proc. of SOFSEM 2010: Theory and Practice of Computer Science*. (2010), 96–107.

[19] D. Raggett. Testbed for abduction over relationships. 2013. At: http://www.w3.org/2013/01/abduction/

[20] Richter, K., Nichols, J., Gajos, K., and Seffah, A. The many faces of consistency in cross-platform design. In Proc. of Extended Abstracts of CHI'2006. ACM Press, New York (2006) 1639–1642.

[21] Seffah, A. and Javahery, H. Multiple User Interfaces: Multi-Devices, Cross-Platform and Context-Awareness. John Wiley & Sons (2003).

[22] Sumner, T., Bonnardel, N., and Kallak, B.H. The Cognitive Ergonomics of Knowledge-Based Design Support Systems. In *Proc. of CHI'97*. ACM Press, New York (1997), 83–90.

[23] Vdovjak, R., Frasincar, F., Houben, G.-J., and Barna, P. Engineering semantic web information systems in Hera. *Journal of Web Engineering* 2, 1/2 (2003), 3–26.

[24] Wegner, P. Why Interaction is more Powerful than Algorithms. *Communications of the ACM* 40, 5 (May 1997), 80–91.

Teaching UX: Designing Programs to Train the Next Generation of UX Experts

Guiseppe Getto
East Carolina University
2108 Bate Bldg.
Greenville, NC 27858
+1 (517) 574-8965
guiseppegettoatwork@
gmail.com

Liza Potts
Michigan State University
291 Bessey Hall
Lansing, MI 48824
+1 (517) 355-2400
lpotts@msu.edu

Michael J. Salvo
Purdue University
500 Oval Dr.
West Lafayette, IN 47907
+1 (765) 494-3772
salvo@purdue.edu

Kathie Gossett
Iowa State University
203 Ross Hall
Ames, IA 50011
+1 (515) 294-7460
kgossett@iastate.edu

ABSTRACT

This experience report describes core values and approaches to teaching and developing programs in User Experience (UX). What binds these values and approaches together is a deep engagement with ongoing trends and best practices in the field of UX over the past several decades. Examples offered are contextually embedded, yet each expression is consistent with underlying core competencies gleaned from a ten-plus year history of teaching and practicing UX design, information architecture and information design, visual rhetoric, ethics, and usability in the technical communication classroom. The best practices we articulate below are applicable in the context of corporate training, team building and preparation, and consulting, in addition to academic contexts.

Categories and Subject Descriptors

K.6.1 [**Project and People Management**]: Training

Keywords

User Experience, Usability, Programs, Teaching, Training, Jobs

1. INTRODUCTION

Over the past 10 years, User Experience design (UX) has emerged as a recognizable focus for a variety of related practices in technical communication. Understood broadly as a field that spans information architecture and information design; usability, user-centered design, and participatory design; document design, visual design, and 'big data' analysis; institutional and intra-office communication, team building, document and project management—UX as a central area of study informs the constantly evolving identity of the technical communicator. As Johnson-Eilola and Selber (2013) argued, we must think of contemporary technical communication as a "problem-solving activity" insofar as contemporary communication problems are subjective, rarely solved permanently, and engaged by multiple actors [1]. The contemporary practice of technical communication thus has much in common with the central practices and core values of UX.

Like the figure of the technical communicator, the rise of the UX expert has heralded a variety of paradigm shifts that impact the place of UX expertise within professional discourse and practice. Once conceived of as the design professional solely responsible for making sure that software was created with users in mind, contemporary UX experts are industry leaders who mobilize empirically data of to design products that are not only usable, but will be used once they are launched.

At the same time, however, programs that train future UX professionals are nearly non-existent. Some UX professionals are trained as technical communicators who specialize in UX late in their undergraduate or graduate programs through internships, solitary courses, or intensive and—often self-propelled—study. Some emerge from related disciplines like Human-Computer Interaction (HCI) or Information Technology (IT), fields which arguably focus more on the analytical study, design, and maintenance of Information and Communication Technologies (ICTs) than on the creation of successful user experiences. Many more UX professionals are self-taught, having gotten involved with tech firms as designers, developers, or consultants in the 1990s, when companies first started to value the experiences of their users as important to product development and deployment.

Ultimately, our goal in this brief report is to start a conversation around the development of educational experiences within technical communication programs that could foster the next generation of UX professionals. Interdisciplinary programs in tech comm, in which a variety of skill sets that are central to UX theory and practice converge, are ripe for such development. We begin below by detailing the evolution of the field and professional practice of UX, from its inception as a kind of analytical study of user-centered design principles to its modern day place as both research methodology and deployment of participatory design theories and projects. From there we map the current state of academic programs in technical communication that feature UX coursework and/or principles. We then discuss the emergence of full programs in UX, focusing on a new major at Michigan State University as a case-in-point. We close by providing implications for the future of such work, including some shifts we see as necessary within the field of technical communication if UX is to fully take root within its borders.

2. Evolution of UX Core Values

One of the first articulations that placed users at the center of the professional practice of design, in 1988 Donald Norman published *The Psychology of Everyday Things*, or POET as it was nicknamed by design professionals [2]. This title is emblematic of still-operative interests in human psychology amongst user-centered designers. The idea that user-centered design is really the study of the motivated use of discourse hearkens back to rhetorical theorist Kenneth Burke's interest in revealing motives, which is arguably a major underpinning of rhetorical analysis and practice within technical communication programs, a point we return to later. Norman later retitled his book *The Design of Everyday Things*, or DOET, and thus reoriented the goals of design as inclusive of a larger audience, one beyond design specialists, psychologists, and technicians [3]. While usability, ergonomics, and behavioral psychology were taking shape as academic fields of interest in the wake of this landmark publication, a decade passed.

2.1 From (Unspoken) System to User

In 1998, ten years after the first appearance of Norman's book, Robert Johnson published *User-Centered Technology* [4]. Johnson's book was a watershed moment in the development of UX, as Johnson named the current-traditional practices of industrial design as system-centered. In a time when computing technologies and devices were largely the provenance of a white-coated scientific priesthood and every computational cycle represented specialist values put to functional use, a system-centered paradigm made much sense. However, with the dawning personal computer revolution bringing access to more and more consumer-level computer users, or "end users" as they would soon be called, a new era of computers and information spaces designed for non-expert users was ushered in.

This turn from system- to user-centered design paradigm is ably retold many places, perhaps none more engaging than in Tracy Kidder's *Soul of a New Machine* (2000), which also begins to articulate the late 20th century arrival of technical communication as a professional practice and mapping strategy for showing users how to utilize new computing machines made available during this time [5]. As Dorrmehl (2012) explained, from the standpoint of design professionals of this era these new machines—first designed, developed, and introduced to market by Wozniak-Jobs—seemed to frivolously spend all their computational power on new interfaces for non-specialist users (e.g. Graphical User Interfaces or GUIs) [6]. Within this context, it was Johnson (1998) who first articulated a concern with interface and activity as user-centered, calling attention to the system-centeredness of existing design and development paradigms, and ushering in a generation of technical communicators who focused as much on usability as they did on software documentation, a focus which has quietly gained traction within the field since *IEEE Transactions* published its usability-focused special issue in 1989 [4] [7].

2.2 From User to Users

In the late 1990s and early 2000s, information architecture and information design captured the focus of the field of UX, as web-based publication Boxes and Arrows (2001) followed the publication of Jacobson's Information Design (1999) [8] [9]. While the former provided a forum where practitioners and academics communicated in a timely, open-access manner, the latter took seriously the idea of information science as work key to the digital age. Shortly thereafter, Christina Wodke's *Information Architecture: Blueprints for the Web* (2002) first employed personas as a conceptual tool, introducing the consideration of multiple users with possibly divergent goals, purposes, and aims deployed amidst an array of technological artifacts, including but not limited to those present within the World Wide Web [10]. In technical communication, a parallel inquiry has resulted in an interest in multiple communication stakeholders, as evidenced by the recent work of both Johnson-Eilola and Selber (2013) and Michele Simmons (2008) [1] [11]. In both fields, users began to be conceived of as having different levels of commitment, investment, and power in their relationship to technological artifacts.

2.3 From Users to Participants

As Courage and Baxter (2005) argued during the first decade of the 21st century, engaging users and building an audience for product deployment necessitates user participation at all levels of use and design [12]. A product may look good, may be exceedingly useful for a certain demographic, but without engagement of users 'where they live,' the product may roll out to total digital silence. Several of the authors of this report receive e-mails on a daily or weekly basis from designers trying desperately to build a constituency for their application, website, or startup, after this selfsame artifact has already been fully developed. It is saddening to see promising new products and projects grind to a screeching halt when developers suddenly realize they have no user base.

As we point out below, from an educational standpoint this shift from user-centered design to participatory design means building relationships with stakeholders ahead of time so that UX trainees can learn engagement from the ground up, by doing it. From a research and development standpoint, however, the new emphasis on participation means doing the same thing within industry while projects are still in their infancy. Only by recruiting participants for user tests, getting buy-in for a new prototype of an existing product, and/or finding skilled designers and interested stakeholders to partner on a new startup or venture, can a potential user experience that could be awe-inspiring become an actual experience that real, live users use to better their lives.

3. Balancing Theory and Practice in UX Program Development

If there is one truism of working in technology-driven fields, it is that those fields are constantly in flux. We can never teach all of the tools our students or trainees need for their future or ongoing careers simply because these tools have not been invented yet. Instead, we must instill in our mentees the notion that technological innovation is not only inevitable, but a positive, kinetic impulse that can propel them forward. Rather than teaching a set of tools or products, learners need to gain an understanding of how to adapt, learn, grow, and most of all, embrace change. Fortunately, the field of technical communication strongly values such philosophies; they are one of our greatest strengths as a field [1] [13] [14] [15] [16].

This is not to say that any program will succeed if learners are prioritizing theory over practice. A balance between the two is necessary, and teaching tools is an opportunity for students to put theory into practice. It doesn't necessarily matter if those tools come in commercial packages, open source packages, or in the form of pencils, paper, and post-it notes. It is most important that learners understand that the form, content, and context of the tools they use must match the exigencies of the job at hand. Below we talk about some important contexts for the development of UX learning, including classes, programs, and full-blown degrees.

3.1 A Note about Program Names

Depending on which departments or industries are involved, you may have to negotiate the name of the program you are developing. It is important that the program name translates well to the market you are located in. Otherwise, the program risks looking out of date or out of touch with current best practices. Names with the term "design" or "writing" or "architecture" are all useful, but know that they will indicate a certain skill set and/or mindset to hiring managers. While graduates of a program will have the opportunity to explain their degree names during interview processes, they may never get the opportunity if the hiring manager has already passed up their resume. It is also true that user experience itself is having issues with its own naming conventions [17]. We at the university-level can be of service here by stabilizing these names and giving stronger meaning to them through developing programs that become permanent parts of academic institutions.

3.2 UX Classes and Workshops

The easiest to design and the first step in the development of a full UX program, classes and individual workshops can introduce learners to UX tools broadly or specifically, can foster different learning configurations, and can begin to give a new program traction within an already-existing program. Below we discuss the current state of UX learning within programs in technical communication and provide some heuristics for developing new courses and workshops within these and other established fields and industries.

3.2.1 UX for Undergraduate Students

Currently, only twenty of the seventy-two undergraduate programs in Technical Communication or Professional Writing listed on The Association of Teachers of Technical Writing website have at least one regularly scheduled course in UX [18]. Out of those twenty programs, most have only one course at the undergraduate level, and many of these courses embed UX within another area (e.g. document design, visual rhetoric, or web design). In addition, many programs offer a UX course as a "special topics" course once every few years. These courses usually fill, but with no follow-up or more advanced course offerings, students who take these single-instance or special topics courses often find themselves interested in a field with good career potential without a way to learn the fundamentals needed for entry level positions in UX.

In order to assist students in overcoming this issue, several programs have begun to form partnerships with academic centers and/or industry-based organizations—partnerships that can provide students additional training through internships or work-study credit. For example, at Iowa State University the undergraduate and graduate programs in Professional Communication have formed a partnership with the User Experience Laboratory, a lab run through the Human Computing Interaction graduate program, and which provides year-round internships for students who are interested in gaining more experience with UX tools and methods.

3.2.2 UX for Graduate Students

At the graduate level, there is a slightly higher concentration of UX offerings within tech comm: twenty of the fifty-eight MA, MS, or graduate certificates in Technical Communication or Professional Writing offer at least one regularly scheduled course in UX [18]. As with undergraduate programs, however, many more of these degrees offer experiences in UX-related topics that are embedded within another, broader topic. This also holds true for the Ph.D. level, where out of twenty-four programs only nine offer Ph.D.-level classes specifically geared toward UX, but again: many more programs offer broader courses (e.g. New Media Writing, Writing for the Web, etc.) that cover aspects of UX. In addition to coursework at the Ph.D. level, there are options (e.g., qualifying exam reading lists, dissertation research topics, etc.) that allow advanced graduate students the opportunity to specialize in UX theory and/or methods beyond coursework. However, it should be noted that these options focus almost exclusively on the theoretical rather than practical aspects of UX work.

3.2.3 UX within Industry

In a 2013 article in a leading software industry publication, Baldwin wrote about the "Rise of the UX Expert" [19]. Within industry-based firms and collaboratives, a variety of UX learning, training, and knowledge-making is going on, from workshops to conferences to paid consulting to actual classes—both in-person and online. A variety of businesses, both large and small, are starting to understand the power of UX for developing products that become part of consumer lifestyles, and for increasing communication across departments that have traditionally been separated, such as IT, marketing, management, and development [20] [21].

In some ways, academia could learn from these types of collaborations, because the goal of them is often to encourage team members within existing organizations to adopt UX as a problem-solving strategy. Here are the heuristics Ivins (2013) recommended, for instance:

- Overview of the Core Areas of UX (User Research, IA, IxD, and Content Strategy)
- UX Problem Solving
- Remembering that We're Always Designing for People, Not Requirements
- Being a Good Listener and Communicator
- Facilitating Collaboration Across a Team [22]

These heuristics are emblematic of the kinds of thinking we have encouraged as UX educators. Like Ivins, we think it important to balance conceptual understanding, tool use, and practice. Developing successful courses in UX means constantly iterating through these different levels of understanding, such as by introducing a UX concept, trying out the concept via an introduction to a specific tool, and using the tool to practice the concept in a way that at least simulates a design context.

In industry partnerships mentioned above, students go beyond this type of situated learning to actually acting as UX designers with real clients. In these situations, clients must enter these relationships with the understanding that student contributions to their organizations will not be at the level of a professional UX consulting firm the organization might hire. Potential clients for these types of interactions should have this explained to them before they agree to work with students, and furthermore clients should certify that they understand they will be expected to also act as mentors to students. The buy-in for prospective clients can be presented—besides the lure of free labor—as the opportunity to create the type of professional that can be of use to not only their organization but to other organizations within their industry. Without consistent, contextualized training, UX expertise will quickly be drained from industries that need it the most.

3.3 Full UX Programs

Despite the relative absence of courses dedicated to UX, as we have mentioned: many technical communication programs provide some measure of coursework about usability, content management, and/or information design. At a minimum, the topic is discussed during classes on technical writing. Over the past few years, with increasing demand for user experience experts, we have also seen a move to update technical communication programs or create new programs focused on this topic. Other programs have created distinct technical tracks that focus on specific aspects of user experience, such as content strategy, information design, and usability [23]. Some programs also have certificate programs that are related to user experience, both at the graduate and undergraduate level [24]. There is also increasing discussion between industry and academia regarding ways to address this increased demand in the future [25].

Tech comm programs dedicated to such innovation have the ability to draw in new majors to their colleges, to create new partnerships with industry professionals, and to help fill a need for a more humanities-focused, technology-savvy workforce. By foregrounding the need to be interdisciplinary, we can build new coursework that draws on skills and knowledge from across the university. In doing so, we can encourage the kind of collaboration necessary to research and build world-class products and services. To prepare students for careers as researchers, analysts, strategists, designers, and developers, however, we will also need to include class experiences that are outside the traditional semester model, including workshops, field trips, design days, "hackathons," service-learning projects that span multiple semesters, and internships.

3.3.1 Emergence of Degrees in UX

We are just beginning to see the emergence of full-fledged degree programs in user experience. Many of these programs are growing out of existing technical communication and professional writing programs. At Michigan State University, for instance, scholars are launching a new B.A. in Experience Architecture [26]. The program goals' include instilling the foundations, principles, and best practices of user experience architecture in existing and new majors. A key component of the program includes the ability to build technologies from a humanities-centered perspective. As such, students in the program will work to gain advanced communication and design skills as well as an ability to think critically, analytically, and creatively when confronted with conflicting information or complex problems. Drawing on courses from across the university, the interdisciplinary program includes classes from professional writing, studio design, computer science, and philosophy, and is meant to prepare students for careers that range across software development, user experience architecture, project management, user research, information architecture, content management, interaction design, and web development [27]. All of which are careers in demand with starting salaries around $70,000 in spite of the recent downturn in the economy [19].

4. Conclusion and Implications

In the last few years, several industry leaders have expressed the need for more programs centered on user experience [17]. The field of technical communication has a long tradition of innovating in response to industry trends. Partnering with industry practitioners should be a major goal within the next decade, both to better understand the needs of industry and to influence the trajectory of our professional practices. Partnership goals may include the typical models of internships and service-learning programs, as well as more innovative configurations in which students, scholars, and UX experts collaborate on existing new learning models and projects. Connecting student experiences and academic research projects to industry practitioners and contexts is key to ensuring both learners and professionals enrich their individual knowledge bases as well as their portfolios.

As the UX profession continues to grow and mature it will need qualified practitioners who have been trained in not only the best methods and practices of the field but who also understand how to adapt, learn, and embrace technological innovation. In addition, it will be important for these future practitioners to understand the complexities of humanistic approaches to both technology development and problem solving. Our field's strengths in information design, project management, and content strategy coupled with our foundation in rhetoric are a strong fit for leading the development of programs that produce professionals capable of creating robust digital projects and services built around exciting new user experiences.

5. REFERENCES

[1] Johnson-Eilola, J. and Selber, S. 2013. *Solving Problems in Technical Communication*. University of Chicago Press, Chicago, IL, 3.

[2] Norman, D. 1988. *The Psychology of Everyday Things*. Basic Books, New York, NY.

[3] Norman, D. 2002. *The Design of Everyday Things*. Basic Books, New York, NY.

[4] Johnson, R. 1998. *User-Centered Technology*. State University of New York Press, Albany, NY.

[5] Kidder, T. 2000. *The Soul of a New Machine*. Back Bay Books, New York, NY.

[6] Dormehl, L. 2012. *The Apple Revolution: Steve Jobs, the Counter Culture and How the Crazy Ones Took Over the World*. Virgin Books, London, UK.

[7] *IEEE T. Prof. Commun.* 4 (Dec. 1989), 210-316.

[8] About Boxes and Arrows. *Boxes and Arrows* website. *http://boxesandarrows.com/about-boxes-and-arrows/*.

[9] Jacobson, R. *Information Design*. 1999. MIT Press, Cambridge, MA.

[10] Wodtke, C. 2003. *Information Architecture: Blueprints for the Web*. New Riders, Boston, MA.

[11] Simmons, M. 2007. *Participation and Power: Civic Discourse in Environmental Policy Decisions.* State University of New York Press, Albany, N.Y.

[12] Courage, C. and Baxter, K. 2005. *Understanding Your Users: A Practical Guide to User Requirements Methods, Tools, and Techniques.* Morgan Kaufman, Burlington, MA.

[13] DeVoss, D. Teaching philosophy. Personal website. https://www.msu.edu/~devossda/philosophy.html.

[14] Defining technical communication. *Society for Technical Communication* website. http://stc.org/about-stc/the-profession-all-about-technical-communication/defining-tc.

[15] Code of ethics. *The Association of Teachers of Technical Writing* website. http://attw.org/about-attw/code-ethics.

[16] About us. *SIGDOC* website. http://sigdoc.acm.org/about/.

[17] Anderson, J. Who are we and what are we doing? *UX Magazine.* (May 2013). http://uxmag.com/articles/who-are-we-and-what-are-we-doing.

[18] Academic programs. *The Association of Teachers of Technical Writing* website. http://attw.org/programs/academic-programs.

[19] Baldwin, H. Tech hotshots: The rise of the UX expert. *Computerworld.* (Jan. 2013), http://www.computerworld.com/s/article/9235552/Tech_hots hots_The_rise_of_the_UX_expert.

[20] O'Connor, F. With revenue at stake, companies want business-savvy tech workers. *Computerworld.* (Apr. 2013), http://www.computerworld.com/s/article/9238658/With_reve nue_at_stake_companies_want_business_savvy_tech_worke rs.

[21] Arad, D. Hire a user experience manager: 10 reasons why you should do so. *Usability Geek.* (Apr. 2013), http://usabilitygeek.com/hire-a-user-experience-manager-reasons-why.

[22] Ivins, J. What I learned from teaching UX, part 1. *Jessicaivins.net.* (Mar. 2013), http://jessicaivins.net/blog/20130311-What-I-Learned-From-Teaching-UX-Part-1.html.

[23] Professional Writing courses. *Writing, Rhetoric, and American Cultures* website. http://wrac.msu.edu/professional-writing/courses/.

[24] Certified user experience professional (CUEP) training program. *Texas Tech University Department of English* website. http://www.english.ttu.edu/usability/cueptraining.asp.

[25] Benavente, S., Rude, C., Hart-Davidson, B., and Andersen, R. Results of the April 2013 technical communication industry research needs survey. *CIDM Information Management News.* (May 2013), http://www.infomanagementcenter.com/enewsletter/2013/20 1305/third.htm.

[26] Undergraduate degree: experience architecture. *Michigan State University Office of the Registrar* website. http://www.reg.msu.edu/academicprograms/ProgramDetail.a sp?Program=5743.

[27] A guide to UX careers. *Onward Search.* Infographic. http://www.onwardsearch.com/UX-Career-Guide/UX-Career-Guide-Infographic.pdf.

Reducing Complexity Using an Interaction Room – An Experience Report

Simon Grapenthin, Matthias Book,
Volker Gruhn

paluno – The Ruhr Institute for Software Technology
University of Duisburg-Essen, 45127 Essen, Germany
{simon.grapenthin, matthias.book,
volker.gruhn}@paluno.uni-due.de

Christian Schneider,
Kai Völker

Barmenia Versicherungen
Barmenia-Allee 1, 42119 Wuppertal, Germany
{christian.schneider, kai.voelker}@barmenia.de

ABSTRACT

Large-scale information system evolution projects often place high demands on both business and technical stakeholders' cognitive and communication skills. Especially if the need for evolution is not confined to a particular feature, but affects the whole value chain, finding dependencies and interrelationships between processes and components is challenging as it requires cross-departmental understanding. These issues can be even more challenging for management stakeholders who need to make high-level and far-reaching decisions on implementation strategies despite not being deeply involved in the technical details. One of the main problems in such projects is that the stakeholders who have expert knowledge typically have only little methodical experience, while the method experts lack the business experience. In this paper, we report on experiences and lessons from a large systems evolution project in a German insurance company, where we applied a new approach – the so-called "Interaction Room" – to improve stakeholders' understanding of the project's risks and dependencies in a pragmatic way, without overwhelming them with a heavyweight analysis method.

Categories and Subject Descriptors

K.6.1 [**Project and People Management**]: Systems analysis and design, systems development; H.1.2 [**User/Machine Systems**]: Human Factors; D.2.9 [**Management**]: Productivity

Keywords

Software evolution; complexity reduction; heterogeneous teams; cognitive load of methods; Interaction Room

1. INTRODUCTION

The evolution of business processes – and thus of the information systems supporting them – can be driven by various reasons. Sometimes, new functionality has to be added to react to market demands; sometimes, an information system has to be migrated from an outdated technology stack to a more contemporary one;

and sometimes, the need for change arises out of the need for compliance with legal regulations. If such changes mainly affect a particular part of an enterprise – e.g. a department or a few business functions – the impact on the underlying information systems is limited, and their business and technical complexity can be managed through traditional systems analysis methods.

However, when business functions that support the organization's entire value chain need to be adapted, the complexity can rise to a level where it is very hard for any stakeholder to keep a clear understanding of both the high-level picture and project goals and their low-level technical dependencies and problems: Highly interdependent requirements may be distributed over the whole value chain, so their interrelationships with and impacts on business functions and their IT implementation may not be immediately obvious. Apart from the challenge of understanding the system itself, and weighing different implementation options, complex evolution projects typically involve stakeholders from many different departments and backgrounds, who need to have a common understanding and vision of the system in order to work effectively together. Communication demands therefore increase together with cognitive demands in such cross-functional, cross-departmental stakeholder involvement.

In this paper, we describe our experience with an approach fostering collaboration, joint system understanding and reducing complexity in a German insurance company's large-scale evolution project, which was triggered by far-reaching regulatory requirements that affected the organization's whole value chain.

2. INITIAL SITUATION

In this section, we will explain the project scope and the system design approach the company would usually follow for this kind of project, which will lead to our motivation for using an Interaction Room instead, and our experiences with it.

2.1 Project Scope

European Union (EU) regulation 260/2012 [5] regulates the unification of the electronic payment services in the EU towards the Single European Payments Area (SEPA). The regulation formulates different requirements for electronic payments (e.g. affecting the direct debit procedure) and has far-reaching consequences for any enterprise's value chain. Among other changes, there are several regulations about the storage and lifecycle of a SEPA mandate, as well as requirements about the additional preliminary information on an encashment (the so-called pre-notification). Furthermore, there are several time constraints related to SEPA mandates, pre-notifications and call types which need to be observed.

In this paper, we report on the SEPA Impact Analysis Project (or "SEPA project" for short) of Barmenia Versicherungen, a mid-sized German insurance enterprise that consists of three companies dealing with health, life and composite insurances. The project was carried out from August to October 2012 with the goal to analyze the impact of SEPA on Barmenia's current value chain, and to identify and elaborate risks, opportunities and implementation options for becoming SEPA-compliant. Our project team consisted of a project manager (PM), several technical experts from different departments (e.g. accountancy and cashing), as well as a method coach from academia. The project team's task was to produce several sets of implementation options (so-called decision templates), each of which included several alternative paths to become compliant with a particular aspect of the SEPA specification (e.g. pre-notifications). A decision-making body consisting of Barmenia's CIO and several department heads then evaluated these sets of alternatives and selected one out of each for implementation.

This paper focuses on the method by which the project team analyzed Barmenia's value chain in order to arrive at the decision templates that were ultimately presented to the decision-makers. In the following sections, we will first give a brief overview of how such decision proposals were usually generated, and then describe the novel approach we undertook in this project.

2.2 Previous Project Format

Previous system analysis projects took the form of recurring meetings of up to 10 people, which lasted up to 90 minutes. Beyond the net meeting time, further individual effort had to be invested by the PM for technical understanding, meeting preparation and result documentation.

Because no written enterprise-wide business process model was previously available, it had to be spelled out specifically for the process segments relevant to the project. To accomplish this, the PM would usually make assumptions on how a project's relevant processes work and model them within a tool. Then, she would initiate meetings to discuss her assumptions with business and technical experts. Once the discussion about a particular process part had come to a conclusion, the PM would work the results into the process model. This recurring procedure would be carried out until the PM felt sufficiently familiar with all relevant parts of the business process.

When the relevant parts were understood and modeled, the meeting topics changed to elaborate decision templates. For this, the PM would pick a process part and discuss that part with technical experts. Once the alternatives were elaborated, the PM would formulate and document a decision template with the different implementation options, which would then be presented to the decision-making body. Since the decision-makers cannot be deeply involved in the details of any given project, it is the responsibility of the PM to provide them with the appropriate information to make sound decisions.

This procedure works well in analysis projects that only deal with a particular department or system component, but not with the company's whole value chain. In the SEPA project, however, we faced a set of quite far-reaching requirements – since the EU regulation affects payment processes for claims, contracts and cashing across the whole enterprise, the cognitive load to consider all relationships and dependencies between the affected processes and systems was much higher than usual.

We had to take these relationships into consideration. An adequate decision template representation would have been highly complex following the old approach, and the cognitive load for the decision-making body would have been even bigger, so we chose not to follow the usual value chain analysis process for the SEPA project, but instead applied the Interaction Room method.

3. PROJECT EXECUTION

An Interaction Room (IR) is a physical room dedicated to a specific project that is equipped with wall-sized white boards and pin boards. Each board is dedicated to the representation of a particular aspect of the project, which can either be a model sketch of affected processes or components, or a view on a specific question (e.g. requirements). The model sketches in an IR remain deliberately abstract, informal and incomplete, as they are not intended to replace formal system specifications. Rather, they should serve as a catalyst for the discussion and mutual understanding of a project and its possible pitfalls.

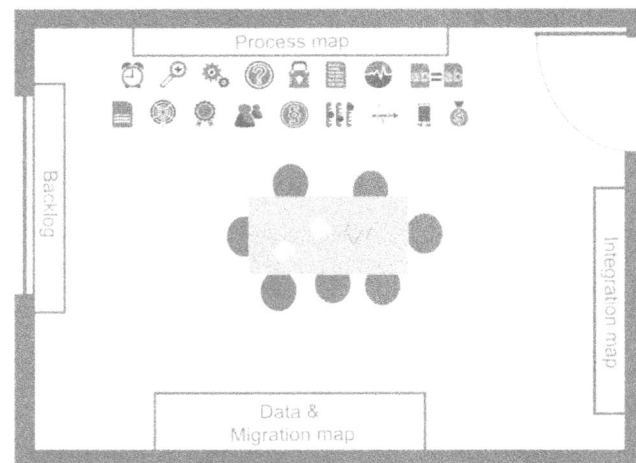

Figure 1. Basic Interaction Room Layout

The basic setup of an IR (as we introduced in [3]) includes four main perspectives (Fig. 1): The process and data maps represent the dynamic and static aspects of the business domain. The migration and integration map focus on the often-overlooked technical aspects of data migration from legacy systems, and the integration of the system into the organization's overall application landscape. The backlog contains project requirements; in this case, the business requirements that had to be fulfilled for Barmenia to become SEPA-compliant. As illustrated by the icons in Fig. 1, we also used a set of value and effort annotations that stakeholders could add to the models in order to make priorities and risk factors explicit (see Sect. 3.5).

With the help of this setup, the goal of our project was to understand the impact of the SEPA requirements on the business processes, identify how they would have to be adapted, and suggest possible ways of implementing these changes in Barmenia's systems, so management representatives could decide which of the proposed implementation strategies to pursue.

3.1 Basic Project Organization

The project was organized around two tracks of recurring meetings – "operational meetings" that took place about every other day, where the business and technical experts produced decision templates with proposals for implementation strategies;

and monthly "decision meetings" of the upper management, who decided which of the proposed options should be implemented.

The operational meetings had a technical leader (the PM) and two methodical leaders (one from Barmenia's staff and one from the university), who moderated the meetings with their modeling and IR method expertise. Each meeting had a particular topic (e.g. process modeling with a focus on changes of customer data), and meeting participants were invited according to their expertise in the meeting's topic. A typical operational meeting started with an explanation of the meeting's topic and goals, followed by an overview of the steps to be executed to reach the goals.

To reach our overall goal, defined as "analyzing needs for change and consequences to become SEPA-compliant", the project proceeded according to the following steps:

1. Analyze and prioritize the SEPA requirements.

2. Document, adapt and understand the process model of the value chain with respect to SEPA-relevant aspects.

3. Map the SEPA requirements to process parts/activities, and visualize implementation options.

4. Assess priorities of implementation options to prepare decision-making.

In the following subsections, we will describe the four steps in more detail, and show how we employed the IR's facilities in the process. Interspersed with our report on the steps taken in this project, we document lessons we hypothesize to be generalizable to other projects. In our ongoing work, we are striving to test these hypotheses in further projects.

3.2 Requirements Analysis and Prioritization

To obtain an overview of the SEPA requirements, we gathered them from the official regulations and organized them in a traditional backlog [1]. Since we aimed to create a high-level view of the project requirements, we formulated clear and concise terms on the front side of blue story cards (e.g. "delay before debit"). More detailed information was provided on the back side of every story card (e.g. "default delay is 14 days, but reduction allowed under certain circumstances"). To structure the requirements, we grouped them by themes (e.g. pre-notification, SEPA mandate, etc.) and noted the themes as headlines on white cards in our backlog. To prioritize more critical requirements, we highlighted them with an exclamation mark (e.g. one major requirement was the SEPA mandate, which has to be manually signed).

The backlog was not only supposed to create an overview of prioritized requirements, but also to visualize the decision-making progress: As we formulated decision templates over the course of the project, we noted them on yellow cards. We developed one decision template for every requirement, and placed an abstract about the implementation options on a card next to the corresponding requirement (e.g. "use default debit delay or reduce delay to five days?"). Since the decision templates were the output of the operational meetings and the input of the decision meetings, we had a clearly documented interface for handing results over between the two meeting tracks. Analogously, every time a decision was made in a decision meeting, that decision was written on a green card that replaced the yellow card with the template (e.g. "reduce debit delay to 5 days").

Lesson: An Interaction Room can be effectively used for communication between separate stakeholder groups (e.g.

technical/business and management) if there is a clear interface for the artifacts they exchange.**

3.3 SEPA-affine Business Process Modeling

Since no explicit written representation of the process model existed yet (especially none focusing on the SEPA-relevant parts), we documented Barmenia's long-established process practice in a process model that covered all steps from claims to cashing. While the stakeholders involved in this activity were experts in their respective fields of business, about one third of them had not modeled a business process before, and 80% of the remaining stakeholders dealt with modeling processes less than 10% of their overall working hours. To make the vast (but implicit) process knowledge that these stakeholders possessed explicit, it was important to adopt a pragmatic approach allowing them to focus on describing their business domain and analyzing its SEPA affinity. To keep the complexity at a manageable level, we applied a top-down approach that was structured as follows:

1. Note SEPA-relevant functions on file cards. To reduce the modeling complexity for the inexperienced stakeholders, we let them note their main business functions with respect to SEPA on cards first.

2. Order the cards into a chronological sequence: After gathering the functions, we told the stakeholders to put their cards into a chronological sequence.

3. Transform card sequences into a process representation.

To prepare the actual process modeling, we introduced just a small subset of UML activity diagram elements, namely activities, flows, decisions, and conditions, and asked the stakeholders to use these to structure the information on their file cards in more detail. Again, we aimed to reduce complexity where possible (e.g. we did not force the stakeholders to name activities in active voice at first), so they could focus more on the business aspects than correct UML notation. This dovetails with a core principle of the IR – that the formal correctness of a modeling language or notation plays a minor role in obtaining a common understanding of a process.

Lesson: Encourage stakeholders to model process aspects themselves in order to elicit their tacit knowledge, relaxing the need for syntactical accuracy where it does not interfere with understanding.

While the stakeholders were quite able to produce the process models for the claims and cashing part, the transformation from claims to contracts and contract-related issues turned out to be too complex for them to model independently (due to certain legal complexity in the domain and company structure), so we followed a more guided, iterative approach there:

In the first iteration of looking at the contract-related processes, we concentrated on new contracts only, because they were the least exposed to frame conditions and thus more easily understood. Based on the file cards, we established a moderated group discussion in which the moderator elicited detailed structural information about the process from the group, and modeled that information on the board "live" as the discussion progressed. Because the moderator had UML experience, we could employ further activity diagram elements such as initial and activity final nodes, forks, joins and merges.

Lesson: For more complex processes, have a dedicated, experienced modeler translate the stakeholders' discussion

into model sketches "live". **This allows stakeholders to focus on the business domain instead of the tool/notation.**

In the next iteration, we focused on insurance contract changes – an area that turned out to be more complex since we recognized that there are seven reasons for contract change that have a least one SEPA-relevant impact (for example, if a contract's premium payer wants to change his bank account, a new pre-notification has to be sent to him, unless the new account still resides with the same bank). Since we found that some of these rules were easily forgotten as we built the process models, we introduced a dedicated zone (the so-called "practice zone") on one of the IR's walls where we documented the various reasons for change with their resulting impacts. Having this representation reduced stakeholders' cognitive load, as they were able to primarily concentrate on building the process representation, but still could access the information on change reasons ad hoc.

Over the course of the project, we found it helpful to collect various bits of reference information in the practice zone that were important for structuring and understanding the process, but could not be kept in memory at all times, and would have been cumbersome to look up every time.

Lesson: Having miscellaneous but important bits of information in sight at all times allowed the team members to focus on the task at hand without worrying about overlooking important analysis criteria, and enabled stakeholders to access the information without disturbing their primary focus.

The practice zone also turned out helpful to deal with another possibly disruptive situation: While eliciting the structure of the business processes, some stakeholders tended to provide much too detailed information, which was not technically wrong, but easily led the group on tangents away from creating a process overview. On one hand, we were dependent on the tacit knowledge of these stakeholders, so we did not want to demotivate them by repeatedly telling them to stick to a higher level of abstraction – but on the other hand, we had to maintain the focus of our discussion so as not to continuously distract the other stakeholders.

We therefore established an area within the practice zone that we called the "memo list": Every time a stakeholder provided more detailed information than was necessary at a given time, we asked the stakeholder to note this information on a file card and tack it onto the memo list. This way, the information was not lost, and we could refer back to the memo list when the issue was discussed (or about to be re-told in detail again).

Lesson: A memo list helped us to "off-load" important but currently non-relevant information for later reference, while keeping the ongoing discussion focused and avoiding items from being brought up repeatedly.

While experienced modelers tend to create a complete process representation in sequence, this was not possible with our group of relatively inexperienced stakeholders. Rather, our iterative approach let the process representation evolve over time. Since the process models were therefore not in a finished state after any meeting, but remained sketchy, we had to spend some effort on post-processing them. To prepare for the next meeting, we refactored the process sketches into "clean" models by restructuring and adjusting them to close minor specification gaps or clear up the layout. We explicitly decided to invest this extra effort outside the meetings since we wanted the stakeholders to develop the process models based on their own understanding,

and avoid the impression that they should just sign off on complete models that we created beforehand (based on assumptions might not have been correct, but likely would not have been questioned without the in-depth discussion that their own model construction in the meeting required). According to our timekeeping, our effort spent on model refactoring was less than 16% of the joint effort spent on model creation, which we consider appropriate.

Lesson: Collaborative model development encourages more in-depth discussion than just reviewing models prepared a priori by individuals (and thus seems likely to reveal more issues), but requires extra effort for refactoring the models into a clean, consistent state.

3.4 Match Requirements to Process Activities

To visualize which SEPA requirements impact which activities in the process model, we labeled each SEPA requirement in our backlog with a colored identification mark and mapped the most critical requirements to the process activities. We first discussed the most obvious way of implementing it, and highlighted the corresponding activities. Beyond this, we explicitly also strove to develop new ideas by brainstorming about unconventional implementation alternatives. We collected and discussed all arising ideas, and retained those options that were realistic.

This mapping of requirements to process activities revealed two types of insights: Firstly, by visualizing different implementation options within the process model, we could identify consequences of SEPA for the processes and underlying information systems more easily, given the context information. Secondly, we could identify process parts in which plenty of requirements had to be realized, so we were able to identify hotspots of change.

This information did not only provide helpful context in the operational meetings, but also provided important information for the decision meetings: Since different process parts are typically realized by different information systems, a change hotspot concentrates requirements which could be realized within one information system, while other information systems do not need to be changed. Knowing how many information systems would need to be changed in a particular implementation option was therefore an important criterion in assessing the options.

Lesson: Making implementation options explicit by mapping requirements to a process model helps to come up with unconventional solutions, and to identify hotspots of change.

3.5 Value and Effort Annotations

Another important criterion for assessing implementation options was the priority of business processes. To ascertain this, we annotated the process parts with so-called value and effort drivers, another key method of the IR [3] that was inspired by the concept of value-based software engineering [2]. Using value and effort annotations, we can highlight process parts of particular value (e.g. affecting the company image or incurring financial responsibilities), process parts that will require particular effort (e.g. to implement time constraints or security standards), and process parts that pose other problems which do not meet the eye directly (e.g. uncertainty due to tacit or incomplete technical knowledge, or implementation complexity due to outdated technology). By annotating process parts with these indicators, we aim to foster a deeper understanding of the most relevant and most success-critical process parts among all stakeholders.

In practice, the annotations take the form of magnetic icons that can be applied to the model sketches on the white boards. Every icon has a dedicated meaning, which can be elaborated into a concrete requirement. For example, the padlock in Fig. 1 stands for a security requirement such as "data needs to be stored in auditable form". Such requirements are documented in the model only if all stakeholders agree, in order to make sure the need is well-reasoned despite the pragmatic way of its elicitation.

To prioritize the business processes and assess the implementation options with these annotations, we encouraged the stakeholders to apply them to the process models after a brief introduction to their meaning. We iterated through the process and discussed every placed annotation, until we could come to a consensus on the precise meaning of each annotation that could be documented for consideration in the preparation of decision templates.

4. DECISION-MAKING PROCESS

The process of making implementation decisions to achieve SEPA conformity comprised two main parts. First, the decision templates had to be prepared as outputs of the operational meetings. After this, the PM invited the decision makers to the IR for a decision meeting, in order to discuss and choose a course of action for a decision template.

4.1 Decision Preparation

To prepare a decision template, the participants of the operational meeting had to evaluate various implementation options, as described in the previous section. According to feedback we received from the PM, the effort for preparing a template for a decision meeting this way was much lower than what the usual analysis procedure (Sect. 2.2) would have required, because the requirements were already mapped to the process. Furthermore, as the process parts were prioritized later on, she found that the annotations helped to focus discussion on details and raised technical issues that might not have been discovered otherwise.

4.2 Decision Meetings

A decision meeting was called whenever a decision template was completed. For this, the PM invited the management stakeholders into the IR where the business and technical stakeholders had been working before. The PM started with a summary of the current project state as a re-introduction to the topic. Since decision meetings took place approximately monthly and lasted about one to two hours, the management stakeholders were not highly involved in the project and had to be brought up to speed on the business and technical details each time. The PM could explain and illustrate implementation options to decision-makers with the aid of the IR's process map, requirements backlog and practice zone items under consideration of their dependencies. In addition, she explained the process assessment made by the business and technical experts, including advantages and disadvantages of implementation options, and value and effort drivers expressed through the annotations.

In the large majority of cases, implementation decisions could be made by the management stakeholders based on this information right away. Less than 10% of the decisions were postponed when the decision-makers felt they had insufficient information. This is a significant improvement in decision-making efficiency over a previous project (not performed using an IR) with similarly high-level management stakeholders involved, where the rate of postponed decisions was about 33%.

Of course, despite this, we cannot yet confirm that this increase in efficiency is due to the use of the IR from just two anecdotal data points. In our future work, we will further investigate the IR's role in facilitating efficient project understanding and decision-making, looking at decision speed as well as decision quality.

5. PROJECT OUTCOMES

Using the process described above, the SEPA impact analysis project at Barmenia was accomplished on time and in budget. To obtain feedback from the stakeholders on their opinion of our approach, we performed two surveys – one of the business and technical stakeholders who participated in the operational meetings, and one of the management stakeholders participating in the decision-making meetings.

5.1 Survey of Operational Meeting Participants

In the survey of the technical and business stakeholders, we used questionnaires to ask how effective they found the process model sketches, practice zone, value and effort annotations, and overall IR method, for understanding the business processes, SEPA requirements, and decision template preparation. To gather insights about their perceived efficiency, we asked them to rate whether the above items helped them to prepare the decision templates faster, and related our approach to the usual procedure described in Sect. 2.2.

Since the team comprised only nine people, the questionnaire obviously yielded insufficient data for a quantitative analysis of the results. However, subsuming the questionnaire's results qualitatively, we can report highly positive feedback about the method and the IR elements that were employed in the project:

The collaborative development facilitated by the process model sketches was particularly well-received. Stakeholders found them helpful to get familiar with the problem domain, and thought they worked well to obtain an overview of the project's dependencies. The efficiency with which they could be used was also emphasized. Since the moderators did the entire model refactoring (e.g. cleaning up the layout of white board sketches, correcting minor mistakes etc.), the stakeholders were not burdened with a task that might get cumbersome otherwise. For us, the effort spent on model refactoring seemed appropriate and well-invested.

Furthermore, the introduction of the practice zone was perceived as very useful to reduce complexity. The constant availability of additional information (e.g. the overview of reasons for contract change and corresponding process impacts) was found especially helpful. In our future work, we will examine if there are different practice zone elements that are particularly suitable for particular project types, so we can propose default items to place here.

The effectiveness of the IR concept as a whole also received positive reviews. The stakeholders found that the physical setup helped to facilitate discussion and understanding of all project aspects. The pragmatic approach to business process sketching and the elaboration of the decision templates was particularly highlighted in this respect, while the room's impact on understanding the SEPA standard's specific business and technical requirements played only a minor role.

While consensus prevailed in the assessment of most IR concepts, we observed divided opinions on the value and effort annotations. While the stakeholders agreed that the annotations helped to understand the process complexity better, some did not see their usefulness for creating the decision templates. We will need to correlate this feedback with evaluations of future projects to determine whether the reason for this was that we introduced the concept too late or with insufficient explanation in this project, or that it indeed may not be appropriate for this purpose.

5.2 Survey of Decision Meeting Participants

The second survey among the management stakeholders contained a subset of the questions of the first questionnaire: We asked only about the effectiveness and efficiency of the IR's overall method, because the decision-makers did not work as intensively with the individual room elements as the other stakeholders. We also altered the question if the IR helped to prepare decision templates faster than usual to the question if the IR helped to make decisions faster than usual.

The results of this questionnaire were unanimously positive: The question on the IR's impact on the efficiency of the decision-making process was answered positively without reservations by every one of the management stakeholders. In the open feedback question, the decision-makers furthermore pointed out that the IR works as a facilitator for cross-department communication, provides a project and system overview with an appropriate level of abstraction, and guides discussion to the most critical project issues, while helping to recall and not miss any issues that still need to be discussed. A most encouraging summary of the survey results is the CIO's decision that Barmenia will use the IR approach for future large IT projects as well.

6. RELATED WORK

Agile methodologies suggest team rooms for interaction and collaborative work (e.g. [7]). These rooms are mainly intended for the development team's daily work, and their walls are often covered with highly implementation-specific, technological artifacts. The idea of using dedicated physical rooms for system development bringing users with different backgrounds and viewpoints together can be traced back to the Joint Application Design (JAD) approach that was developed by IBM in the late 1970's [4]. We adopted this intention by focusing our IR method on pragmatic modeling and annotation techniques to facilitate cross-domain discussion and joint understanding of those project aspects that are particularly success-critical.

The use of collaborative modeling, public representations and physical artifacts has been investigated by many researchers (e.g. [6]). We follow their findings by keeping our models deliberately informal and using low-tech approaches that keep the contribution barrier low. We believe that this is particularly important because team members that are experts in their respective technical or business domain, but have no modeling or tool experience, should not be deterred by a steep learning curve from contributing their knowledge to the project.

The idea of extending models with extra information is not new – there are several approaches for adding additional information to process models (e.g. [8], [9], [10], [11]). However, our annotations aim to identify critical issues within a process or system, rather than precisely specifying a particular functional or non-functional aspect (e.g. security requirements, as in [8], [9]).

7. CONCLUSION

In this paper, we presented our experience from a mission-critical systems analysis project carried out in an Interaction Room. The project – determining an insurance company's necessary business process and information system adaptations in order to achieve compliance with the new European payment standard SEPA – deals with far-reaching requirements that affect the whole value chain of the organization, so it was paramount to arrive at reliable decisions based on a joint understanding of all cross-department impacts and ripple effects.

Over the course of the project, we confirmed the IR's core design tenet that inexperienced stakeholders' cognitive load can be reduced (and refocused on the more important questions of the problem domain) by not insisting on the exchange of formally correct specifications, but encouraging cross-department collaborative modeling to make tacit knowledge explicit, and to jointly identify and address challenges and risks.

In future industrial projects, we will collect more data to evaluate the efficiency of the IR's methods, and the validity of the hypotheses that the lessons learned in this project suggest. This research will be carried out both at the Barmenia insurance company, who already decided to use the IR for future projects (thus providing opportunities for longitudinal studies), as well as at other industrial partners, which will provide opportunities for examining the method's general applicability across domains and project types.

8. REFERENCES

[1] Beedle, M. and Schwaber, K.: *Agile Software Development with Scrum.* Prentice Hall, 2002.

[2] Boehm, B.: Value-based software engineering. *ACM SIGSOFT Softw. Eng. Notes,* 28(2):4, 2003.

[3] Book, M., Grapenthin, S., and Gruhn, V.: Seeing the forest and the trees: Focusing team interaction on value and effort drivers. *Proc. ACM SIGSOFT 2012 / FSE-20, New Ideas Track,* art. no. 30. ACM, 2012.

[4] Carmel, E., Whitaker, R.D., and George, J.F.: PD and joint application design: A transatlantic comparison. *Commun. ACM* 36(6):40-48. ACM, 1993

[5] European Union: Regulation No 260/2012 – Technical and business requirements for credit transfers and direct debits in euro. http://eur-lex.europa.eu/LexUriServ/ LexUriServ.do?uri=OJ:L:2012:094:0022:0037:EN:PDF

[6] Goldschmidt, G.: The dialectics of sketching. *Creativity Research Journal* 4:123-143. Taylor & Francis, 1991.

[7] Pietri, W.: An XP Team Room. http://www.scissor.com/resources/teamroom/, 2004

[8] Rodriguez, A., Fernandez-Medina, E., and Piattini, M.: Security requirement with a UML 2.0 profile. *Proc. 1st Intl. Conf. on Availability, Reliability and Security (ARES 2006),* pp. 670-677. IEEE Computer Society, 2006.

[9] Rodriguez, A., Fernandez-Medina, E., and Piattini, M.: A BPMN Extension for the Modeling of Security Requirements in Business Processes. *IEICE – Trans. Inf. Syst.* E90-D(4), pp.745-752. Oxford University Press, 2007.

[10] Saeedi, K., Zhao, L., and Falcone Sampaio, P.R.: Extending BPMN for Supporting Customer-Facing Service Quality Requirements. *Proc. IEEE Intl. Conf. on Web Services (ICWS 2010),* pp. 616-623. IEEE Computer Society, 2010.

[11] Zou, J. and Pavlovski, C.: Control case approach to record and model non-functional requirements. *Inf. Syst. and E-Business Management* 6(1):49-67. Springer, 2008.

Icon Design for User Interface of Remote Patient Monitoring Mobile Devices

Ljilja Kascak
School of Industrial Design
Georgia Institute of Technology
North Ave, Atlanta, GA 30332
ljilja@gatech.edu

Dr. Claudia B. Rébola
School of Industrial Design
Georgia Institute of Technology
North Ave, Atlanta, GA 30332
crw@gatech.edu

Richard Braunstein
School of Industrial Design
Georgia Institute of Technology
North Ave, Atlanta, GA 30332
RichardBraunstein@ykk-api.com

Jon A. Sanford
School of Industrial Design
Georgia Institute of Technology
North Ave, Atlanta, GA 30332
jon.sanford@coa.gatech.edu

ABSTRACT

The purpose of this paper is to describe the studies undertaken in order to improve and simplify user interface (UI) design of a Remote Patient Monitoring (RPM) device, specifically the BL Healthcare Access Tablet. Current icon designs for UIs of the RPM devices are not well designed to reflect the needs, experiences and limitations of the end-user. Complex and unclear UIs and instructions make compliance with self-management schedules often poor. The issue of compliance, with the need for effective communication between chronic disease patients and healthcare professionals emphasize the need for the appropriate UI and communication technology. Improvement is made from the perspective of the user experience (UX) / UI redesign. Usability studies were conducted, followed by the UI redesign and icons design with the aim to address the UX design. A mobile application concept for the RPM is developed, that could be used on existing tablets and smartphones, thus eliminating the need for the current costly hardware.

Categories and Subject Descriptors

H.5.2 [**Information Interfaces and Presentation**]: User Interfaces – *Graphical user interfaces (GUI)*.

Keywords

Icons design, interaction design, remote patient monitoring, telehealth, user experience, user interface.

1. INTRODUCTION

Remote Patient Monitoring (RPM), as one of the telehealth care modes [1], is a home-based monitoring system to support patients with chronic conditions [2]. It is proven to be useful to homebound older adults who have difficulty in accessing care due to disability, transportation, or isolation, effectively engaging them in self-care disease management [2]. RPM is effective technology for recording and storing patient data, such as vital signs or symptoms [3]. Data from the medical peripherals are sent via Bluetooth onto the home monitoring devices and transmitted to health care professionals for review. The opinion from the health care provider is then sent back to the RPM device.

Chronic disease patients are personally responsible for their daily care. They must actively participate in their treatment in order to achieve effective management of chronic diseases [3]. However, due to complex and unclear UIs and instructions, compliance with daily self-management plans is not adequate [4], [5]. One of the problems that can make older adults experience dissatisfaction while using technology is usability. Several studies reported that certain fonts are difficult to read, metaphors and icons difficult to be interpreted, and that memory and motor problems can make it hard to operate a system [6].

Although information technology (IT) integration in the medical field has increased during the past decade, UI design was not optimized [7]. Usability testing was not required for UI design of the health IT systems [7].

Usability needs to be assessed when designing for older adults, taking into an account choice of the icons, fonts, and font sizes [6]. Successful implementation of RPM requires easy to use devices with good UI design. A good UI design is intuitive, easy to use, and inexpensive to maintain, to support, and to train the users [8]. It can lead to safe and effective equipment operation, installation, and maintenance [9]. In order to deliver good UI design, human factors should be considered early in the design process, and user testing should be conducted throughout the whole design process involving participants from the end-user population [9].

The purpose of this paper is to describe the studies undertaken in order to improve and simplify UI design of RPM devices, specifically the BL Healthcare Access Tablet. Concern over health risks due to non-compliance with self-management schedules is addressed in this case study by the UX/UI redesign and icon design. Following this line of work, there is a need to develop easier to use and improved UI of the RPM devices. This paper describes UI redesign, usability studies, and icon design for the proposed RPM mobile application concept, which could be used on existing tablets and smartphones.

2. BACKGROUND

RPM technology addresses the needs of older adults in efficient and effective way, and helps in facilitating greater independence of older adults [4]. "People want to take a more active role in managing their health care - both to reduce costs and improve their quality of life," said Katherine Holland, general manager of IBM Life Sciences [5] (p.28-34).

Current market solutions for RPM are stationary hubs that connect via Bluetooth with medical peripheral devices. RPM hubs take and record health-related readings, send data to the server, making those accessible to the healthcare providers.

According to the study "Wearable Dry Sensors with Bluetooth Connection for Use in Remote Patient Monitoring System" [6], RPM devices have many design requirements with portability being one of the most important ones.

Mobile computing poses a series of challenges for UI design and development. UIs must now accommodate the capabilities of various access devices, in this case tablets, smartphones, and medical peripheral devices. In addition to this, UIs need to be suitable for different contexts of use, while preserving consistency and usability [7]. RPM mobile application UI needs to accommodate use on both the tablets and the smartphones.

Older adults have a specific relationship with technology. This mostly comes from the fact that hardware and software have not been designed to suit their needs [8]. They are considered a market niche for the sales of RPM technology products [9]. Technology through RPM supports physical independence and stimulates social and psychological engagement. It is important to share with machines a common language in order to naturally interact with them [10]. Furthermore, Norman [10] brings up that technologies are not capable to adapt their language to different classes of humans, unless they are designed to do so.

Familiarity of the technology language to tell about its usage, objectives and meanings, covering issues of usability, accessibility, accountability, and acceptability has a great importance in the communication between older adults and technology [9]. Also, perception of high benefits associated with the adoption of technology is valuable motivation for older adults to accept perceived costs and effort associated with using a technology [11].

Icons designed for usability improve the user experience of an UI [4]. Usable icons need to be clear and legible, simple, consistent, and familiar [12]. They should enhance recognition, be meaningful, and hasten option selection [12]. Choice of the color and type improve instruction [13]. An important principle of good icon design is to always provide a text label [12].

As discussed by Bernard, older adults prefer larger font sizes and sans serif fonts over serif fonts [14] [15]. In in a study by Bernard, Liao, and Mills [15], serif fonts (Georgia and Times New Roman) were compared to sans serif fonts (Arial and Verdana) at 12- and 14-points. Overall findings resulted in older adults' preference for the 14-point fonts that promoted faster reading and were found more legible. The sans serif fonts were more preferred than the serif fonts. Sorg [16] found that older adults preferred to read sans serif font Helvetica, compared to serif font Century Schoolbook.

Usability testing requires relatively small test groups [12]. Nielsen [17] states that "elaborate usability tests are a waste of resources. The best results come from testing no more than 5 users and running as many small tests as you can afford." When dealing with homogeneous group of users, observing five users can identify a high percentage of the most critical errors [17]. For efficient and productive usability testing five is the optimal number of users [17-19]. Usability testing with more than five users is proven to be waste of time and money, which could be spent on assessment of design changes [12] and more tests.

3. PURPOSE OF THE STUDY
3.1 Design Criteria
Literature review resulted in the list of problems that were summarized into the following design criteria:

- Design RPM customizable mobile application concept that could be used on existing tablets and smartphones,
- Design simple and clear icons for UI,
- Design icons that are easy to be interpreted by the older adults,
- Have bigger graphics and font sizes for both smartphone and tablet,
- Choose fonts that are easy to read by the older adults.

The significance of this study is advancement of new designs of RPM devices by developing RPM mobile application concept that could be used on existing tablets and smartphones, thus eliminating the need for costly hub units. Portability provides chronic disease patients with the advantage to get medical advice and send vital sign measurements from any place, integrating RPM into their daily lives. Additional benefit to the patients is that "convergence with consumer electronic products will enable patients to use devices they are already familiar and comfortable with" [20].

3.2 The BL Healthcare Access Tablet
A case study was undertaken with the BL Healthcare Access Tablet, as one of the RPM devices that are widely adopted on the market. The BL Healthcare Access Tablet UI provides various applications that could be accessed form the home screen (See Figure 1). Vital signs monitoring is the main function that provides connection with medical peripheral devices. Charts function visualizes vital signs data. Setting up the sessions and messaging with the healthcare provider are two functions that provide communication with the healthcare professionals. In addition to this, there are a few other wellness and education-related functions like the Workout Tracker and Medical Terms.

Figure 1. Graphic UI of the BL Helathcare Access Tablet.

4. METHODOLOGY
The icon design study was organized into three phases: 1 – User Experience, 2 – Evaluation / Testing, and 3 – Concept Refinement.

4.1 Phase 1 – User Experience

The purpose of the phase 1 was to improve the UX of The BL Healthcare Access Tablet with the goal of improving its icon design for UI, by conducting usability studies. Specific goals included:

- Usability Testing 1: one hour-long observation with the group of older adults testing the UI of the chosen RPM device,
- Usability Report 1: analysis of the results retrieved from the observation, and
- Icon Redesign: application of the results to the RPM device icon redesign; initial concepts development.

Usability Testing 1 was conducted with six volunteers from a local Naturally Occurring Retirement Community (NORC). One-hour-long observation was performed with each volunteer individually, followed by an interview. Volunteers were asked to perform task of using the Sleep Journal UI of The BL Healthcare Access Tablet, on both the iPhone and the iPad. The Sleep Journal function was chosen for the testing purposes because of the important relationship between the sleep quality of the older adults and their chronic conditions [21]. Daily task of conducting the sleep quality survey is reported this way. The tasks were video recorded.

List of the interview questions was presented to the volunteers. Navigation through the Sleep Journal UI, level of satisfaction, and visual interface were tested during the interview. Screen size management and differences, including the ease of use, were tested using both the iPhone and the iPad. Comments on differences and screen size preferences were taken in the overall impressions section.

For the first list of questions volunteers were given the five-point Likert scale (Very easy, Easy, Neutral, Difficult, and Very difficult or Excellent, Good, Neutral, Not so good, and Not good at all). The questions regarding the satisfaction with the RPM mobile application had the following answers: Very satisfied, Satisfied, Neutral, Dissatisfied, and Very dissatisfied.

Icon redesign for UI followed the Usability Report 1 with various designs of visuals (icons, color coordination, and button sizes). Exploration of different icons for text buttons representing different functions of the RPM mobile application took place during this phase. Three sets of icons for the buttons were designed for the following functions of the mobile application: video call, charts, messages, settings, sleep journal, contacts, and sessions.

4.2 Phase 2 – Evaluation / Testing

Phase 2 was dedicated to the evaluation of the improved icon concepts by conducting additional usability testing with the purpose of choosing the final concept. Specific goals included:

- Usability Testing 2: one hour-long observation with the same group of older adults testing the improved icon concepts on the smartphone.
- Usability Report 2: Analysis of the observation and choosing the final concept.

Usability Testing 2 was conducted with five out of six volunteers from the Usability Testing 1. It took place at the same Naturally Occurring Retirement Community (NORC). One-hour-long observation was performed with each volunteer individually, followed by an interview. Volunteers were asked to perform task of using the mockup UI on the iPhone. HTML with JQuery Mobile mockup was made for the purpose of this usability testing.

Mockup application had all the functions of the RPM mobile application:

- Charts, as the main function of visualizing and recording the body vital measurements,
- "Alert" button, which calls 911 in a case of emergency (in the case of this mockup personal number was used),
- Video call, including the voice call option (the same personal number was used for the mockup version),
- Sleep Journal, daily survey of the patient's sleep quality (survey question pages were designed),
- Messages, providing the health-related messaging (in the case of a mockup the first page was designed),
- Sessions, allowing for scheduling the check-ups and visits to the doctor's office (scheduling the checkup by inserting name and date preferred),
- Contacts (Contacts sample page was designed),
- Settings, which provides for customization based on the chronic condition, personalization based on the user's preferences, and medicine reminder (Settings sample page was designed).

Volunteers were asked to go through the task of using all the functions on the home screen (video call, charts, messages, settings, sleep journal, contacts, and sessions) and the "Alert" button. Observation was video recorded.

The goal of the second usability study was to test the icon design for UI and interaction design with the mockup mobile application concept including: navigation through the UI, visual interface including its icons, colors, sizes, shapes, and graphics, screen size management, level of satisfaction, information inclusion, ease of use, and overall impressions.

List of the interview questions was presented to the volunteers. The same list of questions used during the Usability Testing 1 was used for the Usability Testing 2. For the first list of questions volunteers were given the 5-point Likert scale. The same criteria was used as the one in the Usability Testing 1. Interview continued with the same list of open-ended questions used for the purpose of the Usability Testing 2, asking for their overall thoughts on device itself.

In addition to that, three sets of icons for the home screen buttons were tested. Volunteers were asked to associate each function of the RPM mobile application concept with one of the three icons. The goal of this task was to find the icon that potential users associate the best with the given function. All the functions (video call, charts, messages, settings, sleep journal, contacts, and sessions) were available on the mockup home screen.

4.3 Phase 3 – Concept Refinement

Phase 3 consisted of the final concept development. Final icon concept was designed based on the results of the Usability Report 2. Concept refinement consisted of the following phases:

- Design of the icons with the color coordination,
- Choosing the right font and font size,
- Peer Review,
- Prioritizing the functions of the RPM mobile application,
- Future design considerations.

The final concept development started with designing the icons for the Home Screen buttons that represented each of the functions RPM mobile application provided. It continued with choosing the right font and font size for the functions of the mobile application. Different icons for all the functions were designed and tested in a Peer Review with a group of five volunteers that were considered experts in the field, with the goal of choosing the most adequate one for each of the functions. Color-coordination for the icons and fonts for the functions were also tested here.

5. RESULTS

5.1 User Experience

5.1.1 Usability Testing 1
The goal of the usability testing was to test navigation through the Sleep Journal UI, visual interface (icons, colors, sizes, shapes, and graphics), screen size management, information inclusion, ease of use, and subjective satisfaction with UI of The BL Healthcare Access Tablet's Sleep Journal.

5.2.1 Usability Report 1
Usability Report 1 summarized all the results of the Usability Study 1 (See Graph 1). Satisfaction with the UI, icons, colors, size, shapes, and graphic, as well as the ease of use and navigation through the UI were rated as excellent by all the volunteers. The executive summary reported that all volunteers had an issue with the touchscreen navigation of both the iPhone and the iPad. Problems included increasing the size of the screen unintentionally when tapping.

One volunteer had a negative comment on the screen size: "Small size is not good for eyes." This volunteer would have used the iPhone when needed outside the house. The other volunteer wanted to have bigger size of the scale graphics on the iPhone.

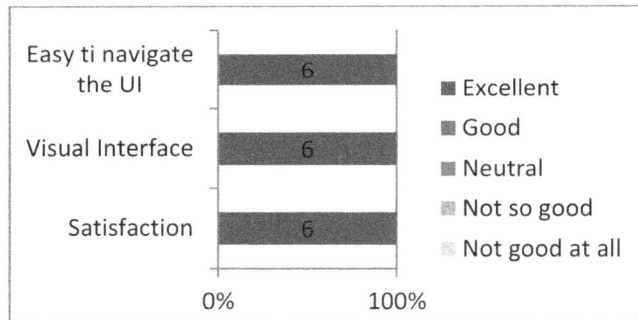

Graph 1. Results of the Interview Questions:Usability Report1

Problems found with the UI reported confusing time navigation using the time picker and four questions that were found unclear. Positive findings reported excellent colors, size, shape, and graphics, easiness of use and navigation, and overall satisfaction with the product.

5.3.1 Icon Redesign
5.3.1.1 Initial Concept Redesign
Three sets of different icons for the buttons were developed for the following functions of the RPM mobile application: video call, charts, messages, settings, sleep journal, contacts, and sessions. Volunteers tested sets of icons with the goal of choosing the most relevant and appropriate icon for each function. We asked volunteers to choose the icon that they associate the most with the function (See Figure 2).

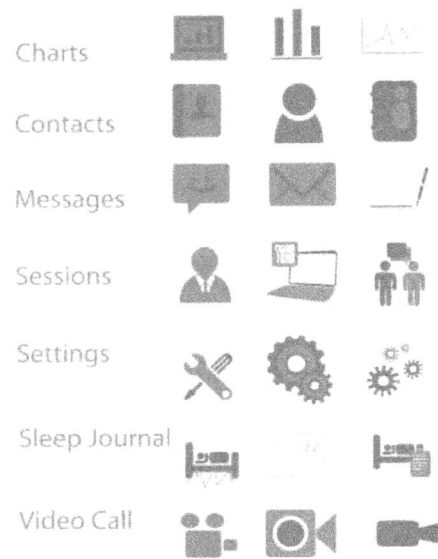

Figure 2. Three Sets of the Icons for the Buttons.

HTML5 with jQuery Mobile was used to develop the prototype of the RPM mobile application for the purpose of the Usability Testing 2. The prototype had a log in page, the Home Screen with all the functions of the RPM mobile application (video call, charts, messages, settings, sleep journal, contacts, and sessions), the first page of all the functions of the application, and three pages of the Sleep Journal function.

5.2 Evaluation / Testing

5.2.1 Usability Testing 2
Goal of the usability testing was to test navigation through the UI, visual interface (icons, colors, sizes, shapes, and graphics), screen size management, information inclusion, ease of use, and subjective satisfaction with the RPM mobile application UI.

In addition to this, three sets of icon designs were tested and associated with words representing the functions of the RPM mobile application (video call, charts, messages, settings, sleep journal, contacts, and sessions), with the goal of choosing the most adequate ones for the final concept development.

5.2.2 Usability Report 2
Usability Report 2 summarized all the finding from the Usability Study 2. Executive summary included results of the interview questions presented in the Graph 2.

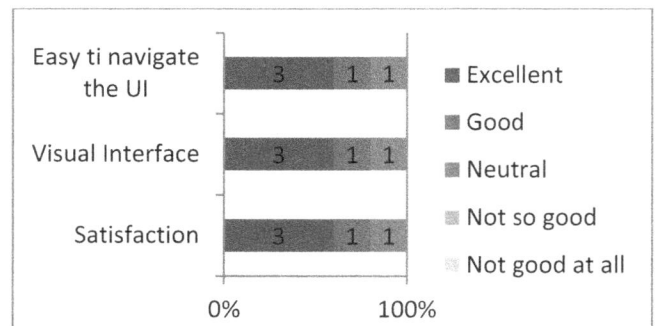

Graph 2. Results of the Interview Questions:Usability Report2

Results of the icons testing can be found in the Table 1 (V was used for the term volunteer). Volunteers of the Usability Testing 2 associated word "Chart" with the icon that had the image of the chart. Word "Contacts" was associated with the image of the address book. Volunteers associated word "Messages" with the word cloud with smiley face. "Sessions" was associated with the icon of the professional, while "Settings" was connected with the gears. Cloud with letters Z that writes represented the "Sleep Journal", and camera was associated with the "Video Call".

Table 1. Results of the Icons Testing

Functions	V1	V2	V3	V4	V5
Charts	3	3	2	3	3
Contacts	1	2	2	1	1
Messages	3	3	1	1	1
Sessions	2	1	1	3	1
Settings	3	1	3	1	1
Sleep Journal	2	3	2	3	2
Video Call	2	2	2	2	2

Icons that were associated with the functions of the mobile application the most are presented in a Figure 3.

Figure 3. Icons That Were Associated the Most With the Functions of the RPM Mobile Application.

5.3 Concept Refinement

5.3.1 Peer Review

Choice of fonts was determined based on the results of the research and the Peer Review with a group of five volunteers that were considered experts in the field. Research reported that older adults prefer larger font sizes, specifically 14-point font size. They also prefer sans serif fonts over serif fonts [14]. Choice of the following sans serif fonts was presented to the participants: Arial, Arial Rounded MT Bold, Calibri, Estrangelo Edessa, Helvetica, Mangal Bold, Raavi, Trebuchet MS, Verdana, and Vrinda (See Table 2). 14-point font size was used. Results of the peer review reported that Mangal Bold was preferred font.

Table 2. Results of the Peer Review: Fonts

Charts	**Charts**	Charts	Charts	Charts
1	1	0	0	0
Charts	Charts	Charts	Charts	Charts
4	0	0	0	0

Based on the results of the Usability Study 2 and the Usability Report 2, icons for the RPM mobile application functions were designed. Reference colors for the icons design were black, white,

and cyan. Black and white were used as contrasting colors, and cyan was used as an accent color. The order by which they were presented is the following one: Contacts, Sessions, Video Call, Charts, Messages, Sleep Journal, and Settings (See Figure 4).

The "Alert button" was designed based on the results of the Usability Testing 2. All the volunteers of the study required the "Alert button" to be prominent, spread across the whole page, and located at the top of the screen. Design of the "Alert button" explored different sizes and representations of the alert signage. It was designed as a red button, associating one with the importance of its function.

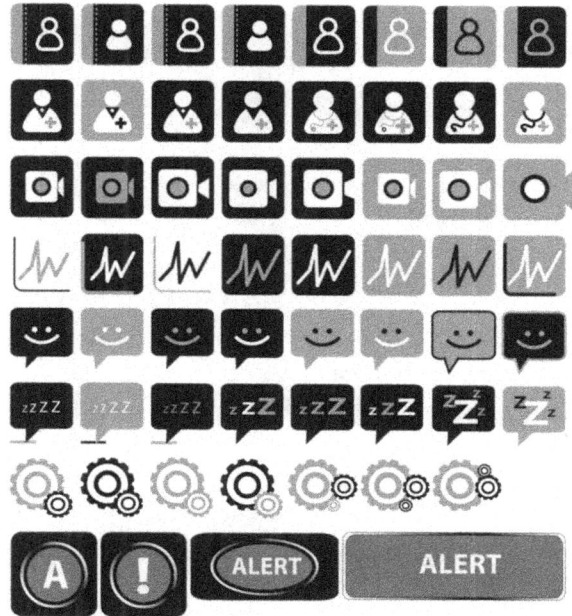

Figure 4. Icons Concepts for the Final Concept Development.

Results of the Peer Review finalized icons design for the buttons of the Home Screen that will represent all the RPM mobile application functions (See Table 3).

Table 3. Results of the Peer Review: Icons for the Buttons of the Home Screen

Functions	V1	V2	V3	V4	V5
Contacts	6	2	2	4	2
Sessions	6	2	1	3	2
Video Call	8	7	1	7	8
Charts	4	3	1	1	4
Messages	5	2	1	3	2
Sleep Journal	1	2	2	7	7
Settings	2	3	3	2	3
Alarm	2	2	2	2	2

Color-coordination was also explored based on the Usability Study 2 findings. All the volunteers preferred bright colors and contrast. Color coordination was presented to the volunteers (See

Figure 5). Based on the results of the Peer Review, icons design was finalized. As the reference, the initial set of icons with the reference colors was placed next to the icons with different bright colors options (color coordination). Volunteers were asked to choose one of the color options for the icons.

Volunteers preferred the original choice of black, white, and cyan, and also warm color options in Video Call, Charts, Sleep Journal, and Settings.

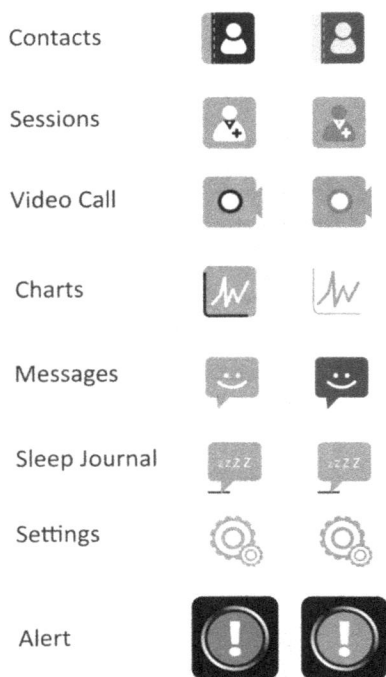

Figure 5. Color Coordination for the Icons.

Charts icons number 1 and number 4 got equal number of votes. In order to keep consistent appearance of all the icons, Chart icon number 4 was chosen for the final design (See Table 3).

Table 3. Results of the Peer Review: Icons for the Buttons

Functions	V 1	V 2	V 3	V4	V5
Contacts	1	1	1	1	1
Sessions	1	2	1	1	2
Video Call	1	2	1	2	1
Charts	1	2	1	2	1
Messages	1	2	1	2	1
Sleep Journal	1	2	1	2	1
Settings	1	2	1	1	1
Alert	2	2	2	2	2

Since most of the icons have cyan as a background color, cyan was chosen as the background color for the final Chart icon as well. Cyan was slightly changed into a more pleasing and more neutral color (See Figure 6).

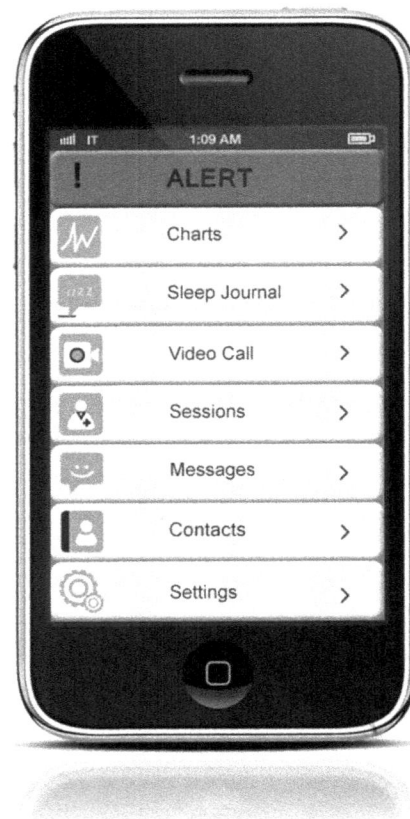

Figure 6. Final Icons Design.

6. CONCLUSION
6.1 Discussion

The icon design study improved the UX/UI aspect of the RPM devices, specifically The BL Healthcare Access Tablet. Its unique approach of eliminating the need for the hub unit and its manufacturing by designing customizable RPM mobile application concept led to the improvement of the whole RPM system.

Icons for UI of the RPM mobile application were simplified and adapted for the use by the older adults. Fonts that are easy to read and icons that are easy to interpret were chosen, providing easier use and greater satisfaction with the product and the service. Icons were designed to be recognizable and meaningful. In addition to this, bigger graphics and font sizes for both smartphone and tablet were chosen, to accommodate the needs of the older adults.

RPM mobile or tablet application can be used to record, visualize, and send data to the server. This way data could be accessed from the server by the healthcare provider's office. Other RPM functions, like video conferencing, scheduled sessions, recording daily sleep journal, or medicine reminder can also be done through these devices.

The Mobile Health Application has a log-in page to allow for caregivers and patients to have separate entries to the application and provide for additional security of the data. Application has the following functions that could be accessed from the main page:

- The Alert button, which will call 911 by pressing it once in a case of emergency,

- Charts, which collect, record, and visualize various vitals such as blood pressure, weight, body temperature, blood glucose levels, etc.,
- Daily Sleep Journal, a short survey of health and sleep-related questions,
- Video call, which allows for video conferencing, virtual clinic visits, health counseling, video visits for case management, coordination of care between multiple parties, wound/skin inspection using plug-n cameras, directly observed therapy, and video conferencing with family members,
- Scheduled sessions with the healthcare provider,
- Health-related messaging,
- Contacts,
- Medicine reminder, that is incorporated into the Settings function,
- Settings, where patients can personalize their mobile application and healthcare providers can customize the application based on the chronic disease.

The Mobile Health Application is customizable for the patients with different chronic conditions. It can be personalized by the users by uploading different images and backgrounds.

UX redesign had the greatest impact on users by adding the portability to the RPM and giving them the opportunity to use the RPM mobile application outside their homes. This flexibility gives the chronic disease patients more freedom and may enhance their daily amount of physical activities, thus further benefitting their health. Additional benefit to these patients is commodity of using the devices they are already familiar and comfortable with.

6.2 Future Work

Next steps include adding other important features to the mobile application UI, with related icons. Several additional features are possible that could help in patients' health management:

- Educational videos,
- Health-related games and readings as a part of the library,
- Social aspect of connecting with other patients.

Development of new technologies allow for advanced types of social networking for patients [22]. Social support can increase patients' possibility for success in achieving health-related goals [22].

In addition to having more features, the case study requires future steps of conducting the additional usability studies and further refinements of the final icons concept.

7. REFERENCES

[1] Black, S. Mobile Telemedicine: A Computing and Networking Perspective, 2008, 161–172.

[2] Chiang, L. C., Chen, W. C., Dai, Y. T. and Ho, Y. L. The effectiveness of telehealth care on caregiver burden, mastery of stress, and family function among family caregivers of heart failure patients: A quasi-experimental study. International Journal of Nursing Studies, 2012.

[3] Suter, P., Suter, W. N. and Johnston, D. Theory-based telehealth and patient empowerment. Population health management, 14, 2, 2011, 87-92.

[4] Thong, J. Y., Hong, W. and Tam, K. Y. What leads to user acceptance of digital libraries? Communications of the ACM, 47, 11, 2004, 78-83.

[5] Fraser, H., Kwon, Y. J. and Neuer, M. The Future of Connected Health Devices. Ritrieved from touchhealthsciences.com, 2011, 28-34.

[6] Gargiulo, G., Bifulco, P., Cesarelli, M., Jin, C., McEwan, A. and van Schaik, A. Wearable dry sensors with Bluetooth connection for use in remote patient monitoring systems. Studies In Health Technology And Informatics, 161, 2010, 57-65.

[7] Eisenstein, J., Vanderdonckt, J. and Puerta, A. Applying model-based techniques to the development of UIs for mobile computers. In Proceedings of the Proceedings of the 6th international conference on Intelligent user interfaces (Santa Fe, New Mexico, USA, 2001). ACM, New York, NY, 2001.

[8] Dourish, P. Accounting for system behaviour: Representation, reflection and resourceful action. Computers and Design in Context, MIT Press, Cambridge, MA, USA, 1997, 145-170.

[9] Leonardi, C., Mennecozzi, C., Not, E., Pianesi, F. and Zancanaro, M. Designing a familiar technology for elderly people. Gerontechnology, 7, 2, 2008, 151.

[10] Norman, D. The design of future things. 2007. New York: Basic Books, City, 2007.

[11] Melenhorst, A.-S., Rogers, W. A. and Caylor, E. C. The use of communication technologies by older adults: exploring the benefits from the user's perspective. SAGE Publications, City, 2001.

[12] Battleson, B., Booth, A. and Weintrop, J. Usability testing of an academic library web site: a case study. The Journal of Academic Librarianship, 27, 3, 2001, 188-198.

[13] Nielsen, J. a. H., J. T. Usability engineering. Academic press Boston, 1993.

[14] Bernard, M. L. Criteria for optimal web design (designing for usability). Retrieved on April, 13, 2003.

[15] Bernard, M., Liao, C. H. and Mills, M. The effects of font type and size on the legibility and reading time of online text by older adults. ACM, City, 2001.

[16] Sorg, J. A. An Exploratory Study of Type Face, Type Size and Color Paper Preferences Among Older Adults. Pennsylvania State University, 1985.

[17] Nielsen, J. and Hackos, J. T. Usability engineering. Academic press Boston, 1993.

[18] Rowan, M., Gregor, P., Sloan, D. and Booth, P. Evaluating web resources for disability access. ACM, City, 2000.

[19] Nielsen, J. How to conduct a heuristic evaluation. On the World Wide Web, 1994.

[20] Malkary, G. Healthcare without Bounds: Trends in Remote Patient Monitoring, April 2006, Spyglass Consulting Group.

[21] Foley, D., Ancoli-Israel, S., Britz, P. and Walsh, J. Sleep disturbances and chronic disease in older adults: results of the 2003 National Sleep Foundation Sleep in America Survey. Journal of psychosomatic research, 56, 5, 2004, 497-502.

[22] Czejdo, B. D. and Baszun, M. Remote patient monitoring system and a medical social network. International Journal of Social and Humanistic Computing, 1, 3, 2010, 273-281.

Towards Simplifying Learning Systems: A Critical Review

Frantzeska Kolyda
School of Electronics and Computer Science
University of Westminster
London, UK
+44 (0)20 3506 4844
kolydaf@westminster.ac.uk

ABSTRACT
The concept of learning itself involves a significant amount of complexity. Therefore there is a need to design and implement learning systems that are not complex, confusing or complicated. This paper discusses, based on a review of the literature, how we could simplify educational technology and learning systems by focusing on one of the most important user centered design principles, i.e. understanding learner's needs and establishing requirements. It is also important to consider the learning context before focusing on the characteristics and system requirements. In conclusion, nowadays, more than ever before, new and emerging technologies could make possible the design of powerful learning systems that could transform the quality of learning as long as they are easy to use, intuitive and provide an engaging user experience.

Categories and Subject Descriptors
K.3 **[Computers and Education]**: Computer Uses in Education - *Computer-assisted instruction (CAI), Computer-managed instruction (CMI)*.

H.5 **[Information Interfaces and Presentation]**: User Interfaces - *User-centered design, Theory and methods*.

Keywords
Learning Systems, Educational Technology, Learning, User-centered Design.

1. INTRODUCTION
Interaction design involves designing interactive systems and products to support the way we communicate and interact in our everyday and working life [1]. Consequently, learning systems should be designed focusing on the above goal. In order to achieve this, there is a need to understand human capabilities, cognitive limitations, people's desires and motivation. This will

help us identifying the learners' needs, establishing the system's requirements and translate these into an appropriate and optimized design that could enhance and facilitate learning. How could we simplify complexity of educational technology and learning systems?

2. LEARNING
The concept of learning itself involves a significant amount of complexity both as a process as well as an outcome. According to Hodkinson and Macleod [2], "learning is a conceptual and linguistic construction that is widely used in many societies and cultures, but with very different meanings, which are fiercely contested and partly contradictory. Learning does not have a clear physical or reified identity in the world". As learning is complex enough, educational technology and learning systems should be particularly simple. We could simplify complexity of learning systems by focusing on the primary user of such systems i.e. the learner and the learning activity. As Norman [3] emphasizes, we need to start with an understanding of people i.e. learners: user needs first, technology last.

Over the last 20 years, psychologists are trying to understand the influence of the social and cultural environments that are involved in someone's learning and cognitive development [4] and more emphasis is now being placed on seeing learning as a very social process. This idea of learning as a collaborative and socially situated process has led to a number of researchers e.g. [5, 6, 45] nowadays focusing on how educational technology could act as powerful social resources in someone's learning context.

When learners acquire information in a meaningful context and are able to relate it to their prior knowledge and experiences, they could form connections between the new information and their prior knowledge to develop larger and better linked conceptual understanding [7].

3. LEARNER NEEDS AND CHARACTERISTICS
Numerous researchers, e.g. [8, 9, 10, 11, 12, 13] have emphasized the common idea that technology can create learning environments that would not otherwise be possible without technology. Hence how can we simplify the complexity of learning systems in order for them to facilitate and enhance learning? The key answer to this question is to know the users and their needs. Knowing and analyzing what is meaningful to the learners and their possible interactions with educational technology is fundamental. We need to study learners' preferences, desires and adopt their perspective. Understanding their needs as users means that we can design educational technology that makes the learning object meaningful and

provides learners with a context in which learning becomes a tangible need [14].

It is important to understand why and how learners differ because then educational technology could be designed and used in such way that learners could achieve their full potential and guided though the learning process. Intelligence, personality and cognitive styles contribute to variations among individuals. Cognitive style refers to "an individual's preferred and habitual approach to organizing and representing information" [15]. Although within the literature, the term "learning style" has been used in two ways: a) as "cognitive style" and b) as a term to indicate a wide description of rather consistent behaviors in relation to the way people learn, in both ways the term meant to cover "a range of concepts which have emerged from attempts to describe aspects of student learning" [16]. Research into the field of individual differences and learning styles is particularly significant in order to design instructional material through technology. In this way it is possible, if we adapt the instruction, to accommodate learners' differences in styles or preferences [17] and help them approach their learning in the best possible way. Riding and Rayner [15], argue that academic performance is related to the development of learning strategy, the learning process and individual differences.

In addition, it is important to study the relation between educational technology and certain processes that learners employ in their learning, i.e. their learning strategies. Mayer [18] defines learning strategies as "the behaviors of the learners that are intended to influence how the learners process information". Investigating the learning strategies that students are engaged in when learning from and with certain computer applications could be beneficial. It could provide an assessment of the way computer-based learning strategies differ from the strategies used in the traditional learning environment within the school (lectures, tutorials, use of textbooks). Although the use of computer applications in the classroom becomes greater there is a dearth of research (particularly in primary education) regarding the kind of learning strategies students use when working with technology. The use of certain learning strategies in the course of learning could affect the encoding process and consequently, the learning outcome and performance [19].

Adaptive learning environments through the use of educational technology could also play an important role on enhancing the learning process. Adapting content and instruction to particular learner characteristics, needs and abilities is a particular important area of research, e.g. [20], nowadays especially since the recent advances in technology have created a number of exciting opportunities for personalized learning and instruction. However, as Mavrikis et al [21] highlight, computational analysis and reasoning in supporting learning with and from exploratory environments will be of little benefit when designing these exploratory environments without subtle understanding of the interaction between the learner and the system and the types of support they need.

4. LEARNING CONTEXT

It is important to increase our understanding regarding the relationship between learning and context so that we could specify the requirements for the design of learner activity and technology. The nature of context is crucial for someone's development, Luckin [22] concludes that different contexts will lead to different social interactions and consequently to the development of different mental processes within the individual. Luckin [5]

defines a learning context as "an Ecology of Resources: a set of inter-related things/elements that provide a particular context". Past research has confirmed the importance of exploring the learner's context but has been largely limited to specific environmental locations. Nowadays, the capacity to create learning context is widely available and the challenge is to develop ways in which technology can support learners to effectively create their own learning contexts [22].

Luckin [23] argues that we need a framework which helps us design educational experiences that match the available resources to each learner's needs. According to Luckin's Ecology of Resources framework, there are four different types of resources: a) Tools: learning materials, b) People: teachers, peers and adults, c) Knowledge and Skills: the teachers' expertise and d) Environment: the setting in which learning is taking place.

In addition to the issues discussed above regarding the learning context, it is also significant to consider the overall power of contexts in educational research which makes the need for qualitative approach necessary in trying to understand school life and particularly designing successful learning systems for use in formal learning.

5. CHARACTERISTICS OF SUCCESSFUL LEARNING SYSTEMS

Sinclair et al [24] analyzed a range of digital technology implementation projects with focus on mathematics and which have been implemented at a national scale in various parts of the world. The researchers highlighted that although early work with digital technologies mainly focused on individual learners or school-based groups, these large-scale projects that they analyzed demanded a much more systemic approach that considered issues such as teacher adoption and curriculum integration. Sinclair et al [24] noticed a shift in focus towards the teacher's role and participation that was emerging across these projects. Furthermore, it appeared that the majority of these projects were focusing on the use of one "multi-purpose digital technology". The majority of digital technology implementation projects that have been undertaken at a national scale in different parts of the world are still focusing nowadays on a mandated curriculum. Nevertheless, there are some exceptions where certain projects encourage new content or new variations of curriculum content [24]. For example, by offering different ways of approaching primary school mathematical ideas, they focus on scaffolding learning. For instance, the use of a visual animation could enhance understanding of a difficult mathematical idea, or an abstract mathematical idea.

Nowadays, innovative technology and open-ended environments afford new forms of interaction that offer great opportunities for exploratory learning as well as personalization. Nevertheless, in the classroom there is a need to obtain a balance between allowing students to express their own ideas and follow their own paths, and at the same time steering them towards the activities and ideas that are concerned with the curriculum material [25]. A potential solution to this problem could be to equip the teacher with tools that could provide the latter with valuable insights as to how the students progress so that the teacher could still orchestrate the classroom but without becoming intrusive as this would almost certainly lead to the elimination of any exploratory learning opportunities.

Exploratory learning seems to have great potential nowadays through information visualizations, online environments, powerful simulations and augmented reality. Nevertheless, there are not enough examples of innovation [26] and this type of learning appears to be underused and undervalued within the school classroom. Possible reasons for this could be the obvious limited amount of time that teachers have to use such environments, the complexity of designing such environments and also, the difficulty of assessing and effectively evaluating what needs to be learned at school through such exploratory environments.

There is little doubt that interactivity facilitates learner's exploration of the learning environment and as Salomon [27] underlines, interactivity adds a completely different value to the learner's engagement in the activity. In addition, it makes possible the testing of ideas and receiving guidance and informative feedback.

Guidance and feedback is another characteristic of successful learning systems. In contrast to other mediums of learning (e.g. books), a well-designed interactive learning system can provide important guidance and informative feedback [27]. In fact, it could be said that it creates for the learner a "Zone of Proximal Development", the distance between the learner's actual developmental level and their potential level of development under guidance and help [28]. However, it is obvious that different kind or amount of feedback can have different effects on learning. For example, when the students start an interactive activity the amount of guidance and feedback is greater in comparison with what they receive as they move on and complete a number of activities and acquire certain skills.

New and emerging technologies require reconsidering the concept of scaffolding within software. Luckin [23] introduced the "Zone of Available Assistance" (ZAA) and the "Zone of Proximal Adjustment" (ZPA) in an attempt to clarify the relationship between the ZPD and educational technology. Luckin used ZAA to describe the types of resources, both human and artifact, available within a particular context to help a more able partner to offer appropriate help to a less able learner. The ZPA represents a selected subset of the ZAA that are the resources which are the most appropriate form of help for a specific learner at a particular moment in time. However, Luckin argues that the existence of a rich set of resources within the ZAA is not sufficient to ensure the required interactions in order to create a ZPD for the learner.

The computer-based learning environments should not only present information but also provide guidance for how to process the presented information (i.e. determine where to focus, how to mentally organize it and how to relate it to prior knowledge) [29].

Learning systems should be designed in such way that [44] a) cognitive processing which does not facilitate the instructional goal (i.e. extraneous processing) is reduced while b) cognitive processing that is needed to represent the material in working memory (i.e. essential processing) is managed and c) cognitive processing that is needed for deeper understanding (i.e. generative processing) is supported. This is, according to Mayer [44], the triarchic model of cognitive load.

Research, e.g. [30, 42, 43] emphasizes that there is a need to develop educational computer environments that will foster meaningful learning and that this could be achieved through active learning. However, we need to consider what we actually mean when we refer to active learning. Is the latter related to the learner's physical behavior (e.g. the level of hands-on activity) or to what is going on in the learner's mind (e.g. the level of integrative cognitive processing)? As Mayer [29] highlights:

"Research on learning shows that meaningful learning depends on the learner's cognitive activity during learning rather than on the learner's behavioral activity during learning... My point is that well-designed multimedia instructional messages can promote active cognitive processing in learners, even when learners seem to be behaviorally inactive".

In successful educational games, difficult concepts could be explored through gaming that motivates and engages students. In addition to this, students' interactions with a game could be logged and then analyzed in order to acquire valuable information regarding their learning, for example, what section they found difficult or easy etc. Such data-mining in a school environment could reveal which curriculum areas lead to achieving the required learning outcomes, which as Noss [8] explains is particular difficult information to collect traditionally.

Furthermore, educational games or other technology enhanced learning systems could help learners apply their knowledge in real life. Simulation authoring tools such as SimQuest [31] enable students to explore the physics of motion in a real life context. Immersive virtual environments such as EcoMUVE [32] teach secondary school students about ecosystems and causal patterns [34]. Simulation tools and micro-world environments such as ThinkerTools [33] allow primary and secondary school students to run simulations of objects moving and observe the affects of various forces such as impulses, gravity and friction. Gee [45] argues that good computer game design can help us understand how to design good learning because good games are mainly learning and problem-solving experiences.

There is also a need for better understanding whether and how specific characteristics of a particular type of educational technology could be effective in promoting learning since by expanding our knowledge in this area we create the foundation for further research that could lead to the implementation of systems capable of making a real difference in schooling."Technology by itself cannot be expected to revolutionize education, but rather should be seen as one of a collection of tools that might spark and facilitate innovative thinking" [35].

6. ISSUES OF ASSESSMENT
In order to be able to design simple and effective learning systems an investigation is required from a number of different perspectives (e.g. types of assessment, relevant measures of learning) and an understanding of the difficulty of evaluating the system's effectiveness on learning. Lee (cited in [36]) argues that there are several questions about evaluating educational technology as well as some serious problems in using more authentic assessments (e.g. performance assessments) to measure change over time such as low reliability. In school education it is quite difficult to assess long-term change (such as learning) due to changes in classroom conditions for example, change of a teacher. Lee argues that outcomes such as performance assessments, engagement, academic self-concept or aspirations are more complex to measure than the assessment scores (e.g. standardized tests) therefore, there is concern regarding the reliability and validity of other measures (that could be used in order to measure the impact of technology).

Ridgway and McCusker [37] agree that educational technology raises important questions about "what is worth learning in an ICT-rich environment, what can be taught, given new pedagogic tools and how assessment systems can be designed which put pressure on educational systems to help students achieve these new goals" [37].

In addition, as Jonassen [38] underlines, the most important reason for assessment and evaluation is to provide learners with feedback that facilitates their comprehension of how much they have learned in order to "better direct their learning". Jonassen embraces the opinion that technology should be used to support meaningful learning and engage students in critical thinking but at the same time he highlights the fact that critical thinking is difficult to assess because, apart from all the other reasons, it is quite complex to define.

Assessing the process of learning as opposed to simply the result is crucial. Being able to assess competencies such as students' ability to a) analyze and solve complex problems, b) synthesize information and c) apply knowledge to new situations. At present, assessment in school is designed to simply indicate if students have learned but it is not sophisticated enough to assess student inquiry learning or students' thinking during learning. Educational technology has the potential to engage students in immersive, meaningful and challenging learning activities that could provide the teachers as well as the students themselves with rich insights into their reasoning and knowledge [39].

In order to assess the simplicity and consequently effectiveness of educational technology and learning systems there is a need to determine the purpose of the assessment and to identify the best ways to measure the key (and usually multiple) outcomes. For example, are we measuring the learning outcome or creativity or higher order thinking or any changes in learning attitudes? According to Rutter, "the long term educational benefits stem not from what children are specifically taught but from the effects on children's attitudes to learning, on their self-esteem, and on their task orientation" (cited in [40]).

A learning system that supports and facilitates learning activities could gather valuable data while the learning activity is taking place. While the learners are working their inputs are captured and their learning paths are documented as well as the amount of time spent in each activity. This process needs to be straight forward and the recorded results appropriately collected and with various options of analysis and presentation. If such process is complex, confusing and time-consuming or if the collected data is overwhelming and the system does not offer a simple and easy way to analyze it then all the great system's functionality and powerful features do not serve their purpose i.e. to provide teachers and facilitators (or even learners themselves) with a simple and easy way to enhance their classroom learning through better control and awareness of classroom's performance that could consequently lead to opportunities for formative assessment.

7. CONCLUSIONS

This paper has attempted to discuss briefly the need to consider the learner's characteristics and needs as well as the learning context before focusing on system requirements and specifications. There is a need to consider how we can design non complex learning systems that could enhance learning and how we can measure that enhancement [39].

Further research is required on the way games, simulations, virtual words and collaborative environments could be implemented to motivate students while assessing complex skills and aspects of thinking in different situations. For example, a research project in Sweden [41] focused on kinesthetic learning (i.e. how we learn and acquire understanding through bodily interactions and through moving into a large space setting). Researchers explored how abstract notions of energy and energy

consumption could become something that could be experienced and interacted with in a physical manner using our body and movement. They argued that: "by adapting the interchange needed between the different spaces, it is possible to build activities and learning environments that allow for both a rich experience of small details in the personal space to a joint understanding of concepts in the larger whole, through both system and real world feedback and interaction" [41]. This seems quite an interesting approach to design for alternative pedagogical practices.

Learning systems could enable both learners and teachers to reflect upon activities and keep track of the learning process as well as present the information and learning material in rich and interactive ways.

Nowadays, more than ever before, new and emerging technologies could make possible the design and development of powerful learning systems that could transform the quality of learning, teaching and assessment through unique opportunities of individual and appropriate feedback and personalized learning as long as such systems are easy to use, intuitive and provide a positive, immersive and engaging user experience. Our focus should always be first in better understanding how people learn, what are the requirements of education and learning and then following a user-centered design approach implement systems for learning.

8. REFERENCES

[1] Rogers, Y., Sharp, H., & Preece, J. 2011. Interaction design: beyond human-computer interaction. Wiley. London.

[2] Hodkinson, P., & Macleod, F. 2010. Contrasting concepts of learning and contrasting research methodologies: affinities and bias. *British Educational Research Journal*, 36(2), 173-189.

[3] Norman, D. A. 1999. *The invisible computer: Why good products fail, the personal computer is so complex, and information appliances are the solution.* MIT Press, Cambridge, MA.

[4] Selwyn, N. 2011. *Schools and schooling in the digital age: A critical analysis.* Routledge, Abingdon, Oxon.

[5] Luckin, R. 2011. *Re-designing learning contexts: technology-rich, learner-centred ecologies.* Routledge, Abingdon, Oxon.

[6] Greeno, J. G. 2006. Learning in activity. In R. K. Sawyer (Ed.), *The Cambridge handbook of the learning sciences* (pp. 79-96). Cambridge University Press. New York.

[7] Sawyer, R. Keith. 2006. (Ed.).The Cambridge handbook of the learning sciences, vol. 2, No. 5.Cambridge University Press, Cambridge.

[8] Noss, R. 2012. *Public lecture: Learning the Unlearnable: Teaching the Unteachable.* Melbourne Graduate School of Education, University of Melbourne. http://vimeopro.com/mgse/deans-lecture-series/video/53119963 (Access Date: 01/12/2012).

[9] Noss, R., et al. 2012. *System upgrade: realising the vision for UK education.* London.

[10] Druin, A., & Solomon, C. 1996. *Designing Multimedia Environments for Children.* Wiley & Sons. New York.

[11] Fraser, A. B. 1999. Colleges Should Tap the Pedagogical Potential of the World-Wide Web. *Chronicle of Higher Education, (section: Opinion & Arts), 48,* B8.

[12] Papert, S., & Harel, I. 1991. Situating Constructionism. In S. Papert & I. Harel (Eds.), *Constructionism*. Ablex Publishing.Norwood. NJ.

[13] Soloway, E., Guzdial, M., & Hay, K. E. 1994. Learner-centered design: The Challenge for HCI in the 21st Century. *Interactions, 1,* 36-48. DOI= http://doi.acm.org/10.1145/174809.174813

[14] Sedighian, K., & Sedighian, A. S. 1996. *Can educational computer games help educators learn about the psychology of learning Mathematics in children?* In 18th Annual Meeting of the International Group for the Psychology of Mathematics Education. Florida, USA.

[15] Riding, R., & Rayner, S. G. 1998. *Cognitive Styles and Learning Strategies*. David Fulton Publishers. London.

[16] Eysenck, M. W. E. 1994. *The Blackwell Dictionary of Cognitive Psychology*. Blackwell Publishers. Oxford.

[17] Moallem, M. (2002). The implications of research literature on learning styles for the design and development of a web-based course. *Proceedings of the International Conference on Computers in Education 2002,* 1 (pp. 71- 74). IEEE Computer Society. Washington, DC.

[18] Mayer, R. E. (1988). Learning Strategies: An Overview. In C. E. Weinstein, Goetz, E. T. & Alexander, P.A. (Eds.), *Learning and Study Strategies: Issues in Assessment, Instruction and Evaluation* (pp. 11-22). Academic Press. San Diego.

[19] Weinstein, C. E., Goetz, E. T., & Alexander, P. A. 1988. *Learning and Study strategies: Issues in Assessment, Instruction and Evaluation*. Academic Press. San Diego.

[20] Vandewaetere, M., Desmet, P., & Clarebout, G. 2011. The contribution of learner characteristics in the development of computer-based adaptive learning environments. *Computers in Human Behavior,* 27(1), 118-130.

[21] Mavrikis, M., Gutierrez-Santos, S., Geraniou, E., & Noss, R. 2012. Design requirements, student perception indicators and validation metrics for intelligent exploratory learning environments. *Personal and Ubiquitous Computing*, 1-16.

[22] Luckin, R. 2006. Understanding learning contexts as ecologies of resources: From the zone of proximal development to learner generated contexts. *In World Conference on E-Learning in Corporate, Government, Healthcare, and Higher Education*, 2006(1), 2195-2202.

[23] Luckin, R. 2008. The learner centric ecology of resources: A framework for using technology to scaffold learning. *Computers & Education*, 50 (2), 449-462.

[24] Sinclair, N., Arzarello, F., Gaisman, M. T., Lozano, M. D., Dagiene, V., Behrooz, E., & Jackiw, N. 2010. Implementing digital technologies at a national scale. In *Mathematics Education and Technology-Rethinking the Terrain* (pp. 61-78). Springer. US.

[25] Noss, R., Poulovassilis, A., Geraniou, E., Gutierrez-Santos, S., Hoyles, C., Kahn, K., ... & Mavrikis, M. 2012. The design of a system to support exploratory learning of algebraic generalisation. *Computers & Education*, 59(1), 63-81.

[26] Luckin et al 2012. *Decoding Learning report*. Nesta. London.

[27] Salomon,G. 1990. Cognitive Effects with and of Computer Technology. *Communication Research, 17*(1), 26-44.

[28] Smith, P. K., Cowie, H., & Blades, M. 1998. *Understanding Children's Development* (3rd Ed.). Blackwell Publishers. Oxford.

[29] Mayer, R. E. 2005. (Ed.). *The Cambridge handbook of multimedia learning*. Cambridge University Press.

[30] Mayer, R. E. 2009. *Multimedia Learning.* (2nd ed). Cambridge: Cambridge University Press.

[31] SimQuest. 2011. SimQuest. http://www.simquest.nl. University of Twente. Netherlands.

[32] EcoMUVE project. 2011. EcoMUVE. http://ecomuve.gse.harvard.edu. Harvard Graduate School of Education. Cambridge, MA.

[33] White, B.Y. 2011. ThinkerTools software. National Science Foundation, University of California. Berkeley. http://ott.educ.msu.edu/2002pt3/thinkertools.htm. (Access Date: 10/01/2013).

[34] Noss, R., Cox, R., Laurillard, D., Luckin, R., Plowman, L., Scanlon, E., & Sharples, M. (2012). *System upgrade: realising the vision for UK education*. London Knowledge Lab.

[35] Bitter, G. G. & Pierson, M. E. 2004. *Using Technology in the Classroom* (6th Ed). Pearson

[36] Haertel, G. D., & Means, B. 2004. *Using Technology Evaluation to Enhance Student Learning*. Teachers College Press. New York.

[37] Ridgway, J., & McCusker, S. 2004. *Literature Review of E-assessment - Report 10*. NESTA Futurelab. Bristol.

[38] Jonassen, D. H. 2000. *Computers as Mindtools for Schools: Engaging Critical Thinking* (2nd Ed.). Prentice Hall. Columbus, OH.

[39] Technology Enhanced Learning (TEL) project publication. 2012. Does Technology Enhance Learning? *TEL Programme publications*. http://www.tlrp.org/docs/enhance.pdf. (Access Date: 01/12/2012).

[40] Fisher, R. 1995. *Teaching Children to Learn* (1st Ed.). Nelson Thornes. Cheltenham.

[41] Johansson, C., Ahmet, Z., Jonsson, M., Tholander, J., Aleo, F., Sumon, S. 2011. Weather Gods and Fruit Kids – Embodying abstract concepts using tactile feedback and Whole Body Interaction In *proceedings of the 9th International Conference on Computer Supported Collaborative Learning* . (July 2011), 160-167. Hong Kong, China.

[42] Evans, C., & Gibbons, N. J. 2007. The interactivity effect in multimedia learning. *Computers & Education*, 49(4), 1147-1160.

[43] Shieh, R. S. 2012. The impact of Technology-Enabled Active Learning (TEAL) implementation on student learning and teachers' teaching in a high school context. *Computers & Education*, 59(2), 206-214.

[44] Mayer, R. E. 2009. *Multimedia Learning.* (2nd ed). Cambridge: Cambridge University Press.

[45] Gee, J. P. 2008. Learning and games. In Salen, K., (ed.) *The ecology of games: Connecting youth, games, and learning, 3,* 21-40.

Enhancing Communication and Collaboration through Integrated Internet and Intranet Architecture

Ganapathy Mani
George Washington University *and*
The GEF, The World Bank Group
Washington, DC
gans87@gwu.edu

Juman Byun and Patrizia Cocca
Global Environment Facility
The World Bank Group
Washington, DC
jbyun@thegef.org, pcocca@thegef.org

ABSTRACT

When it comes to enhancing collaboration and communication in an organization, particular types of technologies with different properties, frameworks and platforms are used to accomplish different types of tasks. These technologies are often disconnected and require separate maintenance and coordination. This system leads to more complex processing and communication that creates confusion in collaboration. It is also time consuming, have little or no flexibility and accumulates data overhead. To address these issues, we propose a new Integrated Internet and Intranet (I3) architecture, information flow models and optimization techniques to streamline the communication and enhance the collaboration. With an efficient Big Data processing design and optimization techniques, we reduce the complexity and enhance the computer-human interaction. Our implementation of this architecture in a non-profit international organization showed significant improvement in communication and collaboration by reducing the number of emails, duplicates of documents, man-hours, and number of steps for each task.

Categories and Subject Descriptors

H.4 [**Information Systems Applications**]: Miscellaneous; H.5.3 [**Information Interfaces and Presentation**]: Group Organization InterfacesWeb-based interaction; D.2.8 [**Software Engineering**]: Metricscomplexity measures, performance measures

Keywords

Intranet, Computer-Human Interaction, Internet of Things (IoT), Internet of Technologies, Document Collaboration, Communication Optimization

1. INTRODUCTION

For the last two decades, information technology — using computers, software and tools of telecommunication to store, retrieve and analyze data — has changed the world, for the

most part, for better. Combining it with the Internet, since 2000 we have been experiencing an exceptional transformation in the field of digital communications [4]. We are entering into an era that is characterized by our ability to aggregate, analyze, visualize and utilize the data not only to enhance the way we communicate and collaborate but also to make those tasks easier. Several types of computer and telecommunication technologies are used by the organizations to accomplish various types of tasks and most of the time each of the tasks is to be managed separately. Most common of these technologies are data management, document management, web services, collaboration through emails and telecommunications (with or without video), applications for hand-held smart devices and local intranet portals (a restricted, private, local communication network using local web services).

Data management technologies are used for processing, storing, retrieving and analyzing data collected from wide range of sources. For an organization, data management technologies are used for maintaining records about their projects as well as their employees. Data management in any organization is built with databases that are the tools for collecting and organizing information. Databases can store information in tables or lists or in a document-processing program (e.g. QuickOffice) or spreadsheet (e.g. Microsoft Office Excel). Databases can be accessed through the Database Management Systems (DBMS) where the user can interact with the database using Structured Language Queries (SQL) — *CREATE, DROP, SELECT, INSERT, UPDATE, DELETE, COMMIT, ROLLBACK* etc. — specific for the database management systems [14].

DBMSs based on relational model — relations between individual and/or group of database tuples — are known as Relational Database Management Systems (RDBMS) [26]. There are open source RDBMSs like MySQL and PostgreSQL as well as proprietary software or closed source software like Microsoft SQL Server. Due to the needs of security and customer service, majority of the organizations prefer proprietary RDBMSs [10]. But it does not work with other web services or local form-based applications of a different platform. For example, windows form based applications are hardly compatible with open source database management system. With the RDBMS as the back-end server, web services or local form services (e.g. windows-based forms) can be used to create a user interface to add, remove or retrieve data from the databases.

In the web services, there are proprietary services like Windows Communication Foundation (WCF) supported by programming languages C Sharp and Visual Basic, and there are open source services like Apache supported by programming languages like Java, Hypertext Preprocessor (PHP), and Content Management Frameworks or CMF (e.g. Drupal and Joomla). Windows Presentation Foundation (WPF) is an example of proprietary local form-based application services with C# and VB languages, and Java, C++ are the open source examples of local form-based applications. Both open source and proprietary services have their advantages as well as disadvantages but each one is good at handling specific tasks. For example, Drupal can facilitate users with customized, responsive themes that can be installed and maintained easily with low cost. On the other hand, Microsoft SQL Server provides excellent, secure environment with robust support from the vendor. Unfortunately, Drupal and Microsoft SQL Server are not compatible in so many levels [1]. It is a still-in-progress process with less enthusiasm from the proprietary vendors. So the users are left with very few restricted options.

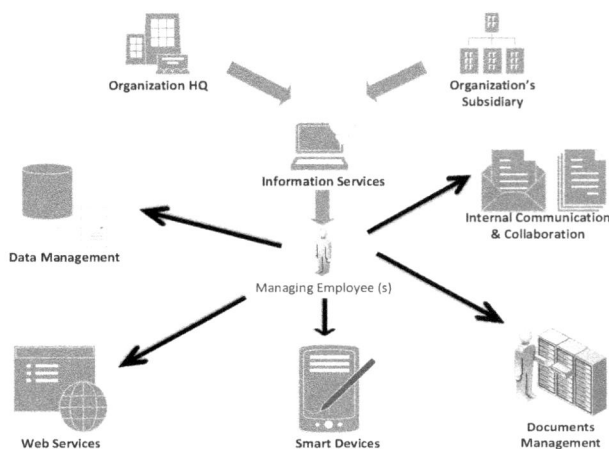

Figure 1: Disconnected information services managed separately by employee(s)

Most of the time collaborations happen through emails among team members in any organization. Collaborations mean teams contributing to the tasks that require supervision, providing feedback, approval and content editing. In particular, document collaboration is vital for all the organizations, but there are only few document-processing applications available with less or no compatibility between them thus there are very few document collaboration portals are available. Collaborating through email creates communication overhead of tens or even hundreds of emails and duplicates of the same documents thus confusing the team members. The enormous number of emails — accumulated due to collaboration — for any given task makes searching and finding the required documents harder. The famous word processing application is from Microsoft — Microsoft Office — is widely used by many organizations [8]. When it comes to collaboration, Microsoft SharePoint has comprehensive solutions including document libraries, lists and workflows that are designed to streamline and enhance the collaboration. Microsoft SharePoint is a Windows Communication Foundation, web application platform which is used as the intranet content management and document manage-

ment [16]. It has broader capabilities like calendar, blogs, team sites, record center, etc. The SharePoint can be used as a server farm hosting several sites as internal intranet or external intranet where people from outside the organization can access it with right credentials. But SharePoint is not compatible with the open source content management systems like Drupal [9] or Joomla. This can create a major inconvenience for most of the private and public sector organizations.

Non-profit international organizations, for example, have to deal with bureaucracy with extensive paper work. Each task has to pass through several levels of hierarchy to get a review and/or approval. If there are any changes needed for the approval, the task has to start from step one. Despite the innovations and advancements in information technology to digitize the tasks, international organizations have to take several factors into consideration while designing the computerized workspace. Some of these documents are meant to be on the public website of the organization and some of them are for internal purpose only. SharePoint can handle document permission and collaboration but it will not be able to integrate with open source content management systems which are browser and platform independent. So the employees have to separate those documents automatically and post them online. These bureaucracy and paperwork not only reduce the productivity and stall the communication among employees but make the organizations to comply with something which is not an environmentally friendly (e.g. excessive use of paper).

1.1 Complications with Big Data

International organizations (both profit and non-profit) work with wide range of countries from the most developed to the least developed in the world. To comply with the technology available in each country, the international organizations use different methods of collecting valuable data. For example, [20] introduces several data collection methods and tools that can be used for a particular data collection environment. Especially, the authors points to technology availability in the countries as one of the main factors of affecting data collection. Most of the data collection in the developing and poor countries are done with general word processing software like Microsoft Office, Microsoft Works, Notepad, WordPad, and QuickOffice [28]. The organizations collect data (project documents, funding applications, surveys, videos, audios etc.) and save through these word processors as well as other file formats. In effect, thousands of records are stored in different file formats and saved either in a project management portal or simply in a local drive. But storing and categorizing these electronic documents become harder thus invoking the need for on-the-fly classification and categorization of the incoming data [6].

Finally, when it comes to applications for hand-held smart devices, the development as well as installation framework mostly favor the open source services [21]. This creates an even more disconnected information technology environment in an organization. In this paper, we propose a fourfold solution:

1. Implementing a new integrated architecture - The architecture will create an internet of technologies i.e. integration of internet and intranet. This allows the users — employees of the organizations — to perform any operation only once in any one of the services (in-

ternet or intranet) and the other will be automatically updated based on the content's permissions settings (private, public or read/write).

2. Designing a new information flow model - The new information flow model is mainly used as a policy framework which starts from the user and go through the intranet to the internet. This will allow the users to use only one service and go through a minimum number of of steps for each task.

3. Developing optimization techniques - Enhancing computer and human interaction is a vital part of the employees' performance of any organization. From office work space to surgical training [24], web based interactive designs are vital part of an efficient system. We propose One-Click-One-Email method as well as some visualization techniques to optimize the tasks and reduce the number of steps involved.

4. Implementing a new on-the-fly document processing method based on "Meta Data Templates (MDTs)" - MDTs are composed of predefined attributes of types of data (project types, application types, survey types etc.). These templates can be applied to each incoming document and determine the appropriate category to store in a well-structured database.

2. RELATED WORK

Soonhee et al. examines the impact of information technology as well as organizational context on employees' efficiency and knowledge sharing capabilities within organizations [19]. The author identifies and analyzes three major information flow mechanisms for employee knowledge sharing: sharing knowledge through interaction among employees, sharing knowledge among colleagues in the group or teams and acquiring knowledge from other departments. The study shows that the impact of information technologies' through user-friendly information systems will ease and optimize the knowledge management and employees' efficiency. Our idea of integrating internet and intranet would optimize and enhance the knowledge sharing. The study by *Buhalis et al.* shows the impact of information technology in tourism management and the impact of internet revolution in the user as well as employees perspective. The study analyzes the consumer demand for the last 20 years and technological innovations that made eTourism as a successful business model for many organizations [7]. Based on this study, collaborative mechanisms are very few and far behind. I3 architecture is specifically build to address these issues. *Jafari et al.* uses digital rights management systems (DRM) to secure data in the field of medical research. The DRM system provides "persistent access control" where the electronic data can be governed by a policy that is expressed in machine readable format [18]. The study proposes a new information flow to secure data in medical research at the same time the information technology architecture reduces the number of steps for each document to go through security checks. Just like this information flow model, we propose the I3 information flow model. Compared to the study [18], our information flow model carries low security overhead and excellent security with minimal management. The study [17] discusses the enhancement of human-computer interaction using EyeTracking technology thus optimizing the

training environment. Our architecture uses several visualization techniques to enhance the users' experience.

A review study by *Liu et al.* discusses the key issues in the structured document retrieval (SDR) in engineering document management. The study concludes that SDR can make positive impact on engineering document management process from the beginning of document preparation to delivery in the future [23]. Our implementation follows the same structured document management with the on-the-fly document processing. *Rodriguez et al.* studies the communication, control, and coordination problems in a distributed development environment. They propose that to reduce the communication's effect on distributed teams and groups, the system should include communication tools like chats and instant messages for enabling synchronous and asynchronous communications like threads and forums. The technologies should also include coordination and control aspects for the employees to streamline the communications. Most of all, the study makes an important point of "close integration often builds on proprietary data models that lock in users with one supplier", hence they recommend open source software for the information services [27]. Selecting appropriate information technology tools is suggested in [12]. The study identifies the factors that contribute to efficient knowledge management tools that include determining system requirements, using and testing the tools in the development phase thus allowing multiple opportunities for feedback and interaction, developing the tools to approximate the structure as well as information workflow of the entire systems and replacing the existing knowledge management system with the new developed systems by the new knowledge management approach "burning the bridges". In our paper, we consider both of these ideas and select appropriate tools (open source as well as proprietary) for communication and collaboration. Finally, the suggested architecture in this paper is motivated by the new approach to the technology architecture — proposed in [5] — called internet of things. In this paper, the methodology uses internet of technologies where all the software and hardware specs of an organization is connected to each other thus promoting communication instantaneously and performing updates simultaneously.

3. INTEGRATED INTERNET AND INTRANET (I3) ARCHITECTURE

In order to solve the problem of disconnected information technology structure, the internet (public web site, web services etc.) and the intranet (local communication network) should be integrated. The I3 architecture will contain three major elements: a storage mechanism with relational database management systems, an internal communication system with local content management and document management tools, and an external communication system with public web site, and smart device applications. Figure 2 shows the outline of I3 architecture. The internal communication system is local and subjected to security and permissions at each level of the network. For example, a document can be set to be visible to only selected group of people in the internal communication system. But the internal communication system will be able to interact with external communication system through Representational State Transfer (REST) or Simple Object Access Protocol (SOAP) web services and Application Programming Interface (API).

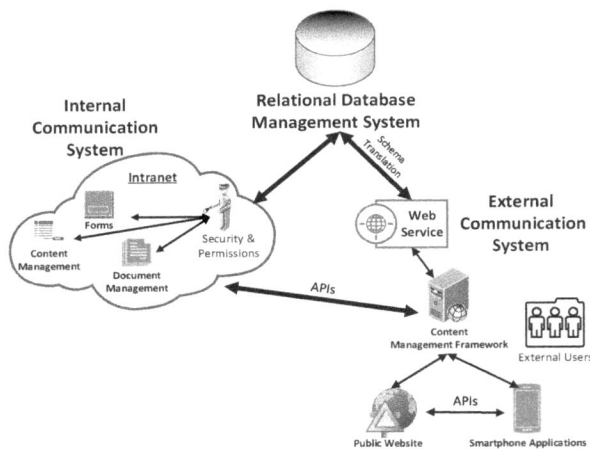

Figure 2: Architecture formed by the integration of internet and intranet services

APIs facilitate an intermediate communication that can get data from the intranet and transfer to the internet for display and vice versa. It also allows users to update both internet and intranet services at the same time. SOAP and REST web services are web APIs that are designed to exchange structured information from distributed web services and computer networks. On the other hand, the external communication system has the web services connected to the content management framework. Open source CMFs are presumably the best for an external website because of their platform independent features and flexible installation and low-cost maintenance. For example, some of the .NET Framework features need special plugins like Silverlight in browsers and some solutions are very particular to internet explorer environment. But open source CMFs can work with all the browsers with default plugins and do not need any special plugins. Compared to proprietary solutions, open source CMFs are widely used by many fortune 500 companies. Plus, proliferation of hand-held smart devices has created demand for dynamic and flexible applications. I3 architecture has the following unique advantages,

- Since RDBMS is connected to both the internet and the intranet, the users have to update the database only one time either through intranet or the public website.

- Document collaboration becomes easier — posting the appropriate documents publicly based on their approval status or properties becomes easier as well.

- Intranet can streamline the communication and collaborations inside an organization and can be connected to the external website thus users will have reduced workload and consume much less time overhead.

- I3 architecture allows new technologies to be connected with it by interacting with the new technologies through specific APIs and web services.

4. I3 ARCHITECTURE IMPLEMENTATION

In order to achieve maximum efficiency in communication and collaboration in any organization, a best information services structure is needed. For the best information services structure, best information technology tools are needed at least with the capability of indirect communications with the other open source or proprietary services. Most important parts of the integrated architecture are RDBMS, web services and development framework, content management systems for websites, document management as well as content management in the intranet, Application Programming Interface (API) and hand-held smart devices application development framework.

4.1 Storage Tools

The relational database management system must have a universal database structure — databases in table or list format. This is also known as "Universe of Discourse" [15] as it helps us to capture semantics of the basic database structure and implement the model on different platforms. Having a universal structure increases the interoperability of the data. As shown in Figure 3, the RDBMS system must be used for

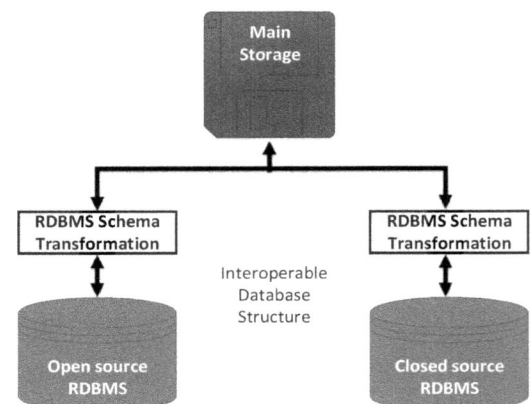

Figure 3: Interoperable Storage Structure

copying and translating the database to a different platform. This translation can occur by RDBMS schema transformation or through an application programming interface.

4.1.1 Microsoft SQL Server and MySQL

Although Microsoft SQL Server has many features as MySQL, MySQL tops the list because of itâĂŹs a platform independent product. MySQL has unique query cache which stores the query as well as the returned result set. In most cases, MS SQL Server can only be used for Windows products and applications where MySQL can be used for more than 24 platforms. But Microsoft offers SharePoint which the best document and content management system [22]. Hence in I3 perspective it is wise to choose Microsoft SQL Server for the RDBMS.

4.2 Internal Communication Tools

Internal communication tools for the information services are nothing but an intranet with flexible at the same time reliable web service framework. The intranet should offer broader solutions for document management as well as content management. In particular, document collaboration should be comprehensive and simple. Team members editing documents, asking other members to provide feedback for the documents, sending approval requests to the team leaders and publishing them are the vital parts of the internal communication tools functionality. Plus, private social networking, blogs and wiki pages are instrumental when it comes to readability and user experience of the system.

4.2.1 SharePoint

Microsoft SharePoint is the widely used as the intranet communication system with comprehensive functionality on document collaboration and content management. 78% of the fortune 500 companies are SharePoint users [11]. SharePoint allows the flexibility of keeping web service to be internal communication system or external communication system. SharePoint allows the developers to integrate the custom windows-based or web-based applications as well as third party APIs to the intranet thus enhancing the functionality of the site. SharePoint also provides blogs and wiki pages that are vital for the internal training and private social networking in an organization. One of the biggest advantages of SharePoint is version control of libraries and lists. Instead of sending multiple copies of a single document back-and-forth in tens of emails, users can easily use the SharePoint document library to see the modifications and keep track of every single version of the library or list item. Several workflows can be designed and customized for getting feedback from colleagues and approval from the team leader. SharePoint has highly customizable permission settings from top level sites to library and lists level items.

List items like event in calendars, documents in document libraries can be automatically posted in open source content management framework like Drupal. Integration possibilities: direct Integration, client-side integration, and usage of web services. Direct integration involves using SharePoint foundation server-side object model which directly interacts with the database inside SharePoint server farm. Client side integration involves using JavaScript, C Sharp and Silverlight where we can extract the data from the database with Language-Integrated Query (LINQ) [25]. But the third option using REST API is the simplest one because of the protocols flexibility with both Drupal and SharePoint server. For the current I3 implementation REST API was used.

4.3 External Communication Tools

External communication tools basically involve web services, web servers, web pages, web content management system and applications for smart devices. Basically, all these are interconnected among themselves as well as the RDMBS. Public website is used for posting documents, results, events, news, mission as well as vision of the organization to the shareholders, donors or to the public. Depends on the RDBMS an organization can select their type of web services and content management systems. There are open source content management systems specific to a particular proprietary web framework. For example, DotNetNuke is an open source content management system which uses .NET framework as their base development platform. But the problem is that it may not be entirely platform independent. So it is better to choose an open source content management solution like Drupal. These open source CMFs are platform independent and they do not need any special plugin or web framework to work on the client side. External communication tools also consist of smart devices'

applications, which extract data directly from the RDBMS or through a markup language like Extensible Markup Language (XML) or JavaScript Object Notation (JSON). XML and JSON are the set of rules for encoding documents or text-based forms in the format of machine-readable as well as human-readable.

4.3.1 Drupal

Drupal is a free and powerful, open source content management framework that is based on the language PHP and distributed under GNU Generic Public License. Worldwide about 2.1% [9] of the websites are using Drupal (e.g. whitehouse.gov, nasa.gov etc.). Drupal is easy to install and it provides us with highly customizable and responsive themes. Installation and maintenance cost for Drupal content management system is very low. For this implementation, Drupal framework was chosen to be the public website. Drupal can also be integrated with all open source frameworks and wide range of proprietary frameworks like .NET framework. Drupal is integrated with .NET framework through JavaScript or SOAP/REST APIs.

4.3.2 PhoneGap and Sencha Touch

PhoneGap [13] is an open source mobile application development framework based on the open source software Apache Cordova. Using PhoneGap, we can develop mobile applications for all the platforms from iOS to Android. Sencha touch is a JavaScript library which is used with PhoneGap to enhance the user interface of the mobile web application. For the implementation of I3 these technologies were used with HTML5 and jQuery for application development.

4.3.3 Big Data Processing

Any management system may face the following drawbacks while managing the overwhelming number of electronic records (images, video files, audio files, spreadsheets, project documents and reports etc.) — Big Data,

1. Complex queries have to be designed in order to store, categorize and search the documents thus effectively slowing down the system

2. Relying on obscure keywords to search the documents and other types of records leads to false-negative [1] or false-positive[2] search results.

3. Since the data is irregular and in different forms, it becomes difficult to parse or interpret.

In this paper, we propose new clustering method to classify and categorize on-the-fly electronic documents. For each document uploaded to the intranet goes through a program with Meta Data Templates (MDTs) for checking the document to determine its destination database or SharePoint (Lists or Libraries). This program module is built with C Sharp language with code optimization (reducing time and space complexities). The program checks whether the documents match one of the templates of various project types (climate change, natural resources, biodiversity etc.). The document type can be determined through naming conventions, document extensions, etc. Once the type of the document is determined, the program aromatically moves the

---

[1]The search query did not return the results that are related to it

[2]The search query returned more results than required

document from one document library to another appropriate document library. This reduces manual work of the employees to classify documents and store the documents.

5. I3 INFORMATION FLOW MODEL

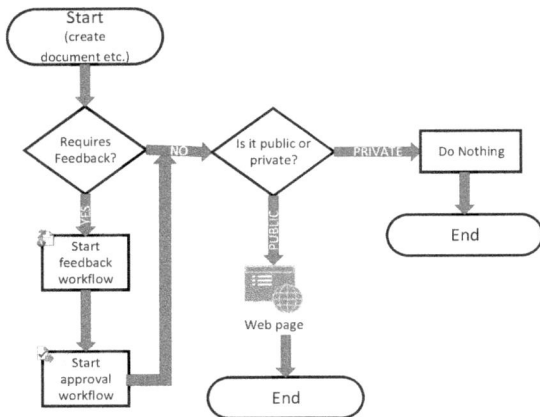

Figure 4: Information workflow model of the implemented I3 architecture

In order to avoid confusion in the information sharing and collection, we propose an information flow model to be followed. If there is no information flow policy to be enforced and documents are building up in the document libraries, then we have to manually identify each document which has to be public and which has to be private. In computer-human interaction point of view, instead of having multiple input and output (update) targets, it will be easier for the user and the processes if there is one simple input and update target. To accomplish it, the following steps are to be followed (see Figure 4):

1. Start the information flow by creating a document, event, announcement etc. in the intranet using Share-Point document libraries or lists (calendar, announcements etc.) and specify the document type at the end of the document title as (public or private). *Note: The other way to do it is to create two new "content types" in SharePoint named public items and private items. Now, we can create documents that belong to a particular type and it will be easier to design SharePoint workflow with the content type information.*

2. Initiate SharePoint feedback or approval workflows depends on the needs of the document (manually or automatically)[3] or you can create alerts for the document so that if the document was modified you will receive an alert through email. *Note: Workflows can be customized to carry out your own actions. New workflows can be designed using Microsoft Visio or SharePoint Designer software.*

3. Check the name of the document in the workflow. If the document title contains the word public or private

---

[3]SharePoint workflows have the options of initiation: manually and automatically

at the end then store or publish accordingly. (We can also check the content types).

4. Send the document through on-the-fly Big Data processing module which is composed of MDTs

5. End the information flow

This information flow is the fundamental structure of the I3 architecture and it can be extended or changed depending on the organizations need. But one thing to remember here is that to use one module as input and update the internal as well as external communication tools.

6. IMPLEMENTATION

The I3 architecture was implemented in the Global Environment Facility (GEF)[2] an international organization and a part of the World Bank Group management. The GEF manages over $4 billion environmental projects in over 180 countries. The organization had two different database repositories for their Project Management Information System (PMIS) as well as their public website. The PMIS system was built using Visual Basic and Microsoft SQL Server 2008 and it stores information about each project as well as their extensive documentation. The public website is built with Drupal and MySQL. A module built with Visual Basic is responsible for transferring the necessary data from MS SQL Server to MySQL. The website is not only an information source about the organization but used for publishing projects documentation and results. Since it's a non-profit international organization, it has to publish the status (ongoing, completed, dropped) of the projects and project documents. These public documents are manually uploaded by the employees of the organization thus resulting in the use of more man-hours and exhausting work of categorizing the documents.

The intranet module was set up using SharePoint 2010 and connected to the public website publishing portal through APIs. A smart phone app called "The Greenline" [3] is developed to get the data from the website. The Greenline is built for tablets (initial version for iPad) using HTML5, CSS, JavaScript and jQuery.

7. OPTIMIZATION TECHNIQUES

In any organization, the ease of access and the ease of use are vitally important for the productivity of employees thus the organization as a whole benefits from it. When it comes to all non-profit international organizations, public sector industries and some private organizations, most of them have extensive bureaucracy that requires each approval process or feedback process have to go to several supervisors through email for it to get approved. These processes involve heavy paper work as well as tens of back-and-forth email conversations. Reducing the paper work and approval steps would streamline the communication and fasten up the approval process. Another problem when it comes to document management systems is that very little or no information available about the average or visual representation of the underlying data as well as document statistics. Even though SharePoint type of intranet systems have lot to offer, without optimizing these small backlogs, the I3 architecture will not be efficient. Thus we propose two fundamental optimization techniques:

1. One-Email-One-Click: reducing the number of emails and clicks required for approving or providing feedback for tasks

2. Visualization of document statistics: providing an interactive tool for analyzing the document statistics using document type, size and other attributes.

7.1 One-Click-One-Email

Most of the tasks in organizations involve a form-type input sheet to enter details about their request. For example, travel approval request, vacation approval request and sick days approval requests are some of the basic examples of the requests come from employees to their team leader or branch manager. Since there are local requests, often times these are done through paper or sending emails back-and-forth to get the full details of the situation. SharePoint offers a wide range of solutions for these particular problems through their in-built, customizable workflows. We can set the workflows to start when there is a new item added to the request, or the existing item is changed, or the workflow can be started manually. Each library and list in SharePoint have three basic functionality: add new item, display item, and edit item. There are three *.aspx* files named *NewForm.aspx, DispForm.aspx and EditForm.aspx*. Through SharePoint designer, we can access all three files and alter the input variables (texts, radio button, check box values and other inputs). This would be the first step towards the technique One-Click-One-Email. Changing those forms according to your content type or the columns in the SharePoint lists can create a form-type of input module for the *NewForm.aspx* file.

One-Click-One-Email means that for single processes, the requesting employee gets only one email as a notification for the approval or rejection, he/she clicks only one button to submit the request after entering the details in the form. With these two steps, the requesting employee's part will be over. The approver will get an email with all the details of the *NewForm.aspx* inputs and he/she will have a "Approve or Reject" button (or link) in his/her email. He/she can either approve or reject the request by clicking that approve or reject button. Interestingly, there will be a multiple-line text box for the comments from the approver. So the approver can comment on whether there needs to be any changes, any suggestions after approval and any reasons for rejecting the request. All in all the process will only take One-Click-One-Email for the requesting employee and the approver.
Note: All of these emails can be configured and initiated by altering the built-in workflows of the SharePoint.

7.2 Visualization

In international organizations, visualizations are very important due to their diverse group of employees from various countries with different languages. In order to accommodate them and make the document management as well as the project statistics should be understandable by all employees regardless of their education, language fluency and other factors. The visualization effect can be clearly felt in a few days of implementation where nearly 100% of the employees were satisfied with the interface. Data management statistics are saved in the Microsoft SQL Server database and copied by a routine and transferred to MySQL database which is the back-end of open source content management framework

Drupal. Using Google Charts—an application programming interface with rich web interface for graphs—this data can be represented fairly easily. With their Google Translate library, we can enable the feature of translating from one language to another.

8. PERFORMANCE ANALYSIS

Our I3 architecture was implemented in the GEF, a nonprofit international organization with over 200 employees in its headquarters at Washington, District of Columbia (DC), United States. The organization had two separate repositories for their project management system as well as for their public website. The project management system was built using visual basic and Microsoft SQL server 2008. The repository stores the information of the projects and their related documents. The public website is built with Drupal and holds public documents uploaded separately by employees. The existing systems do not have any information exchange between them and the employees do not have a private domain to keep their private files and other information. They also did not have any document collaboration mechanism or document management system. All the files were being stored in local drives and folders. The performance analysis will be between the existing system and the new system of I3 architectures. We consider each new improvements proposed in this paper and compare them with the old system to measure and quantify the performance. We consider the following factors,

- Number of emails for document collaboration (creating, editing, approving, publishing)

- Number of duplicates of documents created through those emails

- Time taken from creating a document to publishing it online

- Time spent on manually organizing the documents

- Number of steps involved in important tasks of the organization

8.1 Data collection methodology

For the old system, we used staff emails to get the information about how many documents were created, managed and published. Since each document process involves all members in a team, we gathered emails of one staff member from each team to get the details of number of document duplicates sent in back-and-forth emails and the time it took for them to publish the documents online. For the new system, we used SharePoint 2010 workflows and customized web parts to keep track of the document process and record the time when a document status is updated to "published". This recorded time is nothing but the difference between the time when the document is created and published.

8.2 Impact of I3 Architecture

The new system will have SharePoint 2010 installed and connected to the public website built with Drupal 6 as well as project management system built with VB and MS SQL Server 2008. The implemented I3 architecture will be replacing a number of old document collaboration techniques (sending emails, file circulation, etc.).

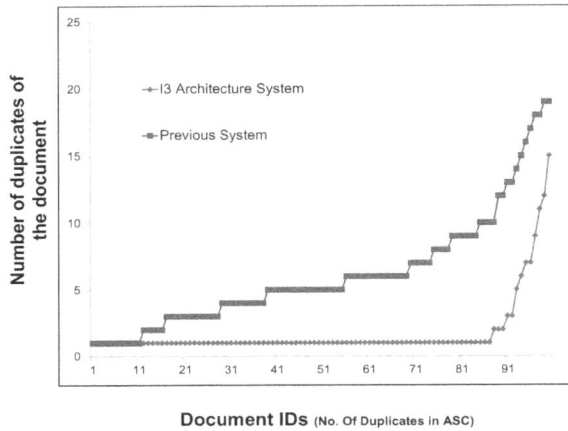

Figure 5: Number of duplicates of each document created by each system

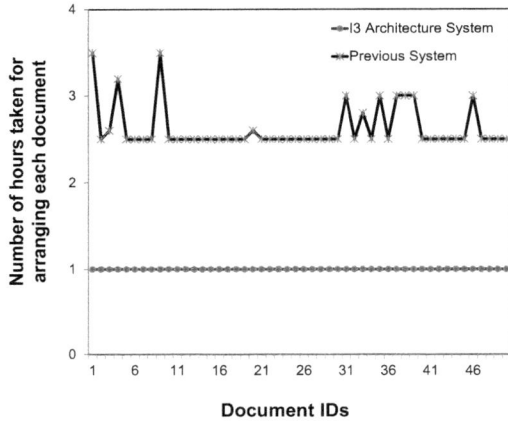

Figure 6: Number of hours (rounded to the nearest value) taken by the employees from creating the documents to publishing online

As we can see in Figure 5 chart that the previous system created several document duplicates for each document and the maximum was 20 duplicates. These documents were ordered in ascending order based on the number of duplicates created for each document. When compared to the old system the new I3 architecture document management system is more efficient (over 85% of the time) when it comes to document collaboration. These duplicates are calculated by the number of emails that are having the same document, with the same document name (without any naming conventions in pace), and the number of document duplicates present in the employees local drive folders.

The chart in Figure 6 shows the number of hours it took for the employees to arrange the edited versions of the documents and publish them online. The hours are calculated by the time taken to finish the work based on their "clock-in" and "clock-out" times.

8.3 Impact of One-Click-One-Email technique

To test the performance of this technique, we chose five important tasks that require approval from the team leader and each time they have to fill-out a form for each task and submit to an employee. The employee then takes it to the team lead and if the team leader suggests any changes, those changes will be notified to the requester by an email or direct conversation. Each time when there is a change in the requirement, the requester has to submit another form reflecting the suggestion and changes from the team leader. As figure 7 shows that the previous systems approval process

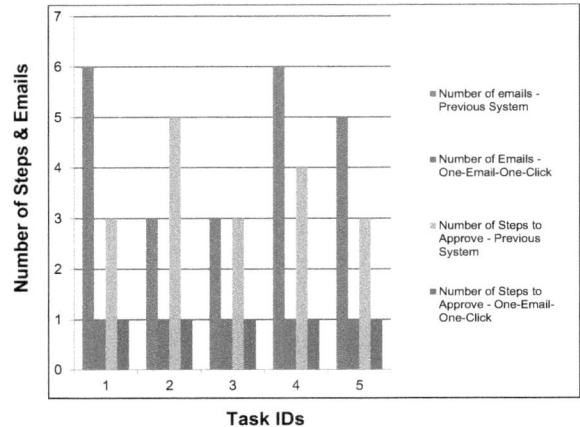

Figure 7: Impact of One-Click-One-Email technique in number of emails and steps involved in 5 different tasks

involving too many back-and-forth email communication as well as steps to go through for the approval. But when it comes to One-Click-One-Email methods all the requester and the team leader will only receive one email and they both have to click one button to submit as well as Approve or Reject the request.

9. CONCLUSION

In this paper, we proposed a new Integrated Internet and Intranet (I3) architecture, an information flow model, a Big Data processing model as well as optimization techniques to enhance and streamline the communication and collaboration in an organization. Through our implementation, we showed that our new I3 architecture gives significant advantage to the employees and streamlines the communication and collaboration process compared to the old system. The suggested information flow model can be used as a fundamental policy for implementing I3 architecture because it reduces the workload of the employees. The Big Data model proposed here is a generic model thus can be used for various scenarios and frameworks. Finally, our optimization techniques produced significant results in reducing the number of tedious steps involved in any given task. In the future, we plan to extend our research to analyze the networking, security and privacy factors affecting our new architecture and information flow models. We also plan to extend the the proposed Big Data generic model for efficient information retrieval and data analysis.

10. ACKNOWLEDGMENTS

We thank the employees of the Global Environment Facility for their cooperation and valuable suggestions. We also thank Prof. Simon Berkovich for providing his inputs to this study on the Big Data processing. Finally, we thank Dr. Abdou Youssef (Chair, CS Dept. at GWU) for providing the required office space and equipment for this project.

11. REFERENCES

[1] Compatibility of Drupal and SQL Server. https://drupal.org/node/1394, 2013.

[2] Global Environment Facility. http://thegef.org/, 2013.

[3] The Greenline. https://itunes.apple.com/us/app/the-greenline/id635788241?mt=8, 2013.

[4] P. Andersen. *What is Web 2.0?: ideas, technologies and implications for education.* JISC, Bristol, UK, 2007.

[5] N. Bari, G. Mani, and S. Berkovich. Internet of things as a methodological concept. In *4th International Conference on Computing for Geospatial Research and Application (Com.Geo), 2013.* COM.Geo, July 2013.

[6] S. Berkovich and D. Liao. On clusterization of "big data" streams. In *Proceedings of the 3rd International Conference on Computing for Geospatial Research and Applications*, COM.Geo '12, pages 26:1–26:6, New York, NY, USA, 2012. ACM.

[7] D. Buhalis and R. Law. Progress in information technology and tourism management: 20 years on and 10 years after the internetâĂŤthe state of etourism research. *Tourism Management*, 29(4):609 – 623, 2008.

[8] J. J. Cadiz, A. Gupta, and J. Grudin. Using web annotations for asynchronous collaboration around documents. In *Proceedings of the 2000 ACM conference on Computer supported cooperative work*, pages 309–318. ACM, 2000.

[9] S. Corlosquet, R. Delbru, T. Clark, A. Polleres, and S. Decker. Produce and consume linked data with drupal! In A. Bernstein, D. Karger, T. Heath, L. Feigenbaum, D. Maynard, E. Motta, and K. Thirunarayan, editors, *The Semantic Web - ISWC 2009*, volume 5823 of *Lecture Notes in Computer Science*, pages 763–778. Springer Berlin Heidelberg, 2009.

[10] J.-M. Dalle and N. Jullien. Open-source vs. proprietary software. *Guest lecture at ESSID Summer School, Cargèse*, 2001.

[11] J. Diffin, F. Chirombo, D. Nangle, and M. de Jong. A point to share: Streamlining access services workflow through online collaboration, communication, and storage with microsoft sharepoint. *Journal of Web Librarianship*, 4(2-3):225–237, 2010.

[12] D. Flynn, E. Brown, and R. Krieg. A method for knowledge management and communication within and across multidisciplinary teams. *Workshop on Knowledge Generation Communication and Management (KGCM 2008)*, November 2008.

[13] R. Ghatol and Y. Patel. Using phonegap plug-ins. In *Beginning PhoneGap*, pages 271–292. Apress, 2012.

[14] P. Greenspun. *Database Backed Web Sites: The Thinking Person's Guide to Web Publishing.* Ziff-Davis Pressl, NYC, USA, 1997.

[15] T. Halpin and H. Proper. Database schema transformation and optimization. In M. Papazoglou, editor, *OOER '95: Object-Oriented and Entity-Relationship Modeling*, volume 1021 of *Lecture Notes in Computer Science*, pages 191–203. Springer Berlin Heidelberg, 1995.

[16] C. Holland, M. Catignani, and C. Porter. *Microsoft SharePoint 2010 Web Applications: The Complete Reference.* McGraw-Hill, NYC, USA, 2011.

[17] J. F. Huston. Making usable documentation: iterative instructions and media richness. In *Proceedings of the 30th ACM international conference on Design of communication*, SIGDOC '12, pages 27–30, New York, NY, USA, 2012. ACM.

[18] M. Jafari, R. Safavi-Naini, C. Saunders, and N. P. Sheppard. Using digital rights management for securing data in a medical research environment. In *Proceedings of the tenth annual ACM workshop on Digital rights management*, DRM '10, pages 55–60, New York, NY, USA, 2010. ACM.

[19] S. Kim and H. Lee. The impact of organizational context and information technology on employee knowledge-sharing capabilities. *Public Administration Review*, 66(3):370–385, 2006.

[20] P. Liamputtong and D. Ezzy. *Qualitative research methods.* GEF, www.thegef.org, 2006.

[21] F. Lin and W. Ye. Operating system battle in the ecosystem of smartphone industry. In *Information Engineering and Electronic Commerce, 2009. IEEC'09. International Symposium on*, pages 617–621. IEEE, 2009.

[22] D. Litchfield, C. Anley, J. Heasman, and B. Grindlay. *The Database HackerâĂŹs Handbook.* Self, France, 2005.

[23] S. Liu, C. McMahon, and S. Culley. A review of structured document retrieval (sdr) technology to improve information access performance in engineering document management. *Computers in Industry*, 59(1):3 – 16, 2008.

[24] G. Mani and W. Li. 3d web based surgical training through comparative analysis. In *Proceedings of the 18th International Conference on 3D Web Technology*, Web3D '13, pages 83–86, New York, NY, USA, 2013. ACM.

[25] E. Meijer, B. Beckman, and G. Bierman. Linq: reconciling object, relations and xml in the .net framework. In *Proceedings of the 2006 ACM SIGMOD international conference on Management of data*, SIGMOD '06, pages 706–706, New York, NY, USA, 2006. ACM.

[26] R. Ramakrishnan and J. Gehrke. *Database management systems.* Osborne/McGraw-Hill, NYC, USA, 2000.

[27] J. Rodrìguez, C. Ebert, and A. Vizcaino. Technologies and tools for distributed teams. *Software, IEEE*, 27(5):10–14, 2010.

[28] M. Willis-Shattuck, P. Bidwell, S. Thomas, L. Wyness, D. Blaauw, and P. Ditlopo. Motivation and retention of health workers in developing countries: a systematic review. *BMC Health Services Research*, 8(1):247, 2008.

The Ethics of Agile Ethnography

Andrew Mara
North Dakota State University
Fargo, ND U.S.A.
Andrew.Mara@ndsu.edu

Liza Potts
WIDE Research
Michigan State University
East Lansing, MI U.S.A.
LPotts@msu.edu

Gerianne Bartocci
Netflix
Los Gatos, CA U.S.A.
gkbartocci@gmail.com

ABSTRACT
In this paper, we describe methods for evaluating the ethics of agile ethnographic research. The large variety of how the term ethnography is used and a lack of a clear scope of associated activities limits the capacity for communication design researchers to accurately and ethically conduct ethnographic field research in various settings. This paper discusses possible ways to conduct ethical ethnography by providing a common definition and case studies to support an agile, rich, iterative, contextual research process.

Categories and Subject Descriptors
H.5.3 [Group and Organizational Interfaces]: Computer supported cooperative work, evaluation/methodology, organizational design

Keywords
Ethnography, Design Research, Agile, Workplace Research, Field Research, Internet Studies

1. INTRODUCTION
Ethnography is a "strategy of inquiry in which the researcher studies an intact cultural group in a natural setting over a prolonged period of time by collecting, primarily, observational and interview data" [1]. Now a popular method in experience design, ethnography can be a problematic term due to the variety of definitions attributed to it. The term ethnography evokes an image of the lone anthropologist surrounded by natives learning about foreign cultures and immersing themselves in the natives' day-to-day lives.

Yet, today ethnography is used to represent many different types of communication design work and research. Some researchers practice it as a large-scale, time-intensive observational and contextual research, while others are using contextual inquiry and diarying in short research/design cycles. The large variety of uses of the term and a lack of a clear definition has limited the capacity for design researchers to accurately conduct ethnography and has limited the field. Critical to these discussions is the necessity of ethical practice guidelines; however, in order to come up with an inclusive ethical framework to consider methodological decisions, it is first important to identify the conceptual horizon within which ethnographic decisions take place. As Fetterman reminds

us, "ethics guide the first and last steps of an ethnography" [2]. If a designer wants to take surer first steps, and knows when to close the final steps of research more confidently, understanding the possible range of ethnographic definitions, settings, potential benefits, and probable pitfalls can create a more effective design research program.

In this paper, we discuss possible ways to conduct ethnography by providing a common and detailed definition to support a rich, iterative, contextual process to inform communication design that foregrounds ethically-aware research practices. The complexity of this research method means that any ethical decisions must be made situationally [3]. First, we will provide a landscape review of ethnography from an anthropological perspective, reminding experience designers of its anthropological roots. Then, we will trace the use of the term tracking its evolution conceptually and practically; for example, today the term is used to represent the methods used in contextual research rather than the body of written work. By historicizing the term, we will then be able to best define a common definition. In conclusion, addressing a call to action from Potts & Bartocci [4] to find an umbrella under which we can place the plethora of contextual design research methods, we will outline the role of ethnography in experience design.

2. DEFINING ETHNOGRAPHY
We will start by summarizing the landscape of traditional ethnography and its anthropological roots. In anthropology, ethnography is represented by the written body of work that arises from years of anthropological fieldwork, an exercise often much too long for typical industry projects. While initially focusing on what Michael Agar defines as a "community approach" versus a "problem approach," anthropologists used to create a detailed recording of any and all aspects of native life. Yet, many of these previously unknown cultures have now been documented, and the discipline has shifted to towards the "problem approach" by adapting their earlier methods to a more agile-style process. This "problem approach" has opened the research process to include the subjects of the research as participants. Such adaptations of ethnography by anthropologists and other social scientists have opened the door for its application to experience design.

"Classical" ethnography traditionally requires "6 months to 2 years or more" in the field [2]. Despite a dominant characterization of ethnography as a long, field-centered, endeavor, there is a millennia-long tradition of alternative ethnography practices from which researchers can draw lessons. Ethnography, which dates back to the third century B.C. and Herodius' History, can be easily divided into four main waves: a first wave of documentation to facilitate colonial conquest; a second wave of ethnography designed to help the cultures being eradicated by colonization; a third wave associated with the postmodern discovery of the power of language; and a final, contemporary wave associated with postcolonial awareness of how identity can be subsumed into damaging power structures [5].

Each wave provides a design researcher a set of tools and lenses with which to view the work facilitated by the tools. The first wave's interest in collecting artifacts and stories from outside cultures still informs how contextual design does its primary work. The second wave's interest in mitigating harm, third wave's interest in the power of language and metaphor, and fourth wave's interest in identity all can provide ways of approaching and re-approaching the use of ethnography in design research. The broader notion of ethnography we base our definition upon centers upon systematized observation of authentically motivated activity performed with locally available materials through locally meaningful symbolic activity. Although our use of ethnography involves qualities from each of the four waves of ethnography as outlined by Claire [5], our discussion of ethics in regards to these practices involves the strategic choice of conducting systematic observation in short cycles, with opportunities to share and correct build into each iterative cycle.

3. AGILITY

Although agile ethnography draws lessons from the long ethnographic history we detail, its origins as a practice also has roots in experience design. Today some researchers practice ethnography as a large-scale, time-intensive observational and contextual research, while others are use contextual inquiry and diarying in short research/design cycles.

This variety of uses of ethnography makes the term hard to define, and limits the capacity for design researchers to apply ethnographic principles that could benefit their projects. Instead of providing an exhaustive definition (something that seems unwise, considering the history of large-scale shifts in associated practices), we instead want to focus on how a process akin to agile programming might attune the researcher to a wider range of strategies in conducting ethnographic research.

Agile programming, which altered the process of programming away from a creating polished product with minimal bugs and full features, and instead toward more compressed cycles of failure and overcoming failure, informs our switch away from a definitive sense of boundary marking for ethnography. Instead, we advocate for an agile ethnographic method that embeds ethical evaluation throughout the process so that course corrections can be integrated at moments of inevitable breakdown and failure. By viewing failure and breakdown as useful, agile ethnography can help design researchers integrate local knowledge into an iterative design practice. Also, by extracting the most salient aspects of ethnography, such as rich field observation and careful micro-methods, researchers can extract lessons and discern best practices. These best practices will support an agile and iterative ethnography more suited to an agile design process.

4. ETHICS AND ETHICAL CONCERNS

Ethnography is already a complicated activity, dependent upon "the location where the participant accomplishes whichever tasks need to be studied. Such locations can include offices, schools, hospitals, homes, and shopping malls. In such locations, it is the job of the researcher to understand the context in which this work is taking place. Researchers are encouraged to 'co-design the system with users'" [4]. Researchers, by their very presence become part of the work scene they are observing. Responsible researchers acknowledge that their presence ultimately shifts the organization, workplace, or network they are observing, and align

their work with the ethical goals and imperatives of these aggregations of people and purposes. Towards this end, researchers implement protocols that alert their collaborators to possible benefits and potential pitfalls of the research, and enjoin those being observed to clarify their activities and the meaning of those activities. Each step of the research process should be shared as openly as possible, so that the data set is rich, open, and accurate. In the end, the researcher is hoping to gather the best data, understand the most useful lenses through which these data might be interpreted, and to alter or create new processes that authentically help users.

4.1 Ethical Principles

When conducting agile ethnography, the lean and iterative nature of the process makes ethical concerns both important and difficult. There are many chances to make mistakes, a positive development for ferreting out task breakdowns; however, each possible mistake is also a chance to erode the trust necessary to carry out research that is both useful and authentic. In order to capture necessary lessons and to rapidly rebuild trust that may erode with each mistake, the researcher must place the concerns of any collaborators front and center. Clay Spinuzzi, in his workplace ethnography text Topsight [6] formulates ethics around the concept of permission (p. 55) and reciprocity (p. 37). Spinuzzi builds the process of gaining (and earning) permission upon particular written genres that capture the intentions of the researcher in a way that members of the researched organization can understand—a research proposal, a consent form, a site letter, and interim report, and a recommendation report (p. 37). While these are all document genres that may be clear to professional and business communicators, they only scratch the surface of possible communication genres that an ethnographer might use to convey the risks and the benefits of cooperation with a researcher. In order to better map out the potential and the peril of these interactions, an ethnographer should map the ethical dimensions of a situation by tracking the three Cs of ethnography during each iteration of an ethnographic research project—consent, context and contribution.

4.2 Consent genres

Spinuzzi provides a case study example of how he as an ethnographic researcher negotiated ethical ground rules in an algorithm-optimizing SEO company through preliminary relationship building, advocate cultivation, and documentation of agreements. In order to negotiate these ground rules, Spinuzzi had to first understand the context of a small company he was studying, which he negotiated with the use of document genres that are common in United States technical companies. If he were operating in other environments with less-stable genres or more widely-varied interpretations of genres were commonplace, the negotiation of ethnographic consent would have to be transacted differently. Key in ascertaining consent is context. Contexts that we are suggesting in our cases involve a wide range varied demands, possible dangers, and potential benefits. Online spaces, transcultural organizations, and multinational workplace settings all involve a range of histories, power, structures, and agencies that need to be accounted for in order to both gain permission, and to outline the potential benefits to everyone.

Rather than using the term "permission," we use the term consent as something that must be constantly maintained. While permission can be both granted and rescinded, once it is granted, there is an assumption that it is given for the duration of the work—something that must be explicitly worked out before a project cycle begins anew (another reason for a shorter project iteration). The final term, contribution, emerges from a sense of reciprocity in the project. The ways that research and the researcher might help those being researched should be front and center during the entire process.

5. SPACES AND CASES

In order to describe how ethical concerns might differ, and how the ethnographer might address these concerns in different ways, the authors will describe three different cases, the ethical constraints, and how they overcame constraints in particular settings. The first site, multinational corporate settings, creates challenges when discoveries of worker inefficiencies might imperil a worker's status or self perception. The second site, transcultural international organizations, poses problems with gaining consent because of the layers of cultural context that are hidden beneath a more simplified organizational identity. The final site, digital spaces, constitutes its ethical challenges around the difficulty of characterizing the significance of online activities. By describing the individual challenges in conducting ethnographic research in each of these settings, we hope to locate the role of ethics as the beginning and end points of agile ethnography cycles.

5.1 Multinational Corporate Settings

Design and agile ethnography conducted in multinational corporate settings consists of day-to-day observation of work patterns to document and solve the specific design problem being addressed. The end goal is to provide a picture of the landscape and design requirements to improve and make that work more efficient through technology to support the end users—employees. But transcultural corporate settings, as ethnographic sites, are riddled with complex social and power relationships that are not only reflective of a top-down hierarchical business structure but also reflective of acquired "power" across the organization due to knowledge gathering and bartering. These complex relationships make it hard to build trust in agile ethnographic exercises because the researchers are dropped into these complex relationships by contributors to that relationship (stakeholders).

Agile ethnographers researching in the multinational corporate settings are faced with a multitude of ethical challenges. First and foremost, our primary obligation "is to do no harm" [7]. Yet, when we say do no harm, we must do no harm to any all that we are working with. It represents a set of layers - the participant, the participant's work circle, project stakeholders, and the corporation, and any external properties potentially affected by the work [8].

We must also consider the constraints put on us as researchers in the multinational corporate setting due to the project parameters and agreement with our client (the transcultural corporation) [8]. Baba reminds us that it clear through Warner's work "that understanding of what is going on in a formal organization requires an intellectual scope that transcends the organization per se, something that is difficult to do if one is too closely aligned with or reigned-in by an organization and its requirements and constraints (e.g., funding contracts, nondisclosure agreements, access negotiations)" [8].

One of the strengths of consulting for transcultural corporations is that we, as outsiders, have an outside perspective and can sidestep some of the organizations' complex power relationships. Yet, this opportunity presents an ethical challenge. When our goal is to not do harm, we, as outsiders, are not always immediately aware of the ways in which we can do harm. It is in this exact situation that an agile ethnographic approach is vital to the ethical success of the project. We must constantly assess and re-assess our knowledge of the organizational dynamics to ensure that our research stays focused on the goals at hand and does no harm.

We do not set out to hurt people; our job is to solve their projects and make their work lives better and easier. But our insertion into their world and our need to document and report on what we have learned has the potential to do harm to participants, their circle, and the organization as a whole. The opportunities to unintentionally hurt people stem from the collection tool and documentation required from the research. As researchers, we want to collect as much information as possible—work samples, recordings, pictures, videos - to ensure we have as much data as possible. But, we are not fully aware of other political exercises going on around us and the hidden agendas of particular employees. The information collected and shared could end up being used or interpreted in a different way.

For example, in the multinational corporate setting, an agile ethnographic team wants to see how employees really work, what tools/objects/references they use to do their job and expect these to be outside of the company process. In fact, researchers want to see these workarounds because they represent tactical problem solving, which can help researchers define root causes to the problem. Yet, because project stakeholders are part of the workplace power structure, they may want to further their own agendas by reporting behaviors or feel obliged to report these "workarounds" or unhappiness/issues as something subversive to the current power structure. For example, on one project, we spoke with an individual that was very concerned about showing us a spreadsheet he created on the side to complete part of the work he needed to complete in another spreadsheet. It took time to get him comfortable with sharing that with us but even then we could not get a copy of the spreadsheet he created. As members of a design team, his spreadsheet represented ingenuity and showed us how he processed information and did his job. Yet, it was outside of the currently established process and could have potentially caused him organizational problems since he was not following that process to the letter. As outsiders, corporate ethnographers are limited in our understanding of these internal power dynamics and the underlying goals for each individual so we need to assume that anything could potentially cause harm to an individual.

Ethical multinational corporation ethnography means that researchers need to consider ethics throughout the process from research design through reporting. And this ethical landscape must include all those that could potentially interact with/touch the information collected and reported. We must also address our own perspective as researchers that have been hired by the organization to address this problem. We are constrained by particular things—like contracts—that will ensure we protect the organization but could also limit our collection and reporting abilities.

For project stakeholders within the multinational organization, the researchers need to clearly articulate to stakeholders the goals for the research and the expected outputs ensuring that clients understand that the goal is not to report on employee effectiveness but to determine how to best solve a larger problem. Researchers must also maintain all control of the research assets that could potentially identify a specific participant (e.g. notes, recordings). "Dissemination and sharing of research data should not be at the expense of protecting confidentiality" [7]. In fact, specifically in these corporate settings, we do not conduct the sessions with our project stakeholders and request that only the consulting research team observe the sessions. The addition of client stakeholders in sessions with participants ensures that current power dynamics will limit interactions and keep participants from being more honest about how they work and it provides the stakeholder an opportunity to use what is reported against that employee. Through the data collection and analysis phase, the research team needs to also temper their knowledge of the participant's work and reported behavior in the observed knowledge about the power dynamics. Most importantly, when reporting findings, information must be abstracted enough such that it could not be traced back to any one participant, even if it means you do not use a quote to punctuate a point. This is a complex negotiation process that must be ongoing and clear to project stakeholder and participants [7].

For participants, the most important way to build trust with your participant (the employee) is to be as transparent as possible throughout the process. The 2012 American Anthropological Association Statement on Ethics states "[a]nthropologists should be clear and open regarding the purpose, methods, outcomes, and sponsors of their work. Anthropologists must also be prepared to acknowledge and disclose to participants and collaborators all tangible and intangible interests that have, or may reasonably be perceived to have, an impact on their work" [7]. We must be clear also about the collection tools being used by a participant so they understand what data could potentially be available. They should always have an opportunity to no to certain collection methods not only at the start of the session but at any point throughout the session. In fact, we as researchers should pay attention to their level of comfort and use our understanding of their behavior (e.g. nervous twitching, eyes straying to a recorder) and offer again as needed to stop that form of data collection.

Agile ethnographic lends itself well to a very appropriate ethical approach. This agility, ability to move on the fly and constantly be evaluating and re-evaluating our collection and analysis, ensures that we have the ability the reflect upon what we are learning about the complex relationships in transcultural corporate spaces and constantly inform our own approach as well as our interactions with our clients (the corporate space and stakeholders). And the next step is to ensure that we are always clear about our position to our participants and clients; "[t]ransparency, like informed consent, is a process that involves both making principled decisions prior to beginning the research and encouraging participation, engagement, and open debate throughout its course" [7]. Once you marry the concept of a reflective transparency into the agile ethnographic approach when considering the ethics of your work, you have the opportunity to ensure that you operating with the highest potential for an ethically successful project.

5.2 Transcultural International Organizations

Transcultural and transnational work sites can challenge some of the assumptions in ethnographic research because of the nature of the international networks created in these organizations. The networks that traverse national boundaries can both create and alleviate problems, depending upon the perspective taken. Ethnographic methods need to account for the ways that cultural expectations and subjectivity in these culture-spanning workplaces complicate ethnographer assumptions. What may seem like a straightforward transaction in one national culture, can take on an entirely different hue in an adjoining national culture.

Despite these differences, networks between nationalities and cultures persist because of their usefulness. Arjun Appadurai [9] characterizes the contemporary assemblage of ethnicities and roles into a single setting as an "ethnoscape." The assemblage can consist of a surprising variety of roles and cultures that bear both the markers of this difference and deploy this difference in a way helps create distinctiveness. Appadurai defines ethnoscapes as "the landscape of persons who constitute the shifting world in which we live: tourists, immigrants, refugees, exiles, guest workers, and other moving groups and individuals constitute an essential feature of the world." [p. 33] Transcultural international organizations succeed insofar as they can negotiate these networks in productive ways that create surprising reciprocities.

In order to deal with some of the vagaries and multiplicities of international ethnography, UNESCO advocated for "ethnographic action research" [10] in order to model how to ethically employ ethnographic research in a way that foregrounds consent and contribution in a contextually sensitive way. The UNESCO report compiles some of the ethnographic methods that have been most useful in international settings (including participant-observer, questionnaires, interviews, and diaries). This compilation acknowledges both the changing nature of international agencies, and some of the useful groundwork that has been laid with contemporary ethnographic research. The emphasis in this document is on elevating all participants to a more egalitarian level with that of the researcher. Ethnographic action research involves a kind of radical transparency that not only involves participants in planning the research, but sharing giving researcher reflections and other preliminary insights with other participants to help guide the research process. This kind of radical transparency helps the researcher ask more targeted questions, but also allows for a more through inquiry into the effectiveness of the design research as the process is unfolding.

Ethnographic research on the Green Belt Movement in Kenya involved several of the techniques interacting with a social media coordinator from San Francisco who was preparing both an international social media campaign called "The Size of Wales" and the first ever "Wangari Maathai Day" with a Kenyan and Ugandan staff (itself made up of many different tribes, or what Dr. Maathai called "micronations"). An American interlocutor cautioned me during my investigation of their methods of doing work, as the Green Belt Movement's history involved periods of political conflict and imprisonment that hinged on notions of ethnicity, nationality, gender, and colonial positioning.

The founder of The Green Belt Movement, Wangari Maathai, who eventually received a Nobel Peace Prize for her work in this organization, began the organization as a way of ameliorating the environmental and gender damage that occurred with development and industrialization of the Kenyan nation. Even though Kenya eventually won independence from an English government that created a series of concentration camps for the Kikuyu fighters (Maathai's ethnically-identified group), Maathai still had to struggle to establish her organization because of gender, interpersonal, and regional conflict that was sown during the colonial period. She was thrown in prison for her environmental work and was denounced by the President of Kenya because of the threat she posed to established gender, economic, and political heirarchies. Through a long and difficult history, the Green Belt Movement transitioned from being viewed as an interloping force for outside meddling with development to one which was advocating for a vital and central environmental program (Dr. Maathai, before her passing in 2011, eventually served in Parliament and was the Assistant Minister for the Environment and Natural Resources for President Kibaki) [11].

These historical complications, still far from settled, reflect an organization that connects outside political influences (the West, China, other African countries, multinational corporations, etc.) with a national plurality made up of 42 ethnic micronations. Finding a comprehensive set of rules as an ethical framework is both unworkable and unrealistic. Instead, ethics in this setting involves formulating your ethnographic research as part of the scene that you are surveying, and involves seeing research as an activity that willingly must reciprocate the trust that is being invested into the researcher. Appadurai admonishment to view even outsiders (tourists, refugees, and even ethnographers) as providing important roles of how things function in the scene should guide the work of the ethnographer. Conducting an ethnographic study of the work of the Green Belt Movement meant understanding how the local work of employing Kenyan women in the tree nurseries and planting in-country—work proceeded from the oral and performative genres of the seminar given in local dialects—differed from the internationally-focused work of social media. Both kinds of work happened under the auspices of the same organization, but each activity needed different cycles of research, different methods to tease out where communication could be improved, and different ways of gaining consent and reciprocation.

Like most workplace ethnography, a researcher in an international transcultural setting must both control her/his assets and consider the implications of deploying these assets. Efficiency may not be a primary, or even desirable, goal for a social and environmental justice group. Instead, the researcher should proceed carefully in what my co-researcher and I playfully called "soccer logic." Soccer, which is characterized by short bursts of speed punctuating longer back-and-forth flows, can inform how research proceeds in these complex organizations. The ethical principles that must infuse the research process must account for both long and unstructured as well as short-and-intense sessions. Like other workplace contextual inquiry, the key to ethical ethnography in complex transcultural organizations is to first adopt a position of humility, with the aim to make your research useful to the community you are studying. The problems you are solving are part of the tactics of communities that connect through a particular organization. There are good reasons that these tactics are being used. Because most of this work is so situational and tactical, it is impossible to fully get permission (either through Memoranda of Understanding or through an Institutional Review Board) to document what one might find. Instead, the ethnographer must build trust incrementally. The phase which we encountered during our Kenyan research, "TIA" (This is Africa), which roughly translates to "you aren't in control," applies generally to transcultural organizations. The ethnographer can suggest, but must be very willing to hear no as an answer, even if it is implied.

Consent evolves in a transcultural organization, so the researcher needs to schedule a lot of unstructured time to ascertain where harm and contribution can occur. Using a multiplicity of ethnographic tools mentioned in the UNESCO report, the ethnographer must maintain assets within clear view of the collaborative subjects, and should share reflections where possible, to help participants understand the implications of their participation from the situated perspective of the researcher. Like the corporate researcher that Spinuzzi [12] describes, building trust can be tedious and arduous, but can ultimately lead to more optimal solutions to persistent, and often invisible problems.

5.3 Digital Spaces

Digital spaces can be especially challenging, with regards to ethics. There is a wealth of data on the internet on any number of topics across any number of spaces. Given the availability of data, the ease of collecting it, and the need to understand the context in which these conversations take place. While researchers can easily fall into looking at social networking sites as Big Data repositories, it is important to understand these digital locations as cultures or even a collection of subcultures. Once we can see them as cultural spaces, we can then understand how we can, as researchers, be involved in these cultures in order to understand the participants, interfaces, and systems.

In online ethnography work, we are thankfully past the stage of pioneering [13]. There are several resources available to us to navigate ethical issues in these spaces, including a set of ethics recommendations from the Association of Internet Researchers (AOIR) that can help guide their research. This document, written by Annette Markham and Elizabeth Buchanan, with contributions from the AOIR Ethics Working committee, is freely available online [14]. It is a major update from the earlier ethics guidelines from AOIR, released in 2010. Taking into consideration new devices, the increase in global participation on the internet, and the growth in research into ethical issues, this update serves as a useful resource.

The authors of this document acknowledge how quickly technologies change, and do not espouse a set of rules so much as a present a document that is designed to "emphasize processes for decision-making and questions that can be applied to ever-changing technological contexts" [14]. In doing so, AOIR's document lists six fundamental principles to guide the ethics of internet research. These fundamental principles include understanding "harm" as something that is contextual, human subjects research issues, balancing the needs of research with the rights of subjects, and the deliberative process of ethical decision-making. Each of these principles should be consulted in depth and adopted when conducting research in digital spaces and offline spaces. What makes this document different from other statements on ethnographic research is its focus on public/private content, personhood, and other internet-specific ethical questions.

As with any other kind of ethnographic research, it is critical to understand the communities in which we conduct our research. While many of us practice the "researcher as lurker" technique [15], it is critical to be knowledgeable of the spaces in which we study phenomenon. To gain such an understanding, we need to be participant-researchers. Becoming a participant-researcher online means that researchers must strive to "become immersed in the social situation being studied and should use that experience to try to learn how life is lived there, rather than coming in with a particular pre-formed research question or assumptions about the issues that will be of interest" [16]. Here, too, we must be aware of how our behaviors can alter the ways in which the culture we are studying continues their activities. While it is true that "the only real way to learn to be a researcher is by experience" [13], it is critical that our learnings is not causing harms to the participants we are studying.

So what constitutes harm online? Unfortunately, much like offline ethnography, there are many ways to cause harm. Not announcing yourself as a researcher can be a form of harm if this information would somehow alter the communication between yourself and the participant. Taking on other identities in an attempt to obtain information from participants is also highly unethical. Not taking into account different viewpoints and even dismissing those perspectives that do not match up with your own can also cause harm. Taking in all viewpoints as legitimate can also cause issues. Instead, focusing on "dialogical processes" that can help sort through these views and understand shared norms is important to representing these communities accurately and ethically [17].

It is important to note that the same rules of offline ethnography apply to online ethnography. While some Institutional Review Board (IRB) are now better at understanding internet research, other IRBs are still unclear about how and when to ask for informed consent. If you are going to conduct interviews with participants, you must consult IRB just as you would with offline interviewing. If your work includes accessing privately held content, you need to consult IRB. To be clear, this means that if you are accessing content that requires you to have a password to see it or special access to acquire it, you need to discuss the project with IRB. That said, if the data is publicly available, you could very well find yourself in an ethical dilemma regardless of IRB oversight. As it is noted in AOIR's ethics document, "people may operate in public spaces but maintain strong perceptions or expectations of privacy" [14]. Such binaries of public/private are no longer enough to guide us ethically. This issue is yet another reason why it is of critical importance that researchers understand the cultures in which they are researching.

Publishing information can also create ethical dilemmas. How you will anonymize content to protect your research subjects can be particularly tricky, as search engines can often easily pull up quoted material and connect that material to your otherwise anonymous participant. These "outings" can be dangerous, even for publicly-available data. If your work touches on hacktivism, activism, terrorism, or disaster, publishing identifying information can put your participants at risk. It is important to "recognize that members of a studied group may have mixed feelings about reports published on their activities" [15]. There are some simple questions to ask yourself before publishing any identifiable information:

- Will publishing this piece of information add to the argument?
- Will publishing this identifying piece of information upset or risk my participant?

Considering the proliferation of mobile devices, creating boundaries around what is offline and online is not simple. In an early text on the internet and ethnography, Hine points out that we need to study both: to combine the two requires a rethinking of the relationship between ethnography and space, to take account of the Internet as both culture and cultural artefact" [18].

6. CONCLUSION

Returning to Fetterman's admonition that "Ethics guide the first and the last steps of an ethnography" can help tie the loop between project cycle. By seeking consent first through contextually communicating the possible promise and pitfall of ethnographic research, the researcher can better collaborate and contribute to the workplace that she or he is studying. Whether it is a multinational corporation, an informal online workplace, or an international environmental justice organization, each setting contains its own challenges. Workplaces have intensely-contested economic, juridical, and national interests in play, and creating a process that ties the work of the researcher to the researched individuals and cultures through tight, iterative cycle can serve as a way of keeping the dangers and the promises in full view.

7. REFERENCES

[1] Cresswell, J.W. 2009. *Research Design: Qualitative, Quantitative, and Mixed Methods Approaches*. Third edition. Thousand Oaks: Sage.

[2] Fetterman, D. M. 2010. *Ethnography: Step by Step*. Third edition. Los Angeles: Sage.

[3] Christians, C. 2005. Ethics and politics in qualitative research. In N. Denzin & Y. Lincoln (eds.) *The Sage Handbook of Qualitative Research*. Thousand Oaks, CA: Sage.

[4] Potts, L. and Bartocci, G. 2009. <Methods>Experience Design</Methods> 2009. SIGDOC Proceedings of the 27th ACM international conference on design of communication. 17-22.

[5] Clair, R.P. 2003. The Changing Story of Ethnography. In *Expressions of Ethnography: Novel Approaches to Qualitative Methods*, ed. Robin Patrick Claire. New York: Stat Univrsity of New York Press.

[6] Spinuzzi, C. 2013. *Topsight: A guide to studying, diagnosing, and fixing information flow in organizations*. Austin: CreateSpace.

[7] American Anthropological Association. 2012. Statement on Ethics: Principles of Professional Responsibilities. (November 2012). Retrieved July 26, 2013 from http://www.aaanet.org/profdev/ethics/upload/Statement-on-Ethics-Principles-of-Professional-Responsibility.pdf.

[8] Baba, Marietta L. 2009. W. Lloyd Warner and the Anthropology of Institutions: An Approach to the Study of Work in Late Capitalism. *Anthropology of Work Review* 30, 2 (Fall 2009), 29-49.

[9] Appadurai, A. 1996. *Modernity at Large: Cultural Dimensions of Globalization*. Minneapolis, Minn.: University of Minnesota Press.

[10] Tacci, J., Slater, D., & Hearn, G.N. 2003. *Ethnographic Action Research: A User's Handbook*. UNESCO, New Delhi, India.

[11] Maathai, W. 2006. *Unbowed*, New York: Knopf.

[12] Spinuzzi, C. 2010. Secret Sauce and Snake Oil: Writing Monthly Reports in a Highly Contingent Environment. *Written Communication*, 27 (4): 363-409.

[13] Hine, C. 2005. Introduction. *Virtual Methods: Issues on Social Research on the Internet*. Ed. Christine Hind. Berg: New York.

[14] AOIR. 2012.Ethical decision-making and Internet research 2.0: Recommendations from the aoir ethics working committee. Authors include Annette Markham and Elizabeth Buchanan, with contributions from the AOIR Ethics Working committee. http://aoir.org/reports/ethics2.pdf.

[15] Rutter and Smith. 2005. Ethnographic Presence in a Nebulous Setting. In *Virtual Methods: Issues on Social Research on the Internet*. Ed. Christine Hind. Berg: New York.

[16] Markham, A.N. and Baym, N. 2009. *Internet Inquiry: Conversations About Method*. Los Angeles: Sage.

[17] Ess, C. 2009. *Digital Media Ethics*. Polity Press: Malden, MA.

[18] Hine, C. 2000. *Virtual Ethnography*. Thousand Oaks: Sage.

Linked Open Data for Cultural Heritage

Evolution of an Information Technology

Julia Marden
Pratt Institute School of
Library Information Science
144 West 14th Street
New York, NY
jmarden@pratt.edu

Carolyn Li-Madeo
Pratt Institute School of
Library Information Science
144 West 14th Street
New York, NY
cmadeo@pratt.edu

Noreen Whysel
Pratt Institute School of
Library Information Science
144 West 14th Street
New York, NY
nwhysel@pratt.edu

Jeff Edelstein
Pratt Institute School of
Library Information Science
144 West 14th Street
New York, NY
jedelstein@pratt.edu

ABSTRACT

Communication design encompasses how information is structured behind the scenes, as much as how the information is shared across networks (Potts & Albers). Information architecture can profoundly alter our perceptions of society and culture (Swarts). Today cultural heritage institutions like libraries, archives, and museums (LAMs) are searching for new ways to engage and educate patrons. This paper examines how linked open data (LOD) can solve the communication design problems that these institutions face and help LAM patrons find new meaning in cultural heritage artifacts.

Categories and Subject Descriptors

H.4 [**Information Systems Applications**]: Miscellaneous; D.2.8 [**Software Engineering**]: Metrics—*complexity measures, performance measures*

General Terms

Theory

Keywords

Linked Open Data, Cultural Heritage, User Experience, User interface

1. INTRODUCTION

Communication design encompasses how information is structured behind the scenes, as much as how the information is shared across networks [22]. Information architec-

ture can profoundly alter our perceptions of society and culture [24]. Today cultural heritage institutions like libraries, archives, and museums (LAMs) are searching for new ways to engage and educate patrons. This paper examines how linked open data (LOD) can solve the communication design problems that these institutions face and help LAM patrons find new meaning in cultural heritage artifacts.

Although nascent in practice, many LAMs are beginning to adopt linked open data as a way to organize and disseminate their catalogs of holdings. Linked open data organizes information using four basic rules:

1. Use URIs as names for things.
2. Use HTTP URIs so that people can look up those names.
3. When someone looks up a URI, provide useful information, using the standards (RDF, SPARQL).
4. Include links to other URIs, so that they can discover more things.

For example:
Moby Dick (subject) is a book (predicate) written by Herman Melville (object). We can express this using URIs and RDF triples as:

```
<http://dbpedia.org/page/Moby-Dick>
<http://dbpedia.org/page/Herman_Melville>
<http://purl.org/dc/terms/creator>
```

LOD is freely available to access, download, and use. It is distributed on an open license (1-star); as machine-readable, structured data (2-star); in a nonproprietary format (3-star); made available via World Wide Web Consortium (W3C; 4-star); and is linked to other people's data (5-star). This five-star model, envisioned by Tim Berners-Lee, is the widely accepted framework for evaluating LOD projects[1][?].

While this model does well to evaluate how well the data is structured and shareable, it does not answer the primary question of this paper: how can linked open data help cultural heritage institutions design a communications system that better shares their holdings with the public?

A linked dataset converts a basic catalog of cultural heritage items into RDF triples using a predefined vocabulary[6]. These datasets can then be matched with other RDF triples to offer a richer cultural heritage experience. LOD gives LAMs the opportunity to set their collections free from silos and place them in multiple contexts by pairing them with different LOD sets from around the world. Essentially, LOD allows users to interrelate communication artifacts without needing the interpretation of an archivist, curator or librarian. This ability for users to create their own relationships between artifacts is an important aspect of communication design (What is Communication Design? Clay Spinuzzi)

This paper will examine how LAMs are adopting LOD projects to address five major challenges within communication design:

1. Museums, libraries, and archives often possess specialized or rarefied information. How can they present that siloed information in a way that establishes their collection as a trusted information source?

2. How can these groups combine these siloed collections to create a new and sustainable, high quality datasets on a particular subject?

3. How can these institutions bring their backend development to the forefront and empower other cultural heritage holders to share their collections in a more open network?

4. How can cultural heritage institutions create a better user experience that empowers patrons to draw their own conclusions about cultural heritage artifacts?

5. How can these groups take advantage of the linked open data framework to expand the definitions of what cultural heritage can be?

2. METHODOLOGY

Working from within the framework of Tim Berners-Lee's Five Star model for linked open data, we sought to address common communication design problems faced by cultural heritage institutions, with a focus on how these problems can be resolved through the adoption of linked open data. Our goal is to illustrate how a spirit of openness and an adherence to linked open data web technology standards can benefit both institutions and users.

For this paper we chose to examine linked open data projects from around the world that had a common goal of improving the cultural heritage experience for their users, typically the citizens of a particular nation. Through the examination of their project documentation, applications, and datasets we first considered their contributions to the linked open data community and then grouped them according to the design problem they excelled at resolving through the use of linked open data.

Reflecting the realities of grant-based project development, this survey of the linked open data for cultural heritage landscape includes projects that are incomplete, unfinished or currently still in development. Although not all of these projects would receive a five-star rating on Berners-Lee's evaluation scale in their current state, their project documentation illustrates a dedication to the linked open data movement and a strong adherence to its standards. Furthermore, each of these projects would rate within the spectrum of the traditional five-star rating system.

The following research reflects the projects we found most exemplary of a particular design problem. It is by no means a complete survey of the linked open data landscape.

3. OPENING SILOED INFORMATION TO ESTABLISH AN INSTITUTION AS A PUBLISHER OF HIGH QUALITY DATA

Many institutions have the potential of turning information that was previously only used for internal purposes – such as cataloging information – into distinctive and informative datasets. These datasets, built off of years of institutional growth and careful work can benefit both the institution and the larger community by expanding the semantic web and establishing an institution as a trusted source of high quality data. The most robust of these datasets have been converted into RDF triples and are shared via an open API or through a SPARQL query endpoint. These linked open data requirements also enable users to have greater accessibility, while this access is lighter and easier to handle for the hosting institution. The Library of Congress and The Hungarian National Library are two national libraries who have released datasets, one to maintain the value of their already well-used cataloging information and the other to promote their more siloed collection to an international audience.

Beginning in 2009, the Library of Congress (LOC) converted its famous subject headings and authority names into linked open data through the Library of Congress Linked Open Data Service porta[12]. This project is part of the larger Bibliographic Framework Plan, an initiative to encourage libraries to transition their collections from MARC records towards RDA and linked open data[15].

The goals of the LOC's Linked Open Data Service are twofold, benefiting both the Library itself as well as human and machine users. With a linked open dataset, users can download authority names and files in bulk, which results in fewer taxing downloads on the LOC's web servers. These users can now also link to the LOC's data values and utilize the LOC's concept and value relationship mapping within their own metadata[20], all at no cost.

For individual human users, the Linked Open Data Service portal's search tool works similarly to the traditional authorities portal but features more information, an updated look, and a simplified results pages. Searching under a related name (e.g., Lady Day for Billie Holiday), users are taken directly to the authority file where popular LOC information can be found; the file's URI, links to alternative formats, and exact matching concepts from other schemes are also provided.

For the LOC, its only logical to coin authoritative and reliable URIs from existing vocabularies and authorities. In order for the LOC to maintain their influence among catalogers it was imperative that they convert their authorities into linked open data.

The success of the LOC's Linked Open Data Services is multifaceted. Through exposing its authority files to linked open data, the LOC has increased the relevancy of its holdings for a new generation of users. Along with updating their dated Authorities portal it connected its holdings to other libraries and alternative schema, therefore making this corpus of knowledge lighter and more flexible for both the LOC's internal use and for its users.

The releasing of linked open datasets can also increase the influence of smaller libraries in the field, as illustrated in the Hungarian National Library's conversion of its authority files, digital library and OPAC to linked open data[16]. Beginning in April 2010, the Hungarian National Library's shared catalog was one of the first successful linked open data projects. The Hungarian National Shared Catalog is part of The European Library, a major provider of cataloging data to the Europeana Project. By sharing their information through the Europeana.eu internet portal this small national library has connected their information with 2,000 other institutions across Europe. The Hungarian National library incorporates RDFDC for bibliographic data, FOAF for name authorities[7],, SKOS for subject and geographical terms, DBpedia name files, CoolURIs and owl:same AS statements[?], which all help weave its dataset into the fabric of the linked open data community. Furthermore the documentation and creation of their linked open data processes has enabled the library to branch into other interesting projects, and has acted has a guide for other institutions.

Releasing accessible, easy to use datasets is a powerful and meaningful project for institutions with large amounts of information. Although the creation of a dataset may appear to be only the first step towards a larger linked open data project, it can be a standalone project with meaningful results for the end user. Linked open datasets are easier to access as well as to transform them into new information, as examined in the next section.

4. COMBINING SILOED COLLECTIONS TO CREATE NEW AND SUSTAINABLE GROUPS OF CULTURAL HERITAGE ARTIFACTS

Individuals, archival collections, repositories, libraries and other cultural institutions of all sizes and prominence in the field can utilize LOD to combine previously siloed collections. Through the utilization of collaborative knowledge bases and linked open datasets, cultural heritage institutions can enrich their own collections through collaboration, or even foster the creation of a new, authoritative and sustainable subject specific datasets. Alternatively, an existing cultural heritage institution can offer their patrons additional context for understanding their collections by integrating preexisting linked open datasets into their websites and apps, and by encouraging patrons to forge new connections.

A small but ambitious project laid the framework for some of the best practices for the creation and linking of open data. Civil War Data 150 (CWD 150) championed for public engagement, collaborative app development and the growth of a collaborative knowledge bases such DBpedia or in the case of this project, Freebase[8].

A partnership between the Archives of Michigan, the Internet Archive, and Freebase, CWD150 was a multifaceted project that encompassed, and planned to encompass, a number of different data sources, tools, and applications as well as a social media component. Along with promoting the digitization of archival documents from the Civil War, CWD150 championed the adoption of linked open data and the strengthening of Freebase. Libraries, archives, museums, and even individual researchers were encouraged to contribute data to the projec[?].

The issues that led to the termination of the project are not stated anywhere on the project's website, but it can be assumed that this ambitious project did not have the staffing necessary to fulfill all of its goals.

An ongoing project that has received continued funding and growing interest in the Linked Jazz Project. The Linked Jazz Project utilizes linked open data technologies in order to enhance the discovery and understanding of cultural heritage assets. Through processing of archival jazz interview transcripts from disparate institutions the project follows linked open data web standards from the minting of new URIs to the development of RDF triples and the creation of a powerful API. Transcripts are first exposed to natural language processing tools, which pull out full names (entities) and partial names. These entities are then mapped against DBpedia, and previously unrecognized entities have URIs created for them[21].

Utilizing a crowdsourcing tool, these annotated transcripts are then analyzed by users who assign relationships between the interviewee and the names mentioned in the transcript using a linked open data friendly vocabulary. These relationships are then available as RDF triples, an API and a network visualization[1]. Through the analyzing of transcript data and the exposure of this data to linked open data technologies the Linked Jazz Project works to expose the relationships of the jazz community and introduce these relationships to a larger audience.

Finally, the LOCAH project[3] was an effort to publish data from the finding aids of Archives Hub and the catalogs of more than 70 major UK and Irish national libraries[2]. LOCAH, like PCDHN is an example of multiple institutions collaborating to merge their data together in order to create new research paths for their users[4].

In a brief feature article on the project, Adrian Stevenson describes its value as allowing the development of new channels into the data. Researchers are more likely to discover sources that may materially affect their research outcomes, and the hidden collections of archives and special collections are more likely to be exposed and used[?]. Variations in the data from institutions posed a challenge to end-users; although the libraries and archives providing the data adhered to standards, these standards can be hard to implement uniformly and can interfere with machine-processing [23].

Linking Lives[4]expanded on LOCAH by bringing in more external datasets and creating a model for a Web interface that allowed researchers to search the new joined archives by name-based biographical pages. While in concept phase, Linking Lives illustrates the potential richness of a collection based on the holdings of multiple institutions[23]. Linking Lives focuses on individuals as a way into archival collections as well as other relevant data sources[?]. One goal was to expose archival collections to researchers, who might not be familiar with primary sources or who might not think of searching archival collections when starting biographical research.

When institutions embark on a project to collect or join disparate data sources there are a number of considerations that should be remembered during planning. Institutions must be prepared to face issues that can arise from the merging of datasets of different qualities by planning for data cleaning. Additionally, projects will benefit from ex-

---

[1]http://www.linkedjazz.org

tensive funding not only to combat surprise costs such as difficult data merges but also ensure for money to promote and maintain data after it is linked. Contributing to collaborative knowledge bases such as DBPedia or Freebase can also ensure that the project's legacy lives on regardless of funding availability through the coining and publishing of publicly accessible URIs.

However, even with the financial and data challenges, smaller institutions can offer their patrons a much richer experience by linking their datasets with other-related LAMs to provide a richer database for research.

5. BRINGING BACKEND DEVELOPMENT TO THE FOREFRONT IN ORDER TO EMPOWER OTHER CULTURAL HERITAGE HOLDERS

With linked open data in its infancy, a spirit of openness fostered by successful linked open data projects can help to improve user experience, define best practices and foster interest in the technology. The documentation and dissemination of backend development is key to demystifying linked open data for both users and potential creators by explicitly outlining the development of and potential uses for powerful linked open data applications. Linked open data projects such as the projects created by The New York Times exemplify the creation and stewardship of linked open data's future in cultural heritage.

The New York Times has adopted linked open data to maintain and share the newspaper's extensive holdings and is actively encouraging reuse via public APIs[17]. The datasets are based in large part on the newspaper's 150-year-old controlled vocabulary, The New York Times Index, an authoritative, cross-referenced index of all of the names, articles, and items that appear in the newspaper.

As of the spring of 2013, the New York Times has released fifteen APIs, ranging from Movie Reviews to the TimesTags API, which matches queries to the New York Times controlled vocabulary. The documentation for the suite of APIs is hosted in the Developer section of the New York Times website[17], which includes a glance view of the API as well as suggested uses for each API and a forum for users and developers. All of the New York Times APIs are available in a JSON response format and a smaller subset is available as XML or serialized PHP.

The New York Times publicizes its projects through its blog, Open: All the News Thats Fit to print(f)[18]. In addition to creating prototype tools such as Who Went Where, a search engine that enables users to search for recent Times cover- age of the alumnae of a university or college, the New York Times also promotes the use of its APIs and source code. In a blogpost introducing the search engine the step-by-step process behind the creation of a API based application is also explained. Open has been a regularly updated blog since the New York Times Company began its foray into the use and promotion of open source software in 2007.

Who Went Where showcases the value of the New York Times and its APIs, as an elegant example of a straightforward application of these LOD APIs. Who Went Where is a JQuery application that queries DBpedia's SPARQL endpoint. The power of this tool is amplified by the documentation surrounding it, including the source code, which is freely available.

6. USING LINKED OPEN DATA TO IMPROVE CULTURAL HERITAGE USER EXPERIENCE

LAMs have a vested interest in improving user experience for their patrons in order to compete with the other major technological influences on culture– smart phones and the internet. A backend that runs on linked open data can radically alter the traditional library, archive, or museum experience. Several organizations and informal groups have made headway in conceptualizing user interfaces that expand users ability to experience and interact with cultural heritage. Many of these projects are still at a proposal stage, but highlight what can happen when linked open data is integrated with a cultural heritage website or application.

EUscreen, is Europeana's main aggregator for audiovisual media. Building on a network of content providers, standardization bodies, television research partners, and specific user groups, EUscreen provides multilingual and multicultural access to European essential components of European heritage, collective memory, and identity. By its nature, audiovisual media, particularly analog recordings, such as pre-digital television, radio, sound recordings and film, are difficult to access. EUscreen's linked open data pilot was created to address the need to make these artifacts openly accessible to a wide audience of users[10].

EUscreen's content selection policy and metadata framework borrows from existing standards such as the metadata schema of the European Broadcasting Union to tag a multiplicity of content through Europe and encourage exploration, comparative study, and serendipitous discovery. The different metadata models of the contributing institutions (XML, RDF, EBU Core ontology, 4store triple store repository, and SPARQL query)[9] are aggregated into a single EBU Core metadata structure and published to the EUscreen portal[11]. From there Europeana aggregates the content and makes it available through its website. Users can take advantage of this rich linked open data backend to find digital media from dozens of countries, in multiple languages and genres, dating back to the beginning of the Twentieth Century.

On a more conceptual level, the Agora project is a collaborative effort involving several Dutch cultural heritage institutions concerned with historical context and methods of manipulating and redefining context through social media platforms[5].. One major aim of the project is to shift the viewpoint of historical narrative from that of the curator or institution to that of the viewer.

The project's tagline, Eventing History, plays on the concept of inventing history. The project aims to put the power of defining what constitutes a historical event into the hands of app users. Members of the project have expressed the desire to do away with the conventional version of history by creating applications that connect artifacts in disparate collections and allowing users to link and discuss artifacts, locations, and events as they see them[5].

The demo, which is geared for touchscreen devices, allows users to unite objects from multiple collections based on a common historical event or actor. Artifacts which wound up in different collections over the years can now be regarded in the same frame of reference.

The project is ambitious in ideology and scope but technological documentation is not a strong point. Development of the project is partially fueled by the dissertation research of graduate students and the fate of the project beyond participant graduation is uncertain. Although Agora has begun some user interface development, its mark may be more philosophical than as the producer of a usable application.

Rich linked open data empowers users to better navigate cultural heritage collections and draw their own conclusions about the meaning and significance of artifacts.

7. EXPANDING THE DEFINITION OF CULTURAL HERITAGE

In addition to the technical requirements, LOD projects are executed with a spirit of openness and collaboration, that can not only simplify but also redefine the cultural heritage user experience.

We think of the traditional cultural heritage user experience as a consumer experience. Libraries, archives, and museums preserve and curate a cultural heritage experience. Patrons come to each institution to consume that pre-packaged experience. A linked open data project can remove the barriers between curator and cultural consumer.

More and more, governments and private citizens are taking on a role of promoting use and reuse of open datasets. In September 2011, the Dutch Heritage Innovators Network[13] began the Open Cultuur Data [2] initiative to encourage cultural institutions to release their data under open standards and encourage users to develop new uses for this data. They facilitated the creation of datasets from eight organizations: the Rijksmuseum, Amsterdam Museum, EYE Film Institute Netherlands, National Archives, the Netherlands Institute for Sound and Vision, and National Heritage Sites of the Netherlands[19].

The datasets were made public in time to be relevant to developers entering the Apps for the Netherland contest, a government-sponsored nationwide contest encouraging developers to create smartphone apps that would engage users with the rich heritage of the Netherlands. INE hosted several hackathons before the contest deadline, creating a supportive environment for developers to use the new open cultural heritage datasets in the creation of cultural heritage apps with a strong user interface. Thirteen apps were created during the initial contest, including three award-winners:

- Rijksmonumenten.info [3]. This app that allows users to browse more than 61,000 buildings in the Netherlands and take geotagged photos of each building to share via Wikimedia. It won an education award.

- ConnectedCollection [4]. This app that is targeted more toward the cultural heritage organizations themselves, allowing them to install a widget on their site that shows users related objects from partner institutions. They won funding to continue development.

- Vistory [5] This project used a linked open dataset of images and video. Users can discover historical films shot near their location, and contribute to the geotagging of historic videos.

---

[2] http://www.opencultuurdata.nl
[3] http://rijksmonumenten.info
[4] http://www.opencultuurdata.nl/?p=583
[5] http://www.vistory.nl/what-is-vistory.shtml

Each of these apps redefine who is a creator and who is a preserver of cultural heritage. The developers take on a preservation role, and the users gain the ability to draw new meaning and create new understandings of cultural heritage.

However, although these projects exemplify the philosophical intent behind linked open data, many of the datasets used were in unlinked formats. Among government agencies and developers, the spirit of open data is catching on much more quickly than the technical specifications for linking.

Japan has become a leader in linked open government data, hosting the 2011 and 2012 Linked Open Data Challenge Japan [6] along with nonprofit and business leaders. Winners in 2012 developed linked open data apps to improve user experience and discovery. One app tracked the spending of tax dollars in local government; another helped users to explore photos related to the history of Hakodate, the first Japanese port opened to foreign trade.

Japan demonstrates that giving people access to linked open data sets can blur the lines between national and cultural heritage identities. Users can track tax dollars to see how much is spent on a local museum, or gain easier access to primary source knowledge about important periods in history. Their apps have richer potential because the datasets are compatible and reusable using linked data standards.

Looking at these examples, we find that just as the open government data movement could benefit from adopting linked open data standards, cultural heritage LOD projects could benefit from adopting contest models that encourage users to access datasets and transform them into meaningful new experiences for other users.

We believe linked open data has the potential not just to preserve cultural heritage for users, but to offer users new opportunities to understand, manipulate, and recreate cultural heritage experiences. Embracing the philosophy behind open government data, that citizens have a right to access and contribute to data, we believe users have the same right to contribute to their cultural heritage experience.

8. CONCLUSION

As Hart-Davidson and Grabill put it, "Technology drives change because it alters culture." [14] Certainly we've seen this with the advent of mobile devices, but perhaps we haven't paid as much attention to the ways that information architecture has changed our culture. Linked open data offers a new way for cultural heritage institutions to share their holdings with a wider audience, and to change the traditional relationship between the holder of knowledge, the interpreter of knowledge, and the consumer of knowledge. With a strong user interface built upon a linked open data set, users with all levels of expertise can access and analyze information once siloed in many different LAMs. This new way to interpret and access cultural heritage information might allow us to update how we define cultural heritage itself.

9. REFERENCES

[1] Linked data, June 2009.
[2] Archives Hub. Archives hub, n.d.
[3] Archives Hub. Linked open copac and archives hub (locah), n.d.

---

[6] http://lod.sfc.keio.ac.jp/challenge2012/

[4] Archives Hub. Linking lives: Using linked data to created biographical resources, n.d.

[5] L. Aroyo. Agora creating the historic fabric for providing web-enabled access to objects in dynamic historical sequences - isab 2012 site visit, Dec. 2012.

[6] C. Bizer, R. Cyganiak, and T. Heath. How to publish linked data on the web., 2007.

[7] D. Brickley and L. Miller. Foaf vocabulary specification 0.98, Aug. 2010.

[8] Digital Library Federation. Civil war 150: Notes toward a linked data case study, 2011.

[9] European Broadcasting Union (EBU). Metadata specifications, n.d.

[10] EUscreen. About euscreen, n.d.

[11] EUscreen. Euscreen linked open data pilot, n.d.

[12] T. Gheen. Library of congress launches beta release of linked data classification, July 2012.

[13] B. Grob, L. Baltussen, L. Heijmans, R. Kits, P. Lemmens, E. Schreurs, N. Timmermans, and E. van Tuijin. Why reinvent the wheel over and over again? how an offline platform stimulates online innovation. paper presented at museums and the web 2011, philadelphia, pa, Apr. 2011.

[14] W. Hart-Davidson and J. Grabill. The value of computing, ambient data, ubiquitous connectivity for changing the work of communication designers. *Communication Design Quarterly*, 1(1):16–22, September 2012.

[15] Library of Congress. Library of congress linked data service: About, n.d.

[16] National Szechenyi Library. Hungarian national library opac and digital library published as linked data, nd.

[17] New York Times. Api documentation and tools. developer network beta, 2013.

[18] New York Times. Open [web log site]., 2013.

[19] J. Oomen, L. Baltussen, and M. van Erp. Sharing cultural heritage the linked open data way: Why you should sign up. paper presented at museums and the web 2012, san diego, ca., 2012.

[20] Open Metadata Registry. International standard bibliographic description (isbd) elements., n.d.

[21] M. C. Pattuelli, M. Miller, L. Lange, S. Fitzell, and C. Li-Madeo. Crafting linked open data for cultural heritage: Mapping and curation tools for the linked jazz project. *Code 4 Lib*, 21, July 2013.

[22] L. Potts and M. Albers. Defining the design of communication. *Communication Design Quarterly*, 1(1):3–7, September 2012.

[23] J. Stevenson and A. Stevenson. Lifting the lid on linked data: Linked data and the locah project. presentation at european library automation group (elag) conference, prague, czech republic., May 2011.

[24] J. Swarts. Communication design. *Communication Design Quarterly*, 1(1):12–15, September 2012.

Simplifying Complexity: Modeling the Process of Collaboration Between Artists and Scientists

Zoe McDougall[‡], Sidney Fels[¥], Dominic Lopes[§], Heather L. O'Brien[β]

Interdisciplinary Studies Graduate Program[‡], Department of Electrical & Computer Engineering[¥],
Department of Philosophy[§], The iSchool[β]
University of British Columbia, Vancouver, Canada
zedoe@alumni.ubc.ca, ssfels@ece.ubc.ca, dom.lopes@ubc.ca, h.obrien@ubc.ca

ABSTRACT

This paper presents a modal model to describe and facilitate communication design in collaborative settings. This model was conceived of as a tool for understanding the nature of collaboration between artists and scientists in an interdisciplinary case study, but can be used cross–disciplinarily and ultimately prescriptively. The model may reveal shifting patterns of interaction between collaborators over time and through multiple processes. Patterns may be revealed in setting and attaining benchmark goals as well as in general group communication. Different collaborative modes (ontological relationships between collaborators) and modes of being (phenomenological relationship between collaborators) form the basis for sixty collaborative possibilities with two or more collaborators.

Categories and Subject Descriptors

A.0 [**General**]: Conference proceedings.

Keywords

Collaboration, Models, Charles S. Peirce, Communication.

1. INTRODUCTION

Interdisciplinary collaborations are increasingly popular in both academic and professional settings. Additionally, national and international incentives exist to further these pursuits [9]. Such collaborations often promote a group composition that combines scientists and artists, who in the process of collaborating may not only acquire new perspectives on their own work, but collaboratively are better equipped to address larger issues of human experience and understanding [13]. As noted by Lin and Beyerlein [8], despite the importance of collaboration being widely recognized, its nature has remained obscure. The numbers of interdisciplinary collaborations that are taking place are disproportionately matched to the relative scarcity of comprehensive documentation about them. Multiple online and offline communities and forums exist specifically to address concerns between artists and scientists in collaborative relationships. These social constructs largely exist to actively reconcile the historical disparity that has existed between the two fields while approaching an understanding of collaborative

SIGDOC 2013, September 30-October 1, 2013, Greenville, NC, USA.
Copyright 2013 ACM 978-1-4503-2131-0/13/09...$15.00.
http://dx.doi.org/10.1145/2507065.2507069

endeavours. Lin and Beyerlein have identified a need to focus on the nature of interdisciplinary collaboration as it pertains to "social constructs" [8] and Beyerlein et al [1] suggest that social interaction and communities of practice are the optimal unit of analysis. Pursuant to a better understanding of the nature of collaboration and its processes, this paper will: a) outline the development of a modal model of collaboration; b) discuss examples of the model put to descriptive use in a specific case of artists and scientists collaborating (a case study that included engineers and performance artists developing and performing with a real–time speech synthesis interface); c) discuss how the model could be used to prescriptively aid further collaborations.

2. RELATED WORK

Models provide predictive and explanatory power for understanding our interactions with the environment, with others and with artifacts of technology [10]. Several attempts have been made to model interdisciplinary collaboration and as Gentner and Stevens state: recently "[computational] models have moved from early models which emphasize information flow and channel capacity to exceedingly rich, finely structured formalisms for representing both data and processes in a uniform framework" [7]. They identify the technique adopted in models research as "overlap and conquer" [7]. Through collaboration of different disciplines and domains of expertise a "kind of powerful unifying theory" could be arrived at [7]. So it follows that a good model of collaboration would be arrived at through collaboration. After a brief discussion of existing models, we discuss a modal model developed out of collaborative observation and participation, group discussion and trial and error.

There are several existing models of collaboration specific to certain disciplines or multi–disciplines. The next section discusses but a few examples appearing in both linear two–dimensional and three–*n* dimensional form.

2.1 Two Dimensional Models

Bronstein's model of collaboration is outlined in two parts. She identifies consistently appearing components of interdisciplinary collaboration through theoretical literature as it pertains to social work practice (figure 1) and then surrounds those components with identified influences on them (figure 2) [3].

Bronstein's models are linear ones that: a) function as a checklist as to what interdisciplinary collaboration is in the identified context and b) model static influences on collaboration as if they exist in isolation from each other. Bronstein's model does not give us any insight into an actual collaboration. It models general components of, and influences on collaboration but neglects the process and interactive nature of collaboration, which involves people with identified roles and characteristics that can shift and change over time. Components of, and influences on collaboration not only affect the collaboration but also affect each other. The structure of this model is too general to give insight into an actual social work collaboration and too specific to be applicable to collaborations in a wider context.

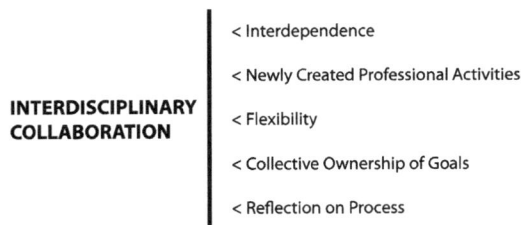

INTERDISCIPLINARY
COLLABORATION

< Interdependence

< Newly Created Professional Activities

< Flexibility

< Collective Ownership of Goals

< Reflection on Process

Figure 1. Components of an Interdisciplinary Collaboration Model (Based on Bronstein, 2003, 299)

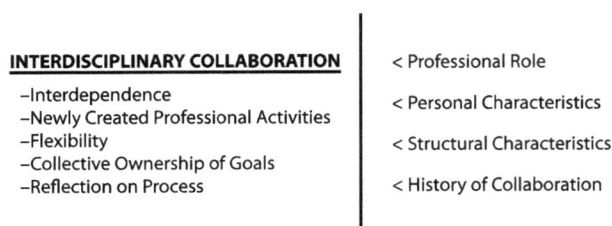

INTERDISCIPLINARY COLLABORATION

–Interdependence
–Newly Created Professional Activities
–Flexibility
–Collective Ownership of Goals
–Reflection on Process

< Professional Role

< Personal Characteristics

< Structural Characteristics

< History of Collaboration

Figure 2. Influences on Interdisciplinary Collaboration (Based on Bronstein, 2003, 303)

Another model of collaboration is the Seven Layer Model of Collaboration developed by Briggs et al. It shows "seven key areas of concern for designers of collaboration support systems" arguing that the identified areas address collaboration at differing levels of abstraction thereby affording separation of concerns at design time [2]. The seven **layers** of the model are depicted as being connected by *issues and outcomes* (see figure 3).

The model depicts arrows pointing from each **layer** to the one above it: **Scripts** to **Tools**, **Tools** to **Techniques**, etc. Design changes to a layer are said to possibly affect layers below, but not necessarily layers above. At and between each layer, the different issues and outcomes "may be addressed with different concepts, techniques and tools" [2]. The separation of layers is meant to simplify or reduce cognitive load for designers for the purpose of improving completeness and consistency of their designs [2] hopefully resulting in higher productivity in collaborating groups.

Although this model is more process–centred it is still a linear representation of a process that is non–linear. The purpose of the model is to reduce cognitive load on collaboration systems designers but it may be unnecessarily oversimplified or too rigidly dictated. Collaboration is more cyclical and recursive in its manifestations and it calls for a model that better represents its processes and its components.

We model collaboration between artists and scientists based on feedback loops (see figure 4). Reflecting on the case study to be discussed in section 4, we identified three factor classes and nine sub-facets of collaboration.

1. Goals
∧
To achieve

2. Products
∧
To create

3. Activities
∧
To move a group through

4. Patterns of Collaboration
∧
To invoke

5. Techniques
∧
To instantiate

6. Tools
∧
Guide what to say and do with

7. Scripts

Figure 3. The Seven Layer Model of Collaboration (Based on Briggs, Kolfschoten, de Vreede, Albrecht & Dean, 2009, 7)

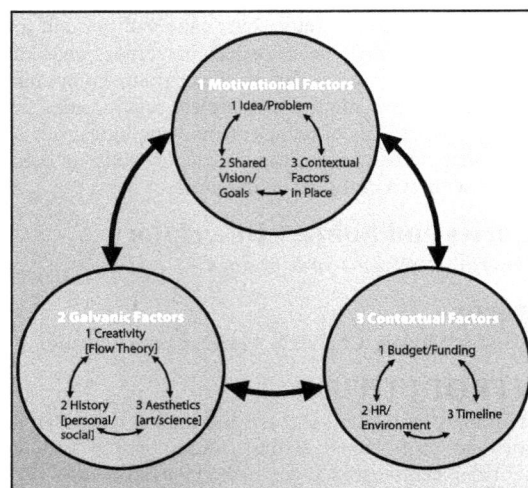

Figure 4. Recursive Phenomenology of Art/Science Collaboration

Figure 4 categorizes the phenomenology of collaboration between artists and scientists as a heterarchical[1] three–class system — each (*factor*) class is further comprised of three sub–facets (each of which can be further ontologically categorized). Factor classes and sub–facets affect and are affected by each other through a recursive pattern of feedback.

1. Motivational factors affect the possibility for collaboration on a practical and inspirational level. They are what provide for the qualitative possibility of a collaboration to take place.

2. Galvanic factors are the foundation of collaboration. Not only do these ground the collaboration but determine cohesion of the group over time, directly affecting the process and products of collaboration through indexical relationships that point to

---

[1] *Heterarchical* here refers to a structure of categories whereby the pattern of relation between categories is equal and inter–reliant. No one category is more important than, entirely dependent on or independent from any other category.

collaborative directions and help to create a collaborative identity.

3. Contextual factors can further mediate and ground the collaboration. They affect whether a collaboration can happen and/or can continue — they represent an argument for or against collaborating/continuing a collaboration on a practical and motivational level.

During collaboration, possible motivational factors are instantiated in actual galvanic factors mediated by continuing reasonable contextual factors. Each factor class affects and is affected by the other two classes, i.e., without practical and reasonable funding, there will be little or no motivation to collaborate and galvanic factors become moot. If any of the factor classes irreparably falls apart so too does the collaboration.

The structure of this model (each triadic relationship) relates to the three universal (phenomenological) categories outlined in C.S. Peirce's theory of predication further explained in section 3.3 as it relates to the modal model of collaboration — a more practical progression from this model.

Figure 4 'simplifies' the process of collaboration by depicting its complexity on an abbreviated level. A model that reflects the feedback and recursion in collaborative systems is a more accurate representation and therefore potentially more useful but this model is most useful at showing how complex collaborations are at even a root level. What drives a collaboration, what holds it together and what makes it generally possible are intertwined relations on a much more complex scale. While all of these aforementioned models speak of, or to the process of collaboration, representing it as such, they are not useful beyond static description and conceptual utility. A truly useful model and tool would be one that had potentially prescriptive qualities as well as descriptive ones and could accurately shift or change over time with the processes it models.

2.2 *n* Dimensional Models

Donald Campbell proposes a model of a different logical type than previously discussed models. Rather than focusing on components and influences, layers or the phenomenology of collaboration, Campbell focuses on collaborative organization. He proposes a "fish-scale model of omniscience" as the ideal intergroup organization for collaboration (see figure 5). But, he states that "due to the ethnocentrism of disciplines", what one gets instead is a "redundant piling up of highly similar specialties leaving interdisciplinary gaps" [5] (figure 6).

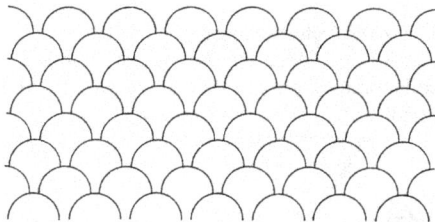

Figure 5. Ideal situation: Fish–scale model of omniscience [5], ©The estate of the late Donald T. Campbell

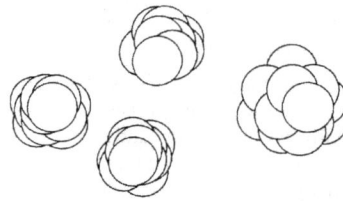

Figure 6. "Present situation: Disciplines as clusters of specialties, leaving interdisciplinary gaps" [5], ©The estate of the late Donald T. Campbell

He states that both of the above figures are oversimplifications, "an analogy in two dimensions of what should be *n* dimensional" [5]. Campbell advocates "collective comprehensiveness through overlapping patterns of unique narrownesses" [5]. This statement parallels the contemporary idea of involving *T and I–shaped people* in collaborations. A T–shaped person "has basic literacy in a relatively broad domain of relevant knowledge (horizontal aspect) along with real depth of competence in a much narrower domain" (vertical aspect). I–shaped people compliment the T's, they are grounded in the practical world of physical materials and tools but have an outstanding capacity for abstract thinking [4]. Campbell's model depicts a conceptual ideal and a reoccurring issue in collaboration group formation. He addresses the larger issue of collaborative member qualifications/abilities, which can ultimately affect every aspect within a collaboration. Regardless of whatever discipline a collaborator originates from, or how structured a collaboration is, collaborative members must have some grounds for communication, which comes from some overlapping comprehensiveness, and/or collaborative aptitude. The actual *people* involved in a collaboration are integral to successfully modeling that collaboration. The people (collaborators) and data collected on the case study followed for the purposes of this research (see section 4) led us to form different ideas about how collaboration works. It showed us that these previously discussed models were limited and we reconfigured our thinking for a new model.

To model the processes and organization of collaborative systems *n dimensionally* with a mind to what could be ideal collaborative relationships, we originally envisioned a three–dimensional physical, structural and conceptual model of interdisciplinary collaboration based in sacred geometry. A model that could provide a functional and theoretical basis for understanding and promoting the processes and organization of collaborative systems as well as its various qualities, aspects and mediated outcomes. The model could be inverted, i.e., represent change over time and collaborative relationships could be mapped on it. However, this model was flawed in that it had little practical or functional basis in the reality of collaborative cases, specifically, our case study. It represented an ideal but no collaboration is ideal. Also the number of faces on the model restricted the number of collaborative relationships, because they were geometrically determined. What follows is a re–envisioning of the three–dimensional model back onto a two–dimensional plane structured as a heterarchical mapping system that can depict 'ideal' and actual collaborative relationships descriptively and ultimately prescriptively.

3. TOWARD A REALITY BASED MODEL OF COLLABORATION

In order to simplify complexity it is sometimes necessary to seemingly complicate it. The process of collaboration is a complex one with unlimited instantiations. Our goal was to develop a model that can be used as a tool — a dynamic map to understanding changing collaborator relationships over time and through processes to look for patterns of collaboration, i.e., patterns that connect or repeat. We wanted to gain insight into how collaborator interactions affect the process(es) and products of that collaboration towards a deeper understanding of what makes for a 'successful' collaboration on various levels. We identified four inadequacies found in other models:

- Unchanging over time and process;
- Too general/non–customizable;
- Too limited in scope or too neat and tidy unlike actual collaboration processes;
- Not practically useful, i.e., conceived of as an afterthought to a collaborative occurrence.

3.1 Developing a Rationale by Definition

3.1.1 Defining Collaboration between Artists and Scientists

Interdisciplinary collaboration is contextual. It is largely defined by its use. For our purposes, we define collaboration between artists and scientists as: an *integrative, interactive* and *recursive* approach to realizing shared goals through sharing knowledge, learning and building consensus across a group of curious, creative and complex process oriented people.

3.1.2 Defining the Building Blocks of a Model (basic process elements)

Figure 7 illustrates the integrative, interactive and recursive relationship of the basic process elements of collaboration stemming from the three keywords in the previous definition.

Aspects of the process(es), depicted in red, affect and are affected by the process and operate at a recursive level. These include basic qualitative possibilities, facts and indexical relations, and group reasoning leading to new or altered process laws for the group. Factors of the aspects, depicted in green, are specific instantiations of incidences between collaborators working in the realms of creativity and possibility, fact and reason. Collaborators *work* at this level within larger recursive process(es). These factors of the aspects form interactive elements within the group that can be represented as more linear relations however contained within the more non-linear process synthesis. The modes of being will be explained further in section 3.3.

In the interest of simplifying figure 7 for utility in a larger modeling system, the basic shape of a triangle can be derived. Within a collaboration there are nested relations that must be accounted for (figure 8). Within a *collaboration* there are *people* who are members of different *fields* of study or expertise. Modeling, however, is not relevant at a collaborative level unless two separate collaborations periodically collaborate with each other.

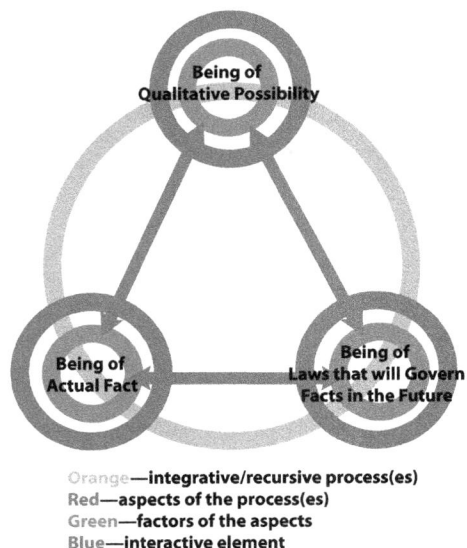

Orange—integrative/recursive process(es)
Red—aspects of the process(es)
Green—factors of the aspects
Blue—interactive element

Figure 7. Defining the Building Blocks of a Model (basic process elements)

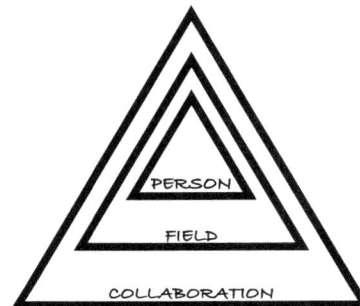

Figure 8. Towards Simplification & Utility: nested relations

Before showing how the model would look at a multi–personnel and multi–field level, it is necessary to discuss further granularity in the form of collaborative modes and different modes of being.

3.2 Collaborative Modes

In looking for salient patterns of collaboration, it is not only important who is collaborating, but in what capacity. We have identified three collaborative modes:

- **1st Order Collaboration**
  Some shared creative act, actual action or analysis — collaborators are in this mode often (when working peripherally on the same issue)

- **2nd Order Collaboration**
  When physically/actively working on some problem together — sporadic occurrences

- **3rd Order Collaboration**
  Intense shared analysis/troubleshooting and creation in a cohesive 'flow'[2] situation — rare and ideal

Collaborative modes are pictorially represented by the alignment of the triangular elements at personal and field levels. A modal model example involving more than one field could be modeled as follows (see figure 9):

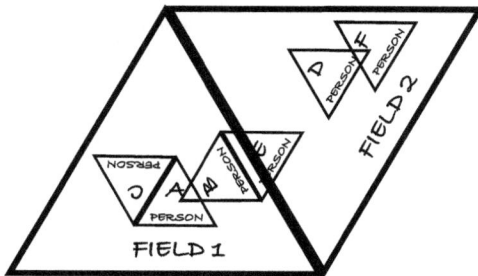

Figure 9. Ontological Field/Personal Level (Relational)

Persons A, B, and C are all members of a field 1 which is in a first order relationship with field 2 at the depicted time, meaning field 1 and 2 are working peripherally and simultaneously on a similar goal. Individual collaborators could be members of more than one field but would generally be working from within one to two fields at a given moment in the collaboration (person E is straddling the two fields depicted while engaging in a 1st order collaborative relationship with person B in field 1). Person B is simultaneously in a 2nd order collaborative relationship with person A who in turn is peripherally working on the same issue as person C. What person B does has a direct impact on person A (2nd order) but A does not directly impact B therefore A is in a 1st order relationship with B (but B is in a 2nd order relationship with A). Person D and F are similarly engaged in a peripheral field.

Figure 9 is a generic example of how a modal model could look. Section 4 will discuss actual model examples from an observed interdisciplinary collaboration/case study between artists and scientists following the addition of a further level of granularity to the model.

3.3 Further Granularity: Different Modes of Being

The triadic structures that operate during collaboration (recursion and feedback) lend to the use of triadic systems theory to attempt to model and understand the relationships inherent to it. Peircian phenomenology and semiotic theory is triadic in structure and presents many possibilities in communication. It is heterarchical rather than hierarchical in structure — no one category is more important or subsumes any other. Phenomenology is:

> "The collective total of all that is in any way or in any sense present in the mind, quite regardless of whether it corresponds to any real thing or not." It "scrutinizes the direct appearances,

---
[2] Flow theory outlines general principles and examples of how to achieve optimal experiences in life [6].

and endeavours to combine minute accuracy with the broadest possible generalization" [11, p.74-75].

Peirce holds the view that:

> "There are three modes of being. We can observe them in elements of whatever is at any time before the mind in any way. They are the being of positive qualitative possibility, the being of actual fact, and the being of law that will govern facts in the future" [12, p.75].

These three modes of being (phenomenological categories) are respectively, firstness, secondness and thirdness (roughly—possibility, fact and reason). Peirce's phenomenology and the semiotic system upon which it is based is a philosophical approach that can lead to shared understanding while not disallowing, albeit encouraging, variation through *possibility* because it is not bound to anything, such as language and is recursive in character. It deals with the nature of being, and like cybernetics and systems theory, can be considered a meta–theory — a theory that includes and can communicate through and about other theories. It is a potentially recursive epistemology in its triadic form and categorical interrelations.

While the three collaborative modes account for ontological/relational interactions at given moments in time, different modes of being account for phenomenological and perceptual relationships. The three modes of being are mapped onto the three sides of the triangle, each colour coded. A 1st order collaborative relationship would only involve one colour/side, while a 2nd order relationship would involve 2 colours/sides and a 3rd order relationship would involve all three colours/sides. A brief description of the three modes of being and depiction of the colour coding follows (figure 10):

- **1st Order Relationships**
  1—creative/imaginative mode (red side)
  2—responsive/action mode (yellow side)
  3—analytic mode (blue side)
- **2nd Order Relationships**
  3,1—imagining solutions, i.e., figuring out, revamping, (adjoined blue and red apex)
  3,2—actively analyzing, i.e., troubleshooting, debugging (adjoined blue and yellow apex)
  1,2—creative act, i.e., building, practicing/performing (adjoined red and yellow apex)
- **3rd Order Relationships**
  3,2,1— *flow* situations, wholly engaged, i.e., intense brainstorming (could be with entire group), performance through a seamless interface (all three sides, red, yellow and blue are involved)

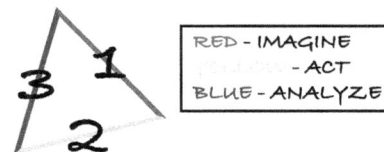

Figure 10. Numbering & Colour Coding 3 Modes of Being

A preliminary example of the modal model depicted at the personal level is as follows (figure 11):

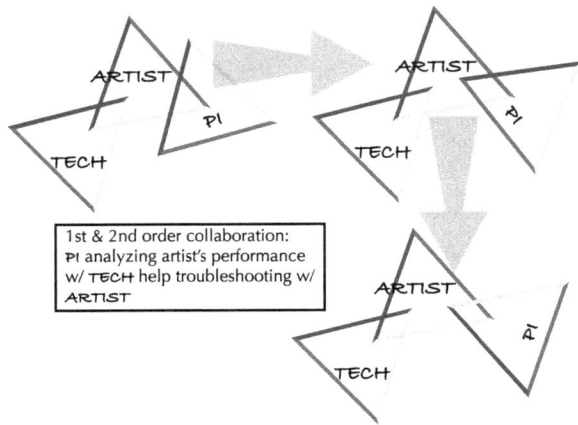

Figure 11. Phenomenological Personal Level (Perceptual)

The artist is in a reciprocal 2nd order active/analytic relationship with the technicians as they set-up and work out any bugs in the system. Simultaneously the artist is in a 2nd order relationship with the principal investigator(s) (PI) as the artist creatively acts on the PI's peripheral analysis of the system (PI is in 1st order collaborative relationship with the artist). If the PI engages the artist to creatively analyze any performance issues, the PI would move into a 2nd order relationship with the artist. The PI could also rotate into a 2nd order active/analytic relationship with the artist or with the technician to troubleshoot any perceived problems.

3.4 Sixty Collaborative Possibilities

There are sixty possible permutations of collaborative possibilities that can be depicted by this model with two or more subjects.

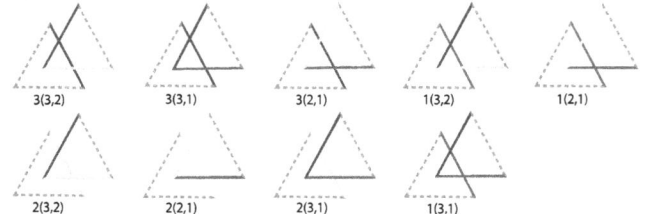

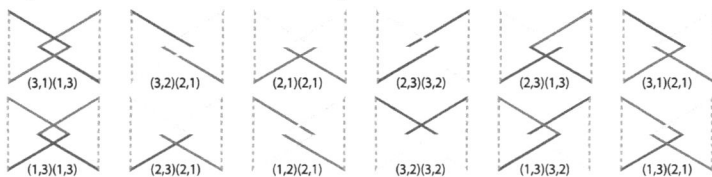

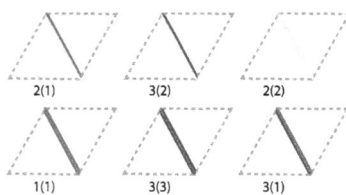

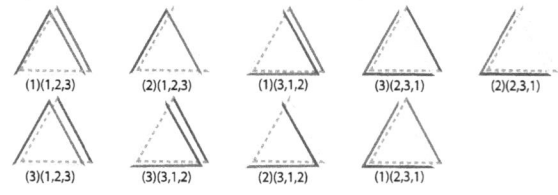

- 5 possible 3rd order collaborative relationships: possible *flow* situations
- 12 possible 2nd order collaborative relationships
- 6 possible 1st order collaborative relationships
- 9 possible 1st/2nd order collaborative relationships
- 9 possible 3rd/1st order collaborative relationships
- 18 possible 3rd/2nd order collaborative relationships
- 1—no collaborative relationship

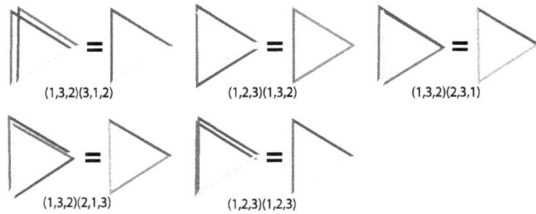

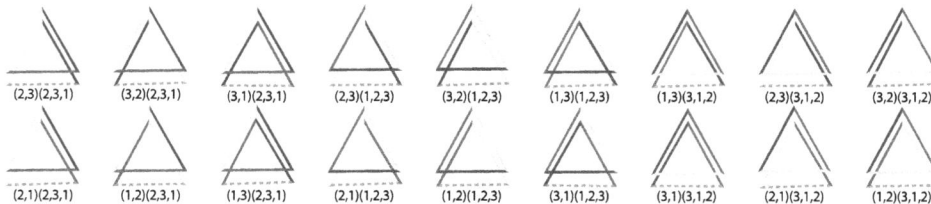

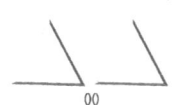

See figure 12 for a map key of the sixty collaborative possibilities.

Figure 12. 60 Collaborative Possibilities (2 or more subjects)

Collaborative relationships can also be expressed mathematically. The number of integers in each grouping indicates the collaborative mode, while the values of the integers, 1, 2 or 3 indicates the mode(s) of being involved.

- One integer=1st order collaborative mode
- Two integers=2nd order collaborative mode
- Three integers=3rd order collaborative mode

Ordered groupings of integers within brackets can also indicate which modes are in relationships with each other. For example:

- (3,1)(1,2,3) Would indicate that person *A* (first set of brackets) is in a 2nd order relationship with person *B* (second set of brackets) who is in a 3rd order relationship with person *A*. *A* is actively analyzing (3) the possibilities (1) presented by *B* and *A* *is* internalizing (1) *B*'s actions (2). *B* is fully engaged (1,2,3) with *A*'s creative analysis.

- Based on the ordering it is also possible to draw the relationship. The 3(blue) from person *A* connects with the 1(red) of *B* and the 1(red) of *A* connects with the 2(yellow) of *B*. The 3(blue) of *B* is unconnected to *A*. See figure 12 bottom row, sixth image.

Section 4 will explain a pictorial and mathematical example of the modal model based on a case study followed for this research.

4. CASE STUDY: DIVAs

The Visual Voice project: gestural control of **DI**gital **V**entriloquized **A**ctors (DIVAs) was a collaborative, highly multi and interdisciplinary research project between scientists, artists and engineers that took place at the University of British Columbia, Vancouver, Canada over four years. In this project, the team created new technologies and approaches to map hand gestures, measured by instrumenting a singer's movements, to control parameters of a digital, artificial vocal tract, enabling the user to sing and speak with her hands in the same way a person uses her vocal tract to speak and sing. Collaborators included a composer, singers, instrumentalists, linguists, cognitive scientists, electrical and computer engineers, software programmers, a fashion designer, a lighting designer, a director, and a librettist. Once trained, a performer onstage can create a chorus of her own vocal tract based voice and her hand generated voice.

DIVAs was observed, recorded and documented (through video, online and written documentation) and some of its collaborators were interviewed. The development of the modal model of collaboration stems from this qualitative research as a tool to further understand the nature of this collaboration and collaborations in general. In looking for patterns in DIVAs we began identifying and modeling benchmarks within the collaborative process. Once more modeling has been completed, we speculate that moments/benchmarks largely devoid of 3rd order collaborative relationships will coincide with turning points in the collaboration, congruous with points of increased and decreased communication (online and off). This speculation has yet to be confirmed or denied.

Rather than looking at 'super–fields' like *art* and *science* or *artists* and *scientists* we found it more productive to look at sub–fields/positions within the particular collaboration like *technical engineers, software engineers, performers, composers*, etcetera. Any given collaborator may occupy several different sub–

fields/positions within the collaborative process over time. Within collaborative processes relationships can simultaneously exist between two, three, four or more collaborators, which shift and change over time. Particular instances of what was relationally and perceptually going on can be mapped and merged together to create a larger picture of the collaborative whole. In the interest of simplicity, basic person and field level relationships should be understood separately before being merged into a larger collaborative picture. The following is a model of one of the final DIVAs performances that occurred at the end of 2011 involving three *performers*, two *composers* (more specifically one composer and one librettist, who will be treated as part of the same field 'composers') and two *technical* engineers. The top portion of Figure 13 shows the three main fields involved in presenting the final performance and their personnel. The bottom portion merges the three fields into a relational pattern and then moves to simplify the resultant pattern by graying out collaborative modes and relationships that are not active.

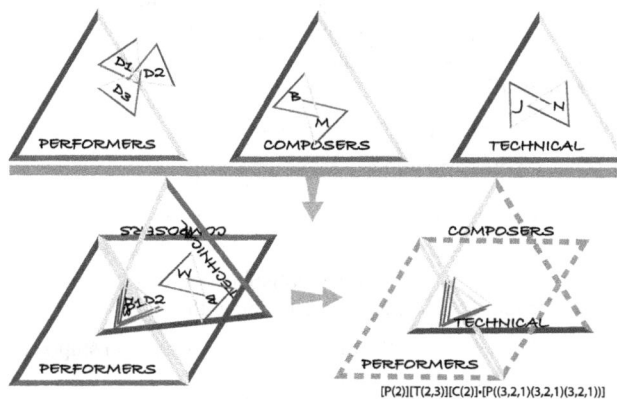

Figure 13. Sample Case Study Models: DIVA

The three performers (D1, D2, D3) are in a 2nd order collaborative relationship with each other (active/creative) and active at a field level in preparation for and entering into their final performance. The composers are in a 2nd order relationship with each other (active creative) in composing and recording their composition. The technicians are in a 2nd order active/analytic relationship with each other in getting the technology to work for the performers and troubleshoot any compositional playback issues. The technical engineers, although existing as individuals to troubleshoot during performance, do not act as individuals during performance. They have little to no bearing on each other (unless there is a problem during performance that both are required to solve) and simply respond to issues that are either within their closest vicinity, or previously agreed to be their responsibility. They need only be represented at field level rather than individually when the three represented fields are merged. Likewise, because the composition is pre–recorded and the composer/librettist cease to be individually active, field level is all that need be modeled during performance. The performers must be represented at both a field and personal level because they affect each other and the technicians if the technology fails. They are peripherally acting on the composition while existing in all three fields — technical, compositional and performance.

Performers move from 2nd order creative/active relationships to 3rd order *flow* relationships with each other as they mindfully respond to each other and the score while being in a 1st order collaborative relationship with the technicians and composers. What the performers do does not affect what the composers do because the composition was pre-recorded and is simply being played back and unless there is a technical malfunction, performers only peripherally affect technicians. The performers themselves could fall in an out of a 3rd order relationship (into a 2nd order one) when cuing on each other or the background composition but for the performance to hang together a 3rd order relationship is predominant.

At a field level technicians are in an active analytic $(2,3)$ 2nd order relationship with the performers and composers. What technicians do can affect the performance if the technology fails. At a personal level they are in a 1st order relationship, as they generally do not affect each other, they are simultaneously keeping the technology running (personal level is not shown in the model as their individual positions are redundant to the performance).

Composers are in an active 1st order collaborative relationship with both the technicians the performers. Because the score was pre–recorded and has been rehearsed to several times it would not actively affect the performers at all times. When performers cued on specific compositional passages the composers are only peripherally affecting the performers.

Mathematically the model can be expressed as:

$$[P(2)][T(2,3)][C(2)]\bullet[P((3,2,1)(3,2,1)(3,2,1))]$$

- [Performers—1st order collaborative relationship/active mode] interacting with
- [Technical—2nd order collaborative relationship/active analytic modes] and interacting with
- [Composers—1st order collaborative relationship/active mode] and
- [Three performers—3rd order collaborative relationships/creative, active, analytic]

5. IDEAS FOR FUTURE STUDY

Because of the modal nature of this model and the possibility for it to be expressed mathematically, there is the possibility for the model to be digitally animated through base triangular components. The components of the model could be programmed to depict the relationships observed and documented in actual collaborative endeavours shifting and changing over time. This movement over time could reveal further patterns of collaboration more fluidly. Any digitally animated expression of the model however, is currently out of the scope of this research. We feel that further testing of the model with actual ongoing collaborations is the most important next step toward possible prescriptive applications of the model. We are continuing to analyze further instances of *collaborative moments* over the duration of the DIVAs case study. Interviews are providing data to identify which 'collaborative moments' would be most informative if modeled in depth. Other existing art/science communities of practice can provide collaborative, social interactions to model to test and explore the possibilities and limitations of the modal model further.

6. CONCLUSION

We believe that further descriptive application of the model is needed in order for it to be refined to possibly function prescriptively for both art–science collaborations and collaborations in other areas. In discovering recurring patterns of collaboration across different projects it will be feasible to reverse

engineer the modal model to function prescriptively as a project progresses. For instance if it is revealed that the majority of collaborative relationships are of the 1st order and fields remain in isolation from each other, the collaboration as a whole may need to be restructured and any indicated restructuring should be undertaken before the collaboration has approached any major benchmark goals. If restructuring is not undertaken soon enough then the fate of the collaboration will most likely be unknown and any resultant products will disappear like so many collaborations of the past and present that are undocumented and do little to further an understanding of the nature of collaboration and the possibilities intrinsic to it. Alternatively, 'successful' collaborations are hard to emulate when no patterns of collaboration are documented or understood. In terms of the DIVAs collaboration, products include photographic, video and audio documentation, written documentation, hardware, software, compositions, and costumes. Challenges to maintaining this documentation and using it to analyze the collaborative model are compounded by time and access to original collaborators who may each possess only some of these products. As with any collaboration, the process can be as meaningful or more meaningful than the resultant products and the process is the easiest 'product' to lose. It is our hope that this modal model or some version of it can be a useful tool in determining the nature of collaboration by discovering and documenting its recurring patterns and pitfalls, thereby preserving the process of collaboration in a more accessible way.

7. ACKNOWLEDGEMENTS

Thanks to the DIVA collaborative group, the UBC Faculty of Graduate Studies, SSHRC, ISGP and the MAGIC (Media and Graphics Interdisciplinary Centre) lab.

8. REFERENCES

[1] Beyerlein, M., Beyerlein, S. & Kennedy, F. (Eds.) 2006. Innovation Through Collaboration. *Advances in Interdisciplinary Study of Work Teams,* (Volume 12). Amsterdam [u.a.]: Elsevier JAI.

[2] Briggs, R. O., Kolfschoten, G., de Vredde, G. J., Albrecht, C. & Dean, D. R. 2009. A seven-layer model of collaboration: separation of concerns for designers of collaboration systems. *ICIS 2009 Proceedings*, Paper 26. Available at http://aisel.aisnet.org/icis2009/26

[3] Bronstein, L. R. 2003. A model for interdisciplinary collaboration. *Social Work*, 48(3), 297-306.

[4] Buxton, W. 2009, July 13. Innovation calls for I–shaped people. *Bloomberg Businessweek*. Retrieved February 20, 2012 from http://www.businessweek.com/innovate/content/jul2009/id20090713_332802.htm

[5] Campbell, D. T. 1969. Ethnocentrism of Disciplines and the fish-scale model of omniscience. In M. Sherif & C. W. Sherif (Eds.), *Interdisciplinary relationships in the social sciences* (pp. 328-348). Chicago: Aldine.

[6] Csikszentmihalyi, M. 1991. *Flow. The psychology of optimal experience.* New York, NY: Harper Perennial.

[7] Gentner, D. & Stevens, A. L. (Eds.). 1983. *Mental models.* Hillsdale, New Jersey: Lawrence Erlbaum Associates, Publishers.

[8] Lin, Y. & Beyerlein, M. 2006. Communities of Practice: A Critical Perspective on Collaboration. In Beyerlein, M.,

Beyerlein, S. & Kennedy, F., (Eds.), *Innovation Through Collaboration. Advances in Interdisciplinary Study of Work Teams,* (Volume 12, pp.53-79). Amsterdam [u.a.]: Elsevier JAI.

[9] Metcalfe, J., Riedlinger, M., & Pisarski, A. 2008. Situating Science in the Social Context by Cross-Sectoral Collaboration. In Cheng, D., Claessens, M., Gascoigne, T., Metcalfe, J., Schiele, B. & Shi, S. (Eds), *Communicating Science in Social Contexts*, (pp. 181-197). Australia: Springer Netherlands.

[10] Norman, D. A. 1983. Some observations on mental models. In D. Gentner & A. L. Stevens, (Eds.), *Mental models* (pp7-14). Hillsdale, New Jersey: Lawrence Erlbaum Associates, Publishers.

[11] Peirce, C.S. 1955. *Philosophical writings of Peirce.* J. Buchler (Ed.). New York: Dover Publications, Inc.

[12] Peirce, C. S. 1992. *The essential Peirce. Selected philosophical writings.* Vol. 1 (1867-1893). N. Houser & C. Kloesel (Eds.). (1998). Vol. 2 (1893-1913), the Peirce Edition Project (Ed.). Bloomington and Indianapolis: Indiana University Press.

[13] Wright A. & Linney, A. 2006. The Art and Science of a Long-term Collaboration. *Alter Ego Conference Papers.* New Constellations, Sydney 17 March 2006. Accessed Sept. 16th, 2009 at http://alteregoinstallation.co.uk/paperspg.html

Visual Research Methods and Communication Design

Brian J. McNely
University of Kentucky
Writing, Rhetoric, and Digital Studies
1315 Patterson Office Tower
Lexington, KY 40506
brian.mcnely@uky.edu

ABSTRACT

Visual research methods include a variety of empirical approaches to studying social life and social processes, including communication and documentation. Developed largely in anthropology and sociology, visual methods typically involve the use of photography, videography, and drawing in qualitative studies of lived experience. Despite the use of visual methods in related fields such as CSCW, HCI, and computer science education, such approaches are underdeveloped in studies of communication design. In this paper, the author provides a historical and theoretical overview of visual research methods before detailing three interrelated approaches that may be productively applied to work in communication design. The author then illustrates how these approaches were adapted to communication design studies in industry and academe before describing implications for future work in this area.

Categories and Subject Descriptors

H.5.3 [**Information Interfaces and Presentation**]: Group and Organization Interfaces – *collaborative computing, computer-supported cooperative work, theory and models.*

General Terms

Documentation, Design, Theory.

Keywords

visual research methods, visual ethnography, WAGR, photo-elicitation

1. INTRODUCTION

Visual research methods, developed primarily in anthropology and sociology, include a variety of empirical means for exploring lived experience *in situ* (see, for example, Banks [3]; Becker [4]; Harper [18]; Morphy & Banks [30]; Pink [32, 33, 34]; Pinney [35]). Today, visual anthropology and visual sociology are thriving subfields that leverage photography, videography, filmmaking, and drawing as integral components of empirical inquiry into social processes and social life. Visual research

methods may also include significant participatory and collaborative components, where research participants use photography, videography, or drawing to represent and reflect upon their own social spaces, artifacts, and interactions. The development of mobile computing technologies, capacious and inexpensive digital storage options, and the decreasing costs of sophisticated photographic and videographic equipment has diminished many technical barriers to implementing visual methods in social inquiry. Yet despite rich traditions of visual research in anthropology and sociology, and despite the use of photography and videography in contemporary computer-supported cooperative work and human computer interaction, empirical visual methods are underdeveloped in design of communication research and theory.

In this paper, therefore, I detail three interrelated visual research methods and describe how they may be used to advance studies and theories of communication design. I follow Spinuzzi in noting that *methods* are the ways in which we investigate phenomena, while *methodologies* entail theories, values, and philosophies that motivate and guide our methods [45, p. 7]. Visual research methods, therefore, may be used to enrich many of the methodological approaches that have been traditionally deployed in communication design. In this paper, I draw on work in writing, activity, and genre research (WAGR; see Russell, [41], for an overview) and the related notion of artifact ecologies from Bødker & Nylandsted Klokmose [6] as a methodological framework for exploring visual methods in communication design. Using visual methods within a WAGR framework entails granular attention to everyday practical activity—to processes in addition to products, and to participant know-how in addition to know-that [see Packer, 31]. In this sense, visual methods may help researchers to uncover and better understand what Shipka called the "mediated action" of communication practice and design—the "varied and various places *in which*, times *at which*, and resources *with which* literate activity is typically accomplished" [42, p. 15].

This paper thus contributes to communication design theory and practice by (a) detailing some of the historical and theoretical foundations of visual methods, (b) by identifying and describing three potentially interrelated visual methods that may be most useful to communication design researchers, and (c) by describing how such methods were applied in cases from both industry and academe. In this way, I hope to build a foundation for the use of visual methods in communication design—a foundation that is currently missing. In the remainder of this paper, I begin by detailing related research in computer-supported cooperative work and human computer interaction. I then describe key developments in empirical visual research methods from anthropology and sociology in order to illustrate some of the breadth and depth of historical and theoretical work in this area. In particular, I describe approaches from ethnoarchaeology, visual ethnography, and photo-elicitation in detail, identifying specific methods from these approaches and how they were applied during communication design research in both industry and academe. Finally, I conclude with some implications and future directions for communication design researchers who may wish to incorporate visual methods into their own work.

2. RELATED WORK

Visual research methods have been used periodically over the last three decades in studies of computer-supported cooperative work (CSCW) and human computer interaction (HCI). CSCW researchers deploying ethnomethodology, for example, have productively used both photography and (especially) videography in data collection, documentation, and analysis of everyday computing environments (see, for example, Dourish [13]; Hutchins & Klausen [20]; Suchman [49]). Additionally, DiSalvo and Vertesi [12], Hall, Jones, Richardson, and Hodgson [17], and Fleron and Pederson [16] have all described the potential of visual methods in studies of human computer interaction. More recently, Farr-Wharton, Foth, and Choi [14] and Jarvis, Cameron, and Boucher [21] have used visual methods (particularly photography) to both study and implement HCI design projects. And work in related areas such as computer science education and game design has similarly advocated for more robust visual research methods, including visual ethnography (see, for example, Fincher, Tenenberg, and Robins [15], and Chan [8]). Research using visual methods in CSCW and HCI has adapted a variety of approaches (described in more detail below) in both studies of practice and design-oriented projects.

In communication design, however, empirical visual research methods have been largely overlooked. In SIGDOC Proceedings (accessed through the ACM Digital Library) searches for "visual ethnography," "visual research methods," "visual methods," and "photo-elicitation" yield no results. This is not to say that communication design researchers have ignored the visual—on the contrary, as a field we have shown particular interest in visual communication from several perspectives. So what accounts for this discrepancy? Visual research methods, typically deployed in rich qualitative studies of practical activity, have been largely absent from studies in affiliated disciplines such as technical and professional communication, composition, rhetoric, and writing studies. Instead, approaches to the visual in these fields have tended to be either orthogonal or parallel to work in visual anthropology or visual sociology. For example, communication design research on information visualization or usability (via eye-tracking devices) might be seen as orthogonal to approaches such as visual ethnography, where photography and videography are used in data collection, analysis, and representation of complex groups over extended fieldwork periods. Similarly, communication design research exploring visual rhetorics might be seen as parallel to empirical visual methods; in studies of visual rhetoric, approaches tend to focus on designed artifacts and their reception and analysis (rather than their production).

Despite the lack of formalized discussion of visual methods within the SIGDOC community, researchers are indeed generating visuals during empirical research and design projects. For example, Racadio, Rose, and Boyd [36] described a mobile application design project informed by anthropology, and they used photography extensively during prototyping, user experience, and implementation. There is an opportunity, however, for more researchers to build robust and theoretically informed incorporations of visual methods into studies of communication design. In particular, visual methods can be more meaningfully deployed throughout communication design research processes, so that photography and videography become more than merely illustrative. In the following section, I describe some of the key developments in empirical visual research methods from anthropology and sociology in order to build a stronger historical and theoretical foundation for adapting such approaches to communication design.

3. DEVELOPMENTS IN VISUAL RESEARCH METHODS

Howard Becker argued that "anthropologists and sociologists have been using photographs ever since the beginnings of both disciplines, but have never been able to agree on just how these images should be used or to what ends" [4, p. 193]. Indeed, much of the overlapping scholarship on visual methods in sociology and anthropology involves comparison, congruency, and even occasional disputes. Historically, the social sciences are disciplines of *words* (see, for example, Clifford & Marcus [11]), and have thus been uneasy with visual representations as valid forms of empirical inquiry. But in the 1960s, social scientists began to better leverage the potential of photography and film for documenting and analyzing aspects of culture and social life [4, p. 194]. Stazs [48], Chaplin [9], and Harper [18] have written histories of visual sociology, while the history of visual anthropology is covered well by Morphy and Banks [30], MacDougall [26], Ruby [39], and Pinney [35]. Beginning in the 1970s and 1980s, anthropology experienced a strong epistemic and reflexive turn, and visual research moved away from traditional (objective-realist) forms of data collection and representation toward explorations of intersubjectivity. More recent work among visual researchers in both sociology and anthropology complicates the ontological properties of photographs, videos, and drawings, taking reflexive approaches to visual phenomena in fieldwork (see Harper [19]; Pink [32, 33, 34]; and Ruby [38]).

Visual sociologists such as Knowles and Sweetman argued that visual methods "include ways of *doing* research that generate and employ visual material as an integral part of the research *process*" [23, p. 5]. Spencer [44] argued that visual material may provide additional, qualitatively different forms of thick description in studies of social life that can help lead to new theories and understandings. Similarly foundational ideas in reflexive visual anthropology may be found in the work of Ruby [39], Banks [3], and Pink [33]. Banks and Pink each draw from their own empirical fieldwork with visual methods to theorize general approaches that have had a lasting impact on the disciplinary development of visual anthropology (and, by extension, related fields). These anthropologists argued that visual research enables wider frames of analysis that may help account for the complex entanglements of human social relations and the spaces and artifacts which mediate them. A common theme in contemporary visual research methods, however, is the understanding that such methods must be deployed within broader methodologies, alongside other forms of fieldwork (such as fieldnotes and interviews, or via the collection and analysis of participant artifacts).

Given the complex and intertwined histories of visual sociology and visual anthropology, a variety of approaches have been developed to address two broad perspectives on conducting visual research: (a) creating visual representations of and about one's object of study as a means for better documenting, analyzing, and understanding participant experience, and (b) working with others to produce or discuss visual representations in a participatory way. What follows is an overview of foundational approaches, accompanied by representative scholarship:

- *Visual ethnography*: Using visuals (typically videography and/or photography) in reflexive processes of intersubjective meaning-making and representation about a particular group or culture. Visual ethnography is a methodology that often combines multiple visual methods (drawing, photography, videography) for exploring lived experience. See Banks [3]; Pink [32, 33].

- *Ethnoarchaeology*: The visual documentation, analysis, and representation of systemic material assemblages. Ethnoarchaeology is a methodology that involves the ethnographic study of contemporary cultures, focusing on relationships between human behaviors and material contexts. See Arnold, et al. [1].

- *Ethnomethodology*: Sociological approach often deployed in CSCW and HCI using (typically) videography to produce detailed analyses of "socially situated talk and visually available behavior" [2, p. 395]. For ethnomethdological studies that theorize visual methods, see Mondada [29], and Ball and Smith [2].

- *Documentary photography*: The use of photography in fieldwork to both document and represent one's object of study. For social researchers (rather than photographers), documentary photography is a visual method (rather than a methodology). See Brown [7]; Harper [18, 19]; Knowles and Sweetman [23].

- *Rephotography*: Also known as repeat photography; involves the *in situ* photographic duplication of an archival (or other extant) image in order to illustrate change (spatial, material, social) over some unit of time. Rephotography is a visual method (rather than a methodology). See Klett [22], and Rieger [37].

- *Content Analysis*: Systematic analyses of (typically) large sets of visual material (e.g., advertisements or archival photographs). Content analysis is a methodology that may involve several visual methods. See Bock et al. [5], and Krippendorf [24].

- *Photo or video diary*: An autoethnographic or participatory method where one compiles visual fieldnotes and perspectives of lived experience. See Chaplin [9]; Mitchell [28]; Pink [33].

- *Photo-elicitation*: An intersubjective method wherein photographs are discussed with research participants in (typically) the context of a semi-structured interview; photos may be produced by the researcher, they may be archival, or even the participant's own. See Banks [3], Lapenta [25], Mitchell [28], Pink [33].

- *Participant drawing*: A participatory method, often used with children, in which research participants produce drawings rooted in lived experience. See Mitchell [28].

- *Photovoice*: Participatory method in which a researcher works with participants to scaffold ways of seeing and representing lived experience through photography; often involves a specific prompt (e.g., participants photograph

what they perceive to be safe community spaces). See Mitchell [28].

By no means is this an exhaustive list of visual research methods or methodologies; instead, I have detailed some of the key forms of visual research currently practiced in the social sciences. While many of these approaches may be adapted to work in communication design, I detail next how aspects of ethnoarchaeology, visual ethnography, and photo-elicitation may be particularly useful in our field.

3.1 Ethnoarchaeology

In ethnoarchaeology, the notion of systemic context entails "the behavioral system in which artifacts participate in everyday life" [1, p. 124]. One of the primary advantages of using photography and videography throughout fieldwork is the ability to capture much more detail than might otherwise be possible through written observational fieldnotes alone. For example, in studies of situated communicative practice, visual methods yield significant granularity, giving researchers the ability to carefully detail and study the material assemblages and arrangements of a given research participant (or group of participants). Over the course of fieldwork, such methods allow researchers to document and analyze changes, adaptations, disruptions, or ad hoc additions to participants' systemic contexts. A significant motive of ethnoarchaeological studies is documenting, tracking, and analyzing inventories of material assemblages. More important, visual documentation of systemic contexts allows ethnoarchaeologists to systematically compare material assemblages across cases. As Shove, Watson, Hand, and Ingram [43] have argued, attending to relationships between people and their systemic context is crucial for understanding how such relationships jointly mediate practice. And visual methods are a primary means for the rich documentation and later analysis of these phenomena. In communication design research, carefully collected visual data can lead to new understandings of how research participants use documentation or devices within rich material contexts.

3.2 Visual Ethnography

In many ways, ethnoarchaeology and visual ethnography may be seen as overlapping (and even complementary) methodologies, since ethnoarchaeology is a variant of ethnographic practice. While it is difficult (and perhaps artificial) to draw clear distinctions between these approaches, there are three important differences. First, unlike ethnoarchaeology, visual ethnography rarely involves systematic documentation of material assemblages. Systemic contexts are certainly explored in visual ethnography, but not typically in the same level of detail seen in ethnoarchaeology. Second, visual ethnography often deploys visual methods in order to understand evolving *processes* of knowledge production, cultural production, intersubjectivity, and lived experience (see Pink [33]). Finally, visual ethnography typically involves sustained fieldwork in a given research site, while ethnoarchaeology is often used in systematic comparisons across field sites. Both ethnoarchaeology and visual ethnography use everyday visual methods in systematic ways: photography and videography, for example, of participants, their processes, and their material environments *in situ*. In ethnographic studies of communication design contexts, therefore, visual methods may help researchers better understand and represent processes of documentation and user experience in rich, granular detail.

3.3 Photo-elicitation

Unlike ethnoarchaeology and visual ethnography, photo-elicitation is a specific field method, and as such, it may be used with a variety of methodologies. Pink argued that researchers "should be interested in how informants use the content of images as vessels in which to invest meanings and through which to produce and represent their knowledge, self-identities, experiences and emotions" [33, p. 82]. The core of photo-elicitation is the collaborative construction of meaning (between researcher and participant) around images (or videos) relevant to the object of study. Photo-elicitation offers design of communication researchers and designers an opportunity to evoke different kinds of participant knowing than they might through verbal interactions alone. When used in conjunction with approaches from ethnoarchaeology and visual ethnography—where images are produced throughout fieldwork processes—photo-elicitation can facilitate salient participant insights across a broad spectrum of experience, from simple member-checks to uncovering crucial forms of participatory understanding. In communication design research deploying visual methods, photo-elicitation may be used in semi-structured or stimulated recall interviews to create pivot points around which researchers and participants may collaboratively understand user experience.

3.4 Applying Visual Research Methods

Ethnoarchaeology's focus on systemic contexts is similar to ethnomethodological work in CSCW and HCI (see, for example, Hutchins and Klausen [20]). For researchers and practitioners in design of communication, using photography to document, analyze, and represent participant artifact ecologies is a robust method for exploring the situations in which, and resources with which, participants use documentation or affiliated applications. Applied to communication design contexts, this approach asks: How do situated artifact assemblages shape and participate in a user's everyday routines? And how might an individual or group artifact assemblage compare to another's? In extended qualitative case studies and visual ethnographies of communication design practice, visual methods facilitate the tracing of change, intentional transformations of documentation, shifts in material assemblages, and participant processes over time. For example, as a given user or group of users becomes more familiar with a documentation task or application, they may change their orientation or perspective—often in subtle ways—and visual methods may help designers and researchers document and explore such processual developments. And using photo-elicitation techniques may aid designers and researchers as they discuss artifact assemblages and processual developments with users. Indeed, participatory visual methods may help researchers and designers develop rich intersubjective understandings and representations of communication design contexts. In the following section, I detail the use of visual methods in communication design studies from both industry and academe.

4. VISUAL RESEARCH METHODS IN COMMUNICATION DESIGN STUDIES

To this point, I have described how visual methods have been used periodically in related fields such as CSCW, HCI, and computer science education, and how research in communication design has largely overlooked foundational work in visual anthropology and sociology. I have provided details about the history and theory of visual research, as well as a sketch of the key visual approaches deployed in contemporary social science in order to address this gap for researchers in communication design. Through more detailed discussion of ethnoarchaeology, visual ethnography, and photo-elicitation, I have identified some specific approaches that may be productively applied to studies of communication design. In this section, I extend the discussion of these approaches by drawing on examples from communication design fieldwork in both industry and academe. I begin by describing the WAGR methodology in more detail, for doing so will delineate the broader strategy driving my use of visual methods in communication design research. I then detail the use of visual methods for studying focus group practice at a media research firm and the relationship between writing and programming among undergraduate computer science students in an advanced programming course. Both examples illustrate how visual methods may provide rich perspectives on—and representations of—participant's communication experiences.

These studies were broadly focused on the relationships between *phronesis*—often tacit participant know-how that helps guide judgment and actions in contingent everyday processes—and activity—unfolding, tool-mediated, and motive-driven objectives enacted through individual and/or collective labor. WAGR is an approach that combines work in rhetorical genre studies and cultural-historical activity theory, and is thus well suited to qualitative studies of everyday practical activity. In WAGR, activities are complex social practices oriented toward a specific *object*: the purpose or linchpin (see Spinuzzi [47]) that brings together people, tools, artifacts, genres, and ideas (see also Russell [40]). These tools, artifacts, genres, and ideas are used in concert as mediational means within a given object-oriented activity and within a given cultural-historical context.

A WAGR methodology, therefore, attends to everyday practical activity and the tools, inscriptions, social connections, and cultural-historical contexts collectively mediating that activity. WAGR approaches account for complex material assemblages, the transformations of inscriptions in actual practice and their instantiations in specific genres, and everyday collaborative actions. The notion of artifact ecologies (Bødker & Nylandsted Klokmose [6]), when coupled with a WAGR perspective, adds careful attention to the systemic contexts in which everyday activities are realized. In WAGR studies of communication design, inquiry follows processes in concert with products and devices, and participant know-how as reflected in situated practice.

WAGR approaches are thus attuned to situated actions and processes that may be analyzed in the data record: these may be observed through traditional qualitative means (for example, in the fieldnotes of a participant-researcher), explained by research participants in semi-structured or stimulated recall interviews, or reflected in a photographic or videographic record (produced either by the researcher/designer, the participants, or both in concert). Ideally, a WAGR methodology is strengthened by a combination of these field methods, giving researchers and designers multiple perspectives on a given activity across multiple observations and contexts of practice. With a WAGR methodology, analysis of the data record may then be pursued in multiple and complimentary directions: through detailed evidence of material assemblages; through participant orientation to those assemblages over time; through the practical, phronetic activity accomplished within those assemblages; and through explorations of the motives driving individual and collective activity toward a particular object.

Visual research methods complement a WAGR methodology in significant ways; through the fieldwork examples that follow, I discuss three such congruencies (see also McNely, Gestwicki, Gelms, and Burke [27] for a visual ethnography of software development guided by a WAGR methodology). First, visual methods allow communication design researchers to construct rich, granular representations of artifact ecologies in everyday practice. For example, by using photographic fieldwork in a manner informed by ethnoarchaeology, we can document and follow the systemic material contexts of our research participants. Stated another way, we can capture and analyze complex artifact ecologies, we can inventory those artifacts and trace changes over time, and we can compare full assemblages across participants with similar or different backgrounds. Second, we can visualize everyday writing work in unprecedented detail, following the transformations of inscriptions (see Spinuzzi [46]) that drive a specific activity. Drawing on work in visual ethnography, we can trace and represent mediated processes and participant know-how. Finally, we can use photo-elicitation as a feedback measure to improve our understanding of participant practice, and to adjust our research focus as fieldwork progresses. For example, by discussing with participants our understanding of their documentation processes as reflected in the photographic record, we can correct misperceptions, gain new insights about participant practice, and refine our understanding of disruptions, ad hoc workarounds, or items we may have overlooked. In the following subsections, I detail how these approaches were adapted in two very different studies of communication design.

4.1 Transforming Inscriptions in Focus Group Research

Over a period of eight months, I conducted an ethnographic study of a media research firm, following a single project among three participants (the director and two project managers), from inception to conclusion (and the public dissemination of their work). The firm has clients in television and digital gaming, primarily, and they are known for developing industry insights about emerging media practices. The project that I studied was an investigation of consumer sentiments about online privacy norms, and this was but one project among several that my participants pursued during the course of fieldwork. As part of their research into online privacy, the firm conducted a series of four focus group sessions with participants in the 18–34 year-old demographic. From a WAGR perspective, their eventual object was a series of professional deliverables detailing findings from their study, lending insights into online privacy concerns among an important demographic. The collective motives behind this work included industry recognition and the beginnings of a program for future client work in the area of online privacy. The assemblages (both individual and collective) mediating activity around this project were incredibly complex (and largely beyond the scope of this paper). I focus here on how visual methods helped me trace a series of written transformations (through attendant artifact ecologies) mediating these researchers' movements from focus group ephemera to formalized findings.

Figure 1 documents a typical focus group artifact ecology arranged by the media researchers I studied. They liked to think of these sessions as fostering attendee creativity, and they provided groups of artifacts and tools to each focus group table in order to facilitate thinking and interaction. Focus group attendees used these tools to generate a series of inscriptions responding to pre-arranged prompts and discussion exercises (mediated by another set of inscriptions, not shown here, that were held by the media researchers and also documented photographically). Following

Figure 1. Collective artifact ecology of one focus group table (four participants).

approaches in ethnoarchaeology, these images help document and represent the material assemblages mediating the experience of focus group attendees. In Figure 2, we can see how initial focus group inscriptions—jottings on butcher paper and sticky notes, visible in crayon and pen in Figure 1—were transformed during full group discussions and interactions by the media researchers (whose handwriting is predominant). Verbal responses from focus group attendees were written (by project managers) on the whiteboards and on large yellow notepads, while sticky note jottings from attendees were placed on the schematic to the right of the image that resembles a traffic light (thus situating specific privacy practices along a "go–slow down–stop" spectrum from green to red). During these 180-minute focus group sessions, inscriptions and verbal interactions were continually transformed as they oscillated between focus group attendees and media researchers; visual methods were instrumental in tracing these fast-moving transformations.

By applying visual ethnography's perspective on social processes and knowledge formation over extended fieldwork, we can see—in Figure 3—how focus group data is further transformed. In this image, a whiteboard schematic (only partially detailed here) represents major project development resulting from nearly three months of analysis of the focus group data detailed in Figures 1 and 2. Stated another way, these inscriptions represent the thematic and formalized transformations of the more ephemeral

inscriptions shown in Figures 1 and 2, and they encompass a whole host of additional inscriptions that I do not have the space to display (email exchanges, qualitative coding trees, analytic memos, notes from brainstorming and debrief sessions, and social media exchanges). Figures 1, 2, and 3 (and a series of related images) were then used in semi-structured interviews with research participants near the end of the project to better understand the motives behind these transformations. I was able to show my participants how I had traced their writing practices throughout the project, and to learn from them how my understanding of the photographic record and observational fieldnotes matched up to their perceptions of work processes. This exercise in photo-elicitation was noteworthy for two reasons: (a) I had documented and understood things about my research participants that they had not been consciously aware of, and (b) their feedback allowed me to refine my fieldwork over the final weeks of the project to focus on further transformations leading to organizational knowledge dissemination.

Indeed, I came to understand the whiteboard inscriptions of Figure 3 as instrumental to the series of final transformations related to this project: It served as an organizational schematic for the industry white paper containing formalized reportage of findings, and it contained key phrases and ideas that were repeated in a series of interviews and articles in the trade press, in a series of blog posts and an interactive information graphic, and through the

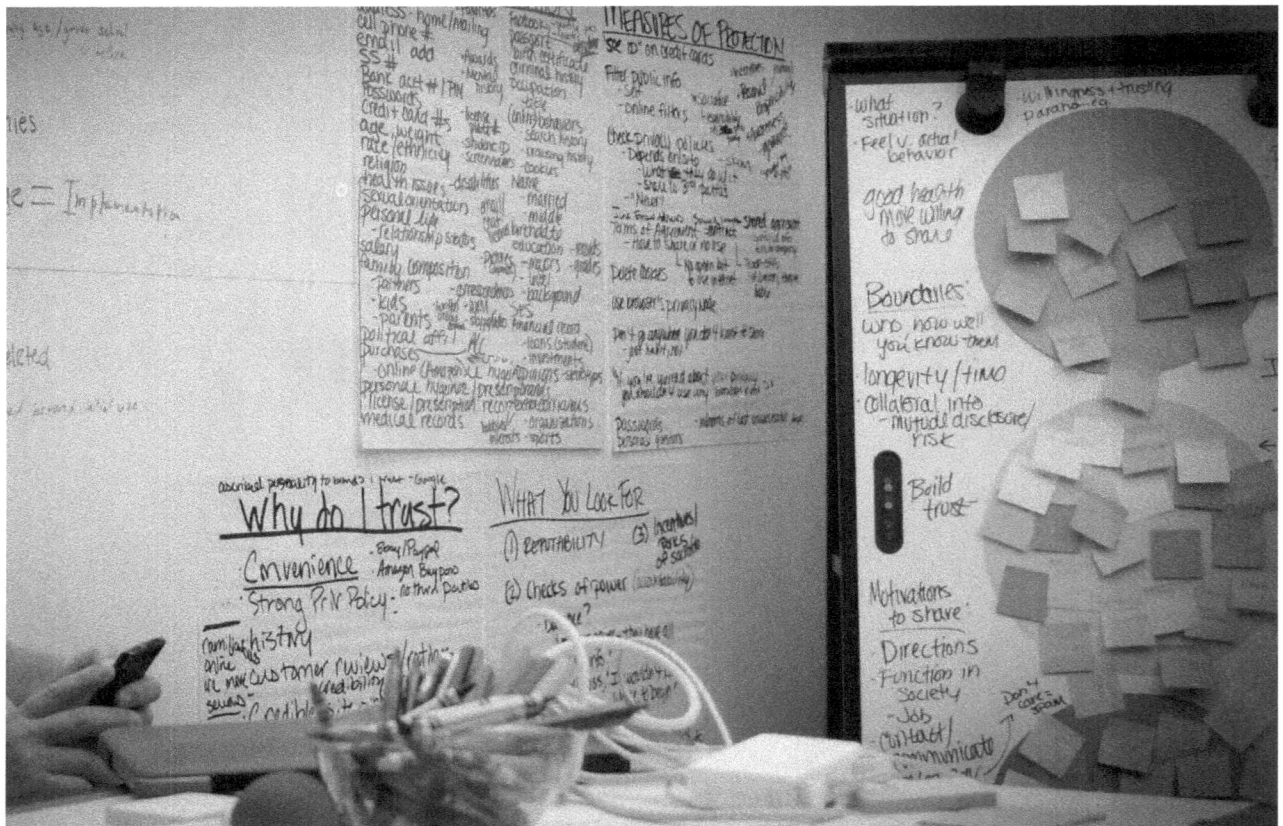

Figure 2. Initial transformations of focus group inscriptions.

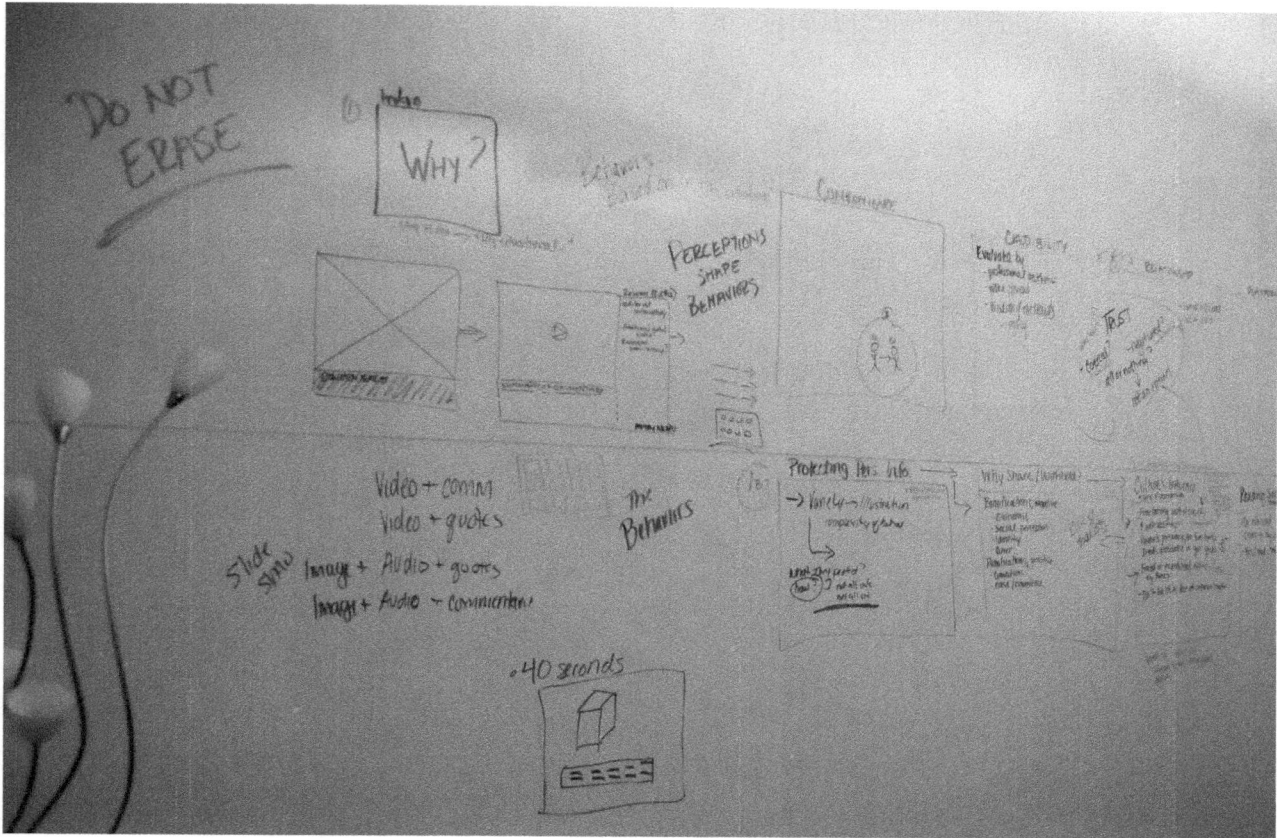

Figure 3. Formalizing focus group findings through further discursive transformations.

atomization of findings via a series of strategic social media posts. In this study, visual methods guided by ideas from ethnoarchaeology and visual ethnography helped me document complex artifact ecologies and trace organizational knowledge through a complex array of layered and transformed inscriptions and genres, while photo-elicitation helped confirm salient observations and directed subsequent research. More important, these visual methods provide rich representations of participant practice, giving other design of communication researchers a visceral sense of how these media professionals worked.

4.2 Writing, Planning, and Small Group Programming Projects

In this example of visual research methods in academe, I describe a different series of written transformations observed during a systematic qualitative case study conducted over the course of a 16-week academic semester. In this project, I explored the role of writing in computer science education by studying a sophomore-level advanced programming course. Taking a WAGR approach, I documented (photographically and in fieldnotes) almost every instance of classroom writing that occurred during the semester. Through a series of three semi-structured interviews conducted with each of ten participants, I explored the relationships between everyday prose, planning, and programming in Java and C#. While evidence of how participants transformed everyday prose as part of complex group programming projects was important, more meaningful findings were generated through photo-elicitation methods during final interviews.

Figure 4 displays a simple sequence diagram created by a small student group (four members) in a class exercise introducing Unified Modeling Language (UML) norms during the tenth week of the semester. This sequence diagram is based on the group's in-progress major project, a system tray program that fetches and displays statistics for a given user of a popular, multiplayer online game. During this 80-minute class session, the instructor modeled UML norms and also worked with each small group to help direct programming decisions and evaluate ongoing progress. While visual methods were significant in documenting writing and planning activities, they were only one aspect of the research process. Indeed, visual documentation coupled with robust fieldnotes created a more holistic understanding of planning and learning processes. This combination of field methods helped me to trace processes, to document those processes visually and verbally, and to better understand how the instructor was teaching and helping students as they diagrammed programming sequences for their group projects.

A more significant aspect of fieldwork and understanding developed through final, reflective interviews involving photo-elicitation, where these details were presented to students who then reflected on their perceptions of the relationships between writing, learning, and programming. In this way, images like Figure 4 acted as meaningful starting points for exploring more nuanced perceptions of writing in computer science education. Yet during initial interviews (which occurred early in the semester and which did not include a photo-elicitation component), participants (save one) expressed little interest in writing.

Figure 4. UML sequence diagram created by a student group during a typical class session.

One of the reasons for studying computer science, participants responded, was an aversion to writing and a preference for mathematics and logic. Few noted writing much of anything beyond what was required in school, and as a group, they simply did not see themselves as writers. However, differences between initial interviews conducted before photographically documenting participant writing work and final interviews in which participants saw themselves transforming programming ideas into writing (and transforming written planning and diagramming back into executable code), were palpable. Participants could see, through photographic documentation, just how much writing and planning work supported their programming efforts. This led them to reflect on similar forms of writing that occurred outside of class, and to consider in much more detail the extent to which jottings, notemaking, code commentary, planning, and diagramming mediated their programming activities (and thus, their learning).

5. IMPLICATIONS AND CONCLUSIONS

In this paper, I have detailed some of the historical and theoretical underpinnings of contemporary visual research in the social sciences. More important, I have described how these perspectives have been underdeveloped in communication design research, and I have suggested three interrelated approaches that may be particularly useful in studying everyday communication, documentation, and user experience. By extending discussion of these approaches through examples from industry and academe, I have argued that visual methods, when coupled with an appropriate methodology (such as WAGR), can promote more granular understandings of everyday communication processes and activities.

There are several implications that emerge from this work, beginning with the obvious: The diminished technical barriers to using visual methods in fieldwork means that communication design researchers can more easily capture and analyze the systemic contexts and material assemblages that mediate a given participant's everyday practice. Moreover, this level of detail may lead to fuller representations of participant environments, as reflected, for example, in Figures 1 and 2. In this way, visual methods are more than merely illustrative; they may lead, rather, to wider frames of analysis, improved understandings of processes and change, and qualitatively different forms of thick description (than fieldnotes alone). And when deployed throughout fieldwork processes, photography and videography can help interviewers elicit different kinds of responses and reflections from research participants. Visual methods thus offer communication design researchers an alternative feedback instrument, where participants are able to reflect upon their own practices and environments by seeing them in a different way.

Of course, this paper is not without limitations. Using visual research methods entails heightened attention to ethical considerations and forms of participant representation. These complex issues warrant additional, stand-alone research. Given the constraints of space, I have touched only on key developments and approaches from two disciplines (visual anthropology and visual sociology) with rich histories and traditions. And I have simply introduced some of the participatory methods that may be particularly useful in communication design. For example, future researchers might ask participants to use photo or video diaries as a way of further documenting *in situ* practice. Similarly, by adapting photovoice methods, communication design researchers might ask participants to visually represent systemic contexts away from research sites, creating points of comparison and analysis between different forms of literate action (for example, "home" and "work"). As an introduction to these methods, this paper serves as a starting point for future work using visual research in design of communication and related fields.

6. ACKNOWLEDGMENTS

I gratefully acknowledge Erika Johnson, who assisted with data collection for the study described in section 4.2, and Paul Gestwicki, the instructor of the course described in section 4.2.

7. REFERENCES

[1] Arnold, J., Graesch, A., Ragazzini, E., and Ochs, E. 2012. *Life at home in the twenty-first century: 32 families open their doors.* Cotsen Institute of Archaeology Press, Los Angeles, CA.

[2] Ball, M. and Smith, G. 2011. Ethnomethodology and the visual: Practices of looking, visualization, and embodied action. In E. Margolis & L. Pauwels (Eds.), *The Sage handbook of visual research methods*, 392–413. Sage, Los Angeles, CA.

[3] Banks, M. 2001. *Visual methods in social research.* Sage, London.

[4] Becker, H. S. 2004. Afterword: Photography as evidence, photographs as exposition. In C. Knowles & P. Sweetman (Eds.), *Picturing the social landscape: Visual methods and the sociological imagination*, 193–197. Routledge, London.

[5] Bock, A., Isermann, H., and Knieper, T. 2011. Quantitative content analysis of the visual. In E. Margolis & L. Pauwels (Eds.), *The Sage handbook of visual research methods* 265–282. Sage, Los Angeles.

[6] Bødker, S., and Nylandsted Klokmose, C. (2011). The human-artifact model: An activity theoretical approach to artifact ecologies. *Human-Computer Interaction 26*, 315–371.

[7] Brown, R. 2011. Photography as process, documentary photographing as discourse. In S. Spencer (Ed.), *Visual research methods in the social sciences: Awakening visions*, 199–224. Routledge, London.

[8] Chan, K. 2011. Visual ethnography in game design: A case study of user-centric concept for a mobile social traffic game. In *MindTrek Proceedings* (Tampere, Finland, September 28–30, 2011). ACM, New York, NY, 75–82.

[9] Chaplin, E. 1994. *Sociology and visual representations.* Routledge, London.

[10] Chaplin, E. 2011. The photo diary as an autoethnographic method. In E. Margolis & L. Pauwels (Eds.), *The Sage handbook of visual research methods*, 241–262. Sage, Los Angeles.

[11] Clifford, J., and Marcus, G., Eds. 1986. *Writing culture: The poetics and politics of ethnography.* University of California Press, Berkeley, CA.

[12] DiSalvo, C., and Vertesi, J. 2007. Imaging the city: Exploring practices and technologies representing the urban environment in HCI. In *Proceedings of CHI '07* (San Jose, CA, April 28–May 3, 2007). ACM, New York, NY, 2829–2832.

[13] Dourish, P. 2001. *Where the action is: The foundations of embodied interaction.* MIT Press, Cambridge, MA.

[14] Farr-Wharton, G., Foth, M., and Choi, J. 2012. Colour coding the fridge to reduce food waste. In *Proceedings of OZCHI '12* (Melbourne, Victoria, Australia, November 26–30, 2012). ACM, New York, NY, 119–122.

[15] Fincher, S., Tenenberg, J., and Robins, A. 2011. Research design: Necessary bricolage. In *Proceedings of ICER '11* (Providence, RI, August 8–9, 2011). ACM, New York, NY, 27–32.

[16] Fleron, B. R., and Pederson, C. 2010. Exploring roles in a photo elicitation dialogue. In *Proceedings of PDC '10* (Sydney, Australia, November 29, 2010). ACM, New York, NY, 175–178.

[17] Hall, L., Jones, S., Richardson, J., and Hodgson, J. 2007. Inspiring design: The use of photo elicitation and lomography in gaining the child's perspective. In *Proceedings of HCI '07*. ACM, New York, NY, 227–236.

[18] Harper, D. 1998. An argument for visual sociology. In J. Prosser (Ed.), *Image-based research: A sourcebook for qualitative researchers*, 24–41. Falmer Press, London.

[19] Harper, D. 2004. Wednesday-night bowling: Reflections on cultures of a rural working class. In C. Knowles & P. Sweetman (Eds.), *Picturing the social landscape: Visual methods and the sociological imagination*, 93–113. Routledge, London.

[20] Hutchins, E., and Klausen, T. 1996. Distributed cognition in an airline cockpit. In Y. Engeström & D. Middleton (Eds.), *Cognition and communication at work*, 15–34. Cambridge University Press.

[21] Jarvis, N., Cameron, D., and Boucher, A. 2012. Attention to detail: Annotations of a design process. In *Proceedings of NordiCHI '12* (Copenhagen, Denmark, October 14–17, 2012). ACM, New York, NY, 11–20.

[22] Klett, M. 2011. Repeat photography in landscape research. In E. Margolis & L. Pauwels (Eds.), *The Sage handbook of visual research methods*, 114–131). Sage, Los Angeles.

[23] Knowles, C., and Sweetman, P. 2004. Introduction. In C. Knowles & P. Sweetman (Eds.), *Picturing the social landscape: Visual methods and the sociological imagination*, 1–17. Routledge, London.

[24] Krippendorf, K. 2004. *Content analysis: An introduction to its methodology.* Sage, London.

[25] Lapenta, F. 2011. Some theoretical and methodological views on photo-elicitation. In E. Margolis & L. Pauwels (Eds.), *The Sage handbook of visual research methods*, 201–213. Sage, Los Angeles.

[26] MacDougall, D. 1997. The visual in anthropology. In M. Banks & H. Morphy (Eds.), *Rethinking visual anthropology*, 276–295. Yale University Press, New Haven, CT.

[27] McNely, B., Gestwicki, P., Gelms, B., and Burke, A. 2013. Spaces and surfaces of invention: A visual ethnography of game development. *Enculturation 15*.

[28] Mitchell, C. 2011. *Doing visual research.* Sage, London.

[29] Mondada, L. 2003. Working with video: How surgeons produce video records of their actions. *Visual Studies 18*, 58–72.

[30] Morphy, H., & Banks, M. 1997. Introduction: Rethinking visual anthropology. In M. Banks & H. Morphy (Eds.), *Rethinking visual anthropology*, 1–35. Yale University Press, New Haven, CT.

[31] Packer, M. 2011. *The science of qualitative research*. Cambridge University Press.

[32] Pink, S. 2006. *The future of visual anthropology: Engaging the senses*. Routledge, London.

[33] Pink, S. 2007. *Doing visual ethnography: Images, Media and representation in research* (2nd ed.). Sage, Los Angeles.

[34] Pink, S. 2012. *Situating everyday life: Practices and places*. Sage, London.

[35] Pinney, C. 2011. *Photography and anthropology*. Reaktion Books, London.

[36] Racadio, R., Rose, E., and Boyd, S. 2012. Designing and evaluating the mobile experience through iterative field studies. In *Proceedings of SIGDOC '12* (Seattle, WA, October 3–5, 2012). ACM, New York, NY, 191–196.

[37] Rieger, J. H. 2011. Rephotography for documenting social change. In E. Margolis & L. Pauwels (Eds.), *The Sage handbook of visual research methods*, 132–149. Sage, Los Angeles.

[38] Ruby, J. 1995. *Secure the shadow: Death and photography in America*. MIT Press, Cambridge, MA.

[39] Ruby, J. 2000. *Picturing culture: Explorations of film and anthropology*. University of Chicago Press.

[40] Russell, D. 1995. Activity theory and its implications for writing instruction. In J. Petraglia (Ed.), *Reconceiving writing, rethinking writing instruction*, 51–76. LEA, Mahwah, NJ.

[41] Russell, D. 2009. Uses of activity theory in written communication research. In A. Sannino, H. Daniels, & K. Gutiérrez, (Eds.), *Learning and expanding with activity theory*, 40–52. Cambridge University Press.

[42] Shipka, J. 2011. *Toward a composition made whole*. University of Pittsburgh Press.

[43] Shove, E., Watson, M., Hand, M., and Ingram, J. 2007. *The design of everyday life*. Berg, New York.

[44] Spencer, S. 2011. *Visual research methods in the social sciences: Awakening visions*. Routledge, London.

[45] Spinuzzi, C. 2003. *Tracing genres through organizations*. MIT Press, Cambridge, MA.

[46] Spinuzzi, C. 2008. *Network: Theorizing knowledge work in telecommunications*. Cambridge University Press.

[47] Spinuzzi, C. 2011. Losing by expanding: Corralling the runaway object. *Journal of Business and Technical Communication*, *25*, 449–486.

[48] Stasz, C. 1979. The early history of visual sociology. In J. Wagner (Ed.), *Images of information: Still photography in the social sciences*, 119–136. Sage, Beverly Hills, CA.

[49] Suchman, L. 1987. *Plans and situated actions: The problem of human-machine communication*. Cambridge University Press.

On Signifying the Complexity of Inter-Agent Relations in AgentSheets Games and Simulations

Marcelle P. Mota, Ingrid T. Monteiro, Juliana J. Ferreira,
Cleyton Slaviero and Clarisse S. de Souza
Semiotic Engineering Research Group
Departamento de Informática, PUC-Rio
Rua Marquês de São Vicente 225
22451-900 Rio de Janeiro, RJ - Brazil
{mmota, imonteiro, jferreira, cslaviero, clarisse}@inf.puc-rio.br

ABSTRACT

This paper reports the results of an empirical study about the semiotic engineering of signs of complexity for live documentation of games and simulations built with a visual programming learning environment. The study highlights the essence of the semiotic engineering process and shows how its outcome has been received by a group of users who can speak for a large portion of the live documentation system's user population. It also shows how the communication of complexity is, in and of itself, a major design challenge, especially when mastering complexity is one of the prime purposes of the documented object. Because the study was carried out in the context of a live documentation system, its conclusions can also illustrate how to conduct semiotically-inspired interaction design.

Categories and Subject Descriptors

H.5.2 [**Information Interfaces and Presentation**]: User Interfaces - Theory and methods; Training, help, and documentation. K.3.2 [**Computers and Education**]: Computers and Information Science Education.

General Terms

Documentation, Design, Human Factors.

Keywords

Meaning of program representations, Semiotic engineering in practice, Live documentation, Computational thinking acquisition, AgentSheets.

1. INTRODUCTION

The importance of developing children's computational thinking (CT) skills at school has been repeatedly emphasized over the last

SIGDOC 2013, September 30 - October 01 2013, Greenville, NC, USA
Copyright 2013 ACM 978-1-4503-2131-0/13/09...$15.00.
http://dx.doi.org/10.1145/2507065.2507070

few years [12][13]. The aim of an increasing volume of research and technology has been to facilitate the teaching and learning of basic computer programming, an inherently complex cognitive activity even if achieved with the aid of 'fun tools' like toys and robots, games and animations. The challenge for researchers and educators is not so much one of *simplifying complexity*, but rather one of providing the appropriate means to *deal with complexity* and *gain mastery* of computers.

This paper reports on empirical research with program representations in AgentSheets, which was carried out to inform the design of extensions to its accompanying live documentation system, PoliFacets. AgentSheets is a visual agent-oriented programming environment with which learners can build games and simulations [17]. PoliFacets supports the exploration of various aspects (facets) of AgentSheets programs, like the depiction and behavior of agents, the structure of game space, the experience of game play and the program code [11]. The interest of this research for design and communication studies is that we follow directives proposed by Semiotic Engineering, an HCI theory that views human-computer interaction as a specific kind of computer-mediated human *communication*. With it systems producers *tell* systems users their design vision as well as how, when, where, why and what for they can use the system [3].

The purpose of the proposed extensions to PoliFacets is to help CT learners and teachers detect and understand the sources of program complexity. One of the main sources of complexity in games and simulations built with AgentSheets is to define and control how agents affect one another when the program is executed. Together, AgentSheets and PoliFacets provide various kinds of representations for understanding *local* and *global* relations, the former being expressed within an agent's behavior rules, and the latter throughout the entire game program. The leap from one to the other, however, is cognitively very challenging for learners. We thus set out to create an intermediate level of representation to deal with a limited scope of inter-agent relations, larger than *local*, yet smaller than *global*. Representations of *regional* inter-agent relations are thus meant to support explorations of bounded chains of influence that one agent has upon the behavior of other agents. By using them, learners (and teachers) should have more options to divide and conquer program complexity while trying to understand and explain the logic of games and simulations.

In the following sections we briefly describe AgentSheets and PoliFacets (section 2), then report how we used a qualitative methodology to carry out a formative evaluation study with users and finally highlight how its procedures and results elicit and express the quality of communication we have achieved (section 3). In the last section we discuss our contribution in view of relevant related work dealing with the signification and communication of complexity in computer-supported program comprehension tasks.

2. AGENTSHEETS AND POLIFACETS

AgentSheets is a visual programming tool specifically designed to promote CT acquisition through the development of games and simulations. Programming is mainly done through drawing and direct manipulation of interface elements and the ultimate targeted users are school children [18].

Although program representations in AgentSheets are very rich (which is appropriate for learning environments), previous studies about this system's interface [5][6] have shown that the overall *communication* of the role and meaning of such representations, as well as that of relations between them, could be improved. The technical outcome of such studies was a live documentation system called PoliFacets [11], with which teachers and learners can explore how the meanings expressed during game play or simulation execution have been *encoded* in program structures by their creators. PoliFacets thus supports *reflection* upon AgentSheets programs, a critically important element in the overall CT learning process. It has been implemented as a Web extension to AgentSheets, following previous successful experiences with the Scalable Game Design Arcade, a Web-based cyber learning infrastructure where learners can assess their progress based on automatically extracted CT patterns that they have used in their games and simulations [2].

To illustrate how AgentSheets and PoliFacets work and relate to each other, we will use a simulation of how industrial pollution affects the environment. An important aspect of this simulation is that it is only *an expression of its creator's understanding* of environmental damage caused by atmospheric pollution and by no means a *computational model* of the actual chemical processes in place. Likewise, the names of program elements have been arbitrarily chosen by the programmer; they aren't necessarily natural language words denoting what such elements *mean* to the programmer or the game players. This characteristic is very important as will be seen in subsequent sections of the paper.

2.1 Creating Simulations with AgentSheets

AgentSheets games and simulations consist of two fundamental components. The first is a set of one or more *agents*, which have a visual depiction (possibly many) and whose behavior is defined by if-then production rules. The other is a set of one or more *worksheets* (or game spaces), where agents are deployed at programming time and where they perform at run time. In Figure 1 we show the deployed worksheet of the environmental pollution simulation we have used in our study. In it there are *agents* like trees and clouds, for instance, placed on top of a background image with a green field, blue sky, wild flowers, and so on.

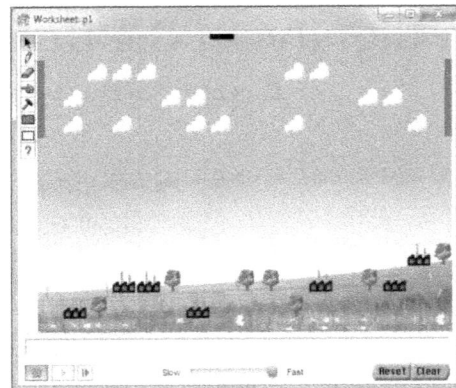

Figure 1. The worksheet

Although, as mentioned, all agents behave in accordance with if-then rules established by the programmer, some may have *void* behavioral rule. This is the case of agents whose sole purpose is to compose the structure of the game space or constrain the behavior of other agents. As an illustration, Figure 2 shows the agents gallery and part of the behavior of agent 'A'. Agents can have multiple depictions, as is the case with agent 'A'. It has two depictions, which are changed as the simulation executes. To specify the agent's behavior a user can build rules by dragging and dropping conditions, actions and even other rules into the appropriate slots. Rules are formed by multiple rows with conditions on the left (If) and actions on the right (Then). When all conditions on the left side are satisfied, actions on the right side of the same row are executed in sequence.

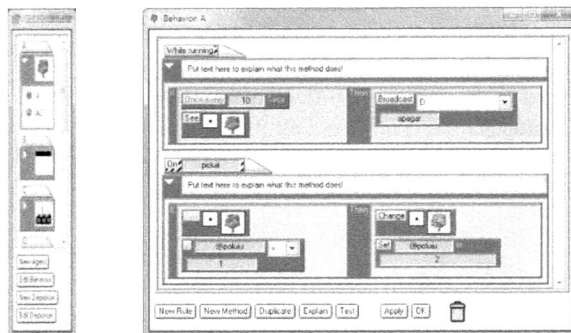

Figure 2. Gallery and part of the behavior of agent 'A'

Figure 2 (when in colors) also shows the effects of AgentSheets' conversational programming style. While a game or simulation is running, the user can see if rule conditions are true or false for a specific agent at particular moment in time. Sequentially tested rules are shown in green (bottom of Figure 2) if they are true and red if they are false (top of Figure 2). Color and animation help users understand why agents do (or don't do) specific actions at run time.

Furthermore, AgentSheets allows users to generate a report with a list of all agents' depictions and behavior rules (see a snapshot in Figure 3). The report is displayed as a Web page, with hyperlinks for quick access to related parts of the report. The language used in the report is exactly the same visual language as used in AgentSheets' programming interface.

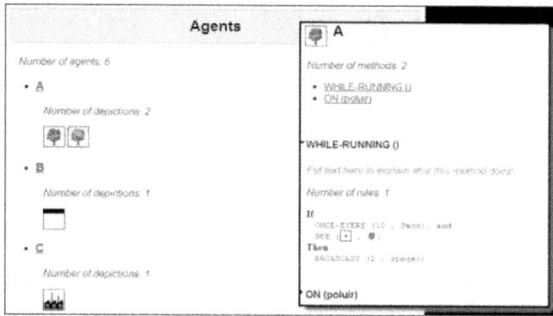

Figure 3. A snapshot of AgentSheets' program report

In spite of its interactive attractiveness, CT learning processes with AgentSheets might benefit from extended representations [6]. This is mainly because while AgentSheets makes *action* easy to take, it doesn't support *reflection on action* [20] to the same extent. This finding has seeded the development of PoliFacets [11].

2.2 Exploring Program Facets with PoliFacets

PoliFacets is a Web-based active documentation system for AgentSheets programs. Once games are uploaded, a range of *facets* are automatically generated. The system allows users to explore such facets by following structured *conversational threads* about facets and significant relations between them. For example, they can ask questions like 'How many agents are there in this game? And what do they do?' or 'Are there stacked agents on the worksheet? Where?'. Content provided in conversations can be automatically generated by the system (based on the parsing and analysis of uploaded games and simulations) or be included by students and instructors, *a posteriori*, by means of structured annotations to program facets.

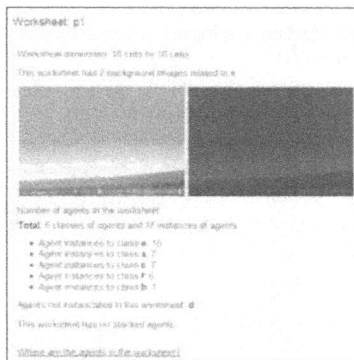

Figure 4. Worksheet details

Insights and understanding promoted by PoliFacets are not easily obtained with interactions with AgentSheets. For example, the worksheet, a critically important component in a game or simulation, may have alternate background images that are switched under certain conditions to produce great visual effects. However, in order to *see* if and how background images are used while analyzing the program in AgentSheets a learner should not only be able to separate (or visually *parse*) the background image from forefront agents in Figure 1, for example, but also spot the specific rule in one of the various agents' behavior where there is a command to switch background image. In PoliFacets this is made immediately clear when the user explores the worksheet facet (Figure 4). Note that other relevant details of the game space, which may actually go unnoticed in the AgentSheets' programming interface, are explicitly represented and

communicated (*e. g.* how many cells there are in the worksheet, how many instances of different classes of agents are deployed, etc.).

In Figure 5 we see a representation of the worksheet in *grid* style, showing the exact positioning of all selected agent intances (compare this structural view with the game space rendition in Figure 1, against the background image that is not seen in Figure 5). In PoliFacet's grids, the user can explore different renditions of the worksheet (viewing the number of existing agent instances in each class, where the agents are located, enabling and disabling agents, viewing and hiding agent stacks, etc.). All such explorations contribute to grasping how the programmer has represented and structured the message that he wants this simulation to communicate.

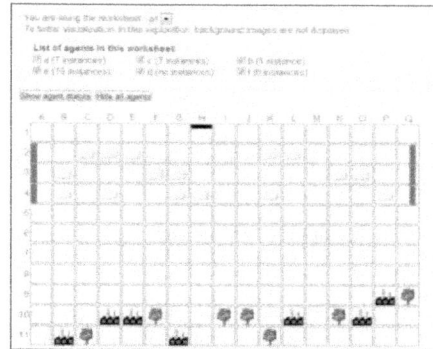

Figure 5. The grid

Another facet called *rules* presents a natural language textual rendition of AgentSheets' visual rules. The rule content is the same, but the variation in form (from visual to textual) supports a more fluid articulation and communication of the rule's *logic*. Figure 6 shows the English translation of the rule shown in the insert of Figure 3. This feature supports different teaching strategies. For example, teachers can begin with the visual programming and then resort to textual rule descriptions when students are *creating* games, but do it the other way around when students are *analyzing* (their own or someone else's) games.

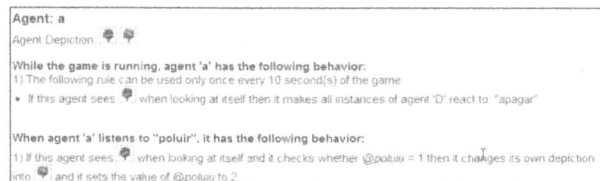

Figure 6. Part of the rules of agent A

One of the main features of PoliFacets [11] is the emphasis on *communicating the designers' intent and message* (namely to stimulate and facilitate reflection upon meanings of/in game and simulation programs). This is achieved by carefully following a Semiotic Engineering perspective [3] on interaction design. Part of this perspective involves having a keen eye for how AgentSheets *signs* are communicated and received by users, especially in view of the overall complexity of programming. Besides various aspects already mentioned and illustrated in paragraphs above, the *signification* (choice of representation) and *communication* (expression of meaning and achievement intent) of relations between agents in the program structure is essential for mastering the cognitive complexity of programming tasks. This is even more important if we consider that visual renditions of agents' behavior during the game play can suggest logical relations that are actually *not* encoded *as such* in the underlying program [5]. In other words, there may be a number of different program structures that yield identical visual effects when the program is executed. Calling the learner's attention to this is of paramount importance in CT acquisition if we want them to appreciate (and eventually master) the power of computing as a new means of expression and action is society.

Table 1: Signs of inter-agent relations in AgentSheets and PoliFacets

	Signs of LOCAL Inter-Agent Relations	Signs of REGIONAL Inter-Agent Relations	Signs of GLOBAL Inter-Agent Relations
AgentSheets	**Static:** Agent's behavior rules **Dynamic:** Conversational Programming Visualizations	**Static:** None **Dynamic:** None	**Static:** Game program report and location in Worksheet **Dynamic:** Game play (*applet*)
PoliFacets	**Static:** Textual (automatic and manually annotated) descriptions of the agent's behavior rules **Dynamic:** None	**Static:** **PROPOSED** **Dynamic:** None	**Static:** Textual (automatic and manually annotated) descriptions of the entire game and agents' locations in *grid* **Dynamic:** Game play (*applet*)

An examination of both AgentSheets and PoliFacets in their current state of development showed us that when trying to trace relations among agents – be it because some agent is misbehaving during execution (which calls for debugging) or because he wants to see what will happen if an agent's behavior is changed (which calls for programming experimentation) – a programmer has two choices. He can either take a *local* perspective and inspect agents' behavior one at a time, or take a *global* perspective and analyze the whole program structure and execution (see Table 1). Stepping from one perspective directly into the other is difficult, which motivated us to create a new sign of complexity for PoliFacets. In keeping with PoliFacets' Semiotic Engineering rationale, our proposal is meant to communicate (and support subsequent exploratory communications about) an agent's *regional* scope of influence upon other agents and to bridge an important gap in both systems. The next section reports what we have found in the ongoing course of Semiotic Engineering research to achieve this end.

3. EMPIRICAL STUDY

The semiotic engineering of a system's interface must always address two aspects of communication: the emission of the designer-to-user intended communication and its reception [4]. Therefore, in view of strong evidence that users need, want or may benefit from some particular piece of communication, the semiotic engineering process starts with the elaboration of *signs* for the emission of the designers' message. In our case this involved the elaboration of signs to communicate a bounded area of influence for all agents in a game or simulation. So, based on previous research studies and on a careful analysis of AgentSheets commands and rule structures, we built a diagrammatic representation of bounded inter-agent relations (see Figure 8 and

additional details in sub-section 3.1). Next, we tested the reception of our message with a qualitative exploratory study, carried out initially with six participants.

In order to create a realistic and semiotically adequate situation for participants to engage in productive communication with PoliFacets' and AgentSheets' representations, we created a specific simulation where we intentionally introduced various kinds of inter-agent relations using moderately complex program structures. That is, we deliberately programmed mutual agent behavior with command structures that *could not* be completely figured out by looking exclusively at individual agents' behavior rules.

The six participants in the first phase of the study (P1-P6) were chosen among teachers and teacher-support team members of the *Scalable Game Design Brasil* project (SGD-Br) [19]. The recruiting criterion was that they had previous experience teaching AgentSheets to beginners or that they qualified to teach introductory lessons about AgentSheets programming. Three of the recruited participants were basic-level game and simulation programmers (P1, P2 and P3), whereas the others had more advanced knowledge (P4, P5 and P6). P4 was the most experienced participant, having taught basic and advanced classes in one of SGD-Br partner schools. P5 and P6 had relatively less experience with AgentSheets, but they had additional programming abilities. P5 had taught programming classes using Scratch [10] whereas P6 not only taught IT classes for middle and high school children regularly, but he also had an active interest in and practice with non-professional programming.

3.1 Procedure and Materials

Our study included two iterations of the following steps: (i) elaboration of the sign; (ii) sign reception test with participants; and (iii) analysis of results. The first iteration (or first phase of the study) showed us how our new message was received and what elements in it were missed or misunderstood. The second iteration (or second phase), after semiotic engineering improvements were made in our message, showed us more clearly if and how the expression of *regional* inter-agent relations can help game and simulation creators gain new perspectives on the complexity of AgentSheets' programs. In the second phase of the study we collected data from five participants, four of which also participated in the first phase.

The materials used in the study were a combination of existing AgentSheets and PoliFacets representations for a specifically designed simulation, along with a manually produced Web page with our proposed diagrammatic representations of regional inter-agent relations (with hyperlinks and tooltips for certain elements of the diagram). A picture of the simulation worksheet has already been presented in Figure 1 (sub-section 2.1) and is shown in more details in Figure 7. Examples of diagrams appearing on the manually composed Web page in the first phase are shown in Figure 8, in this sub-section, and in Figure 9, in sub-section 3.3.

The simulation represents factories that pollute the environment, calling the palyer's attention to the consequences of such pollution. The names of the agents are single letters: A, B, C, D, E and F. We avoided using meaningful names in order to stimulate participants to develop their own interpretation of what the agents are and do. As part of intentional program complexity, we used agent and game attributes or properties set to local and global program variables, as well as methods (to encapsulate a set of rules). Variable and method names, however, were meaningful words, linked to their purpose or content. We estimated that such meaningful names would help participants interpret an agent's behavior more easily and thus be able to assign meaning to them (and possibly name them).

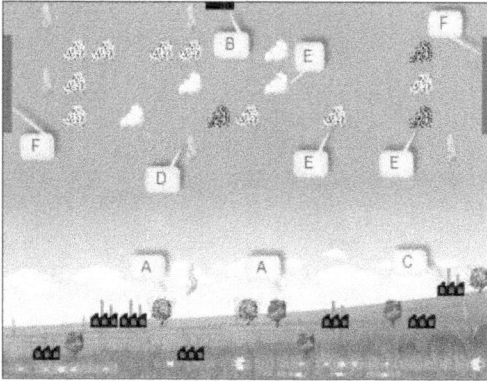

Figure 7. Agents during the simulation

In Figure 7 we show an annotated image of various agents while the simulation is running. The use of letters instead of meaningful agents' names gives the reader (as it also gave the participants) a sense of the complexity of the task, which requires that we constantly combine names and depictions in sense making. This sign-association task lies at the heart of a substantial part of professional programming activities, which justifies the case. The top-level logic of the game is as follows. If agent A is depicted as a healthy tree (🌳), it asks agent D to execute the method "erase" (which may or may not make D erase itself, depending on certain contextual conditions). If agent D (🔧) touches agent E, E's depiction changes to the next polluted stage (— to ☁ or ☁ to ☁). Agent B (⎺) increments a variable used by C (🍾) to control the release of D (🔧) in the environment. Agent F (▮, ▯) generates instances of agent E (—) on the left side of the worksheet and erases them on the right side. Agent E (—) moves from left to right under certain contextual conditions. If its depiction is that of a heavily polluted cloud (☁), it asks agent A to run method "pollute", which turns its depiction into that of a "dead" tree (🌲). When all instances of A are depicted as dead trees, instances of D are no longer erased. The simulation stops when there is a column of D agents (🔧) straight from some C (🍾) into the sky above.

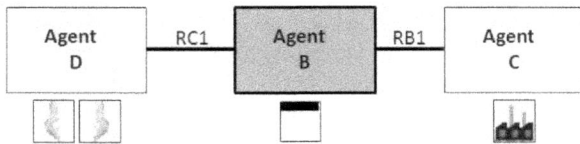

Figure 8. Connections from the agent B

Although the reader is by no means expected to tease out inter-agent relations from the preceding paragraph, the fact that there *are* significant and complex relations among agents should, however, have clearly come across. In Figure 8 we show the proposed diagram for the bounded scope of influence of agent B. Lines indicate that RB1 (rule number 1 of agent B) and RC1 (rule number 1 of agent C) establish the relations between B and C and B and D, respectively. The diagram provides navigation links to rules RB1 and RC1 in the program report (an excerpt is shown in Figure 3). RB1 connects B and C because the two agents share a property, that is, they manipulate the same global variable. RC1

connects B and D because it uses a property shared with agent B in combination with a depiction of D. Just by looking at the simulation it is not possible to identify the relations among B and C or B and D. Moreover, an examination of the entire program code (a *global* perspective) or of the involved agents' behavior rules one set at a time (a *local* perspective) makes it extremely difficult not to get lost in the logic of mutual relations *unless* we use some tracking notation like a diagram, for example.

Our intended message to the users of the proposed diagrams (as illustrated in Figure 8) can be expressed using de Souza's *metacommunication template* [3]. What we meant to say with the diagram and manipulations afforded by the user interface was:

"We [the design team] understand that you [the user] are a CT teacher. We've learned that you need and want to have a deeper understanding of AgentSheets programs in order to decide what strategies you will use in class. We have therefore built a diagram to help you understand relations between agents, realize which ones are important and see how they influence the behavior of agents during game play. As you gain deeper understanding of this facet you will also gain improved skills to express your ideas through games and simulations. Notice how agents are related within certain boundaries – not through the entire game. You can click on hyperlinks to see the complete behavior rules that establish the relations you see. Links lead you to different facets of game representation."

In the first iteration of the procedures, we showed them a run of the simulation and then asked them to give us a verbal description of what they saw. Next, we asked them to tell what were the relations between agents B and C, first, and A and C, second, using only the material they had at hand (the running simulation, the open simulation program in AgentSheets, the program report generated by AgentSheets and the textual rendition of the rules generated by PoliFacets). When they finished this, we showed them the inter-agent relations diagram with representations of bounded scope relations for each one of the agents. We asked them to comment on the diagrams and then tell us how agent D was related to agent F. In order to find the right answer, they should *preferably* use and manipulate the diagram, but they could also use the material provided for previous steps.

3.2 First Iteration: Analysis and Results

The qualitative analysis of the data revealed some recurring categories of meanings from the participants' discourse, which was supported by the observation of their interaction with the provided materials. Categories have been named as follows: affect; iconicity; dominant language function throughout the entire discourse; and transition across referential and metalinguistic language functions.

3.2.1 Affect

Most participants *liked* the diagram from start. A positive reaction to the diagram is important because it increases the chance that users will be initially willing to engage in this sort of communication.

P1 at the first sight of the diagram said: "I already like it! I love icons, graphs and (...) there are figures. I already like it!" P3 had the same kind of reaction: "It's very nice, very clear (...) it will [call the attention to] the need of understanding the code, (...) establishing a relation [between agents]." This participant even anticipated how the proposed diagrams might change the user's experience with PoliFacets: "[The diagram] changed the whole [navigation in] PoliFacets (...) I mean, we begin with an image, in this case with a diagram or a graphic image, and then choose to see the code or [the rules]."

As a counterpoint, P6 reacted badly when he first saw the diagram. He said: "You take something simple and make it so complicated!" However, after he carefully analyzed diagram representations to answer test questions, P6 had a considerably different opinion: "This is good; people [can] understand what is going on (…), it is very useful (…), it is a map (…)."

One of the six participants didn't like of the diagrammatic representation at all. Even after using the diagram to answer our questions, and getting to learn more about what it meant, P2 said: "I got lost with this diagram (...) I think [understanding inter-agent relations] is an incremental success or failure [process], you see? I mean, I don't know why I would see the relations better here than in the [rules], honestly." He summarized his affective reaction to the diagram by saying: "It scares me more than supports me."

Affect, however, did no more than pre-dispose the participants positively (in most cases) or negatively (in a single case) towards trying to understand and use the diagram. The other categories brought up stronger insights on the result of our semiotic engineering effort.

3.2.2 Iconicity

Iconicity is the name we chose to express the fact that participants showed a tendency to interpret relations in a more concrete way (*i. e.* keeping similarities with physical reality) than the style of abstract symbolic signs used to name agents or to compose the diagram suggested. For example, most of participants talked about "toxic rain", "acid rain" or "cataclysm", although none of these expressions had been used in the program. We interpreted this as evidence of how strongly the participants' attention was focused on signs and agents shown during the simulation's execution, which is a natural choice for explanations centered on the *contextual* message of the simulation.

As an example, when asked to explain the simulation, P2 said: "This tiny polluting smoke [here], when it comes near the cloud, it makes the cloud [turn] darker; it pollutes the cloud. Next, you have toxic rain." We must remember, however, that the questions being asked from participants referred to how *program components* (and not domain elements) related to each other. If we look at evidence provided by P2, we see that although he was able to *guess* the relation between clouds and smoke (because the program happened to encode visual effects in a similar way as the phenomenon is articulated by common sense observation and reasoning), he failed elsewhere. For instance, he did not realize the relations between clouds and trees, nor the one between trees and the effects of calls to the *pollute* method.

Likewise, P5 (who is a Science teacher) tried to analyze the simulation scientifically. He, more than any other participant, needed to see acid rain destroy the trees. His explanation of the simulation was: "This is a simulation of factories throwing smoke [in the air]. Because I am a teacher, I know that there is CO_2, which is generating acid rain and the trees are [like] burned out and everything will be burned out." He even complained: "You showed no rain, there is supposed to be rain [falling] from this cloud." This participant's attachment to domain-centered (iconic) signs was so strong that he simply refused to look at the program and explain what the relation between selected agents in it was.

Iconicity also misled participants when trying to tell the relation between agents D ( ) and F (,). The agents themselves are, semiotically speaking, signs of different types (and intentionally so). While D ( ) is acceptably an iconic representation of *smoke*, F (,) might be the iconic representation of whatever holds a similarity with a vertical bar. This was in itself a disorienting fact for an iconic interpretation of *all* signs in the simulation, given that there aren't vertical bars hanging in the skies. As a reminder, agent F (,), as explained in the previous section, generates instances of agent E ( ) on the left side of the worksheet and erases them on the right side. This, however, can be more clearly seen in an examination of the program *code* than in an execution of the simulation or an inspection of agents' depictions.

When giving the answer for the relation between agents D and F, P5 looked at the simulation being executed – not at the encoded program. His explanation for the relation shows how completely misled he was by choosing to privilege icons over symbols: "There is a relation only when this tiny smoke is here, in this area comprised between the two [instances of agent F]. What we see is that the clouds are all within this demarcated area (…). In fact, what you wanted to do was to show the relation between the cloud and the smoke, which is communicated by these little bars here."

P6 gave us very powerful evidence of how iconicity and abstract computing representations and processes generated conflicting interpretations in his mind. At some point he said "Some drop should be falling on the tree (...). Did something happen that I didn't notice? (…) I just saw the tree turning [orange] (...) I do not know if [drops] fell so fast that I didn't see them] Let me play the simulation over again." Later, when trying to tell the relation between agents B and C, P6 went back to the absence of iconic representations of what he thought was happening: "Visually, nothing happens, so let me see. (…) But he [agent B] is a counter, you know, this is what it says here [in the agent's behavior rules]. He's counting something there." So, P6 knew B was a counter, and yet he could not tell what was being counted.

An interesting hint at the meaning of iconicity was given by P4, who is a Math teacher and also the most experienced in programming with AgentSheets among all participants. He was the only one who did not invoke contextual signs (like *rain* and the like) to explain the behavior of agent A. With a remarkably abstract perspective centered on the assumed logic of the program, he explained the relation between B and C like this: "The relation between B and C is that B counts. It looks like C is checking the count; when B counts, [C] checks if B is at 2; then [C] does something; and when the counter reaches 3, [C] will do something else." P4 simply did not care about what the simulation might *mean* and *communicate*. He gave a correct and straightforward explanation based solely on how the rules were programmed. We took this piece of evidence very carefully, however, because although P4 had much less difficulty in dealing with program structures, the ultimate intent of our semiotic engineering of inter-agent relation diagrams is to help teachers and learners realize how abstract (and considerably different) programming alternatives *signify* meaningful things to program creators and program users. Therefore the strength of *iconicity* in trying to make sense of inter-agent relations was not a negative result in terms of previous and ongoing efforts made by the developers of PoliFacets. Participants were, in general, under the influence of the meanings expressed by the simulation. What most of them failed (or had a lot of difficulty) to realize is how those meanings resulted from inter-agent relations in the program.

3.2.3 Dominant Language Function

If we think about the overall goal of PoliFacets – to support teaching and learning of CT and computer programming with an emphasis on meanings – it is critical that PoliFacets be able to communicate how *linguistic* constructs *effect* computations. In other words, how (visual) programming language commands *cause* the kind of agent behavior seen in games and simulations. From a communicative perspective, the relation between language and computation can be framed using a well-known set of *language functions* proposed by Roman Jakobson [9]. According to this author, in communication there are six objects of study: the sender; the receiver; the communication channel; the communication code; the message; and the context. Human language can be used to direct the participants' attention to any one of these objects. So, for example, when communication is full of first-person pronouns ("I", "my", "me", "mine"), the *function* of language is *expressive*. Likewise, when communication provides numerous explanations about the terms being used in a message (*e. g.* "CT stands for *Computational Thinking*" or "*Semiotics* is the study of signs"), language is being used to effect a *metalinguistic* function. The other four functions that language can effect are *phatic* (directing attention to the channel of communication), *connative* (directing attention to the receiver), *poetic* (directing attention to the message itself) and finally *referential* (directing attention to the context of communication, including the physical and social setting where it takes place, the purpose and effect of communication, etc.).

The program *code* is critically important for any piece of software, given that it causes all observable (and non-observable) computations. Therefore, one of the categories that emerged from the evidence collected in our study was the *dominant language function*. It follows from the purpose and the design of our study that we would like participants to use the *metalinguistic* function very abundantly. That is, when asked to explain relations between agents, we wanted them to direct their attention to the code of the simulation, rather than to the message (the simulation itself) or the broader context of communication (the fact that factories can pollute the air and then cause the death of trees, for example).

Three of our participants used predominantly referential function (P1, P5 and P6), with occasional comments on how the message was expressed (poetic function). The other three (P2, P3 and P4) focused on the simulation code, using the metalinguistic function of language more productively.

P1's use of the *poetic* function (focusing on the message), for example, can show the effects of failing to look at the program code. His attempt to explain the relation between B and C goes like this: "Agent C is generating smoke and B... when he sees the cloud, it stops to generate [smoke], right?." Notice how all signs in this piece of discourse (except for agents' names) are borrowed from the *message*, rather than the program code.

A similar situation came about with P5. He was so focused on the context and meaning of the simulation that he expressed the relations between B and C like this: "They are setting a limit to [others], right? It is a limit for [the sky] not to get full of that little smoke." Even after looking at the encoded rules, his (equivocal) conclusion was: "Sure, the role of B is to limit the emission of C." This confusion between what the program is *doing* (the

underlying computation) and what it is *causing* (the observable effects in the simulation) can be expected to be a major barrier for program comprehension and other highly frequent programming tasks such as debugging and program modification.

The discourse of participants could, however, be more closely focused on a *programming* perspective. P2, for example, explained the relation between many agents in the whole simulation by saying: "It gets darker in two stages. In the first one it's somewhat dark, and then it gets [darker] (...). So there should be a counter to say 'when I see [this agent] next [to me], I get somewhat dark first (...) Then when I, for the ith time, get myself in this condition, I get darker' (...)." Interestingly, this *metalinguistic* awareness came about by looking at the simulation, mainly – not the code.

A noteworthy *negative* effect of predominant metalinguistic function was observed in P4's discourse. This participant was so focused on the code that he barely bothered to look one more time at the simulation in order to tell the relations between agents. He looked only at the agents' behavior rules. As a consequence, his initial explanation about the simulation (before he answered specific questions about inter-agent relations) was correct and precise: "After (…) [all] trees 'catch fire' […] smoke keeps building up (...) because it only begins to accumulate after all trees have burned." However, he affirmed quite positively that "agents A and C have no relation with each other." That is, because there aren't any rules for agent A in which agent C is affected (acted upon) and vice-versa, P4 said that the two agents were not related. He missed an *indirect* relation through agent D that was captured in his spontaneous explanation of the simulation (that factories, instances of agent C, generate smoke, instances of agent D, which accumulates after all trees, instances if agent A, have burned). The *negative* effect in this case was not to be guided by the code in trying to answer the question – which was exactly what should be done – but the fact that the interpretation of a *relation* seemed to be strictly *local* (within the scope of an agent's set of rules) and structural, rather than broader and more expressive (taking a *regional* or *global* perspective).

The dominant language function in participants' discourse showed us two things. First, it indicated each participant's positioning when trying to explain inter-agent relations. Explanations where referential or even poetic functions were dominant suggested that their creators were *farther* from the level of abstraction at which *we* – as designers trying to communicate a particular facet of meanings – signified our message and on which we were trying to get users to focus. Second, and possibly more importantly, it showed that in this group there *was not* a systematic correspondence between the dominant function and the level of programming skills. Two skilled participants chose to explain relations choosing mainly the referential function, whereas two less skilled participants chose the metalinguistic one.

3.2.4 Transitions across Language Functions

Although the dominant language function in participants' discourse did not show a direct correspondence with their programming skills, this does not mean that those who favored non-metalinguistic functions failed to recognize that AgentSheets program constructs determined what was seen in the simulation. Throughout the entire discourse produced by participants during the study, we were able to detect transitions across language functions. These transitions were substantially influenced by the study procedures themselves, considering that we asked participants to begin by explaining what they saw in the simulation prior to viewing the underlying program. Only then did we gradually delve into more abstract meanings, by asking them about inter-agent relations as signified in the simulation playback and other program representations. For lack of space (because evidence emerges from contrasting long pieces of discourse collected throughout the entire study), in this sub-section we will only comment on our observations, some of which are supported by quoted passages above.

P5 and P6, for example, had no difficulty in realizing the connection between program code and simulation. They could also express themselves using the metalinguistic function of language in discourse. However, they *preferred* to express themselves using the referential function. They could transition from one to the other effectively. Likewise, P4, who favored the use of metalinguistic expression, had no difficulty in interpreting the simulation with reference to the domain context. Again the transition between functions did not represent a problem.

However, although P2 and P3, for instance, recognized that program structures determine the behavior of agents during simulation (which represents the essence of the metalinguistic function of any language in relation to another), we have no evidence of a complete piece of their discourse with a coherent explanation expressed *only* in metalinguistic terms. The transition between language functions was hard for them; they got confused when trying to establish a connection between program structures (metalanguage) and simulation (object language). Something similar happened to P1, whose explanatory discourse during the study was predominantly expressed with reference to the domain of the simulation. The transition between relevant language functions was not observed in his case.

The importance of looking at how participants transitioned from one language function to the other becomes clearer as we go deeper in the analysis of this category of findings. All participants were teachers or instructors. A good teacher's discourse in class is typically full of language function transitions, which are skillfully used to give the students multiple perspectives on the topic being taught. Consequently, this finding – like the others – called our attention to something we had not thought of in our original design.

After we analyzed findings from the first iteration with a group of PoliFacets users, we improved the semiotic engineering of the metacommunication message conveyed through the prototyped interface and proceeded with the next iteration.

3.3 Second Iteration: Analysis and Results

In her pioneering book about the meaning of computer programming for various groups of people (including children), Turkle [23] distinguishes between hard and soft masters. Hard masters have a plan in mind and work rationally to implement it in the computer. Soft masters interact with the computer and eventually compose a program with meaningful patterns that emerge from interaction. In both cases there is a lot of complexity to be dealt with, although the form it takes and the way it evolves can be considerably different for hard and soft masters.

The first round of evaluation of the semiotic engineering of metacommunication to support the detection and understanding of program complexity in AgentSheets simulations taught us

important lessons. We learned: that a visual representation of complex inter-agent relations was well received (*affect*); that to support correct interpretations of inter-agent relations our extensions to PoliFacets should signify more explicitly elements of both the simulation domain and the program code (*iconicity, dominant language function, transitions across language function*); and finally that a critical feature in our piece of metacommunication, if we want to help PoliFacets users to deal with program complexity, is to provide abundant support for them to navigate smoothly between simulation representations and program structure representations (*transitions across language functions*). The latter, in particular, means that the navigation itself is a semiotically engineered *sign* of how to relate agents to one another. Figure 9 and Figure 10 show the contrast between the first and second (revised) version of the inter-agent relations diagram, respectively.

Looking at how agent C – the center of the diagram – relates to other agents in the simulation, we can see that whereas the old (first) sign had more agents (rectangles) and less connections (lines), the new (revised) sign has more connections and fewer agents. This is because the study showed that representing indirect connections between agent C and agents A and E, in a single diagram, was more confusing than helpful. The new sign thus favors a richer (more scaffolded) representation of how agent C connects only with agents B and D. The annotations to the diagram nodes and edges have also changed considerably. The revised version attempts to evoke program elements that *cause* the relation between agents, in an attempt to support the transition between domain-centered interpretations and explanations of inter-agent relations to program-centered ones.

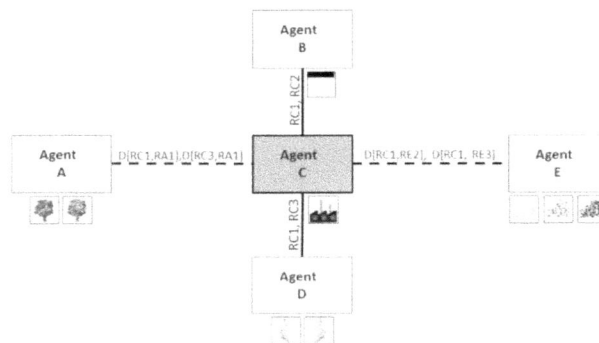

Figure 9. Old diagram of agent C

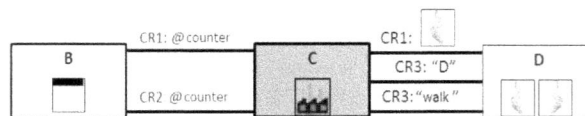

Figure 10. New diagram of agent C

The trade-off in our second round of semiotic engineering has been to shrink the scope of the *region* of influence (agents A and E are no longer represented in Figure 10) and to amplify the communication of the *meaning* of "influence". For example, annotations on edges of the revised diagram explicitly include not only the rule that *causes* the influence (e. g. CR1), but also the program element that originates it (@counter). As a result, the mutual influence between agents C and A can no longer be seen in the *region* of influence of agent C. It will be up to PoliFacets users to find out that C and A are related by exploring agent A's diagram while navigating through the various facets of program meanings in this live documentation system for AgentSheets.

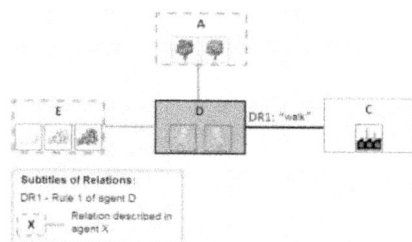

Figure 11. New diagram of agent D

Another element of reengineered signification is the expression of relations defined in the rules of a related agent. In Figure 11, dashed orange squares around A and E mean that their relations with D can be checked only by looking at A's and E's own diagrams. Compared with Figure 9 and Figure 10, this shows that the relation between C and A, or C and E, shown in Figure 9, is still unaccounted for by this strategy. This is because the origin of such relations was not to be found in their own rules (but in agent C's rules, as shown in edge annotations depicted in Figure 9).

We presented the new version of our diagrams to all the participants of our study and to volunteers who had helped us in preliminary pilot tests with the old diagram. We collected the impressions from five of them (P1, P2, P3, P4 and one of the volunteers with advanced knowledge of AgentSheets programming) by means of a questionnaire with open-ended questions. We asked them about: how they compared both versions of the diagram; if/how they would use the new diagram to explain to a learner the effects of a specifically proposed program modification; if/how they would use the diagram to teach AgentSheets programming online or offline; suggestions for improving the diagram; and additional comments.

The result of this second iteration showed that considerable improvements were made in our semiotic engineering process. For example, P2 – the only participant who commented that he did not like to reason based on visual representations – made the following comment: "This new version is more provocative to learning; it teases your chain of thought more strongly by directly expressing relations with attribute names and properties, for example. (...) [It's] more intriguing, I think." Moreover, participants that would fall in Turkle's *hard masters* category (P4 and P7) productively answered questions involving learning-teaching situations. They proposed making sensible use of the new diagram and explored good teaching strategies. However, *soft masters* who participated in this second phase (P1, P2 and P3), although they liked the diagram, showed that they are not yet prepared to use it effectively in dealing with complex situations. We thus conclude that *soft masters* need us to support them further with appropriate explanatory discourse about program complexity and how inter-agent relations play a role in it. In other words, we *can* use the proposed diagrams in metacommunication, but they need to be part of a much richer discourse, with various other signs to convey the essential message.

4. CONCLUSION

This paper presents and discusses the semiotic engineering of representations to signify and communicate complexity in computer-generated live documentation discourse about AgentSheets games and simulations. The emphasis of our research is not on the proposed representations themselves but on the rationale, the criteria and the process we have used to produce them, alternating perspectives between a *sender's* (what *we* mean to say) and a *receiver's* perspective (what *others* take us to mean and would like to mean themselves). This is our contribution to the design of communication.

Our research goals and findings are related to previously published work in different fields of study. To begin with, our choice of diagrammatic representations was motivated by research showing that, unlike sentential representations, diagrammatic ones can communicate more effectively the information about problem components, their roles and relations [7]. Moreover, our attention to the need of *regional* complexity representations was inspired by the work of Stenning and Oberlander [22]. These authors propose that there are three classes of abstract representation systems: those supporting only minimal one-to-one abstractions; those supporting limited one-to-many abstractions; and those supporting unlimited key-switched many-to-many abstractions. Their study on the cognitive roles played by the three systems in learning processes concludes that the expression and manipulation of limited abstractions is critically important for supporting a learner's reasoning.

Limiting the scope of required program abstraction is also supported by previous work in program visualization. Kapec [16], for instance, whose work discusses software visualizations using hypergraphs, concludes that even in small software projects large hypergraphs can be required to express all underlying relations. These are not at all easy to comprehend. By taking one agent at a time as the focus of communication and showing its immediate inter-agent relations, we leave it up to subsequent interaction (like navigation across various facets of meanings in PoliFacets or sequential exploration of agents' area of influence, one after the other) to communicate elements with which users can gradually construe the complexity of the program. The overall complexity is redundantly expressed by mutually-supporting signs like the simulation playback (in visual language) and the program report (in textual language), for example.

Previous work comparing three CT learning environments [24] (Scratch [21], Alice [1] and Greenfoot [8]) concludes that they try to simplify the job of building computer programs in different ways. Alice and Scratch mainly eliminate difficulties with the syntax of program encoding, whereas Greenfoot restricts programming to a tiny set of Java resources. Additionally, all three systems value simplicity and aim at removing or hiding accidental conceptual complexity. This allows users to work only with fundamental programming constructs. The same can be said about AgentSheets [17], which has been the reason for developing PoliFacets [11]. The separation between the *programming* and the *reflection on programming* spaces is how participants of the *Scalable Game Design Brasil* project resolved the tension between AgentSheets learners' difficulty in dealing with program complexity and their need to master it in order to build programs that they really wish to build. So, we keep with the findings from previous work about how the programming environment should be, but elaborate on the semiotic richness that can be explored in live documentation that accompanies such environments. This decision is in line with the opinions expressed by one of the most influential thinkers behind user-centered design, Don Norman [15]. In his 2011 book dedicated to discussing how we live with complexity [14], Norman underlines that: "Modern technology can be complex, but complexity by itself is neither good nor bad: it is confusion that is bad. Forget the complaints against complexity; instead, complain about confusion."

Our study shows that *soft masters*, as Turkle refers to programmers who build software by experimenting with program pieces and looking at interesting emerging effects [23], are not yet helped by the communication we propose to include in PoliFacets. We seem to be speaking only to *hard masters*, whose approach is to work from general goals and principles down into the actual encoding of ideas in the form of program constructs. However, the positive results concerning the *affect* of proposed signs suggests that we can – and must – attempt to build new scaffolds and more elaborate interactive discourse about the diagrams we have proposed. Possibly, this communicative strategy will support *soft masters* more effectively and empower them to deal with the meanings and expressive opportunities lying beneath program complexity.

The next steps in our research is to implement what we have proposed. With a working prototype, we will be able to make empirical observations of how *hard masters* receive our communication in actual teaching-learning situations using AgentSheets and PoliFacets. We must also conduct additional rounds of semiotic engineering studies like the one presented in this paper, elaborating on signs of complexity so that *soft masters* can benefit from them. In one case or another, the longer-term goal of our research is to use Semiotic Engineering principles and methods to design efficient and effective communication about inter-agent relations in AgentSheets games and simulations. This communication should be primarily used in live documentation about AgentSheets, but we believe that it should also provide valuable information for improving AgentSheets' user interface itself.

5. ACKNOWLEDGMENTS

Authors would like to thank *CNPq*, *CAPES* and *FAPERJ*, the Brazilian agencies that support their research in different ways. They also thank *The AMD Foundation* for sponsoring the Scalable Game Design Brasil project, as well as all the participants who volunteered to help us in this research.

6. REFERENCES

[1] Alice - http://www.alice.org/

[2] Bennett, V., Koh, K. H. and Repenning, A. 2011. Computing learning acquisition? Visual Languages and Human-Centric Computing.

[3] de Souza, C. S. 2005. The semiotic engineering of human-computer interaction. Cambridge: Mass. The MIT Press.

[4] de Souza, C. S. 2013. Semiotics and Human-Computer Interaction. In: Soegaard, Mads and Dam, Rikke Friis (eds.) The Encyclopedia of Human-Computer Interaction, 2nd Ed. Aarhus, Denmark: The Interaction Design Foundation. Available online at http://www.interaction-design.org/encyclopedia/semiotics_and_human-computer_interaction.html.

[5] de Souza, C. S., Garcia, A. C. B., Slaviero, C., Pinto, H., and Repenning, A. 2011. Semiotic traces of computational thinking acquisition. EUD'11, Berlin, 155-170.

[6] Ferreira, J. J., de Souza, C. S., Salgado, L. C. C., Slaviero, C., Leitão, C. F. and Moreira, F. 2012. Combining cognitive, semiotic and discourse analysis to explore the power of notations in visual programming. VL/HCC'12.

[7] Glasgow, J., N. H. N. and B. Chandrasekaran. 1995. Diagrammatic Reasoning: Cognitive and Computational Perspectives. MIT Press, Cambridge, MA, USA.

[8] Greenfoot - http://www.greenfoot.org/

[9] Jakobson, R. 1060. Closing statements: Linguistics and Poetics, Style in language. T.A. Sebeok, New-York.

[10] Maloney, J., Resnick, M., Rusk, N., Silverman, B., and Eastmond, E. 2010. The Scratch Programming Language and Environment. Trans. Comput. Educ. 10, 4, Article 16.

[11] Mota, M .P, Faria, L.S. and de Souza, C.S. 2012. Documentation Comes to Life in Computational Thinking Acquisition with AgentSheets. In Proceedings of the 11th Brazilian Symposium on Human Factors in Computing Systems (IHC '12). Brazilian Computer Society, Porto Alegre, Brazil, 151-160.

[12] National Research Council Committe for the Workshops on Computational Thinking. 2010. Report of a Workshop on The Scope and Nature of Computational Thinking. Washington, D.C.: The National Academies Press.

[13] National Research Council Committee on Information Technology Literacy. 1999. Being Fluent with Information Technology. Washington, D.C.: National Academy Press.

[14] Norman, D. A. 2011. Living with Complexity. Cambridge, Mass.: The MIT Press.

[15] Norman, D. A. and Draper, S. W. 1986. User Centered System Design. Hillsdale, N.J. Lawrence Erlbaum.

[16] Peter Kapec. 2010. Visualizing software artifacts using hypergraphs. In Proceedings of the 26th Spring Conference on Computer Graphics (SCCG '10). ACM, New York, NY.

[17] Repenning, A. and Ioannidou, A. 2004. Agent-based end-user development, Communications of the ACM, v.47 n.9.

[18] Repenning, A., Webb, D., and Ioannidou, A. 2010. Scalable game design and the development of a checklist for getting computational thinking into public schools. In Proceedings of the 41st ACM technical symposium on Computer science education (SIGCSE '10). ACM, New York, 265-269.

[19] Scalable Game Design Brasil - http://www.sgd-br.inf.puc-rio.br

[20] Schön, D. 1983. *The reflective practitioner*. New York, NY. Basic Books.

[21] Scratch - http://scratch.mit.edu/

[22] Stenning, K. and Oberlander, I. 1995. A Cognitive Theory of Graphical and Linguistic Reasoning: Logic and Implementation. *Cognitive Science*, vol. 19 (1).

[23] Turkle, S. 2005. The Second Self. Computers and the Human Spirit. Twentieth Anniversary Edition. Cambridge, Mass.: The MIT Press.

[24] Utting, I., Cooper, S., Kölling, M., Maloney, J., and Resnick, M. 2010. Alice, Greenfoot, and Scratch - A Discussion. Trans. Comput. Educ. 10, 4, Article 17.

Interfaces as Rhetorical Constructions: reddit and 4chan During the Boston Marathon Bombings

Liza Potts
WIDE Research
Michigan State University
East Lansing, MI, USA
LPotts@msu.edu

Angela Harrison
Old Dominion University
Norfolk, VA USA
aharrisr@gmail.com

ABSTRACT

In this paper, we describe the rhetorical construction of two community sites and analyze how these sites support the information sharing practices of these communities. By examining activity on web-based discussion boards reddit and 4chan, we show how these spaces are developed and shaped over time by participants making rhetorical moves in order to share content within these ecologies. During the 2013 Boston Marathon bombings, we show how these spaces can be altered, disregarding the more typical practices on these sites. When community members embrace or reject these uses, it is as much a reaction to the content as it is to the cultural misuse of the community. In the case of reddit and 4hcan, this acceptance and rejection is especially true when the makers and maintainers of the system are participants themselves. Through this examination, we conclude that it is important to understand the rhetorical construction of these systems as reflections of the cultures they support.

Categories and Subject Descriptors

H.5.2 Information Interfaces and Presentation: User Interfaces – user-centered design

Keywords

User experience; interface design; digital culture; social web; reddit; 4chan; bulletin boards; disaster; terrorism; digital rhetoric; information design; participation

1. INTRODUCTION

When examining interfaces and discussing their rhetorical structure, information design experts look at issues of usability, playability, accessibility, and other factors when trying to ascertain whether or not a system meets the needs of whatever user group it is trying to support. Similarly, researchers examining the rhetorical implications of design tend to look across activities, systems, and networks [30, 45, 53, 57].

Much of our work as communication design researchers and practitioners lacks a solid understanding of how interfaces are cultural and how participants structure their interactions, much less research on how interfaces are constructed rhetorically.

In this paper, we examine interfaces as rhetorical constructions. Our argument is that interfaces, by their forms of delivery (technology type), memory (recall), arrangement (structure), and style (of content) are rhetorically constructed and impact the methods participants use to share information. We illustrate this in Table 1 by comparing the interface characteristics to the five canons of rhetoric. Used primarily in rhetorical analysis of text and images, these canons serve as a way to analyze interfaces, user experiences, and digital culture.

Table 1. Interface Characteristics and the Five Canons

Delivery	Memory	Arrangement	Style
Platform	Affordance	Layout	Text
System	Meme	Template	Images

Keeping in mind these features listed in Table 1, we can begin to discuss how we are at a point in the design of communication where rhetorical implications are embedded in these interfaces. It is not by accident that there are rhetorical terms in this chart; much of what we teach in our own communication design classrooms is based on these rhetorical terms, which are even more useful when discussing how these choices are reflections of larger rhetorical moves within a given community.

It is important to recognize these spaces as cultures, rhetorically constructed by their communities. When we discuss culture, we are including language, inside jokes, mores, values, and habits within these spaces. We are also pointed to how these spaces are developed and crafted by participants so that they can make certain kinds of rhetorical moves. Rather than seeing these structures as restrictive, we can also observe them as empowering for a given community. How do these structures empower certain kinds of communicating, sharing, and knowledge work?

By examining these spaces, we can discover how new systems, redesigned systems, and other kinds of designer interventions must first begin by conducting community research of these spaces. This kind of research can dig into the surfaces of these spaces in ways in which the interactions of their users will be better contextualized and thus understood.

In his 1997 book Interface Culture, Stephen Johnson [31] argues how interfaces shape how we interact with each other. His central argument could be interpreted as deterministic, rather than symbiotic or even empowering. Rather than expecting interfaces to shape behavior, it is possible that communities encourage interfaces to develop in certain ways in order support of these cultures. This development could be deep in the code itself or through shard conventions for using the system, such as how to structure free-form content, use links, embedded certain types of images, etc.

In this paper, we illustrate how the interfaces of reddit and 4chan are an integral part of their cultures, enabling them to make these rhetorical choices to share information. The structure and form of these spaces was developed not as a reaction to these cultures but to support them. As an example of these behaviors, we discuss how participants on these two sites responded to the Boston Marathon bombings. In doing so, we can analyze how participation is structured because of their interface cultures.

2. ABOUT REDDIT AND 4CHAN

In the wake of the Boston Marathon bombings, images, links, and information quickly moved from 4chan and reddit to Facebook and eventually the mainstream media [56]. This was one of the first crises where both spaces were highly visible to those outside of their communities. By examining these spaces as cultures whose interfaces are integral to the construction of their communities, we can begin to see how such communication flourishes, for better or worse.

Reddit and 4chan are not Facebook and Twitter in terms of presence in the media and numbers of participants. For example, the kinds of images shared on reddit and 4chan are often meme-driven. Many images are labeled as not safe for work (NSFW) or not safe for life (NSFL). These are not the same images that often show up on Facebook and Twitter, where people might post pictures of their children and daily life. Which is to say, reddit and 4chan are not normally thought of as places where much mainstream attention, participation, or even academic research takes place.

It is only recently that we are beginning to see a stronger focus on academic research and mainstream interest in these sites. For example, the 2011 paper published by the MIT Media Lab won the Best Paper award at the International Conference on Weblogs and Social Media for its detailed research of this site [6]. While attention is being paid to these systems, more work is needed to understand how the rhetorical design of these interfaces is key to understanding the cultures in these spaces. These sharp contrasts in memory, arrangement, and style are reasons why reddit and 4chan are useful spaces for examining interfaces as cultures.

Table 2. Interfaces of reddit and 4chan and the Five Canons

Delivery	Memory	Arrangement	Style
reddit	Sources, Links	Threaded, Upvoting	Evidence
4chan	Images, Text	Threaded, Bumping	For the lulz

The information in Table 2 illustrates how these cultures are expressed in terms of language and design on reddit and 4chan. This table contains the rhetorical terms and key examples of how these cultures are constructed through these interfaces. Specifically, we will use this table as we discuss these spaces further, looking at how both are constructed and their use during the Boston Marathon bombings. Across both spaces, the ways in which structure is presented is considerably different. While participants discuss topics by providing links to source material and previous threads, participants on 4chan tend to share images and text as a way of communicating and invoking memory of prior cultural material to create memes, a form of cultural memory for these spaces. As for arrangement, the two systems are considerably different in how content is structured in individual topic posts. Reddit's interface arranges content in a hierarchy, while 4chan's arrangements is much more chaotic. The sites are

equally different in style, with 4chan being more focused on their version of entertainment and humor, while redditors are much more sarcastic and value evidence of some kind (links to primary sources, photographic proof, etc.) to support thread comments.

In discussing these two spaces, in particular their use during the Boston Marathon bombings, we can begin to see how their value as locations of culture can get us to rethink our notions about interface determinism and humanistic agency. It might help communication designers to pinpoint how these spaces are enriched by participants who make these rhetorical choices to accommodate their needs. This kind of research presents us with another reason to value and understand the cultures of our users as we engage in redesign work. In the next section, we will go into greater detail about each platform, describing it in detail to illustrate how interfaces are cultures and cultures are visible within their interfaces.

3. REDDIT

Launched in 2005, reddit is described as "source for what's new and popular on the web" [49]. The form of delivery on reddit consists of a social news website, using a bulletin board style interface. Although it is not as well-known to mainstream internet users the same way that Facebook is known, reddit has seen a huge upswing in popularity. To give a sense of activity on this website, in April 2013, reddit had 69,964,577 unique visitors and over 2.4 million logged in redditors, who cast over 20 million votes [48]. Purchased by publisher Condé Nast in 2006, reddit now operates independently as a subsidiary [40].

3.1 Overview

Reddit is a website where the delivery format, memory devices, arrangement of discussion threads and categorization, and content style all work towards building a distinct culture of sharing information. Halavais refers to reddit along with sites such as StumbleUpon and Digg as spaces where participants are "concentrating attention on sites that have been identified collaboratively" and thus one way to help search work better by locating this content [23]. This concept of locating and sharing content is a core cultural value on reddit.

The reddit interface supports their cultural values by providing ways to for participant to make rhetorical moves. Users on reddit, referred to as redditors, vote on posts made by other redditors in various forums, or subreddits. If a post increases in popularity through the increase of "up" votes, the post can then show up on the front page of reddit. These upvotes is the main form of arrangement across the site. Within these posts, redditors are able to add links within their posts. They do so as a method for referencing source materials, such as news articles, other reddit posts, images, videos, or other materials. This rhetorical move to include references to other material is a key element in using memory and style to reinforce reddit's culture.

Although reddit describes itself as a "type of community where users vote on content" [48], others have described it as a "community of communities" [20]. These communities are referred to as subreddits, and there are over 5,200 active subreddits [48]. There are subreddits devoted to such topics as computer programming, Doctor Who, religions, science, and current events. Each subreddit has a creator who may also be a moderator of that subreddit, regulars who post to the subreddit, and their own culture that may extend into regular jokes, writing patterns, or Rickrolling specific to that subreddit in addition to what already is commonplace on reddit.

3.2 Interface

The interface of reddit is hierarchical and ordered, with discussion threads (or "stories," as reddit's management refers to these posts) moving up or down in ranking, depending on whether the content is voted up or down by other redditors. The same is true for comments posted within a discussion thread; the more popular the comment, the higher it rises to the top of the comment heap. To vote on content, redditors simply click on the up or down arrows located to the left of the post (see Figure 1). If content receives enough votes, it has a chance at making it to the front page of reddit.

As seen in Figure 1, the rhetorical structure of reddit is reflected in the interface with regards to the arrangement of content and the information structure. Posts are made within a subreddit (such as /r/news), and comments are made for those posts. The listings of posts and comments is very hierarchical, in that they can be read from top to bottom. While some discussion posts may rank higher than others, the format of comments remains the same and the comments stay with the original post. Users of the site can expand or collapse different comment threads, moving through the comments easily.

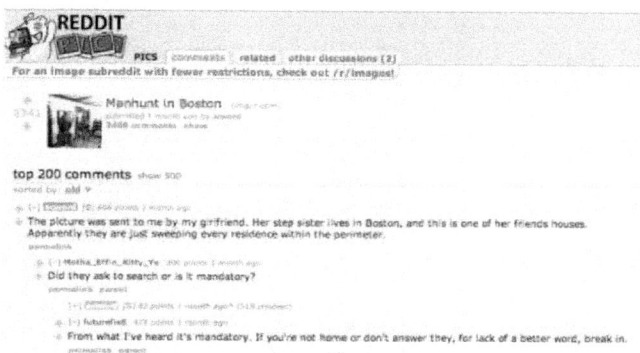

Figure 1. reddit interface.

To navigate the comments, users can sort by a number of different sort types [50]. All of these rankings are based on how other redditors ranked the content using the voting mechanism. There is "top" to sort by the highest ranked comments, "new" lists the most recent comments, "hot" is a combination of the "top" and "new." The "best" sort order is based on an algorithm that attempts to list the best comments first; "Controversial" has a similar algorithm. Regardless of the sort, the comments will be ranked in descending order by whatever sort type the user selects. Thus, their cultural value and rhetorical move of sharing information is evident in the interface, allowing them to rank, sort, and view content based on their collective preferences.

When discussing different issues in a thread, redditors will often submit links in their post to refer to other material. Linking to source material is one of the distinguishing rhetorical choices that redditors make in their posts. The ability to add links in these posts empowers redditors to use memory as a device for linking to relevant material. They accomplish this by using links to add to the conversation. These links may lead to previous posts, memes, images, articles, or other materials. This material typically refers to source material, shares an emotional reaction, or builds upon the argument in the thread. Source material can refer to prior posts, news articles, scientific articles, or other sources. Such activity works towards exchanging information, engaging in the conversation, and participating in the collective rhetorical structure of reddit.

3.3 Culture

Overall, reddit describes itself as "a pretty open platform and free speech place" [51]. Reddit lists five rules that all redditors must follow while on the site [51]. Perhaps the most relevant to the Boston Marathon bombings issue is the "Don't post personal information" rule. This rule lists additional content to describe what reddit means by personal information: Facebook profile links, full names, real-life details, employer names of other redditors.

On reddit, participants have created their own way of enacting their culture through various rhetorical moves. Reddit contains many subreddits on various topics such as geek culture, science, and technology. Every week, another scientist [10], celebrity [4], political figure, everyday person, etc. will post a question and answer session referred to as an AMA (ask me anything) [26]. Their random acts of kindness include sending pizza to those in need, enough so that there is a subreddit dedicated to it [47]. Although there is diversity across reddit, this community inspires a sense of place and unity. In the words of one redditor, "I thought of community as one of those words where it involved everyone but me, and for some reason, reddit just feels like the opposite" [58]. By using various rhetorical moves such as inside jokes, repeated stories, sharing of past threads, and a special tenor in the language, reddit has created a culture that is distinct from other online communities.

Reddit is an open source community, meaning that the software that runs the reddit site is open to updates by reddit participants. The open source philosophy is one in which an ethos of cooperation, freedom, and innovation is held in high regard by redditors. Reddit describes this work as a space in which "community members are constantly tinkering and contributing features, bug fixes, and translations back to the site" [48]. The emphasis on using sources and links for memory, categories for threads, and hierarchies in arrangement in the delivery of reddit are all reflective of these social values.

4. 4CHAN

4chan is an imageboard site created in 2003 by a teenager named Christopher Poole, also known as moot [2]. Originally conceived as a space for anime fans to share and discuss images, 4chan has now has "22 million page impressions every day and 9.5 million unique users each month" [6]. Participants on 4chan are mostly anonymous, meaning that there is no username or user account connected to their posts. The IP address for the computer that any content is posted from is not made public, but it can be seen by the 4chan administrators [1].

Though 4chan consists of many image boards, one in particular stands out from the rest: /b/, the random board. In the space of /b/, the culture is characterized by a distinct rhetorical structure: image-based threads and a chaotic, fast-paced delivery of information. The use of images is the main way in which 4chan enacts its style.

4.1 Overview

4chan consists of six sections: Japanese Culture, Interests, Creative, Adult, Other, and Miscellaneous. One board under the Miscellaneous section, known as the random board /b/, has gained a negative reputation on the Internet. There are few rules on /b/, and the ones that exist state posting anything that violates the law is forbidden and minors should not view mature material [1]. Otherwise, anything can be posted. There are approximately 35,000 threads and 400,000 posts per day on /b/ [6]. Given that the average life of a thread is 3.9 minutes and the median of time a post stays on the first page is 5 seconds [6], the chaotic delivery of information is a constant. It is the birthplace of many popular Internet memes such as LOLcats and Rickrolling, and is supposedly the origin of the group Anonymous [2]. It has been described as "anarchic" [33], a "high school cafeteria" [3], and "a court jester" [33]. A closer look at the interface shows how these descriptions reflect the chaotic, "for the lulz" culture of the site. "For the lulz" is a statement associated with trolling. Trolling is defined as posting "deliberately incendiary content to a discussion forum or other online community . . . for no other reason than to stir up chaos and outrage" [60]. The "lulzs" is the pleasure a troll gets from the act of making people angry. To say that something is done "for the lulz" means that it is done for the personal pleasure of causing anger and discontent in people.

4.2 Interface

4chan is an image board, which is a type of Bulletin Board System [59]. Participants on 4chan are free to post and share pictures in an environment that does not require any login or password. Participants are not restricted from starting threads or commenting upon them, but any time a new thread is started it must have a picture [3]. Each thread is started with a post and accompanying image. Other participants can reply to the post, sometimes with images or sometimes with text. The participants' emphasis on the image is tied to the rhetorical canon of memory, with participants using images to show a collective production of discourse.

The arrangement of this interface structure is unique, if not confusing and chaotic. There are 15 pages on /b/, and as a new thread is started, it is pushed down the line of pages. Any time a thread is commented upon, it is *bumped*, or moved back to the start of the first page. When a thread reaches the bottom of the 15th page it is deleted, or *404*'s. The threads are not nested; rather, they are arranged chronologically. The page needs to be refreshed before seeing new posts. Each post is assigned a number, and when it is referred to in another post its number appears on the new post. Figure 2 shows a several screenshots of a thread. The first screenshot is of an original post. The second screenshot is of a reply to that post. The number 483489093 (OP) indicates the post that is replied to, and the OP stands for "Original Poster." The last screenshot shows what happens to the interface when the number is hovered over. The number turns red and the post that is referred to pops up.

Although 4chan lacks "robust methods for moving information around" [30] in this system, how different threads are organized do seem to work for this community. Conversations are started, always with an image attached, sometimes these conversations spiral off into other topics, some responses to comments are given in the form of images and others in text. Eventually the conversations die without any kind of record. The delivery, memory, and arrangement of the information is fast-paced and chaotic, thus the information that is shared takes a similar turn.

4.3 Culture

4chan's /b/ is notorious; it is not uncommon to see images depicting gore, nudity, and racism, among others. For example, "subject threads range from the mundane to the disturbing—everything from bike-shorts recommendations to found footage of people getting hit by cars or gruesome photos of body parts found in the wreckage of the September 11 attacks" [35]. In the past, /b/ has been cited for a number of negative actions, but it is also responsible for a number of positive actions, such as identifying a woman who was responsible for drowning puppies in a river [9]

and getting a campaign started to send birthday cards to a WWII veteran [28].

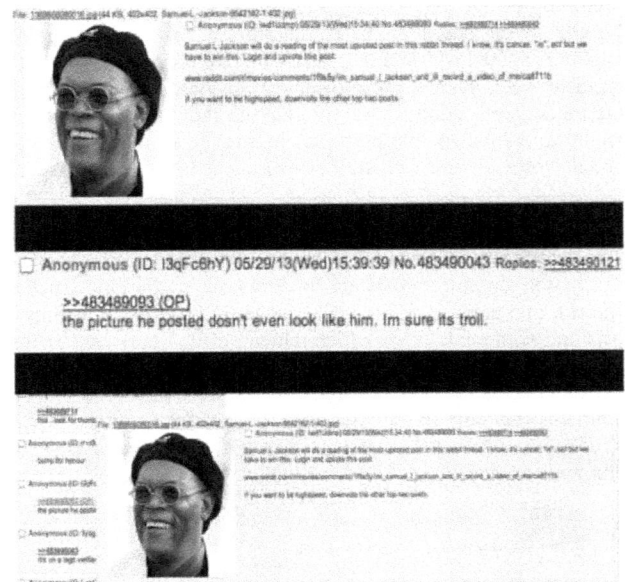

Figure 2. 4chan interface.

The MIT Media Lab study of 4chan pinpointed two contributors to the culture of /b/: anonymity and ephemerality [6]. Since the site does not requite a login or a password, much of the postings on /b/ remain anonymous. As a result, much of the content that passes through /b/ is uncensored. The anonymity is a stark contrast to many of the social spaces that currently exist because whatever is said or done in these spaces is traceable. Part of the allure of /b/, it seems, is that nothing that posted can be easily traced, so people feel more free to post content that may be questionable elsewhere [6]. The traditional rating systems that exist in social sites are also not present on /b/, thus reputation is not of particular concern [6]. The fast-paced nature of the site also ensures that content is chaotic, meaning that the content is jumbled and of a questionable nature. The lack of a reputation system suggests that the content is what drives the site; therefore, content needs to be eye-catching, shocking, or grab attention. Threads that are not commented upon within a particular timeframe disappear, and archives do not exist. All of these factors work into the delivery of information on the site and contribute to its chaotic culture.

5. USE DURING THE BOSTON MARATHON BOMBINGS

On Monday, April 15 2013, two bombs exploded within seconds of each other at 2:49pm near the finish line of the Boston Marathon [41]. Three people were killed and 282 were injured, and Boston became the site of a manhunt as the Federal Bureau of Investigations (FBI) and local authorities searched for the bombing suspects [34]. The manhunt for the suspects lasted several days. During that time, the suspects killed a police officer and were involved in a shootout that resulted in the death of one of the suspected terrorists. Later on the evening of April 19th, the second suspect was taken into custody after he is found in a residential neighborhood.

Across the social web, people were actively trying to share information about the terrorist attack and the subsequent manhunt. During that week, the FBI asked the public for help. They wanted people to send in any photos or videos of the Boston Marathon and its aftermath [14]. Participants across these sites were locating photos and information in an effort to track down the suspected terrorists. Across reddit and 4chan, activity picked up as these users became more active in information gathering, along with photo sharing sites such as Flickr and Imgur [24, 27]. Although it is not clear whether these sites helped or hindered the investigation, our initial research indicates that the interfaces and cultural norms of these spaces helped drive methods of content creation and curation.

5.1 4chan

The same day that the Boston Marathon bombings occurred, a number of articles appeared online that identified two websites—4chan and reddit—as online communities trying to identify who the bombers were. 4chan, while recognized as a site trying to do the same as reddit, was mostly footnoted or mentioned in passing. However, 4chan did play a part in the hunt for the marathon bomber [13, 29. 37]. Examining how the participants on 4chan interacted with one another through the fast-paced space to identify the bomber reveals the chaotic interface culture of the site.

Not long after Boston Marathon bombings, threads started appearing on 4chan that contained images of possible suspects in the crowd. Many of the images, as shown in Figure 3, had arrows and lines drawn around them with accompanying text declaring how the person in the image could be the bomber. Many of the suspect images showed backpacks, which the participants on 4chan used as a springboard to identify the suspects. These images were collected and archived in a post on Imgur, which will be discussed in the next paragraph. The style of sharing information—via image—shows that participants relied more on visual methods of sharing information; the rhetorical memory of the site is rooted in image as opposed to text.

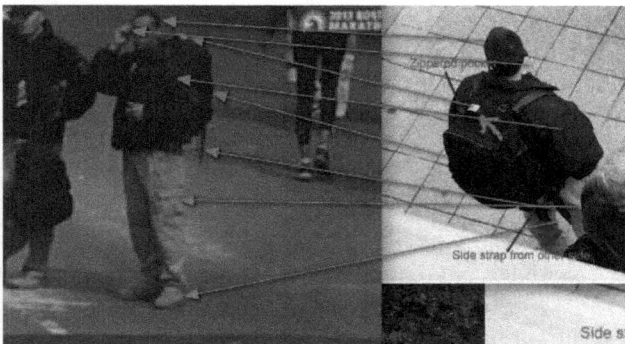

Figure 3. One of the "Think Tank" 4chan Images

On picture-sharing site Imgur, images from 4chan were posted about the bombing. Imgur is a site that "can be used to share pictures with friends, as well as post images on message boards and blogs" [27]. Like 4chan, participants can post and remain anonymous. The 4chan Think Tank was a post made on the same day as the Boston Marathon bombings. It contains 57 images of possible suspects. The images contain the lines and circles that serve as the arguments why these people are suspects, and some have text, like the one shown in Figure 3. The page has over 4 million views [27]. These images appeared in news articles, some of which are about 4chan trying to find the bombers [25, 55]. The use of Imgur also verifies the image-driven nature 4chan's culture, but also serves as the only archive of the deliberations of who the Boston Bomber may have been.

File: 1366214937041.png-(777 KB, 960x708, 11884_10151392936276275_728885636_n.png)

CAN YOU IDENTIFY THIS MAN?

Anonymous (ID: RcBR40ey) 04/17/13(Wed)12:08:57 No.473370235 Replies: >>473370480 >>473371169 >>473371262 >>473371271 >>473371371 >>473371849 >>473372114 >>473372218 >>473372427 >>473373397 >>473373408 >>473374021 >>473374705 >>473375761 >>473376057 >>473376212 >>473376963 >>473376969 >>473377014 >>473377578 >>473377989

Has anyone seen this yet? In any event, /b/, do what it is you do.

Anonymous (ID: ooqHd6hb) 04/17/13(Wed)12:09:48 No.473370361 Replies: >>473370490

A man carrying a massive produced backpack. STOP THE PRESSES.

Anonymous (ID: 7bI2X(U6) 04/17/13(Wed)12:10:39 No.473370480 Replies: >>473370840 >>473371976

>>473370235 (OP)
explosive bag's a foxhead (there's pics of a zipper), no foxhead bags look like what that guy has. try again.

Anonymous (ID: OQWaRJhJ) 04/17/13(Wed)12:10:42 No.473370490 Replies: >>473374286

>>473370361
The bags pretty big, it's not massive though.

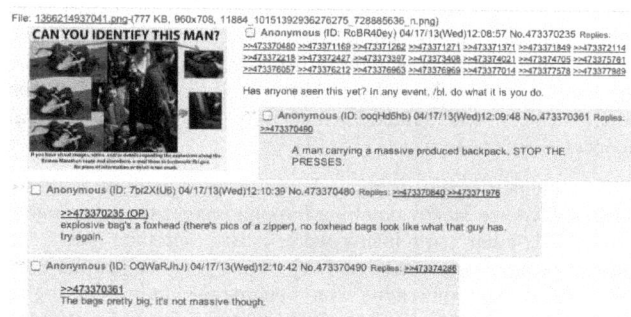

Figure 4. "Can You Identify This Man?" Fake Poster on 4chan

However, what occurred in the threads also warrants some examination, particularly with the style participants use to communicate. Figure 4 shows a fake poster made by a participant that asks, "Can You Identify This Man?" with an email address across the bottom. A version of this poster, with the text cut out, also appeared in the 4chan Think Tank Imgur post. Participants in the thread do not take the poster seriously, commenting, "You're either incredibly [expletive] new, or slower than slowpoke," and "I see the FBI is rocking MSPaint for their wanted signs these days" [5]. Both of these comments suggest that the timing of the post and the composition of the poster are poor, therefore the poster is fake.

Some participants argued about whether the person in the image was the bomber. Others discussed different topics, such as the bombings in Iraq and possible conspiracy theories. It was difficult to follow any kind of linear conversation in the threads, and there is no organization to the posts; they are organized and arranged by timestamp. The disarray of the delivery makes finding any useful information difficult, and when coupled with the "for the lulz" style participants have employed to share information, it is hard to discern what information is genuine or not.

5.2 Reddit

In the wake of the Boston Marathon bombings, activity on reddit largely focused on the delivery and curation of news content [32], sharing information on how to support the victims [7], and sending pizza to local police as a sign of support [46]. The news postings were quite lengthy, updating fellow redditors on what was happening in Boston in the wake of the bombings (Figure 5). The style and delivery of this content followed reddit's typical rhetorical structure created for a current event. This rhetorical structure takes advantage of the delivery, memory, arrangement, and style of reddit's community. seen in Figure 5 illustrates how new edits are made to catalog the events as they happen, with participants adding timestamps and short notes as events unfold.

EDIT 12:41 EST: MIT updated their emergency site again. The shooter remains at large, police continue to search the campus. Please REMAIN INDOORS until further notice.
EDIT 12:45 EST: /u/speedbreeze has a summary in multiple languages. They have fact-checked info, where I relay what I am hearing on the feed.
EDIT 12:47 EST: /u/sceptre886 mentioned the car stolen is a Mercedes ML-350. Tag number 137 NZ1
EDIT 12:49 EST: Shots fired in Cambridge. Shots and Explosions in Watertown.
EDIT 12:50 EST: Shots fired. Grenades spotted.
EDIT 12:51 EST: More shots, explosion. Grenade went off.
EDIT 12:55 EST: Officer down. Explosives at scene. 94 Spruce Street??
EDIT 12:56 EST: Reports of a stolen state police truck. Black, 4 door.
EDIT 12:57 EST: Second officer down. Hand Grenades...automatic weapons fired.
EDIT 12:58 EST: Spruce (sp?) and Lincoin
EDIT 1:00 EST: Dexter and Laural. Suspect injured. Explosives in the area.
EDIT 1:01 EST: Officers ordered back. Map of area thanks to /u/rm-rf_

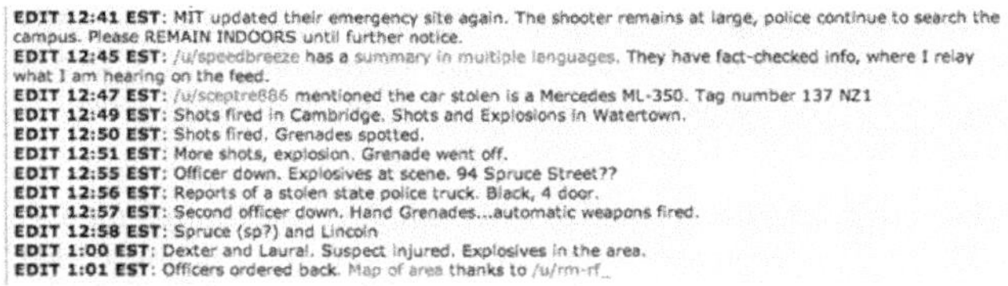

Figure 5. Clip of a news posting on reddit.

While much of this activity was typical reddit behavior, with redditors using its interface to participate in social sharing, it was a newly created subreddit that deviated from this rhetorical structure that garnered considerable attention from the mainstream media. On the FindBostonBombers subreddit, participants were focused on tracking down the suspected terrorists. Before the subreddit was shut down by reddit's leadership team [19], the participants in this subreddit had wrongfully named several innocent people as terrorists [16, 17].

While some participants in this subreddit were aggressively trying to locate the terrorists by combing through images freely available online [14], other participants were calling out their peers for going after innocent bystanders [18]. These posts lacked the kind of proof that other subreddits would encourage, short of trying to link together different images. Pushing away from the style of reddit, this new subreddit divided some of the community, as they questioned the subreddit's use.

The leaders of this subreddit stated that their goal was to support the FBI. One of the moderators of the subreddit stated that he was "inspired by all the people who ran straight toward the blast in the video, trying to help out. This subreddit is kind of like that; it's the human spirit fighting back" [54]. In the past, reddit has participated in smaller scale events and there is a subreddit devoted to crowdsourcing investigations [52].

While the participants wanted to find the "bad guys," it was the behaviors and tone of many of the posts that led to false accusations affecting people outside the community. Participants shared public, personal information about whom they suspected, including photos and Facebook profiles. While this move of sharing material is an attempt to use memory and style, it deviated from the rhetorical structure of the community. Such sharing of personal information is against the rules on reddit. While this could be seen as a cultural shift, the response to these actions by the larger reddit community and their management shows that these behaviors were unwelcome.

The material in this subreddit went viral, leaving reddit and moving across other social web sites and to the mainstream media. One article by *The New York Post* contains some of the pictures that were also in the 4chan Think Tank and declares that authorities are circulating the photos [8]. It is unclear whether they grabbed these images from reddit, 4chan, or Imgur. After the men in the photos were cleared, *The New York Post* received a large amount of criticism [21]. Some in the mainstream media accused the participants in FindBostonBombers of vigilantism [36], while at the same time printing material that they found on reddit as if it were news.

As a result of the issues surrounding the FindBostonBombers subreddit, the leadership of reddit posted an apology on their blog [12]. They reasserted the rhetorical structure of their community. The creator of the subreddit also did an AMA post (ask me anything), where other redditors angrily confronted him. When asked whether or not it was worth it, he replied "not even slightly" [43]. He has since deleted his account on reddit. The subreddit itself still exists, although it seems to be on permanent lockdown as seen in Figure 6 [19].

While many media outlets reacted negatively to the manhunt on reddit [37], other journalists felt that the apology was unnecessary because none of the major media outlets that used reddit's content apologized and they were equally at fault for spreading misinformation [11, 29]. Redditors worked to bury earlier posts

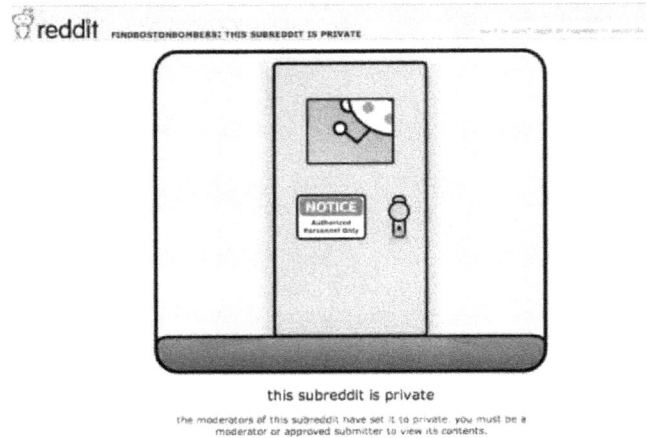

Figure 6. FindBostonBombers subreddit.

that contained this inaccurate information by upvoting information that vindicated the accused. In that aspect, the culture of reddit was well represented by this use of their interface. One reporter from Slate stated "there's no denying that a few professional media outlets have demonstrated far less of a conscience than the users and moderators of findbostonbombers" [44], showing that in spite of the larger impression that reddit was a vigilante mob, there was strong activity to set the record straight.

Overall, the efforts and attitudes in *FindBostonBombers* are not indicative of reddit as a whole, as evidenced by the behavior after these events. On reddit, there was a sense of regret and anger over what occurred on in *FindBostonBombers* [43]. The rhetorical structures of the culture of reddit, with its need for evidence, hierarchy information flows, and link structure, is not a good fit for the kind of activity that went on in FindBostonBombers. It will be interesting to observe how their interface might change further to support these cultural beliefs about these kinds of activities, namely manhunts, in the future.

6. CONCLUSION

In 1998, Robert R. Johnson asked us to "rethink the user as being an active participant in the social order that designs, develops, and implements technologies" [31]. On reddit and 4chan, this active participation can be seen in the interfaces and the rhetorical practices of image sharing, attitudes towards evidence, and link activities among the participants. While many accused the two sites of participating in a dangerous form of citizen journalism, many on reddit and 4chan had the admirable aims of trying to track down the terrorists. The execution of it was problematic at best and destructive at worst.

It is difficult to pinpoint 4chan's goals for finding the bomber, given their chaotic culture. Participants analyzed various images, but due to the fast pace and chaotic culture of the site— information became jumbled and lost. The participants' attitudes, both towards each other and the images shared, were reflective of the site's interface: swift, hectic, and volatile. The priority of the images, coupled with the attitudes of the participants, did not match the seriousness of the topic at hand, but the mainstream media took the efforts seriously, commenting that the result of such crowdsourcing efforts were either helpful or a "witch hunt" [42].

Redditors in FindBostonBombers emphasized that their participation was "playing detective" [39] rather than more typical reddit activities such as news curation, information gathering, or image sharing. In her early work on technologically mediated communication, Gurak noted a similar issue in a forum she was researching where participants experienced an ethos "composed in large part of hyperbolic statements and inaccurate information" [22]. Many of the posts in FindBostonBombers were similarly situated. Those participants were working outside the mores and rules of reddit. In the end, they received negative feedback from their peers and the management of reddit because of how they disregarded their community's values to support their activities.

Examining these spaces as rhetorical constructions, we can see how the forms of delivery, memory, arrangement, and style of these systems led to a variety of different types of information gathering. The design of these systems lent themselves to collecting and distributing information, as evidenced by the high rate of production of text and links on reddit and images on 4chan. However, it was not as good at controlling where that information went. While Monroy-Hernández, et.al. have pointed out that "social media creates an alternate "user-generated" channel of communication that can address weaknesses in information flow," [38] they also acknowledge, like we do, that there are major challenges with regards to misinformation. Looking specifically at these two communities, we propose that further research should be done on how these spaces are rhetorically constructed and what happens when those constructs are disregarded.

7. ACKNOWLEDGMENTS
We would like to extend our thanks to the participants of reddit and 4chan. Major thanks to Alice Daer, whose feedback was pivotal in helping us work through our ideas.

8. REFERENCES
[1] 4chan. 2013. FAQ. http://www.4chan.org/faq

[2] 4chan. 2013. *Know Your Meme*. http://knowyourmeme.com/memes/sites/4chan

[3] Agger, M. 4chanomics. *Slate*. http://www.slate.com/articles/technology/the_browser/2011/06/4chanomics.html

[4] Anderson, G. 2013. Hi @reddit! http://www.reddit.com/r/IAmA/comments/1egkr9/i_am_gilli an_anderson_ama/ ... pic.twitter.com/EXkF0goDUk. *Twitter*. https://twitter.com/GillianA/status/335076734351327235.

[5] Anonymous. Has anyone seen this yet? In any event, /b/, do what it is you do. *4chan*. www.4chan.org

[6] Bernstein, M., Monroy-Hernandez, A., Harry, D., Andre, P., Panovich, K., and Vargas, G. 2011. 4chan and /b/: an analysis of anonymynity and ephemerality online in a large online community. *Fifth International AAAI Conference on Weblogs and Social Media*. Association of the Advancement of Artificial Intelligence.

[7] Boston. 2013. Important links for Boston Marathon 2013 disaster. *Reddit*. http://www.reddit.com/r/boston/wiki/bostonmarathon2013em ergency.

[8] Celona, L., Hamilton, B., and Schram, J. 2013. Authorities circulate photos of two men spotted carrying bags near site of Boston bombings. *The New York Post*. http://www.nypost.com/p/news/national/feds_have_men_in_ sights_j43UJwXZncr0wmysU42scJ

[9] Chen, A. 2010. Puppy-throwing girl caught in Bosnia. *Gawker*. http://gawker.com/5629513/puppy+throwing-girl-caught-in-bosnia

[10] ColCrisHadfield. Post. *Reddit*. http://www.reddit.com/r/videos/comments/1e7bvv/for_my_fi nal_post_on_reddit_from_the/.

[11] Eordogh, F. 2013. Reddit didn't need to apologise after the Boston Marathon bombing. *The Guardian*. http://www.guardian.co.uk/commentisfree/2013/apr/24/reddi t-boston-marathon-bombing-apology-unnecessary.

[12] erik. 2013. Reflections on the recent Boston crisis. *Reddit*. http://blog.reddit.com/2013/04/reflections-on-recent-boston-crisis.html.

[13] Federal Bureau of Investigations. FBI Assists Boston Police Department Regarding Explosions Along Marathon Route and Elsewhere. *Boston Division*. boston-police-department-regarding-the-explosions-along-the http://www.fbi.gov/boston/press-releases/2013/fbi-assists--marathon-route-and-remains-on-scene.

[14] Federal Bureau of Investigations. Additional photos released in bombing case. *News*. http://www.fbi.gov/news/updates-on-investigation-into-multiple-explosions-in-boston.

[15] FindBostonBombers. 2013. Another man spotted wearing backpack. *Reddit*. http://www.reddit.com/r/findbostonbombers/comments/1cix2 2/another_man_spotted_wearing_backpack_with_similar/.

[16] FindBostonBombers. 2013. Blue Robe Guy. *Reddit*. http://www.reddit.com/r/findbostonbombers/comments/1cii4 n/blue_robe_guy/.

[17] FindBostonBombers. 2013. Image overlay of white hat and blue jogging suit. *Reddit*. http://www.reddit.com/r/findbostonbombers/comments/1cke xd/image_overlay_of_white_hat_and_blue_jogging_suit/c9hi nm5,

[18] FindBostonBombers. 2013. The innocent hunt. *Reddit*. http://www.reddit.com/r/findbostonbombers/comments/1cjjl3 /the_innocent_hunt.

[19] FindBostonBombers. 2013. Subreddit. *Reddit*. http://www.reddit.com/r/findbostonbombers.

[20] Fitzpatrick, A. 2013. Don't blame all of reddit for Boston bombing witch hunt. *Mashable*. http://mashable.com/2013/04/24/reddit-boston-bombing/.

[21] Fung, K. and Mirkinson, J. 2013. New York Post's Boston 'Bag Men' front page called 'A new low,' 'appalling.' (photo). *The Huffington Post*. http://www.huffingtonpost.com/2013/04/18/ny-post-boston-suspects-bag-men-front-page_n_3109052.html

[22] Gurak, L.J. 1997. *Persuasion and Privacy in Cyberspace: The Online Protests Over Lotus Marketplace and the Clipper Chip*. New Haven: Yale University Press.

[23] Halavais, A. 2009. *Search Engine Society*. Malden, MA: Polity Press.

[24] Hahatango. 2013. 2013.4_boston.marathon.bombing. Photopool on *Flickr*. http://www.flickr.com/photos/hahatango/sets/721576332524 45135/.

[25] Hoffberger, C. 2013. Did 4chan find the Boston marathon bomber? *The Daily Dot*.

http://www.dailydot.com/news/4chan-boston-marathon-bomber-photo-evidence/

[26] IAmA. 2013. Subreddit. *Reddit.* http://www.reddit.com/r/IAmA/.

[27] Imgur. 2013. FAQ. http://imgur.com/faq

[28] Ingram, M. 2012. 4chan decides to do something nice for a change. *GigaOM.* http://gigaom.com/2010/09/02/4chan-decides-to-do-something-nice-for-a-change/

[29] Inquisitr. 2013. FBI seems to criticize reddit, 4chan for circulating wrong Boston suspect photos. *Inquisitr.* http://www.inquisitr.com/625263/fbi-seems-to-criticize-reddit-4chan-for-circulating-wrong-boston-suspect-photos/.

[30] Johnson-Eilola, J. 2005. *Datacloud: Towards a New Theory of Online Work.* Cresskill, NJ: Hampton Press.

[31] Johnson, Steven. 1997. *Interface Culture: How New Technology Transforms the Way We Create & Communicate.* Basic Books, New York, NY.

[32] JpDeathBlade. 2013. Live updates of Boston Situation [Part 2]. *Reddit.* http://www.reddit.com/r/news/comments/1co395/live_updates_of_boston_situation_part_2/.

[33] Kelly, J. and Sheerin, J. 2010. The strange virtual world of 4chan. *BBC News.* http://www.bbc.co.uk/news/magazine-10520487.

[34] Kotz, Deborah. 2013. Injury toll from marathon bombings rises. *Boston Globe.* http://www.bostonglobe.com/metro/massachusetts/2013/04/22/just-bombing-victims-still-critically-ill-but-count-injured-rises/7mUGAu5tJgKsxc634NCAJJ/story.html.

[35] Lipinski, J. 2012. Chasing the Cicada: Exploring the Darkest Corridors of the Internet. *Mental Floss.* http://mentalfloss.com/article/31932/chasing-cicada-exploring-darkest-corridors-internet

[36] Madrigal, A. C. 2013. Hey reddit, enough Boston bombing vigilantism. *The Atlantic.* http://www.theatlantic.com/technology/archive/2013/04/hey-reddit-enough-boston-bombing-vigilantism/275062/.

[37] Miller, Z. J. 2013. FBI releases photos of suspects; Let the crowdsourcing begin. *Time.* http://swampland.time.com/2013/04/18/fbi-releases-photos-of-suspects-let-the-crowdsourcing-begin/.

[38] Monroy-Hernández, A., Kiciman, E., boyd, d., Counts, S. 2012. Narcotweets: Social Media in Wartime. *Proceedings of the Sixth International AAAI Conference on Weblogs and Social Media.* Association for the Advancement of Artificial Intelligence.

[39] Newman, J. 2013. Reddit and crowdsourcing: Valuable or problematic? *Time.* http://techland.time.com/2013/04/19/reddit-and-crowdsourcing-valuable-or-problematic/.

[40] New York Times. 2012. Left alone by its owner, reddit soars. http://www.nytimes.com/2012/09/03/business/media/reddit-thrives-after-advance-publications-let-it-sink-or-swim.html.

[41] New York Times. 2013. Reconstructing the scene of the Boston Marathon Bombing. *New York Times.* http://www.nytimes.com/interactive/2013/04/17/us/caught-in-the-blast-at-the-boston-marathon.html.

[42] Ngak, C. 2013. Crowdsourcing or witch hunt? Reddit and 4chan users attempt to solves the Boston bombing case. *CBS News.* http://www.cbsnews.com/8301-205_162-57580114/crowdsourcing-or-witch-hunt-reddit-and-4chan-users-attempt-to-solve-boston-bombing-case/

[43] Oops777. 2013. I am the guy that created the controversial and since deleted /r/findbostonbombers AMA. *Reddit.* http://www.reddit.com/r/IAmA/comments/1cvsky/i_am_the_guy_that_created_the_controversial_and/.

[44] Oremus, W. 2013. Reddit vs. the media. *Slate.* http://www.slate.com/articles/technology/technology/2013/04/findbostonbombers_reddit_vs_the_media_in_search_for_boston_bombing_suspects.html.

[45] Potts, L. 2013. *Social Media in Disaster Response.* New York: Routledge.

[46] Random Acts of Pizza. 2013. Sending pizza to Boston PD and other departments involved. *Reddit.* http://www.reddit.com/r/RandomActsOfPizza/comments/1cqup5/sending_pizza_to_boston_pd_and_other_departments/.

[47] Random Acts of Pizza. 2013. Subreddit. *Reddit.* http://www.reddit.com/r/RandomActsOfPizza/

[48] Reddit. 2013. About. *Reddit.* http://www.reddit.com/about/.

[49] Reddit. 2013. FAQ. *Reddit.* http://www.reddit.com/wiki/faq.

[50] Reddit. 2013. Navigation. *Reddit.* http://www.reddit.com/wiki/navigation.

[51] Reddit. 2013. Rules of Reddit. *Reddit.* http://www.reddit.com/rules/.

[52] Reddit Bureau of Investigations. Subreddit. *Reddit.* http://www.reddit.com/r/RBI.

[53] Salvo, Michael J.; Ehren Helmut Pflugfelder; Joshua Prenosil (2010) The children of Aramis. *Journal of Technical Writing and Communication* 40.3 245-263

[54] Shea, M. 2013. Reddit wants the Boston bomber's blood. *Vice.* www.vice.com/read/reddit-wants-the-boston-bombers-blood.

[55] Sheets, C. 2013.10 Boston marathon 'suspects' 4chan and reddit found. *International Business Times.* http://www.ibtimes.com/10-boston-marathon-bombing-suspects-4chan-reddit-found-photos-1199213#

[56] Simpson, C. 2013. F.B.I. released the Tsarnaevs' photos because of reddit and the Post. *The Atlantic* Wire. http://www.theatlanticwire.com/national/2013/04/fbi-released-tsarnaev-brothers-photos-because-reddit-and-post/64416/.

[57] Spinuzzi, C. 2008. *Network: Theorizing Knowledge Work in Telecommunications.* Cambridge: Cambridge University Press.

[58] Youngman, M. 2012. Post. *Reddit.* http://www.reddit.com/r/about_quotes/comments/y5rc8/i_thought_of_community_as_one_of_those_words/.

[59] Yotsuba Society's Guide to Imageboards. 2011. *Yotsuba Society.* http://www.yotsubasociety.org/imageboardguide

[60] Dibbell, J. 2009. The assclown offensive: How to enrage the Church of Scientology. *Wired.* http://www.wired.com/culture/culturereviews/magazine/17-10/mf_chanology?currentPage=all

Sympathetic Devices: Designing Technologies for Older Adults

Claudia B. Rebola
School of Industrial Design
Georgia Tech
Atlanta, GA, USA
crw@gatech.edu

Brian Jones
Interactive Media Technology Center
Georgia Tech
Atlanta, GA, USA
brian.jones@imtc.gatech.edu

ABSTRACT

This paper provides an outline of a framework used in a series of interactive product concepts designed for and with older adults. This framework was developed as part of a research focus, entitled "sympathetic devices," which focuses on the design of communication technologies for older adults. The core elements of the framework are outlined providing examples of product concepts where the framework has been applied in order to demonstrate its capabilities. The significance of utilizing the framework is to better design technologies to help older adults age healthy and independently, specially focusing on the utilization of tangible interactions as an extension of the use of touch interfaces.

Categories and Subject Descriptors

H.5.2 [User Interfaces]: *User-centered design, Haptic I/O, Theory and Methods.*

General Terms

Human Factors; Design.

Keywords

Design; older adults; technologies.

1. INTRODUCTION

Older adults will likely experience decline in one or more abilities as they age, including vision, dexterity, physical function, hearing, and cognition [1]. Product design is a field that can help the older adult population by designing products that meet their specific needs. Yet, designing products, especially technologies for older adults' decline can be a challenging task [2]. Traditional design methods may not be sufficient to develop successful and adoptable products.

This loss of ability may also be compounded by the emotional impact associated with that decline. It is not uncommon for older adults to also experience social isolation and loneliness or even depression as result of such decline. Communities may help alleviate the feeling, but even individuals living in retirement communities have been found to suffer from such conditions [3]. Designed technologies can address the aforementioned issues. Results and experience from conducting focus groups and interviews indicates that older adults want to be connected with friends and family [4], yet it is challenging with the rapid pace of today's society, cultural changes, and new forms of social communication. Older adults are cultural generations linked to technological advancements that are often ignored with current innovative technologies [5]. This poses an additional challenge for developing technologies.

Technology provides promising opportunities to help older adults with their lives; however, older adults may experience a great challenge in using todays high-tech devices. Their attitude towards technology is generally positive — they want technology, but find the interfaces too complex or the cost too high. "Complex" hardware and software, especially screen based, are not an effective use of technology for empowering older adults. Older adults can easily become confused with technology products due to its interfaces and interactions. As a result, older adults become exposed to the issue of the digital divide affected by aging [6].

Also, for a technology to be adopted, older adults need to find them relevant and useful. Adopted technologies are those that respond to basic needs and that are designed around solving problems experienced in everyday activities. For example, everyday activities may involve: 1- socializing, which includes designing technologies for communicating and socializing; 2- remembering: designing technologies to function as memory aids; 3- eating: designing technologies for managing nutrition; 4- moving: designing technologies to promote physical movement; 5- learning: technologies for continuing education; 6- expressing: designing technologies for self-expression, arts and crafts.

2. SYMPATHETIC DESIGN

The field of designing technologies for aging has been growing rapidly due to large number of adults retiring. In the past decade there has been an increasing interest for designers, computer scientists and psychologists to be involved in projects concerning the older adult population [2]. Even though a large number of meaningful products have been developed, little information has been generated in proposing a framework to help organize and aid the design of technologies for older adults.

"Sympathetic design" is an approach of designing technology devices for older adults. It utilizes components to form a framework that has been developed from evidence of research projects related to designing for and with older adults in the recent years [4]. This framework provides and overview of design

SIGDOC'13, September 30–October 1, 2013, Greenville, North Carolina, USA.
Copyright © 2013 ACM 978-1-4503-2131-0/13/09...$15.00.
http://dx.doi.org/10.1145/2507065.2507083

approaches and methods for engaging practitioners in specific activities of designing technologies for older adults. The framework is based in the following dimensions (see Figure 1): 1- product functionality, 2- product interface, 3- co-design activities, 4- universal design; 5- product experience; and 6- technology use.

Sympathetic Devices	Designing Technologies for Older Adults	
Product Functionality	Simplicity	Basic Needs
Product Interface	Tangible	Contextual
Design research methods	Participatory Design	Contextual Design methods
Universal Design	Equitable Use, Flexibility in Use, Simple and Intuitive Use, Perceptible Information, Tolerance for Error, 6- Low Physical Effort, Size and Space for Approach and Use	
Product Experience	Enjoyment	Creativity
Technology Use	Current	Off-shelf

Table 1. Sympathetic Design Framework

First, functionality of the products should be simple to use addressing basic and specific older adults' needs. Second, product interfaces should use physical items/hardware to manipulate actions. Physical tangible computing can afford more accessible interfaces for older adults. Beyond physicality of the interface, contextualization should be exercised. Contextualization is referred as to the physical arrangement of technologies in use.

Older adults should be involved as experts in the product design process. There are a number of design research methodologies that can facilitate the user involvement as co-authors in the design process [7, 8].

Universal design principles must be exercised in the product design to address a wide range of older adults abilities [9, 10]. There are seven principles for designing accessible products and environments to be usable by all people, to the greatest extent possible, without the need for adaptation or specialized design. These include: 1- Equitable Use; 2-Flexibility in Use; 3- Simple and Intuitive Use; 4-Perceptible Information; 5- Tolerance for Error; 6- Low Physical Effort; and 7- Size and Space for Approach and Use [10].

Even though it is not a principle, enjoyment of the product should outweigh effort of use [11]. Lastly, all the aforementioned should be developed with current and off-the-shelf technologies. Emphasis should be given to those technologies that have become established so as to avoid becoming obsolete in a short term.

3. DESIGN APPLICATIONS

This section is dedicated to briefly describe different technology devices that have been designed for older adults following the aforementioned *sympathetic design* framework.

"*Thinking of You*" is a communication device consisting of five square (5x5 inch) stained wooden blocks with a translucent white overlay and a stainless steel hook (see figure 1). Each block can be placed to a magnetic bar that can be mounted to the wall. Each block is associated with a person in their social network by attaching something memorable about that person to the hook. The user may touch a block to send a simple gesture to the person associated with the block. When receiving a gesture, the translucent overlay glows.

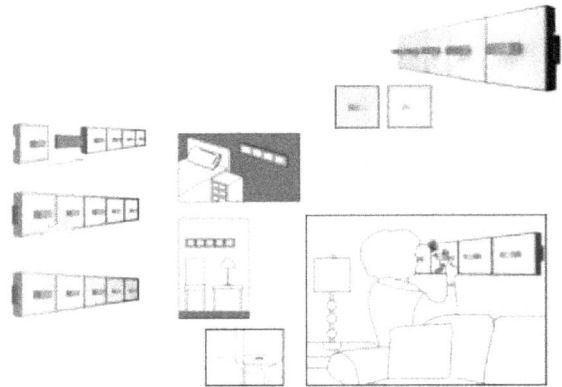

Figure 1. Thinking of You Device

"*TagIt*" is a device to help older adults communicate with their families via a physical interface (see figure 2). It is designed as a stained wood tri-fold frame with metal décor on the two outer panels and a touch screen LCD display embedded in the center. These panels provided a surface on which to attach small magnetic photos surrounded by clear frames. The photo frames glow when a message arrives and touching the photo brings up the associated person's message or media on the LCD screen. The user may touch a control on the LCD to send an audio/video response recorded by the device. The remote recipient may receive messages through email, instant message, or other means that fits their preference and communication style.

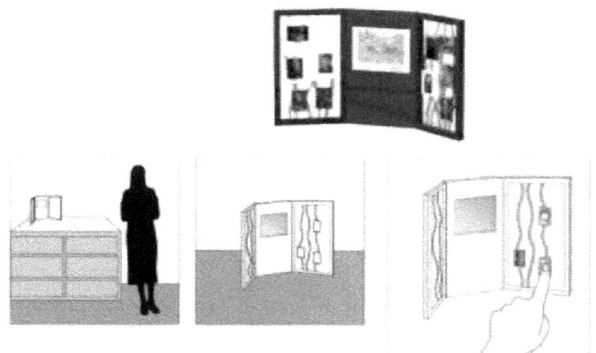

Figure 2. Tag It Device

The "*Altruist*" concept focuses on informing the user of the presence of their connected friends located at common areas of interest, especially in retirement communities (see figure 3). This product aims at helping older adults socialize and get them to go out. The design consists of two part objects that could be used as a keychain or carried in a pocket. Each friend would have one of these objects and be able to join the other's circle of friends by fitting the pieces together for a short time. After joining, the base station plays pre-determined music and colors to specify a location, when one of the circles of friends enters a space.

Figure 3. Altruist Device

The "*Forgetfulness*" concept is designed to aid older adults in remembering to complete tasks, especially around the home (see figure 4). The design utilizes a bracelet with color-coded plastic tags embedded and is intended to replace the string on the finger reminder. The tags may be removed to place on an object, and then a voice message is recorded on the bracelet. Colored lights on the bracelet indicate the tag is missing and that a task should be completed. Pressing a button plays back the messages and returning the tag clears the associated message.

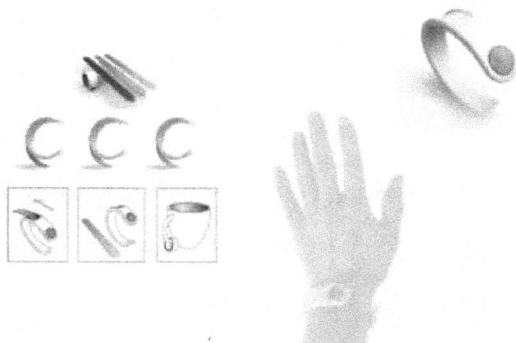

Figure 4. Forgetfulness Device

The "*ShareLab*" concept is designed to provide a simplified method for older adults to share their crafts with others, either for sale or pride (see figure 5). The device is designed to look like a scrapbook, but with an LCD screen and physical slider to move from capturing a photo to editing that photo, then sharing the photo. The share application includes a method of pushing images to monitors around a community or emailing to a friend. The concept also allows receipt of messages in response to shared images.

"*C-Connect*" is a concept to link older adults to cultural institutions, events and databases (see figure 6). Influenced by the design of audio guides from museums, the device looks like an extended smart phone with a small LCD screen and physical controls to select options and playback media. The device can learn preferences and search for information on lectures and similar cultural events, suggesting the most relevant to the user.

Figure 5. ShareLab Device

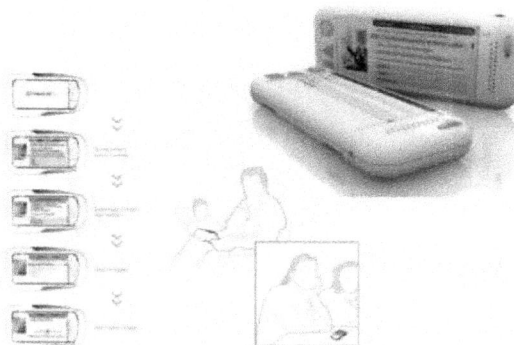

Figure 6. C-Connect Device

The "*Mockingbird*" concept is aimed at allowing older adults to easily capture music, build playlists, and share the music with others (see figure 7). The system consists of a small clip (similar to a refrigerator clip) that when pinched close, would record a short clip of music played nearby. Returning the clip to one of two types of stations, it will upload the clips and online software will match them up with the song ID online and add it to their playlist. In the docked position, the docking station will play the playlist from an online personalized radio site. The clip can also be clipped to a common area music system to share the individual's playlist.

The "*DinnerCloth*" is a concept providing a means for indicating presence of another individual sitting down to dinner, thus providing a sense of connection to friends and family during mealtime (see figure 8). The design is in the form of a placemat with interleaved loops. Two small fiber optic strands with wooden beads at either end are split and one given to the older adult and one to the other family member or friend. Each may then weave their strand in a pattern that associates them with the other individual. When someone sits down with a shared strand, the matching one glows on the placemat and vice versa, thus given a sense of presence at mealtime, when a sense of loneliness might otherwise set in.

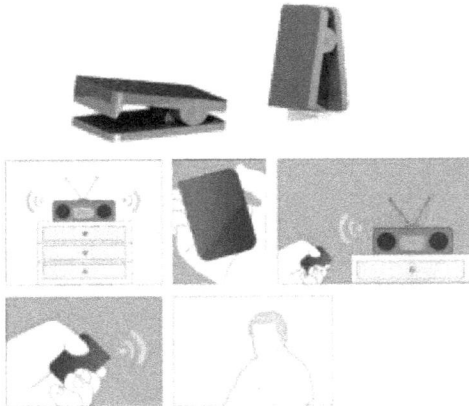

Figure 7. Mockingbird Device

Figure 8. DinnerCloth Device

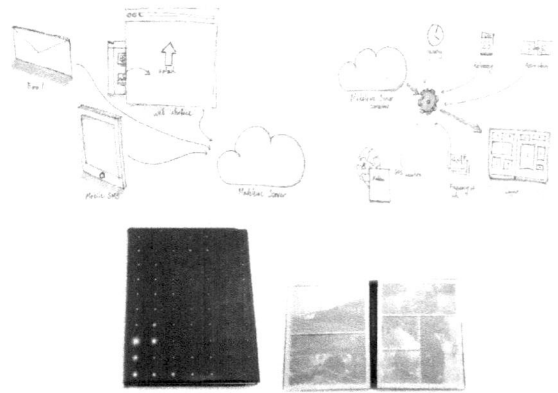

Figure 9. Madeline Device

Figure 10. Onacom Device

Madeline is an electronic photo album that helps older adults explore a serendipitous assortment of family photos in a fun, simple, and engaging way (see figure 9). The product was designed to help answer the question of how to facilitate photo sharing across generations. Madeline operates like a magic book showing different pictures every time it is opened. As such, it has the embedded ability to create new stories every time is opened.

Onacom is one stop-few steps intergenerational multimodal social communication device (see figure 10). It focuses on designing and developing novel interfaces to aid older adults to be more independent in managing communication decisions (e.g. social). The device features improved ways of texting, video conferencing, phone communication and emailing. Several iterations have been produced, from stand-alone devices with removable and tangible parts, to ipad/tablet cases that facilitate the use of interfaces in a more universal manner, especially for the limited vision older adults.

4. CONCLUSION

As the number of older adults will continue to exponentially grow, one of the biggest challenges associated to this rapid increase will be the design of products meeting the demand for better quality living environments of older adults. The design discipline plays a significant role in making the products more approachable for the aging population. This paper discussed an approach to designing technologies for older adults and its applications including the following dimensions: 1- product functionality, 2- product interface, 3- co-design activities, 4- universal design; 5- product experience; and 6- technology use. Different products were presented summarizing the creative outlook responding to the design approach for older adults. The significance of utilizing this framework is to design better technologies that do not downplay the need for products for older adults. Moreover, it works on the premise of moving away from products to be adaptable but adoptable and to address the issue of the digital divide affected by aging.

5. ACKNOWLEDGMENTS

The authors would like to acknowledge all students both students from the School of Industrial Design and School of Interactive Computing involved in the projects showcased in this paper. Special thanks to the Georgia Tech Health Systems Institute and GVU Center Seed grant support, which funded the origins of "Sympathetic Devices". Lastly, the Aware Home Research Initiative for their continuing support towards showcasing the designed technologies at their facilities.

6. REFERENCES

1. Fisk, A., et al., *Designing for Older Adults: Principles and Creative Human Factors Approaches.* Second Edition (Human Factors & Aging Series) ed. 2009: CRC Press.

2. Duh, H.B.-L., et al. *Senior-friendly technologies: interaction design for senior users.* in *CHI'10 Extended Abstracts on Human Factors in Computing Systems.* 2010. ACM.

3. Adams, K.B., S. Sanders, and E.A. Auth, *Loneliness and Depression in Independent Living Retirement Communities: Risk and Resilience Factors.* Aging & Mental Health, 2004. 8(6): p. 475-485.

4. Rébola, C.B. and B. Jones, *Sympathetic Devices: Communication Technologies for Inclusion.* Physical & Occupational Therapy in Geriatrics, 2011. 29(1): p. 44-58.

5. Ingram, M.N., *An examination of the historical time-period and socio-cultural factors that influence the use and non-use of information and communication technologies by older, working-class black americans,* in *School of Information Arts and Technologies* 2013, University of Baltimore.

6. Design and Technologies for Healthy Aging. *Design and Technologies for Healthy Aging.* 2009 [cited 2012 September 6]; Available from: http://datha.gatech.edu.

7. Martin, B. and B.M. Hanington, *Universal Methods of Design: 100 Ways to Research Complex Problems, Develop Innovative Ideas, and Design Effective Solutions.* 2012, Beverly, MA: Rockport Publishers. 207 p.

8. Massimi, M., R.M. Baecker, and M. Wu, *Using participatory activities with seniors to critique, build, and evaluate mobile phones,* in *Proceedings of the 9th international ACM SIGACCESS conference on Computers and accessibility* 2007, ACM: Tempe, Arizona, USA. p. 155-162.

9. Lidwell, W., K. Holden, and J. Butler, *Universal Principles of Design: 100 Ways to Enhance Usability, Influence Perception, Increase Appeal, Make Better Design Decisions, and Teach Through Design.* 2003, Gloucester, MA: Rockport. 216 p.

10. The Center for Universal Design. *The Principles of Universal Design.* 1997 [cited 2012 March 25]; Available from: http://www.ncsu.edu/ncsu/design/cud/about_ud/udprinciplestext.htm.

11. Csikszentmihalyi, M., *Flow : the psychology of optimal experience.* 1991, New York: HarperPerennial. xii, 303 p.

Understanding the Process of Learning Touch-screen Mobile Applications

Lucia Tokárová
Faculty of Informatics
Masaryk University
Brno, Czech Republic
xtokarov@fi.muni.cz

Melius Weideman
Website Attributes Research Centre
Cape Peninsula University of Technology
Cape Town, South Africa
weidemanm@cput.ac.za

ABSTRACT

Mobile devices, together with touch-screen interfaces, have become part of the everyday usage items of many information consumers across the globe. However, it is clear that the learning curve for touch-screen interfaces is steeper than what was expected. This presents some problems especially along with the current trend towards designing more complex mobile applications. The objective of this research was to determine how users interact with applications on touch-screen mobile devices, and how they progress through the various learning phases. A literature study, two pilot studies and a full survey questionnaire were used to gather data and perceptions about the status quo of learning within mobile touch-screen interfaces. Results indicated the presence of recurring patterns in users' preferences. In particular, associations with personal characteristics, namely age, gender and the length of experience, were observed. These patterns might provide fundamental value as a theoretical ground for designing intuitive mobile applications.

Categories and Subject Descriptors

H.5.2 [**Information Interfaces and Presentation**]: User Interfaces – *user-centered design, training, help, and documentation.*

General Terms

Measurement, Design, Human Factors.

Keywords

Learning, learnability, mobile applications, mobile user interfaces, touch-screen devices.

1. INTRODUCTION

Until recently, the primary purpose of most mobile phones was communication in the form of voice calls and text messages. Mobile devices were fairly simple compared to personal computers and the problem of diversity of user knowledge and skills was only marginally important. However, with the emergence of smartphones and tablets, the complexity of these devices has increased dramatically. Furthermore, modifications of infrastructure and distribution of software for mobile devices have expanded the base of application developers. As a result, mobile applications have become more mature, empowering people to perform more advanced tasks. On the other hand, modern mobile user interfaces introduce several challenges, which affected the learnability of mobile applications. These challenges include:

- **Gestural interactions:** Gestural interactions are engaging and intuitive for simple tasks. However, they are less practical for more complex operations, since the range of possible interactions and the precise dynamics of execution is often difficult to discover [14].
- **Small screen size:** Mobile screens provide significantly less real estate for displaying information compared to desktop computers. Therefore, prioritization of content and features is essential. This approach leads to a reduced discoverability of advanced features [14].
- **Predominance of visual feedback:** Touch screen mobile user interfaces rely heavily on visual feedback. The lack of other forms of responses prevents activation of cognitive mechanisms, such as muscle memory, which would aid in the skill acquisition process.
- **Context of use:** Sessions with mobile applications are short [2, 15] and variable in the context of use [15]. User's attentional resources are hardly ever reserved exclusively for a mobile device. It results in the breakdown of fluent interactions with mobile applications and affects the process of learning.

All these factors affect learnability – not only during the first interaction with mobile application, but also during the whole lifecycle of application usage.

The objective of this research was to investigate the process users go through when they are learning how to use applications on touch-screen mobile devices. This study was focused on users' subjective preferences and attitudes towards skill acquisition. It covered the process of application usage, from the first contact, to the reasons for leaving the application.

The primary research question was "How do people perceive the process of learning in the context of touch-screen mobile application usage?" Patterns in responses were analyzed to examine the associations between personal characteristics (age, gender, the amount of experience with touch-screen devices) and users' preferences in various aspects of application usage.

SIGDOC'13, September 30–October 1, 2013, Greenville, NC, USA.
Copyright © 2013 ACM 978-1-4503-2131-0/13/09...$15.00.
http://dx.doi.org/10.1145/2507065.2507066

2. RELATED RESEARCH

2.1 Everyday skill acquisition

Traditional theories on skill acquisition [1, 8] identify three stages of learning (via [16]). In *the initial phase*, beginners focus on understanding the activity and achieving immediate goals. They make perceptually salient mistakes with immediate consequences and they often have someone, such as a parent, friend or teacher, helping them to overcome initial difficulties. *The middle phase* of learning is characterized by practice and gaining experience. Mistakes become less frequent and serious and the activity can be performed with reduced concentration. In this phase, individuals achieve an acceptable level of performance. In *the last phase* of learning, performance becomes autonomous. Since the performance does not need to be actively controlled, most people do not perceive an urge for further improvements. With the minimum amount of regular practice, they are able to maintain the same level of accuracy for months, or even years.

These classic theories explain the process of natural learning, focused on attaining an acceptable level of performance. In contrast, research on the *expert-performance approach* [7] studies strategies that lead to the highest possible level of expertise. The main difference between these two concepts is engagement in so-called *deliberate practice*. Future experts do not stop learning when they achieve an acceptable level of performance. Instead, they keep practicing; they apply problem solving to overcome challenges to achieve ever-higher levels of performance. The most important qualities of deliberate practice include motivation, concentration, regularity, feedback, and design of practice [7].

2.2 Skills in human-computer interaction

Research on skill acquisition in human-computer interaction became important in the 1980s. With the emergence of the personal computer, interactive software was no longer a tool used only by technically oriented users. Yet, operating most programs required formal training and reading paper manuals.

During the 1980s, a number of studies investigated learning and routine use of office systems such as text editors and word processors [5, 11, 17]. This research demonstrated that learning interactive systems has several distinctive qualities. Firstly, exploratory learning seems to be an effective and popular strategy among users. Compared to working through sequenced training materials, individuals are more successful in guided task-oriented investigation [5]. Secondly, users' motivations for learning were focused on attaining practical goals. Software is perceived as a tool. Learners were not interested in understanding system as a whole but rather in how the system can help them accomplish their pursuits [6]. Thirdly, users often generalized their prior knowledge and construct ad-hoc interpretations about how a system works [11]. The problem was that they use their knowledge even when it does not apply, and, as long as they reach their goals, they are reluctant to change their strategies in favor of more efficient procedures. They often persisted in using inefficient strategies and their level of performance stabilized on relative mediocrity [17]. In traditional HCI research, the combination of user's focus on practical goals and persistence in using well-practiced and generally applicable procedures is referred to as the *paradox of the active user* [6]. These findings have initiated further research on learnability of interactive systems and training materials in HCI.

2.3 Diversity in human-computer interaction

A range of studies examined patterns in individual differences towards software usage. For instance, Burnet [4] investigated gender pluralism in problem-solving software, and their results showed significant differences between males and females in terms of feature usage, feature-related confidence, and ad-hoc exploration. The authors associated these differences to the *self-efficacy* (individual's confidence in his or her ability to perform a specific task), the *selectivity hypothesis* (differences between males and females with respect to information processing), and the *attention investment model* (perceived costs, benefits and risks that users consider in deciding how to complete a task in a software environment). However, it can be argued that these differences are not based solely on individual's gender, but other personal characteristics as well.

To illustrate this idea, McGrenere [12] has suggested that the differences might be associated with individual's attitudes. Based on these studies, the author created a scale, which identifies individual differences with respect to the perception of complex software. On one end of the scale, there are *feature-shy* users, who prefer simple user interface without any unnecessary features. On the other end, there are *feature-keen* users, who believe that all interface elements have some inherent value and want them to be visible so that they can gradually explore them.

2.4 Universal usability

The topic has become even more relevant with the adaptation of information technologies outside the work environment. According to Shneiderman and Hochheiser [18], the tendency to make information technologies available to broader populations introduces three major challenges: technology variety, user diversity and gaps in user's knowledge. Universally usable systems have to accommodate users with different backgrounds (age, gender, culture, literacy, skills, knowledge, etc.). Diversity of knowledge and skills is particularly salient, because the level of knowledge and previous experience with interactive systems is generally difficult to estimate. Furthermore, the knowledge changes with practice and exposure to the system. As such, the same user interface should satisfy very different sets of needs of novice and frequent users [18]. Although there has been a persistent interest in this topic, diversity of user knowledge and skills still presents one of the central recurring problems in HCI.

2.5 Learning and mobile touch-screen UIs

Concerning mobile user interfaces, the issue of learning is currently often examined in conjunction with new interaction techniques [3, 9]. However, these experiments are usually conducted in laboratories, with controlled settings, fixed training periods, and homogeneous group of participants. Longitudinal studies are less common, and generally focused on user's performance and subjective preferences towards interactions [10].

A more holistic approach to investigate the process of learning in the context of the mobile environment can be attributed to Oulasvirta [16]. This empirical study is a fraction of the broader research on the self-taught intermediate level of skill and examines learning strategies of three groups of users – novice, casual and expert users of modern smartphones. The authors concluded that superior performance of experienced users (casual users and experts) could be attributed to faster navigation and better knowledge of terminology, not to deeper understanding of the system. Improvement is the result of routine use and three

2006	2007	2011	2012	2013		2012	2010	2008
Nokia N95	Apple iPhone	Nokia Lumia 800	Apple iPhone 5	Samsung Galaxy S4	?	Apple iPad Mini	Apple iPad	Dell Inspiron Mini
2,6"	3,5"	3,7"	4"	5"		7,9"	9,7"	12"

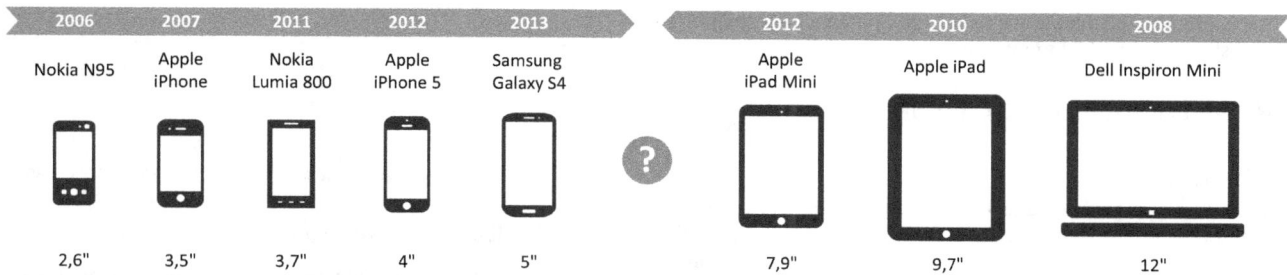

Figure 1. The evolution of screen sizes over the last years

learning events: familiarization, following media and ad-hoc problem solving. Authors also suggested that the self-taught intermediate level of skill is device-specific. However, the experiment was conducted on a Symbian based dual slider phone with many physical controls, and the conclusion may not be fully applicable on current fully customizable touch-screen mobile devices.

2.6 Convergence of screen sizes

Over the past decade, there seems to have been a convergence of miniature, old-fashioned mobile devices (Figure 1, left) and large, bulky personal computers (Figure 1, right). On one hand, mobile devices, such as cell phones, personal digital assistants and feature phones are lightweight and easy to carry. However, small screen sizes and full hardware keyboards made them uncomfortable to use, which has been one of the main reasons for the proliferation of the new generation of mobile devices with multi-touch screens and limited number of hardware controls. To improve the ergonomics and usability, the displays of mobile touch-screen devices have been growing in size. On the other hand, the size of larger personal computer screens restricts portability and flexibility of use – hence the emergence of new categories of devices, such as netbooks and tablets. To increase the mobility of these devices, displays are gradually becoming smaller.

Although the process of learning has been investigated in the related disciplines and HCI as well, the mobile environment and specific features of modern touch-screen user interfaces have introduced several new challenges. In order to design intuitive applications for mobile devices, it has become essential to study the specifics of the new context of use and focus on the user perspective, rather than technical aspects. This paper presents the initial steps towards understanding the process of learning in the context of touch-screen mobile application usage.

3. METHODS

The process of learning was investigated using two methods: a quantitative and qualitative survey. Quantitative data was collected in a questionnaire driven study. The questionnaire design and content was based on a literature review and verified in a pilot study using informal semi-structured interviews with five participants (2 females, 3 males). These interviews helped refine questions and wording and the range of options in close-ended questions. Afterwards, the questionnaire was tested and refined in a second pilot study involving five other participants. Qualitative data was collected in the initial interviews. Also, throughout the questionnaire, open-ended answers were

encouraged and space provided. It allowed users to either comment on questions or expand their answers.

3.1 Questionnaire design

The questionnaire consisted of three parts. The first part (classification, questions 1–6) contained demographic questions. In the second part (screening, questions 7–13), questions on personal experience with mobile devices were included. This part was also used for screening purposes. Only the respondents who reported using touch-screen devices and downloading mobile applications were asked to continue to the last part of the questionnaire. The order of these parts (classification before screening) was intentionally chosen to monitor the diversity of respondents. As a result, a sample of respondents who do not use applications on touch-screen mobile devices was included in the first part of the questionnaire, but did not answer irrelevant questions in the last part. Although it falls outside the scope of this paper, these individuals are likely to be characterized as conservatives or skeptics according to the Moore's theory of technology adoption [13, 18] and as such are relevant for investigation of links between personal characteristics and usage patterns. The last part of the questionnaire (questions 14–24) covered the process of applications usage, focused mainly on the initial and middle phase of learning and the reasons for leaving the applications.

3.2 Analysis

At first, the basic frequencies of responses were processed and examined. To investigate the patterns, contingency tables were created. One dimension of categorical variables included gender, age, the length of experience with mobile devices, and the frequency of application downloads. These variables were selected based on the literature review. The other dimension covered the responses on personal preferences towards application usage, obtained in the last part of the questionnaire.

To investigate the associations between categorical variables, chi-square tests were used. The associations were marked as significant if the Pearson's chi-square test returned a p-value less than or equal to 0,05. Since a high number of issues seemed to be related to age, these associations were investigated in detail. Answers on multiple-choice questions were recoded as "Yes" if the option was checked and "No", if the answer was missing (only the answers from respondents who finished the questionnaire were included). Again, chi-square tests were used to calculate the associations and examine the links between age and individual responses.

Afterwards, all significant associations were investigated in detail by studying contingency tables and the patterns in distribution of responses. Finally, the qualitative data from open-ended responses and pilot studies were used to interpret the results.

4. RESULTS AND DISCUSSION

4.1 Participants

Data collection was conducted using an online survey service. The main reason was the intention to address a wide diversity of respondents in terms of gender, age, culture, level of education, field of employment and personal experience with mobile devices. The target group of participants was not explicitly restricted. In summary, 138 respondents participated in the survey, out of which 127 participants (92%) completed it.

The sample of participants consisted of 40 females (29%) and 98 males (71%). The largest group of participants (39,1%) reported the age between 20 and 29, and 1 participant was younger than 20 years old. The other groups were fairly evenly distributed, with 23,2% participant between the age 30 and 39, 18,1% between 40 and 49 and 18,8% participants 50 years old and above. In an open-ended question, a variety of native languages was indicated. Among 13 languages listed, the most prevalent were Czech (26,8%) and English (26,8%), followed by Afrikaans (20,3%). Other languages included Dutch, French, German, IsiXhosa, Portuguese, Sepedi, Shona, Slovak, and Swahili. The highest level of completed education was distributed among high school graduates (15,4%), bachelor's degree (31,5%), master degree (37,7%) and doctoral degree (15,4%). Eight participants reported other levels of qualification, mainly professional degrees. Respondents also indicated various categories of backgrounds, including Administration, Art and design, Business, Education, Engineering, Information technology, Marketing and sales, Media and culture, and Science.

Concerning the personal experience with touch screen mobile devices, 82,5% of the respondents reported using a smartphone, 48,9% a tablet and 16,1% a dedicated e-book reader. The majority of the respondents (63,2%) have been using touch screen devices for more than two years. The most widely used operating system was Android (55,6%) and iOS (48,7%). The highest number of respondents (39,3%) reported downloading mobile applications at least a few times a month and the most common reason for downloading was utility (81,8%), followed by work-related purposes and entertainment.

Two groups of respondents were eliminated in the screening part of the questionnaire: respondents who do not use touch-screen mobile devices (19 subjects) and respondents who do not download mobile applications (9 subjects). Subsequently, a total number of 99 participants (25 females and 74 males) provided results, which were investigated and summarized further.

4.2 The initial phase of learning

4.2.1 Reading application descriptions

A surprisingly high number of respondents reported reading application descriptions on mobile application markets (Figure 2). 42,4% individuals usually read a description, and 43,4% read it at least briefly. The chi-square test revealed a significant association between the willingness to read application description and two attributes, age (p = 0,003) and the length of experience with mobile applications (p = 0,027). Older respondents and

individuals, who use mobile applications longer, seem to be more likely to read the descriptions.

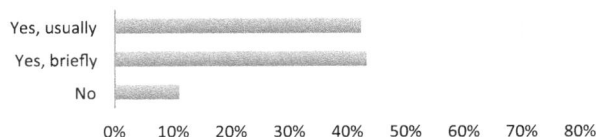

Figure 2. Reading application descriptions.

Additionally, a few respondents commented on the importance of the content and number of user reviews. Interviews also suggested that the decision depends on the motivation for downloading and the source of the first contact with the application (e.g. one individual pointed out that he is more likely to read the description if he is searching for an application on a mobile application market compared to any other source).

4.2.2 Reading introductory instructions

In contrast, after downloading the application, the interest in reading introductory instructions drops recognizably (Figure 3). If introductory instructions are available, 44,4% of respondents usually skip these instructions, while only 21,2% usually read and 34,3% read the instructions briefly.

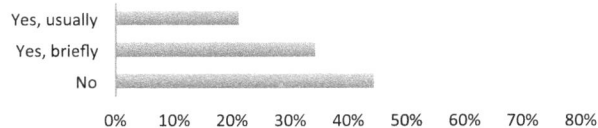

Figure 3. Reading introductory instructions.

Qualitative analysis also pointed to a significant association between willingness to read and age (p = 0,016). In this case, the association is linear, and suggests that the older the respondent, the more likely he or she is to read the introductory instructions.

This association was also observed in the pilot study, where two older respondents (above 50 years old) complained about proclaimed intuitiveness of mobile interfaces and the lack of instructions.

4.2.3 Familiarization preferences

Furthermore, the majority of respondents (65,7%) prefer trying applications on their own (Figure 4). A less popular strategy is presentation of available features (36,4%) and initial walkthrough (33,3%). With mobile applications, video is the least popular strategy (18,2%), presumably because it does not reflect individual pace of familiarization. Also, as interviews suggested, videos might sometimes be confused with an advertisement, and as such, ignored or skipped.

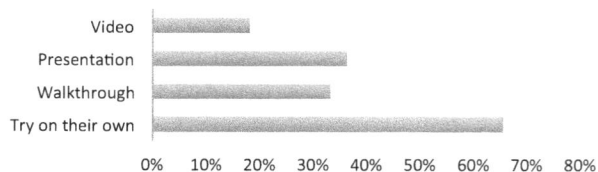

Figure 4. Familiarization preferences.

The familiarization preferences seem to be significantly associated with age. In particular, younger respondents were much more likely to prefer trying applications on their own compared to older respondents (p = 0,037).

4.2.4 Familiarization strategies
Concerning the familiarization (Figure 5), the most common approach is looking for the quickest way to perform the task, for which the application was downloaded (58,6%). Several respondents indicated that in this initial phase, they are likely to spend some time exploring different options (45,5%). Some respondents also admitted that they usually skip all messages and instructions and try the application on their own (38,4%). Only 26,3% indicated that they are most likely to read instructions to find out how the application works. Interviews suggested that motivation and the purpose of the application play an important role as well.

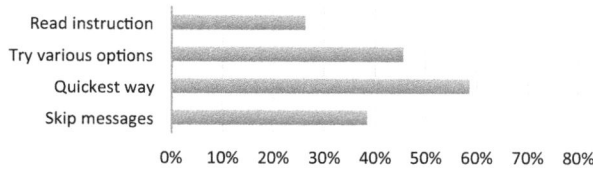

Figure 5. Familiarization strategies.

Again, familiarization strategies seem to be associated with age (p = 0,012). Younger respondents were more likely to spend some time trying various options in the applications, whereas older respondents were more likely to report reading instructions to find out how the application works.

4.3 The middle phase of learning

4.3.1 Problem-solving strategies
The questionnaire indicated that the most common problem-solving strategy (Figure 6) is an ad-hoc exploration. The largest group of respondents (61,6%) reported trying a random course of actions as their usual strategy. A particularly high number of individuals (55,6%) also indicated reading online help. This number might be even higher, because Google search and online instructions were also often mentioned in open-ended answers. Furthermore, 23,2% of respondents reported asking for help (either personally or online), e.g. on social networks.

However, interviews implied that this strategy depends heavily on the individual's motivation and purpose of downloading the application. In 23,2% of cases, it was reported that the problem might be a reason to uninstall the application.

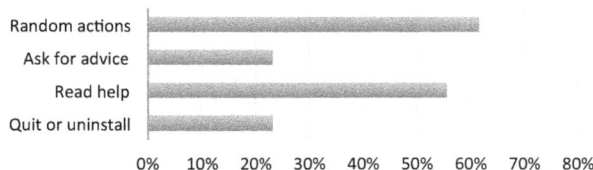

Figure 6. Problem-solving strategies.

Qualitative analysis showed that the problem-solving strategy is associated with several personal characteristics, namely gender (p = 0,043), age (p = 0,008), and the length of experience with

mobile devices (p = 0,001). Females seem to be more willing to read help or ask for advice, while males prefer random exploration. Similar with age, older participants (40 or above) are more likely to read help, compared to younger categories, which are more prone to try ad-hoc strategies. The data set also suggested that novices, who own touch-screen mobile devices for less than six months are most likely to ask for advice.

4.3.2 Exploration of advanced features
When it comes to exploration of advanced features (Figure 7) in mobile applications, the majority of respondents reported that they do not use any special strategies, and they are most likely to notice new features as they appear in applications (55,6%), or stumble onto them by accident, while trying to do something else (45,5%). Other strategies included: following recommendations, reading about the applications, or trying strategies known from other applications. The popularity of these strategies was lower and evenly distributed.

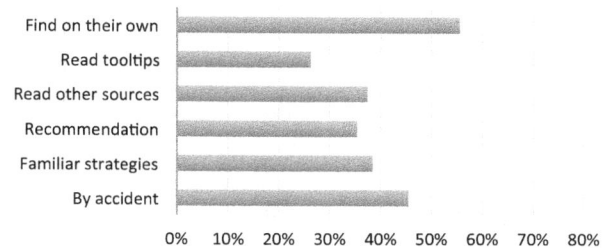

Figure 7. Exploration of advanced features.

Furthermore, learning advanced features seems to be significantly associated with gender (p = 0,011). Females seem to be more likely to follow recommendations, while males reported reading about applications. Age seems to play important role as well (p = 0,023). For instance, older participants were more likely to report following recommendations, while younger respondents were more likely to indicate that they stumble onto new features by accident.

4.3.3 Exploration of gestures
The most common strategy for gesture exploration (Figure 8) seems to be trying gestures known from other applications (60,6%). A relatively high number of respondents also reported that they stumble onto gestures by accident, while they try to do something else (45,5%). Other strategies, such as reading tips in applications, reading about applications, and following recommendations were less popular.

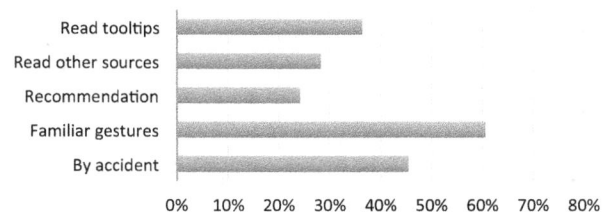

Figure 8. Exploration of gestures.

The analysis showed a significant association with age (p = 0,011). Younger respondents seem to be more willing to try familiar gestures from other applications.

4.3.4 Customization
When asked about customization (Figure 9) of mobile applications, the majority of respondents reported that they usually actively look for application settings (70,7%). A large number of respondents also admitted that they prefer using default options (29,3%). All the other strategies, such as reading about applications, tips, or recommendations, were less common.

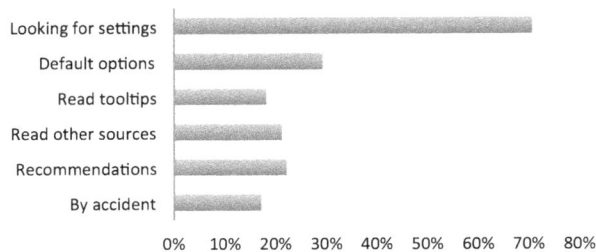

Figure 9. Customization.

Similar to the previous questions, the analysis revealed a significant association with age (p = 0,015), but also with the length of experience (p = 0,043). For instance, novice users are more likely to discover customization options by accident.

However, this result raises an important issue about motivations for finding customization options. As previous studies have suggested [5], for many users, advanced features such as customization, might be either overlooked or perceived to be too demanding for many users.

4.4 The reasons for leaving the applications

4.4.1 Typical problems
For the majority of respondents (71,7%), the most common problem they experience with mobile applications is that the applications do not fulfill their expectations (Figure 10). A large number of respondents also reported that they perceive it as a common problem when a task completion takes too long (38,4%) and when they miss some important features (34,3%).

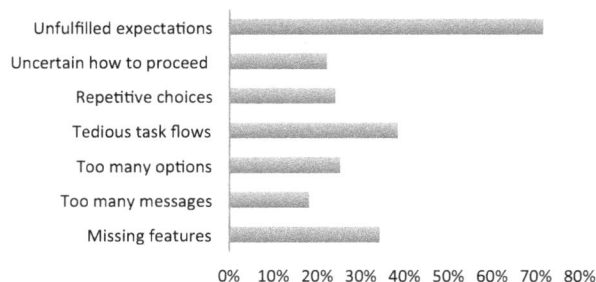

Figure 10. Typical problems.

Quantitative analysis confirmed a significant association with age. Younger participants were more likely to report missing important features and complain about tedious task completion.

Additionally, a wide variety of open-ended answers were provided to this question. Several participants mentioned that they perceive errors, poor design and usability issues as typical problems. Five participants provided more specific examples. For instance, two important issues included the necessity of registration, and long initial setup, especially before trying the application. Paying for advanced features and inappropriate advertising were also indicated as common problems.

4.4.2 Reasons to quit
Finally, the survey suggested that there are two main reasons for individuals to stop using or uninstall the applications (Figure 11). Firstly, the application is not useful (77,8%) and secondly, the application is not needed anymore (65,7%). Many respondents also indicated poor design (43,4%) and missing features (43,4%) as the typical reasons to quit.

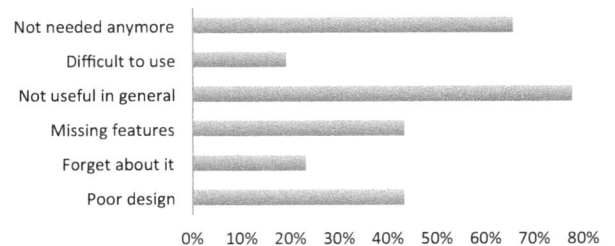

Figure 11. Reasons to quit.

Following the previous question, the typical reasons to stop using or uninstall the applications seem to be associated with age (p = 0,018). For younger respondents it was more common to be discouraged by missing features.

Again, a high number of open-ended answers were provided. Respondents commented on errors, usability issues, advertising and payments as the common reasons to stop using the applications. Data load was also mentioned several times. Either the application uses too much memory, or requires online connection and streams a lot of data. Other issues include the necessity of registration before trying the application and excessive complexity of the user interface.

5. CONCLUSION AND FURTHER WORK
The objective of this research was to investigate how users interact with applications on touch screen mobile devices, and how they progress through the various learning phases. This study was primarily focused on personal preferences and attitudes towards skill acquisition. It covered the whole process of application usage, from the first contact, to the reasons for leaving the application.

To examine this issue, quantitative and qualitative methods were used. Quantitative data was collected in a questionnaire driven study. It allowed the authors to gather a relatively large amount of data compared to interviews and to address a wide diversity of respondents in terms of gender, age, culture, level of education, field of employment and experience with mobile devices. Qualitative data was obtained by open-ended questions and initial interviews and was used to aid in the interpretation of results.

The data showed considerable differences among individuals' learning strategies. However, closer examination revealed some recurring patterns, suggesting associations between personal characteristics and users' preferences. For instance, responses were often significantly associated with age. Older participants were more likely to prefer safer options, such as reading instructions or following recommendations. In contrast, younger participants were more prone to try ad-hoc strategies, whether towards familiarization or problem solving. Some responses were also associated with gender. Females seemed to be significantly more likely to ask for advice or help, or follow recommendations, whereas males preferred random exploration and reading about applications from various sources. The length of experience seemed to play an important role as well. Novice users often preferred safer strategies, like reading instructions, or asking for advice and reported discovering new options by accident. More experienced users were more prone to choose proactive problem-solving strategies. On the other hand, the frequency of application downloads was not a significant indicator. Although the literature review suggested that the frequency of exposure is important, statistical analysis did not show any significant association with this categorical variable.

These results suggest that even though the users' preferences are highly diverse, some patterns in their learning strategies can be observed. In order to design intuitive mobile applications, these patterns might provide fundamental value. It is anticipated that the closer investigation of these patterns might lead to the construction of learning profiles of representative users groups, and subsequently to the design of support mechanisms that will encourage various types of application learners in the process of mobile application usage.

Finally, it should be noted that any questionnaire driven study has several limitations. Participants' understanding of questions and options might bias their responses. Also, the results rely heavily on the subjective views of respondents and the recollection of their behavior. To eliminate these deficiencies, two pilot studies were conducted and the interpretation of quantitative results was supported by the literature review and qualitative data. Yet, the results reflect mainly subjective preferences and might differ from actual users' behavior. Further empirical studies are necessary to extend the understanding of the learning within mobile applications user interfaces – especially user studies with direct access to higher number of participants are essential. Still, the present study provides important initial steps towards this direction, and the results will be used in further research.

6. ACKNOWLEDGMENTS

The authors would like to acknowledge Mrs. Corrie Uys from the CPUT Centre for Postgraduate Studies, for her assistance with statistical analysis.

7. REFERENCES

[1] Anderson, J.R. 1982. Acquisition of cognitive skill. *Psychol. Rev.* 89, 4 (Jul. 1982), 369–406. DOI= http://dx.doi.org/10.1037//0033-295X.89.4.369.

[2] Böhmer, M., Hecht, B., Schöning, J., Krüger, A., and Bauer, G. 2011. Falling asleep with Angry Birds, Facebook and Kindle: A large scale study on mobile application usage. In *Proceedings of the 13th international conference on Human computer interaction with mobile devices and services* (Stockholm, Sweden, August 30 – September 02, 2011). MobileHCI'11. ACM, New York, NY, 47–56. DOI= http://dx.doi.org/10.1145/2037373.2037383.

[3] Bragdon, A., Nelson, E., Li, Y., and Hinckley, K. 2011. Experimental analysis of touch-screen gesture designs in mobile environments. In *Proceedings of the SIGCHI Conference on Human Factors in Computing Systems* (Vancouver, Canada, May 07–12, 2011). CHI'11. ACM, New York, NY, 403–412. DOI= http://dx.doi.org/10.1145/1978942.1979000.

[4] Burnett, M.M., Beckwith, L., Wiedenbeck, S., Fleming, S.D., Cao, J., Park, T.H., Grigoreanu, V., Rector, K. 2011. Gender pluralism in problem-solving software. *Interact. Comput.* 23, 5 (Sep. 2011), 450–460. DOI= http://dx.doi.org/10.1016/j.intcom.2011.06.004

[5] Carroll, J.M. and Carrithers, C. 1984. Training wheels in a user interface. *Commun. ACM* 27, 8 (Aug. 1984), 800–806. DOI= http://dx.doi.org/10.1145/358198.358218.

[6] Carroll, J.M. and Rosson, M.B. 1987. Paradox of the Active User. In *Interfacing Thought: Cognitive Aspects of Human-Computer Interaction*, J.M. Carroll, Ed. MIT Press, Cambridge, MA, 80–111.

[7] Ericsson, K.A. 2006. The influence of experience and deliberate practice on the development of superior expert performance. In *The Cambridge handbook of expertise and expert performance*, K.A. Ericsson, N. Charness, R.R. Hoffman and P.J. Feltovich, Eds. Cambridge Handbooks in Psychology. Cambridge University Press, Cambridge, UK, 685–705.

[8] Fitts, P.M. and Posner, M.I. 1967. *Human Performance.* Brooks/Cole, Belmont, CA.

[9] Jain, M. and Balakrishnan, R. 2012. User learning and performance with bezel menus. In *Proceedings of the SIGCHI Conference on Human Factors in Computing Systems* (Austin, TX, USA, May 05–10, 2012). CHI'12. ACM, New York, NY, 2221–2230. DOI= http://dx.doi.org/10.1145/2207676.2208376.

[10] Li, Y. 2010. Gesture Search: A tool for fast mobile data access. In *Proceedings of the 23nd annual ACM symposium on User interface software and technology* (New York, NY, USA, October 03–06, 2010). UIST'10. ACM, New York, NY, 87–96. DOI= http://dx.doi.org/10.1145/1866029.1866044.

[11] Mack, R.L., Lewis, C.H., and Carroll, J.M. 1983. Learning to use word processors: Problems and prospects. *ACM T. Off. Inf. Syst.* 1, 3 (Jul. 1983), 254–271. DOI= http://dx.doi.org/10.1145/357436.357440.

[12] McGrenere, J. 2004. Iterative Design and Evaluation of Multiple Interfaces for a Complex Commercial Word Processor. In *Multiple User Interfaces: Cross-Platform Applications and Context-Aware Interfaces,* A. Seffah and H. Javahery, Eds. John Wiley & Sons, Ltd, Chichester, UK, 351–372.

[13] Moore, G. 1991. *Crossing the chasm.* HarperBusiness Book, New York, NY.

[14] Norman, D. 2010. Natural user interfaces are not natural. *ACM interactions* 17, 3 (May–Jun. 2010), 6–10. DOI= http://dx.doi.org/10.1145/1744161.1744163.

[15] Oulasvirta, A., Tamminen, S., Roto, V., and Kuorelahti, J. 2005. Interaction in 4-second bursts : The fragmented nature

of attentional resources in mobile HCI. In *Proceedings of the SIGCHI Conference on Human Factors in Computing Systems* (Portland, OR, USA, April 02–07, 2005). CHI'05. ACM, New York, NY, 919–928. DOI= http://dx.doi.org/10.1145/1054972.1055101.

[16] Oulasvirta, A., Wahlström, M., and Ericsson, K.A. 2011. What does it mean to be good at using a mobile device? An investigation of three levels of experience and skill. *Int. J. Hum-Comput. St.* 69, 3 (Mar. 2011), 155–169. DOI= dx.doi.org/10.1016/j.ijhcs.2010.11.003.

[17] Rosson, M.B. 1983. Patterns of experience in text editing. In *Proceedings of the SIGCHI Conference on Human Factors in Computing Systems* (Boston, MA, USA, December 12–15, 1983). CHI'83. New York, NY, 171–175. DOI= http://dx.doi.org/10.1145/800045.801604.

[18] Shneiderman, B. and Hochheiser, H. 2001. Universal usability as a stimulus to advanced interface design. *Behav. Inform. Technol.* 20, 5 (Sep–Oct. 2001), 367–376. DOI= http://dx.doi.org/10.1080/01449290110083602.

API Documentation and Software Community Values: A Survey of Open-Source API Documentation

Robert Watson

Mark Stamnes

Jacob Jeannot-Schroeder

Jan H. Spyridakis

Department of Human-Centered Design & Engineering
University of Washington
Campus Box 352315, Seattle, WA 98195
01.206.685-1557
[rbwatson | mstamnes | jjs5 | jansp] @ uw.edu

ABSTRACT

Studies of what software developers need from API documentation have reported consistent findings over the years; however, these studies all used similar methods—usually a form of observation or survey. Our study looks at API documentation as artifacts of the open-source software communities who produce them to study how documentation produced by the communities who use the software compares to past studies of what software developers want and need from API documentation. We reviewed API documentation from 33 of the most popular open-source software projects, assessed their documentation elements, and evaluated the quality of their visual design and writing. We found that the documentation we studied included most or all the documentation elements reported as desirable in earlier studies and in the process, we found that the design and writing quality of many documentation sets received considerable attention. Our findings reinforce the API requirements identified in the literature and suggest that the design and writing quality of the documentation are also critical API documentation requirements that warrant further study.

Categories and Subject Descriptors

H.5.2 [**User Interfaces**]: Training, help, and documentation

Keywords

API, API reference documentation, Application programming interface, Software documentation, Software libraries

1. INTRODUCTION

Application-programming interfaces (APIs) allow one program or web site to access the data and services provided by another program or website. APIs make programming easier by sharing code and enabling software reuse, and they are multiplying. Microsoft's .NET Framework grew from 35,470 API elements in 2002 to over 109,000 API elements in 2007 [1]. Since that report, Microsoft added several thousand API elements with Windows 8. Each month for the past few years, hundreds of APIs have also been added to the Programmable Web, a site that catalogs web-service APIs [2]. Each new API includes new features, which software developers must learn and apply quickly and correctly. This rapid growth shows no sign of abating, and the demand for increasingly short time-to-market puts tremendous pressure on today's software developers to learn and apply these new APIs.

While the surveys and interviews conducted in past studies of API-documentation requirements paint a consistent picture, recent studies suggest that API documentation might not provide software developers with what they need. One study found "that some of the most severe obstacles faced by developers learning new APIs pertained to the documentation and other learning resources" [3]. Lethbridge et al. [4] reported that documentation was "often poorly written" and "finding useful content in documentation can be so challenging that people might not try to do so." They found that "inline comments [in the source code] are often good enough to greatly assist detailed maintenance work." Another researcher described how API documentation was so bad that "developers may be getting as much as 50% of their documentation from Stack Overflow" (a web site that hosts questions and answers about software development) [5]. Looking deeper into these studies and reports reveals the diverse and complex nature of API documentation and its study.

To consider a different perspective from that of the past studies and to add some context to the recent observations, we look at what software development communities put into the API documentation they produce for themselves. We asked the research question: *do software development communities create documentation that contains, at a macro level, the documentation elements software developers have said they want in earlier literature?*

Past studies applied research methods in which the participants knew they were involved in the research and all produced very similar findings. Our study looks at the question from a different perspective, allowing us to triangulate the findings of past studies. In our study, we examine the documentation produced by the open-source software communities as artifacts of what developers value.

Open-source software is developed and supported by a community of individuals who create, use, and maintain the software and documentation. Therefore, the software and the documentation we find in open-source communities should represent what they value—that is, the members of a software community will tend to write only what they find valuable or useful (be it software or documentation). Because the community that forms around any individual piece of software is specific to that software, we studied a group of open-source software to obtain a more generalized sense of open-source software documentation.

2. BACKGROUND

Our study draws on past research in which software developers were observed, surveyed, and interviewed to identify the aspects of software documentation they need to do their job, or whose absence complicates it. From this research, we summarized the requirements of API documentation and evaluated the API documentation of open-source software.

2.1 Past Studies of Software Developers

Our list of elements that software developers require from documentation comes from past studies of software developers. Nykaza et al. [6] studied the installation of a customer-service call center and interviewed the software developers who used the system's SDK to write the software that adapted the system to the installation. Lethbridge et al. [4] studied software documentation used to maintain the software, as opposed to apply the software in another application. The scenario in Lethbridge et al. differs from that of API documentation written for an external audience in terms of purpose and audience, but includes many of the same requirements of API documentation for learning an API. Robillard surveyed [7] and later interviewed [3] a group of Microsoft software engineers to identify obstacles to learning a new API. Sillito and Begel [8] interviewed software developers at Microsoft about how they learned to develop software on a new software platform. Each of these studies listed some or all of the following API documentation elements as helpful or critical to learning an API.

- Overview documentation.
- Short code "snippets" that demonstrate usage of an API in context.
- Code examples that show best practices with an API.
- Scenario and task-based documentation.
- Limitations and error handling.
- *Meaningful* documentation (as opposed to "filler" or "boilerplate" content that adds little or no value to what is obvious).

Other studies of computer users, users who were not necessarily software developers per se, relate similar requirements of documentation [9] [10].

- Accuracy, completeness, and correctness.
- Scenario and task-focused examples.
- Content that does not repeat the obvious, such as what can be learned from the user interface.

Because software developers are computer users, we also considered those documentation requirements in our study.

2.2 Open-Source Software and Developers

A variety of research has focused on the motivations of software developers who contribute to open source software [13, 17, 18, 19, 20, 21, 22]. Hertel et al. [18] present high-level descriptions of their motivations, citing norm-oriented motives, pragmatic motives, hedonistic motives, and social/political motives, among others. Hars and Ou [17], drawing from psychological theories, distinguish between internal factors and external factors as motivations for contributing to open source projects. Internal factors include intrinsic motivation, referring to an "...innate desire to code," as well as altruistic motivations, and a sense of community identification. External factors include future rewards or the satisfaction of personal needs. Future rewards can include direct revenues from code or coding skills, knowledge gained from the coding experience that can be marketed, along with the self-marketing to potential employers, and just for the recognition from their peers in the community. The personal needs mentioned include the initiation of projects to create products to fill gaps in the current software by opening them to the community.

We believe that the motivation for documenting open source software corresponds to the motivations for developing for open source projects. Documenting open source software remains an important part of realizing the vision of the software developer or developers for the open source project. Oram [23] suggests several reasons why community documentation, that is, documentation generated by developers and individual users with the goal of helping others use the open source software, exists. Much like the explanations for motivations about creating open source software, documentation of open source software can be motivated by factors that are personal and for the betterment of the community who uses the software. The reasons for developing documentation include providing informal support outside of any official documentation to promote the software and helping others on the assumption that the documentation writer will be helped in the future. Helping others in the community also provides a sense of personal gratitude and builds a reputation amongst the open-source community, which can lead to personal growth for the writer. Oram [23] also points out that there are potential financial results for documentation through paid sites. While many of these motivations are external, we feel that the resulting documentation represents the values of the community because the individual members of the community decide to write it.

2.3 Evaluating API Documentation

We studied API documentation as an artifact of the software development communities that exists around open-source software libraries and applications. Studying artifacts is common in contextual design [11] and anthropological research [12]. Because these artifacts are produced by the community, they represent what the community values [13].

We used a heuristic evaluation method [14] to assess the artifacts we found in a way that would be consistent across all artifacts and enable us to study them individually and as a group. We collected the list of elements for our heuristic evaluation from the literature cited in the previous section and Watson [15], who summarized the high-level components of API documentation. Because we were reviewing online documentation only, we also referred to the Association of Support Professionals [16] best support site criteria document for additional insight into creating our list of evaluation criteria.

3. METHOD

We assessed API documentation of open-source software libraries for the presence of the documentation elements and the page design and writing quality. Based on the existing literature, we designed the method to test the hypothesis: *The documentation of open-source software will contain the elements that software developers want, as reported in past research.* To test this, we developed a list of documentation elements identified in past studies and then evaluated open-source API documentation sets, tabulating the documentation elements we found.

3.1 API Documentation Studied

We wanted to find a collection of software that represented a range of open-source software development communities. Our first attempt to select documentation for the study was to take a simple random sample from the catalog of more than ½ million open-source software apps and libraries listed at www.ohloh.net, a catalog of open-source software that has been used in other studies of open source software [24]. However, the vast majority of the software we found using this method had very small communities as measured by users and contributors listed in the catalog. Many of the projects from our initial random sample showed very little activity, appeared to have very few users, or did not appear to be viable projects. We decided that studying inactive or abandoned projects would not accurately reflect the values of an ongoing and active software community.

To make sure we studied viable software communities, we took another sample by selecting the 100 most popular applications listed on ohloh.net. Studying the most popular applications would allow us to study the artifacts of a software community that had enough time and resources to enable the documentation to reach a state that represents the community's values. While this sample does not represent all the software in the open-source catalog, it does represent the more active software projects in the catalog—those that have a large number of the open-source software developers who are the ultimate subject of our research.

Of the 100 open-source projects we started with, we eliminated the projects that did not have a programmable interface intended for software developers. Some of the projects we studied had both an end-user interface and an API for software developers. In those cases, we studied only the API. We also eliminated command-line tools, operating systems, and system-building projects because they represent niche audiences that are distinct from those of general APIs. The result was the 33 open-source software projects listed in Table 1.

Table 1. Open-source API documentation studied

- Adblock Plus
- Apache OpenOffice
- CakePHP
- Common Unix Printing System (CUPS)
- Cygwin
- Django
- Drupal (core)
- Eclipse Platform Project
- FileZilla Firebug
- GIMP
- Git
- GNOME
- GTK+
- Hibernate
- Inkscape
- jQuery
- JUnit
- KDE
- MediaWiki
- MySQL
- NetBeans IDE
- Perl
- PHP
- PostgreSQL Database Server
- Python programming language
- Ruby on Rails
- Samba
- SQLite
- Subversion
- Trac
- VirtualBox-Open Source Edition
- WordPress

3.2 Study Heuristic

We grouped the API documentation elements into three general categories for our evaluation:

- **Overall documentation elements**
  Elements that characterize the general nature of the developer documentation.

- **Documentation entry/home page elements**
  Elements found on the "home page" or top-level page of the developer documentation.

- **API reference topic elements**
  Elements found in the API reference topics.

3.2.1 Assessment elements

Tables 2, 3, and 4 list the specific documentation elements we assessed in each category.

Table 2. Overall documentation aspects

Question	Rating Scale
How did you find the documentation? (the navigation method used)	Link from home page Link from other page Search, internal to the site Search, external to the site
Can you find video tutorials for using the API in the documentation?	Yes No
Can you find sample apps or links to samples in the documentation?	Yes No
*Provide a qualitative estimate of the site quality as a whole.	Excellent Good Fair Poor Terrible Other
How easy was it to find the documentation?	Easy = effortless Hard = not easy
Can you find code tutorials in the documentation?	Yes No
Can you find an API Overview in the documentation?	Yes No
Note any comments from your experience with the site.	Free text comment field

The element noted by an asterisk in Table 2 was reviewed separately from the elements in Table 5. The evaluation of "Provide a qualitative estimate of the site quality as a whole" occurred during the initial evaluation of the documentation to capture a "first impression" of the documentation. After reviewing the ratings of the site quality overall, we added the criteria in Table 5 to identify some of the components that might have contributed to the first-impression rating. The elements in Table 5 were then reviewed in a second evaluation.

Table 3. Entry page documentation elements

Question	Rating Scale
Note the entry page URL	URL of page
Does the entry page have a documentation overview or a link to an overview?	Yes No
Does the entry page have a value proposition for the API?	Yes No
Does the entry page have getting-started content or a link to getting-started content?	Yes No
Does the entry page have a table-of-contents?	Yes No
Note any other comments from your experience with the entry page.	Free text comment field

Table 4. API reference topic elements

Question	Rating Scale
How did you find the API Reference?	Link from home page Link from other page Search, internal to the site Search, external to the site
Note the API reference topic homepage URL	URL of page
Describe the navigation used by the reference topics	Hub-Spoke Menu-Content Other
Did the reference topics provide interactions with the code?	Yes No
How easy was it to find the API reference?	Easy = effortless Hard = not easy
Estimate the API Size (from the number of ref. topics).	Small: APIs with < 10 high-level objects (e.g. classes, objects, etc.) Medium: APIs with 10-99 high-level objects Large: APIs with 100-999 high-level objects Huge: APIs with 1,000 or more high-level objects
Describe how the reference topic pages are organized (multi/single).	Single-Elem/Page Multiple-Elem/Page Other
Did you find code snippets in most of the reference topics you studied?	Yes No

Table 5. Design and writing quality criteria

Question	Rating Scale
Rate the level of design elements used on a reference topic.	High: Many design elements, such as multiple fonts, text layout styles, images, and other visual design elements such as lines, shadings, and adaptive page design. Lo: One or two fonts, minimal use of layout and visual design elements such as lines and shading.
Rate the reference topic pages' content quality in terms of richness and clarity.	High: writing is clear, detailed, and can be understood, even by someone who is not familiar with the API. Lo: writing is unclear, lacking in detail, and is difficult to understand.

The rating scales for the questions in Table 5 were intentionally general to make them easy to rate consistently while providing enough detail to identify the patterns and sites that might merit further study.

3.2.2 Documentation Elements from Past Research

Table 6 shows how the elements we summarized from past research match the assessment elements in our study.

Table 6. Past research and assessment elements

Documentation element from past research	Assessment questions in this study
Overview documentation.	Does the entry page have a documentation overview or a link to an overview? Can you find an API Overview in the documentation?
Short code "snippets" that demonstrate usage of an API in context.	Did you find code snippets in most of the reference topics you studied?
Code examples that show best-practices with an API	Can you find sample apps or links to samples in the documentation?
Scenario and task-based documentation.	Can you find code tutorials in the documentation
Limitations and error handling.	Not studied
Meaningful documentation (as opposed to "filler" or "boilerplate" content that adds little or no value to what is obvious).	Rate the reference topic pages' content in terms of richness and clarity.

The limitations and error-handling element was not rated in this study because we could not characterize it in a way that we could evaluate.

3.3 Study Method and Coding

Four researchers evaluated the API documentation of the selected software projects (Table 1) for the elements listed in the preceding section. Three of the four researchers had used APIs and API documentation in the past to develop software.

The researchers practiced coding API documentation that was not part of the study sample to improve inter-rater reliability and refine the definitions of the documentation elements. Through multiple iterations and review sessions, the researchers determined the operational definitions of each element in the evaluation rubric. At least one coder then assessed the documentation of each API in the final set of APIs and a subset of the APIs was reviewed by the other coders for consistency and agreement. The few disagreements found in this process were reviewed and resolved by agreement of all researchers before the data were analyzed.

4. FINDINGS

We evaluated the API documentation of the open-source software listed in Table 1 to find the documentation elements listed in Tables 2-4. In the first evaluation, we tabulated the characteristics described in our rubric; however, we also identified aspects of the documentation that the original survey did not include. We added the elements in Table 5 to our rubric and then evaluated those elements of the documentation.

4.1 Documentation Elements

Table 7 lists the frequency of the key documentation elements in the API documentation studied. Except for the API overviews, our findings support our hypothesis in that the documentation elements listed as required or desired by software developers in API documentation were found in most of the API documentation we studied.

Table 7. Key documentation elements in documentation studied (n = 33)

Documentation element evaluation question	
Does the entry page have a documentation overview?	82% Yes
Can you find an API Overview in the documentation?	42% Yes
Did you find code snippets in most of the reference topics you studied?	85% Yes
Can you find code tutorials in the documentation	79% Yes
Can you find sample apps or links to samples in the documentation?	55% Yes
Rate the reference topic pages' content in terms of richness and clarity.	82% Good or Exc.

4.2 Design and Writing Quality Evaluation

In our first evaluation of the documentation elements, we found that 21 of the 33 documentation sets (64%) had an overall impression of good or excellent; however, we encountered a broad range graphic-design and writing styles. To characterize this variation better, we added the evaluation criteria listed in Table 5 and reviewed the documentation sets again to evaluate these elements. We found that the qualitative ratings were surprisingly high—specifically, more than half of the open-source documentation we studied (19 of 33) had both high-quality design and high-quality writing (Table 8). This supports the notion that the software development communities value quality in both design and writing, which suggests that craftsmanship is also valued. High-quality writing appeared more often than high-quality design—we found that 82% of the API documentation studied had high-quality writing as compared to the 61% that had high-quality design. Table 8 shows the results of this evaluation. Using a Pearson Chi-Square test, we found significant patterns in the design and writing quality, revealing that writing quality was high in most cases.

Table 8. Design and writing

		Writing Quality		
		Low (n=6)	High (n=27)	Pearson Chi-Square
Design Quality	Low (n=13)	5	8	$\chi^2(1, N = 33) = 5.93, p = .015$
	High (n=20)	1	19	

The following sections illustrate examples of the different types of design and writing we encountered in our study.

4.2.1 Low-Design/Low-Writing Quality

We grouped documentation sets into the *low-design/low-writing quality* group if the reference pages had:

☐ A page design with only one or two fonts, minimal use of layout and visual design elements such as lines and shading.

☐ Page content where the writing is unclear, lacking in detail, or is difficult to understand.

Figure 1 [25] is an example of a reference topic with minimal visual design elements and writing that provides very little detail.

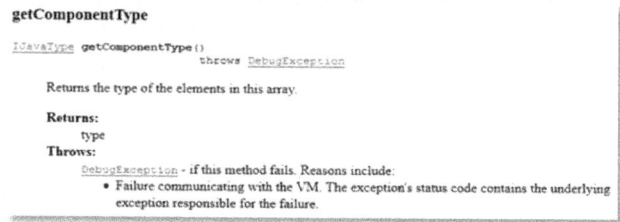

getComponentType

Figure 1. Example of low-design/low-writing qualitydocumentation Copyright (c) 2000, 2007 IBM Corporation and others.

4.2.2 Low-Design/High-Writing Quality

We grouped documentation sets into the *low-design/high-writing quality* group if the reference pages had:

☐ A page design with only one or two fonts, minimal use of layout and visual design elements such as lines and shading.

☐ Page content where the writing is clear, detailed, and can be understood, even by someone who is not familiar with the API.

Figure 2 [26] is an example of a reference topic with minimal visual design elements, but detailed text.

Figure 2. Example of low-design/high-writing quality documentation

4.2.3 High-Design/Low-Writing Quality

We grouped documentation sets into the *high-design/low-writing quality* group if the reference page had:

☐ A page design with many design elements, such as multiple fonts, text layout styles, images, and other visual design elements such as lines, shadings, and adaptive page design.

☐ Page content where the writing is unclear, lacking in detail, or is difficult to understand.

Figure 3 [27] is an example a reference topic with many visual design elements, but writing that lacks detail.

4.2.4 High-Design/High-Writing Quality

We grouped documentation sets into the *high-design/high-writing quality* group if the reference page had:

☐ A page design with many design elements, such as multiple fonts, text layout styles, images, and other visual design elements such as lines, shadings, and adaptive page design.

☐ Page content where the writing is clear, detailed, and can be understood, even by someone who is not familiar with the API.

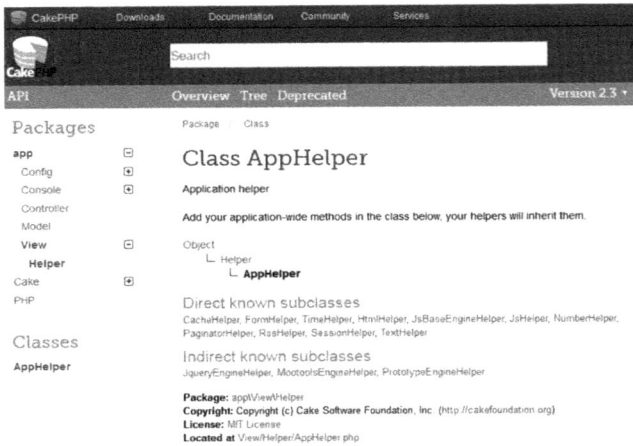

Figure 3. Example of high-design/low-writing quality documentation. Copyright © 2013 Cake Software Foundation, Inc.

Figure 4 [28] is an example of a reference topic with numerous visual styling elements and detailed text.

Figure 4. Example of high-design/high-writing quality documentation. Copyright © 2001-2013 The PHP Group.

4.3 Analysis of Design and Writing Quality

To test for consistency between the detailed quality elements and our initial overall assessment, we compared our initial overall quality assessment to the more specific ratings recorded later in the study by using a Pearson Chi-Square test. Table 9 shows that we found a statistically significant ($p < .05$) relationship between the overall rating and the specific ratings, indicating consistency between them.

We looked for a significant relationship between the frequency of the document elements listed in Table 6 and the quality evaluations using three one-way ANOVA tests. Table 10 shows that the average frequency of the documentation elements found in an API documentation set increased with the assessments of the design and writing quality, as well as the overall impression of the documentation set.

While documentation with high quality writing, design, and with good and excellent overall site quality had more elements then low quality documentation, on average, there was a significant effect seen at the $p < .05$ level in only the writing quality and site quality on the number of documentation elements found. There was no significant effect observed between the element frequency and the design quality.

Table 9. Overall impression and quality dimensions

		\multicolumn{2}{c}{Overall evaluation of API documentation}		Pearson Chi-Square
		Poor - Fair	Good - Exc.	
Design Quality	Low	10	3	χ^2 (1, N = 33) = 15.249, p = .000
Design Quality	High	2	18	
Writing Quality	Low	5	1	χ^2 (1, N = 33) = 6.991, p = .008
Writing Quality	High	7	20	

Table 10. Document element frequency and quality

		\multicolumn{3}{c}{Number of document element categories found}	ANOVA
		Mean	Std. Dev.	N	
Design Quality	Low	3.31	1.601	13	[F (1,31) = 1.877, p = 0.181]
Design Quality	High	4.05	1.468	20	
Writing Quality	Low	2.33	1.366	6	[F (1,31) = 7.537, p = 0.010]
Writing Quality	High	4.07	1.412	27	
Site Quality	Fair - Poor	2.92	1.443	12	[F (1,31) = 6.590, p = 0.015]
Site Quality	Good - Exc.	4.24	1.411	21	

To see which of the individual elements, if any, were associated with high-quality documentation, we looked at the frequency of each of the documentation elements listed in Tables 2, 3, and 4. To find a significant relationship between each one and the quality factors, we used a Pearson Chi-Square test. Tables 11 and 12 show the only significant patterns we found. Of all the documentation elements we evaluated, only the presence of code tutorials and code snippets showed a significant relationship ($p < .05$) with design and writing quality.

Table 11. Code tutorials and quality

		API documentation has code tutorials		Pearson Chi-Square
		No	Yes	
Design Quality	Low	5	8	$\chi^2(1, N = 33) = 3.82$, $p = .051$
	High	2	18	
Writing Quality	Low	4	2	$\chi^2(1, N = 33) = 9.07$, $p = .003$
	High	3	24	

Table 12. Code snippets and quality

		API reference topics have code snippets		Pearson Chi-Square
		No	Yes	
Design Quality	Low	4	9	$\chi^2(1, N = 33) = 4.07$, $p = .044$
	High	1	19	
Writing Quality	Low	3	3	$\chi^2(1, N = 33) = 6.93$, $p = .008$
	High	2	25	

5. DISCUSSION

The presence of most of the key elements in the documentation we studied supports the hypothesis that open-source software development communities, at a macro level, put the same documentation elements into their documentation as the software developers asked for in studies and interviews. That the software communities voluntarily include these elements in the documentation they produce supports the idea that they value these API documentation elements whether they are responding to surveys and interviews, or actually writing software and documentation.

In the course of this study, we experienced several occasions in which we needed to review and revise our evaluation criteria. Initially, we required several rounds of practice evaluations to refine the operational definitions of the elements we were studying. After our first full review, we found high variability in the perceived quality of the API documentation, even though we were studying the most popular open-source software products listed in ohloh.com. To investigate this variation further, we evaluated the design and written quality of the documentation sets in a second review of the API documentation.

5.1 Dealing with the Diversity

Early in the study, we had difficulty identifying some of the documentation elements with consistency using our initial definitions because they did not accommodate the variety of documentation we encountered. While the documentation element definitions seemed clear at the beginning of the project, as we applied them in our initial assessment, it became evident they needed refinement to accommodate the diversity of documentation styles, page formats, and rater experience levels. It took several iterations of trial-and-review to refine the operational definitions of the different elements such that the reviewers could assess the documentation in a reliable, consistent way.

The wide variety of content we encountered and the difficulty we had finding and applying a consistent definition of those elements makes us wonder about the consistency of what past researchers have studied and how we talk about these elements in the literature. In this study, we found that some documentation elements were easier to recognize than others were. For example, Robillard [3] describes a taxonomy of program-code examples that was clear and easy for the researchers to recognize.

- Code-snippet (showing the function being called in a specific context for illustration).
- Sequences of small examples to illustrate functionality (tutorial examples).
- Sample apps (complete and functional programs that use the function).
- Production code (source code of software that is uses the function in a customer-facing application or scenario).

On the other hand, identifying the elements that made up the intent documentation [3] was more challenging. While we tried to operationalize this in a way that mapped to recognizable documentation elements, some intent documentation, such as that which describes specific performance, usage limitations, or error conditions, might be found inside specific reference topics and not in a single topic for an API. Intent documentation that describes higher-level concepts of how to use the API in context, on the other hand, might be more appropriate in an overview or some other type of conceptual topic that focuses on the API as a whole rather than just a single element of the API. Having the information distributed around the documentation could make it hard for developers to know where to find such information, or to know if it even exists at all, until they spend time learning what is and is not documented. It also makes it hard to assess its presence with any accuracy in a survey such as this one.

In addition to the different forms the elements sought by developers can take, the vocabulary used is also critical to discovery. Ko and Riche [29], observed how documentation could exist but remain invisible to the user if they did not know the correct vocabulary to use to find it. Finally, Robillard [3] points out that too much intent documentation can make the documentation difficult to use suggesting that this might be judged better in a specific context, rather than just a simple test for presence.

The diversity of API documentation content and format presented a challenge to our study. On the one hand, technical writing curriculum tells technical writers to know their audience and to write to them [30]. Given that the documentation we studied was written by the community who also use it, it is reasonable to assume they are writing the documentation they need in the format they prefer. Such a focused approach makes sense in a context limited to a single API or library. However, today, it is increasingly common for software developers to use software and documentation from a wide variety of sources as they adopt and apply new technologies. Documentation written to a specific audience can present challenges for developers who come from another perspective or background.

While our survey identified the presence of specific documentation elements, it did not address the usability of the content or its suitability to any task. The elements we studied were presumed to be useful in that they had been identified as necessary or desired in the literature. The diversity of the documentation we reviewed, however, indicates that the problem might be more nuanced than just ensuring the API documentation has a collection of requested elements, for example the matter of craftsmanship in the documentation design and writing.

5.2 Recognizing Craftsmanship

In spite of the diverse character of the API documentation we reviewed, high quality writing and attention to detail was more common than not. The high percentage of documentation sets we found with writing that was clear and detailed indicates quality writing is a common value—one that has not been discussed much in the literature about API documentation. That there was documentation without it, however, indicates that it is a property that cannot be assumed. The use of visual design elements in the API reference topics was also higher than we expected at the beginning of the study, and it, too, is an aspect of API documentation that has not received much coverage.

While the occurrence of high quality design and writing suggests that attention to detail in the content is valued, we do not know if it has any effect on usability or popularity. In our study, for example, we found no significant relationship between any of the quality dimensions and the software's popularity rank or rating in ohloh.com. All the API documentation we studied came from the top 100 open-source software projects in ohloh.net, yet there was considerable variation in the documentation quality.

5.3 Threats to Validity

We assessed the API documentation of open-source software for the presence of specific documentation elements. In any specific documentation sample, the documentation could have been produced by the community on demand, by an organized or professional documentation effort, or some combination—the extent of which we do not know. As open-source software and documentation, we assume that the API documentation represents the values and needs of each individual community.

As open-source software and documentation, it is possible; in fact, it is quite likely, that the API documentation we studied does not represent API documentation as a whole. However, that is not relevant to the research question of the study because we are using open-source and community-generated documentation as an artifact of the software community to gain insight into what they value. In that regard, a selection of open-source and community-driven documentation is appropriate. The literature indicates that there is a high-degree of overlap between open-source and professional, commercial software developers. In many cases, they are the same people. As such, these findings should represent their values whether they are programming for hire or not. While we feel that our findings reflect the values of software developers, these findings should not be generalized to API documentation that was not included in the study.

One aspect of the open-source documentation that became known in our assessment was that many examples of open-source software documentation relied on content that was not part of an organized documentation set. Open-source software developers (if not *all* software developers) are accustomed to using community content such as forum posts, blogs, and other unstructured documentation. While not recorded in our findings, we observed that relying on these unstructured types of documentation appeared to be common. This could, however, cause our study to understate the frequency of documentation elements for a specific API documentation set. For example, it might be common in a particular software community to have code samples or sample programs separate from the API documentation—in which case they would exist for and be known by the community, but could have been missed by our assessment method.

While we made some qualitative assessments of the documentation's visual design and writing quality, this analysis was conducted at a macro level. We did not perform any formal content analysis on the documentation sets we studied. Such analysis exceeded the scope of this research; however, the findings from this study suggest such an analysis would be worthwhile.

6. CONCLUSIONS

The findings of our study of API documentation as an artifact of open-source software communities corroborate the findings of past research into what software developers want and need in API documentation. Past research describes a need for the following elements in API documentation, most of which we found in the documentation we studied.

- Overview documentation.
- Short code "snippets" that demonstrate usage of an API in context.
- Code examples that show best-practices with an API
- Scenario and task-based documentation.
- Meaningful documentation (as opposed to "filler" or "boilerplate" content that adds little or no value to what is obvious).

The fact that most of the communities who support the software we studied provided these elements in the APIs they supported suggests they represent common values among open-source software developers. That the design quality and writing quality of the API documentation we studied were high indicates the developers in these software communities also value these attributes enough to include them in their documentation.

6.1 Documentation is more than the Sum of its Parts

Our study found that open-source software documentation has, for the most part, the elements that the literature identified as necessary. However, we also found that an inventory is not sufficient to characterize a documentation set accurately. Aspects such as design quality, writing quality, terminology, and navigational affordances are also critical elements to consider. While design and writing quality, per se, do not appear as requirements in the literature, the variation of these dimensions that we encountered suggests that the perceived need for such quality varies. Perhaps high-quality design and writing is assumed; however, our study indicates that high quality design and writing is not universally consistent. The variation that we found in these quality dimensions suggests there would be value into further study into how they affect API documentation usability and utility.

6.2 What are we Talking About, Anyway?

While answering some questions, our research also raises others. If the software development communities are producing the documentation that software developers are asking for when surveyed and interviewed, what is the basis of their recent complaints? This study gave us a new appreciation for the level of diversity that exists in the world of "API documentation." Our survey spanned a wide swath of API documentation, much wider than most software developers would tend to encounter in a similar period. At the same time, we touched upon only a very small part of the API-documentation universe. It is possible that past API studies and criticisms are each seeing small and different pieces of a much larger whole—not unlike the fable of the blind men describing an elephant.

6.2.1 Different Worlds

The literature we reviewed indicates that open-source software developers have a lot in common with professional (paid) software developers—in fact, the same people often work on both types of software. It is possible that the findings from our study of open-source API documentation do not generalize to the Microsoft developers' experience in Robillard [7] and Robillard and DeLine [3] or the Android developers' experiences in Parnin [5]. It could be that it is specific examples from these environments that do not meet the needs of the developers—not a general problem with overall documentation that is responsible for the findings in those studies. Further, the difficulty we experienced in operationalizing the element definitions at the beginning of our research suggests that differences in element definitions could be complicating the discussion. While there are differences in in the subjects of each study, the important point to remember is the agreement between their conclusions. However, the definitions and descriptions of the different elements need additional refinement and clarification for practitioners to be able to apply the findings from these studies.

6.2.2 Different Methods
Our study differs from those in the literature we studied in that we studied the products of software communities without involving them directly. We looked at the artifacts that result from their actions, without them knowing we were studying them—in fact, we looked at their work long after they completed it. In that sense, there was no way for our research to influence their actions. On the other hand, in most of the earlier studies, the researchers interacted directly with the participants—the developers. Robillard and DeLine's study [3] focused on learning obstacles by asking, for example, "For each type of obstacle described below, please rate how severe this type of obstacle was in your experience learning the API you mentioned above." Such a leading question could influence the response. While that research focuses on a single aspect of learning APIs, it also highlights the need, in a subject as large and diverse as this one, for multiple studies and multiple study methods to construct a complete picture. Any one method, by itself, is likely to tell only a partial story, at best.

6.2.3 Different Perspectives
While studying the elements of a documentation set provides an inventory of its contents, it does not describe the suitability for a specific task to a specific audience. For the target audience of software developers, the suitability of the documentation to their task is very relevant and likely to influence their opinion of a documentation set. To the software developers using the documentation, if they cannot find what they are looking for, to them, it does not exist—even if we found it in our inventory. This difference does not make an inventory less valuable; however, it might identify ways in which the inventory could be improved. While the different methods provide useful and different insights, it is especially important to recognize when the methods reinforce each other, for example, how our study reinforced the findings from the more direct study methods used to observe software developers in past studies.

7. FUTURE WORK
The diversity of documentation content and content styles we found identified more questions and opportunities for study. It would be valuable to know if variations of these aspects of the documentation influence the software developer's experience and assessment of it. Exploring the influence of these factors, for example, could inform future authoring systems and documentation templates to help make it faster and easier to produce API documentation that software developers need. Our study also reinforced the need to study the documentation in context, so identifying methods and practices to collect and report this information could help identify how to improve existing and plan future documentation.

Because the documentation we studied came from the community it serves, it is reasonable to assume that each specific community tailors the documentation for that community. In that sense, the diverse content we found in our study is a good thing. At the same time, such an uneven content landscape presented a challenge to us as researchers and we suspect that it also presents a challenge to software developers who have to work with multiple libraries and products. It would be helpful to know the impact of variations in content, layout, and organization on search, comprehension, and usability. We suspect these differences complicate developers' understanding and learning in using different APIs. As APIs and API users become more numerous and more diverse, this diversity could add documentation requirements that did not heretofore exist.

Modern software development also appears to encourage just-in-time learning for specific tasks and in moving on to the next task [8]. In such a scenario, software developers coming to any documentation set will arrive with the perspective of a new user more so than that of an expert. Although they might have used the software and documentation in the past, when they return after using other software, they will still need to familiarize themselves with the navigation and terminology all over again, just like a new user. Accommodating these scenarios, which were uncommon in the past, will require additional research to identify the best practices that will empower the users of API documentation today and into the future.

8. ACKNOWLEDGEMENTS
We would like to thank Black Duck Software who hosts OhLoh.com, which provided the catalog open-source software and the data for the software and documentation we studied.

9. REFERENCES
[1] Abrams, B. 2008. *Number of types in the .NET Framework.* Brad Abrams. Retrieved from http://blogs.msdn.com/b/brada/archive/2008/03/17/number-of-types-in-the-net-framework.aspx

[2] Programmable web. 2013. *Keeping you up to date with APIs, mashups and the Web as platfo*rm. Retrieved May 19, 2013, from http://www.programmableweb.com/

[3] Robillard, M. P., & DeLine, R. 2011. A field study of API learning obstacles. *Empirical Software Engineering*, 16(6), 703–732. doi:DOI 10.1007/s10664-010-9150-8

[4] Lethbridge, T. C., Singer, J., & Forward, A. 2003. How software engineers use documentation: The state of the practice. *Software, IEEE*, 20(6), 35–39.

[5] Parnin, C. 2013. *API documentation: Why it sucks. ninlabs research.* Retrieved May 19, 2013, from http://blog.ninlabs.com/2013/03/api-documentation/

[6] Nykaza, J., Messinger, R., Boehme, F., Norman, C. L., Mace, M., & Gordon, M. 2002. What programmers really want: Results of a needs assessment for sdk documentation. In *Proceedings of the 20th Annual International Conference on Computer Documentation* (pp. 133–141). Presented at the SIGDOC 2002, Toronto, Ontario, Canada: ACM.

[7] Robillard, M. P. 2009. What makes APIs hard to learn? answers from developers. *Software, IEEE*, 26(6), 27–34.

[8] Sillito, J., & Begel, A. 2013. App-directed learning: An exploratory study. Presented at the 6th International Workshop on Cooperative and Human Aspects of Software Engineering, San Francisco, CA, USA.

[9] Mitchell, G. E. 1993. What do users really want from computer documentation? In *IPCC 93 Proceedings. The New Face of Technical Communication: People, Processes, Products* (pp. 27–31). Presented at the International Professional Communication Conference 1993, IEEE.

[10] Novick, D. G., & Ward, K. 2006. What users say they want in documentation. Presented at the SIGDOC 2006, Myrtle Beach, South Carolina, USA: ACM.

[11] Holtzblatt, K., Wendell, J. B., & Wood, S. 2004. *Rapid contextual design: a how-to guide to key techniques for user-centered design*. Morgan Kaufmann.

[12] Bernard, H. 2006. *Research methods in anthropology: qualitative and quantitative approaches* (Fourth Edition.). Lanham, MD, USA: Altamira Press.

[13] von Krogh, G., Haefliger, S., Spaeth, S., & Wallin, M. W. 2012. Carrots and rainbows: Motivation and social practice in open source software development. *MIS Quarterly-Management Information Systems*, 36(2), 649–676.

[14] Nielsen, J. 1993. *Usability Engineering*. Boston. MA. USA: Academic press.

[15] Watson, R. B. 2012. Development and application of a heuristic to assess trends in API documentation. In *Proceedings of the 30th ACM International Conference on Design of Communication* (pp. 295–302). Presented at the SIGDOC 2012, Seattle, WA, USA: ACM.

[16] Association of Support Professionals, The. 2013. *The Ten Best Web Support Sites of 2013: Site Scoring System*. ASPonline.com. Retrieved May 19, 2013, from http://www.asponline.com/scoring13.pdf

[17] Hars, A., & Ou, S. 2002. Working for free? Motivations for participating in open-source projects. *International Journal of Electronic Commerce*, 6, 25–40.

[18] Hertel, G., Niedner, S., & Herrmann, S. 2003. Motivation of software developers in Open Source projects: an Internet-based survey of contributors to the Linux kernel. *Research policy*, 32(7), 1159–1177.

[19] Oreg, S., & Nov, O. 2008. Exploring motivations for contributing to open source initiatives: The roles of contribution context and personal values. *Computers in Human Behavior*, 24(5), 2055–2073. doi:doi:10.1016/j.chb.2007.09.007

[20] Shah, S. K. 2006. Motivation, governance, and the viability of hybrid forms in open source software development. *Management Science*, 52(7), 1000–1014.

[21] Wu, C.-G., Gerlach, J. H., & Young, C. E. 2007. An empirical analysis of open source software developers' motivations and continuance intentions. *Information & Management*, 44(3), 253–262. doi:doi:10.1016/j.im.2006.12.006

[22] Ye, Y., & Kishida, K. 2003. Toward an understanding of the motivation of open source software developers. In *Software Engineering, 2003, Proceedings. 25th International Conference on* (pp. 419–429). Presented at the Software Engineering, 2003, International Conference on, IEEE.

[23] Oram, A. 2007. Why do people write free documentation? results of a survey. LAMP: *The Open-Source Web Platform*. Retrieved from http://www.onlamp.com/lpt/a/7062

[24] Ellis, H. J., Purcell, M., & Hislop, G. W. 2012. An approach for evaluating FOSS projects for student participation. In *Proceedings of the 43rd ACM Technical Symposium on Computer Science Education* (pp. 415–420). Presented at the SIGCSE 2012, Raleigh, North Carolina, USA.

[25] Help - Eclipse Platform. (n.d.). Retrieved July 20, 2013, from http://help.eclipse.org/juno/index.jsp?topic=%2Forg.eclipse .jdt.doc.isv%2Freference%2Fapi%2Forg%2Feclipse%2Fjdt %2Fdebug%2Fcore%2FIJavaArrayType.html&anchor=get ComponentType(). Included under Eclipse Public License

[26] Chapter 11. HQL and JPQL. (n.d.). Retrieved July 20, 2013, from http://docs.jboss.org/hibernate/orm/4.1/devguide/en-US/html/ch11.html#d5e2552. Included under LGPL v2.1.

[27] Class AppHelper | CakePHP. (n.d.). Retrieved July 20, 2013, from http://api.cakephp.org/2.3/class-AppHelper.html. Copyright © 2013 Cake Software Foundation, Inc.

[28] PHP: substr - Manual. (n.d.). Retrieved July 20, 2013, from http://php.net/manual/en/function.substr.php. Copyright © 2001-2013 The PHP Group.

[29] Ko, A. J., & Riche, Y. 2011. The role of conceptual knowledge in API usability. In *Proceedings of the Visual Languages and Human-Centric Computing (VL/HCC), 2011 IEEE Symposium on* (pp. 173–176). Presented at the Visual Languages and Human-Centric Computing (VL/HCC), 2011 IEEE Symposium on, IEEE.

[30] Markel, M. 2006. *Technical Communication* (8th ed.). Boston. MA. USA: Bedford/St. Martins.

An Exploration of the Professional Development Potential of Living World Games

Christina Bethel
East Carolina University
Bethelc99@students.ecu.edu

ABSTRACT

By creating and modifying a living world game for professional development (PD), community colleges could more effectively acculturate instructors to community college's values, norms, and practices. I will conceptualize how collaborative game development would function to strengthen faculty learning communities by challenging existing faculty to engage in new literacies that will help them connect with students and other faculty, as well as share disciplinary and professional expertise in new ways. In my poster, I will use screen shots of *Grand Theft Auto IV* to illustrate the potential for living world games as immersive PD that I have collected while conducting a virtual ethnography of the game. I will conclude by exploring potential for building collaborative partnerships between educational institutions, game industry companies, and gamer communities to develop campus-specific living world PD video games.

Categories and Subject Descriptors

K.3.1 [**Computer Uses in Education**]: Collaborative Learning.

Keywords

"living world game," "professional development," "communities of practice".

1. WHY VIDEO GAMES & COMMUNITY COLLEGES?

According to the American Association of Community Colleges, 45% of U.S. undergraduates attend community college, a significant percentage of the U.S. workforce (2013), and many enter fields in which multiple literacies and communication skills are required. Key research interests of community colleges, then, should include examination of communication practices and 21st century literacy skills students must develop to succeed in today's workforce. And according to interdisciplinary scholars James Paul Gee and Jane McGonigal, one of the most important and most undervalued 21st century literacies is gaming literacy. "Games, in the twenty-first century," according to McGonigal, "will be a primary platform for enabling the future" (13). And what do we strive to do through community colleges if not enable the future?

SIGDOC'13, Sep 30 - Oct 01 2013, Greenville, NC, USA
ACM 978-1-4503-2131-0/13/09.
http://dx.doi.org/10.1145/2507065.2507090

To consider Kim Burns' argument that more localized research and interventions are needed to promote community college student success (39) in the context of Wenger's concept of communities of practice, we must understand and value the concepts of boundaries and brokers. Community college learners, both students and teachers alike, strive to cross new academic and professional community boundaries in order to improve the quality of their lives.

Figure 1. Nico's apartment:
where Nico can afford to live on an LCCC adjunct's pay.

According to Murray and Cunningham, many instructors cross boundaries to enter community college communities because they often take positions at community colleges "while they [are] planning for other lives" (26). The authors illustrate that many instructors cross multiple boundaries to join campus communities once hired. It's vital to find ways to broker more effectively for instructors so that they can become effective brokers for students.

Figure 2. Nico has difficulty navigating campus.

The typical preparation, hiring, orientation, and professional development models for hiring community college instructors often result in new community college teachers, teaching live students (sometimes for the first time) while simultaneously beginning to develop new instructor identities and attempting to integrate into new communities. Any one of these individually can be an overwhelming endeavor, and combining the elements leads to understandably poor working conditions.

So how can we fix the system? Gee proposes some answers in a recent blog post "Ten Commandments for Educators" (2013). Most notable for this project are Commandments 1, 5, and 10: reform education, build systems, and encourage failure. My suggestion for "fixing" one element of the "broken" education system is to incorporate living world video game design, development, and production into core community college curricula in order to empower game development students to learn valuable industry skills while improving community college faculty hiring practices and professional development.

2. WHY ETHNOGRAPHY AND LIVING WORLD GAMES?

Marjorie Zielke and her team define a "living world" game as an immersive 3D video game that develops a shared set of beliefs, values, norms, and practices for characters that the player must learn in order to succeed within the game world. They assert that "living world" games are valuable tools for teaching culture, and can be particularly effective for first-person cultural training.

In the introduction to "Serious games for immersive cultural training: Creating a living world," Zielke and her colleagues identify the game *Grand Theft Auto IV (GTA IV)* as a mainstream example of a living world game. I began to collect data for a virtual ethnography of *GTA IV* while I was reading Kinloch's *Harlem on Our Minds*, and processing that data through the lens of ethnography seemed a natural fit for this project.

According to McGonigal, we've reached a stage in technological and cultural development where it's no longer necessary or appropriate to continue using typical, "broken" social and cultural practices with potential gaming solutions, and recent academic, professional, and personal experiences and observations regarding video games lead me to the conclusion that these solutions are both conceptually within our grasp and collaboratively feasible.

Living world games, as defined by Zielke et al, provide a potential solution: community college living world games designed as part of a project-based curriculum in which students collaborate with faculty and staff to collect ethnographic data about campus faculty, staff, students, community, and environment and design a 3D immersive orientation video game for new faculty. Educators, learners, and game designers can collaborate to collect and use ethnographic data gathered to design video games for professional development that take place on virtual versions of real campuses.

3. WHY BUILD GAMES THROUGH COLLABORATIVE PARTNERSHIPS?

However, a game design effort like the one described would take a massive amount of time, energy, and collaboration among an openly networked community of experienced learners, educators, and game developers in order to meet the needs of faculty and students. By building the kind of hybrid industries and unconventional partnerships McGonigal advocates for, by creating and strengthening campus communities of practice, and by focusing on open source and open access tools for design and development, we can overcome the common design gaps that exist in serious games and in many current campus orientation programs. Building partnerships for game development is essential for a variety of reasons, not least of which includes distributing game development costs and providing skill development and internship opportunities for students in game development curricula across post-secondary institutions.

Zielke et al (2010) note one of the conclusions drawn by the military from cultural training: "gathering information from the local population is a major key to success" (2). This is no less true in an educational environment than it is in a military environment:

as educators, we can never fully comprehend how our words or actions affect our students. We don't let our soldiers, doctors, pilots, or astronauts do the bulk of their learning on live individuals, and we've reached a stage in our technological development where we have more responsible options for teaching as well. To interact responsibly with students in any educational setting, we need to develop an intimate understanding of the educational communities we join.

4. ACKNOWLEDGMENTS

My thanks to the following people, who each played multiple roles in my composing process, but primarily: to Josh Moore, Will Banks, and Kirk St. Amant for inspiring the concept; to Wendy Sharer, Mike Albers, and Doug Eyman for helping me find focus; to Jen Heath, Steph West-Puckett, and the TRWP SI 2013 hive for being awesome sounding boards.

5. REFERENCES

[1] American Association of Community Colleges. (2012). Community college-industry partnerships. *About Community Colleges*. Whissemore, T., ed. Retrieved March 29, 2012.

[2] Burns, K. (2010). Community college student success variables: A review of the literature. *Community College Enterprise, 16*(2), 33-61.

[3] Gee, J. P. (2007). *What Video Games Have to Teach Us about Learning and Literacy, Revised and Updated Edition.* New York: Palgrave MacMillan.

[4] Houser, D., and Humphries, R. (2008). *Grand Theft Auto IV.* Rockstar North. PC.

[5] Hughes, M. (2002). Moving from information transfer to knowledge creation: A new value proposition for technical communicators. *Technical Communication, 49*(3), 275-275.

[6] Luzon, M. J. (2005). Genre analysis in technical communication. *IEEE Transactions, 48*(3) 285-295. doi:10.1109/TPC.2005.853937

[7] McGonigal, J. *Reality is Broken: Why Games Make Us Better and How They Can Change the World.* New York: Penguin Group.

[8] Murray, J. P., & Cunningham, S. (2004). New rural community college faculty members and job satisfaction. *Community College Review*, 32(2), 19-38. doi:10.1177/009155210403200202

[9] UT Dallas News. (2009, September 3). ATEC Prof to Take Clinical Concepts to Virtual Worlds. *The University of Texas at Dallas News Center*. Retrieved from http://www.utdallas.edu/news/2009/09/03-002.php.

[10] Wenger, E. (2000). Communities of practice and social learning systems. *Organization, 7*(2), 225-246. doi:10.1177/135050840072002

[11] Zielke, M., et al. (2009). Serious games for immersive cultural training: Creating a living world. *IEEE computer graphics and applications,* 29(2), 49-60.

[12] Zielke, M., et al. (2010). Developing a platform-flexible game-based simulation for cultural training. *Interservice/Industry Training, Simulation, and Education Conference.* Retrieved from http://www.utdallas.edu/~maz031000/.

An Analysis of the Complex Ecological System and Usability of Selected Weather Communication Products for the National Weather Service–Lubbock

Joy Cooney
Texas Tech University
Lubbock, Texas

Heidi Everett
Texas Tech University
Lubbock, Texas

Hilary Graham
Texas Tech University
Lubbock, Texas

Mark Shealy
Texas Tech University
Lubbock, Texas

Ian Weaver
Texas Tech University
Lubbock, Texas

Elaine Wisniewski
Texas Tech University
Lubbock, Texas

ABSTRACT
Our research team was asked by the National Weather Service-Lubbock (NWS-L) to consider the usability of its weather communication products. We specifically focused our study on two types of evaluations: (1) usability testing of GraphiCasts on the NWS-L Facebook page and Submit a Storm Report features with non-expert users and (2) site visits with expert users who use NWS-L products to make high-stakes decisions. The study occurred during an actual severe weather event, so we were able to study real user in a real scenario conducting real tasks. Our participants in the usability testing of the GraphiCasts were planning an outdoor event and the participants in the site visits were reacting to the impending weather. This poster presents our methods, results, and recommendations to the NWS-L.

Categories and Subject Descriptors
H.5.2 [**User Interfaces**]: Graphical user interfaces

H.1.2 [**User/Machine Systems**]: Human factors

General Terms
Documentation, Human Factors

Keywords
complex system; ecological analysis; usability; weather communication

1. INTRODUCTION
The mission of the National Weather Service Weather Forecast Office, Lubbock (NWS-L) is to help protect lives and property by providing information that aids in weather-related decision making. The NWS-L team was interested in simplifying and refining their weather-related communication products (e.g., website, graphics, other materials sent to users); therefore, they enlisted a graduate student usability team at Texas Tech University (TTU) to test the usability of their communication products.

Based on our initial discussions with the NWS-L and our review of academic literature, we decided to study their communication products as both components and tools through usability tests and contextual inquiry interviews in the environments within which they are used. Through our research, we learned that the NWS-L is part of a complex ecosystem comprised of expert and non-expert users, a variety of information sources, the unstable nature of weather, and evolving technologies. Because of this complexity, we selected an ecological framework to understand user experience [1,2].

This poster describes the ecological system; our usability methods; user decision-making models based on severe weather events; and our results and analysis. It also includes our recommendations for simplifying and enhancing the NWS-L weather communication products so that the NWS-L can better fulfill its mission by providing weather-related information for effective decision making.

2. ECOLOGICAL FRAMEWORK
Taking a micro-analytic approach to a macro-sized issue [2], we sought to create an organic picture of user experiences based on an impending severe weather event by analyzing how communication occurs within the ecological system of the NWS-L, its users, and its products. We conducted two types of evaluations: usability tests with non-expert users (drawn from the general public) and site visits with expert users (drawn from those who regularly use NWS-L products to make high-stakes decisions).

3. USABILITY TESTING
We conducted usability testing on two communication products offered by the NWS-L (GraphiCasts on the NWS-L Facebook page and Submit a Storm Report features on the NWS-L web homepage) using a blend of techniques, including observational data through think-aloud protocol and video/audio recordings, self-reported data through pre- and post-surveys, and performance data computer mouse movements and clicks.

SIGDOC'13, Sep 30 – Oct 01, 2013 Greenville, NC, USA
ACM 978-1-4503-2131-0/13/09
http://dx.doi.org/10.1145/2507065.2507088

3.1 GraphiCasts on Facebook

We first wanted to know how well users understand GraphiCasts to make weather-related decisions. We recruited six TTU students (in two groups of three) who were planning an outdoor event to use the GraphiCast to determine if they should plan to hold the event indoors.

Throughout the task, participants were asked to use concurrent Think-Aloud Protocol, verbalizing about information and features of the GraphiCast as well as their decision-making process. A post-task interview was also conducted to further understand the helpfulness of the GraphiCasts, suggestions for improvement to the GraphiCasts, and their typical behavior when assessing the weather. Participants generally felt there was not enough information provided on some of the GraphiCasts to make an informed decision. They had difficulty about the regional context, the symbol conventions, and the timeline of events. We recommend including more information on the GraphiCast to orient users to the location of severe weather, remembering that not all users are regional; also add a projected timeline, key terms, a legend, supplementary headings, or brief text to supplement the visual. The poster will show the GraphiCasts and identify the problem areas.

3.2 Submit a Storm Report Website Features

Based on our attendance at a Severe Weather Incident Webinar hosted by the NWS-L, we learned that the NWS-L wanted its expert users to encourage the public to share weather-related information with the NWS-L via their website using the Submit a Storm Report features. We decided to study the user experience of finding these features.

We recruited five participants from the NWS-L Facebook page who had "liked" the page. Participants were scheduled individually to visit the Usability Research Lab at TTU. After completing a Consent Form and computerized pre-test survey, they were asked to complete two tasks in the laboratory (watch a video of a significant weather event and use the NWS-L website to log their account of the event). Participants were also asked to rate (on a scale of 1 = not easy at all to 5 = very easy) overall, ease, efficiency, and satisfaction when submitting the report.

All participants were able to locate the Submit a Storm Report features; however, the time to locate the correct features and complete the report was inefficient, creating an unsatisfactory user experience. The average number of mouse clicks to locate a correct feature was 3.2 clicks, ranging from 2 to 5 clicks. The average time to locate the correct feature was 2:10 minutes, ranging from 1:01 to 4:30 minutes.

By analyzing comments made during the Think-Aloud Protocol and during responses to the post-task interview, we learned several factors affected the overall usability of the site, including (1) communicating channels do not match user expectations, (2) word choices for navigational tools are not clear, (3) expected placement of key information did not align with conventional website use, (4) website design impedes efficiency, (5) form fields are unclear, and (6) users are unaware that there is an expectation or opportunity for citizen input. Specific findings and recommendations for these factors will be presented in the poster.

4. SITE VISITS

We extended beyond the boundaries of traditional usability testing and conducted a small-scale ecological field study (consisting of expert user site visits and attending an NWS-L severe weather announcement webinar) to better understand users of these products and how these products are used within their respective contexts. On the day of the forecasted severe weather, we visited several webinar participants. These visits afforded us an opportunity to watch emergency managers interact in their workplaces environments during a severe weather situation. We observed and interviewed the expert users to better understand what sources and tools they use, what environments they used them in, and to what extend the tools are useful and usable.

We learned that the webinar content, email updates, and text messages are both useful and usable; the NWS-L is considered the authoritative source of weather information; and none of the expert users rely entirely on NWS-L for all their weather information. The poster will provide more details of the interviews on the site visit, photographs of the work environments, listings of different weather information sources used, and a generic decision-making model used to make weather-related decisions.

5. CONCLUSIONS

To help the NWS-L better fulfill its mission, we have studied how they might improve their weather-related information for decision making. Overall, the NWS-L is the authority on forecasting and communicating the weather. Although expert and non-expert users recognize that the NWS-L offers important weather information, the usability and usefulness of the communication products could be improved for the non-expert users. However, the expert users are satisfied with the information and how it is provided. This poster presentation will provide insightful information to the NWS-L for how their users interact with their weather products and how practitioners and researchers can analyze complex systems.

6. ACKNOWLEDGMENTS

Many thanks to Dr. Joyce Carter for her support and encouragement throughout the project.

7. REFERENCES

[1] Redish, J. (2007). Expanding usability testing to evaluate complex systems. *Journal of Usability Studies*, *2*(3), 102–111.

[2] Still, B. (2010). Mapping usability: An ecological framework for analyzing user experience. *Usability of Complex Information Systems*.

Call to Action: Simplifying Voice Tree Design

Rodrigo Davies
MIT Center for Civic Media
MIT Media Lab, Ames Street
Cambridge, MA 02139
+1 617-299-9831
rodrigod@mit.edu

Sasha Costanza-Chock
MIT Center for Civic Media
MIT Media Lab, Ames Street
Cambridge, MA 02139
+1 617-299-9831
schock@mit.edu

ABSTRACT

Call to Action is an open-source web platform for creating telephone-based services such as hotlines, voice petitions and phone blogging platforms being developed at MIT's Center for Civic Media. It seeks to simplify the design and deployment process for non-technical users, such as community groups. This poster will illustrate the platform's GUI, methodology, typical use cases and future development prospects.

Categories and Subject Descriptors

H.5.2 [**User Interfaces**]: User-centered design

Keywords

Voice trees, ICT4D

PROJECT DESCRIPTION

Call to Action seeks to simplify the often-complex process of designing voice trees and provide a hosted platform for the deployment of these services that meets the needs of community groups and individuals who do not have technical support or expertise.

Development of Call to Action began following the successful deployment of New Day New Standard, a telephone hotline service the team developed with REV-and Domestic Workers United to inform domestic workers and their employers in New York of changes in legislation affecting them.

The success of NDNS led to inquiries from other potential user groups. It was clear that a wide range of community groups could benefit from developing phone-based information services of their own. Since NDNS was created in VoIP Drupal scripting language, though, users without that specific programming experience would need to invest a significant amount of resources to create a similar service. Secondly, our research found that most user communities find creating a voice tree to be a conceptually challenging exercise. We hope to simplify the process with a visually oriented system that mirrors a paper-and-pen workshop method the team uses with community partners.

The platform provides a drag-and-drop graphical interface that enables the user to plan the flow of calls, record custom audio and make use of all the input and output features offered by a regular

telephone. The service requires no software programming experience, and users can build a service in under half an hour.

Users build their services by arranging pre-defined elements onto a canvas and linking these elements with ties. Call to Action was designed with the intention of supporting all possible permutations of a call flow using the fewest possible number of element types. The platform uses seven: 'Welcome Message' (plays audio but has no input node); 'Audio' (plays audio); 'Menu' (plays an audio prompt and accepts a user key press); 'Action' (sends a query to the database); 'Recording (plays an audio prompt and accepts user audio recording); 'Redirect' (re-routes the call to another telephone number); Hang Up (hangs up the call and has no output node). All elements, except the 'Welcome Message' and 'Hang Up', have input and output nodes that must be connected to other elements. Elements are distinguished by color and shapes to help users to quickly identify the elements they need.

Commonly used sequences of elements (such as a caller recording a message to be submitted to the service) are given as grouped templates or 'blocks' that can be imported onto the canvas. After completing a design, the user can save their work for publishing, and retain the files for future editing. As well as facilitating the easy creation of telephone services, the platform gives users advice on how to record effective voice prompts and estimates the call length at each stage of the call flow. This allows creators to optimize their services to suit caller needs.

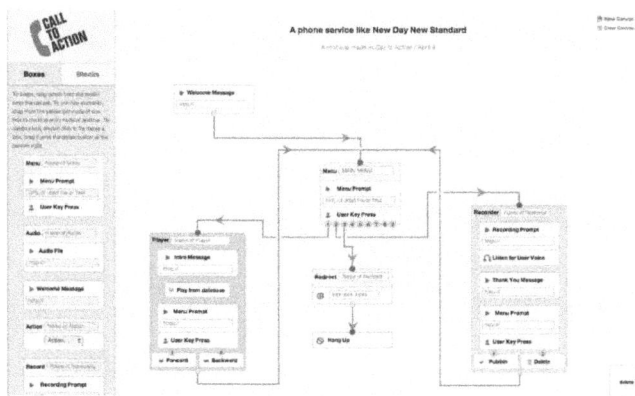

Figure 1. Call to Action design interface

Call to Action uses Javascript to handle the manipulation of elements on the canvas, including the jsPlumb library. The completed platform will output a representation of a user's voice tree design as JSON and XML files that can be used wit VoIP frameworks and APIs such as VoIP Drupal, Asterisk, Twilio and Tropo. The team is also considering developing an end-to-end platform that allows users to save and operate their completed services as nodes on a Drupal instance hosted by the Center for Civic Media.

To date we have released an alpha version of the platform's design interface, and are currently developing the scripting and hosting functions the platform will use. The alpha version is hosted at **calltoaction.mit.edu**. The current tool has been used to support in-person telephone service design workshops with community groups. The finished platform will be a standalone service that groups or individuals can use unassisted.

Redesigning the Library E-lending Experience to Ensure Accessibility and Patron Privacy

Kathleen Dobruse
Michigan State University
East Lansing, MI, USA
dobrusek@gmail.com

ABSTRACT

This poster identifies systematic problems with current user experience models that disadvantage consumers in favor of protecting rights holders' interests. Finally, alternative models that balance library, patron, and publisher interests are discussed.

Categories and Subject Descriptors

H.1.2 [Models and Principles]: User/Machine Systems—*Human factors*, *Human information processing*

Keywords

Ebooks, E-lending, Digital Distribution, Publisher, Third-party Distributor, Accessibility, Availability, Formatting, Privacy.

1. INTRODUCTION

There has been a surge in demand for ebooks, but there has not been a corresponding increased inquiry into the user experience of these systems. There are many ethical and social issues surrounding the increased use of ebooks and ereaders, particularly in public libraries. Rather than simply lobbying for or against increased library spending on ebooks, we must critically question the social and technical implications of these user experiences.

1.1 Defining an Ebook

Ebooks are electronic texts meant to be read on any number of platforms, from ereaders—such as the Amazon Kindle, Barnes & Noble Nook, and Kobo and Sony eReaders—to tablets, smartphones, and personal computers. Ebooks may or may not have a print counterpart, and if such a counterpart exists, they may not be released at the same time.

There are numerous ebook formats available, depending on the distributor and the platform. Some of the more common formats include epub, html, pdf, mobi, and Amazon's azw. Depending on the distributor a library is partnered with, certain file formats may be unavailable, and therefore some patrons may be unable to use their devices to access those particular titles. If a library is partnered with a distributor that only offers ebooks in epub rather than azw format, Kindle users will be unable to read those titles [5].

SIGDOC'13, September 30–October 1, 2013, Greenville, North Carolina, USA.
ACM 978-1-4503-2131-0/13/09.
http://dx.doi.org/10.1145/2507065.2507101

1.2 Third-party distribution

It is only as of April 2013 that all members of publishing's "Big Six" (now "Big Five") publishers have begun to cooperate on some level with libraries to allow for the lending of ebooks [1]. Prior to that, Macmillan and Simon & Schuster did not permit e-lending of their titles at all, while other publishers placed artificial restrictions on library e-lending of their titles [5]. HarperCollins only allowed a title to be checked out 26 times before it "expired" and had to be repurchased. Another strategy employed at various times by different publishers has been to delay the release of the ebook version of their titles for months after the initial release of the print version for fear of hurting their print sales [5].

The current systems for e-lending involve coordination with one or more third-party distributors who aggregate content from multiple publishers. The largest such distributor is OverDrive, which provides more than 700,000 titles—including ebooks, audiobooks, and videos—from 1000 publishers, and is currently the only distributor that permits patrons to download content to their Kindle devices [4]. Libraries that want to offer patrons the ability to download to their Kindles *must* partner with OverDrive, or they cannot serve those patrons.

1.3 Opportunities

A 2011 *Library Journal* survey found that more than half of library patrons purchased books by an author they initially discovered at the library, debunking "the myth that when a library buys a book the publisher loses future sales" [5]. At the same time, a PEW survey found that library patrons are twice as likely to have purchased their most recent book, as opposed to having borrowed it [5]. Taken together, this goes to show that the public library "is an active partner with the publishing industry in building the book market, not to mention the burgeoning e-book market" [5].

Instead of taking advantage of the growing pool of potential customers, publishers are fixated on preventing loss of sales through libraries: "The current models which provide access to digital content to libraries have for the most part been designed to support, safeguard and reflect the commercial interests of publishers, online retailers and rights holders" [3]. Publishers should cooperate with public libraries and reduce the artificial friction that has been introduced to the e-lending system in a misguided attempt to secure profits. As one librarian complained in a recent Pew survey, "'Now some of the publishers have publicly stated that they need to add "difficulty" to the process of borrowing e-books from libraries, either with restrictions on the loan period, or limits on circulations'" [5].

2. CURRENT SYSTEM UNFRIENDLY TO USERS ON MULTIPLE LEVELS

Current systems for e-lending demonstrate little concern for the user experience of patrons. Publishers are attempting to protect their own interests at the expense of patrons' user experiences.

2.1 Difficult to use systems

With ebooks accounting for only 4% of most public libraries' spending, it is much more difficult to check-out a specific ebook than a physical book [5]. A print book not present in one library's collection can often be borrowed from another library through inter-library loan (ILL). However, most publishers and distributors do not support ILL for ebooks [3]. Most libraries rely on ILL to supplement their limited budgets to provide better service for their patrons, and being unable to exchange titles with other libraries limits the value of ebooks.

Even trying to locate titles can be convoluted; as one librarian put it, "'patrons often have a hard time finding titles and then downloading them to their particular device. It is a cumbersome, nonsensical, multi-part process in which we lose too many people along the way'" [5]. Part of the problem with the user experience is that patrons have to leave the familiar ecosystem of their library's website for the unfamiliar environment of a third-party distributor. The search experience often does not match the traditional library catalog search, offering instead a limited keyword search. When a more nuanced search is available, it can require digging to find.

Once patrons have located a particular title, 52% of them reported encountering a waiting list [5]. Patrons are likely to place a request for the title in question, resulting in long waiting lists on many if not most titles. To further complicate matters, patrons may find that they reach the top of the list for several titles at once, and have only a single loan-period to read all of them [5]. Unlike print books, ebooks often cannot be renewed because the system in use literally does not support that function [3]. For patrons whose libraries do offer the opportunity to renew ebooks, the point is moot if there is another patron waiting for that title, which, again, is often the case. Alternately, there are patrons who finish their titles early but do not know how to return their ebooks, artificially extending the wait period for other patrons [3]. Ultimately, many of the regular features of the library borrowing experience are stripped away by the digital distribution system, leaving patrons confused and frustrated. They expect the experience of checking out an ebook to involve no more friction than checking out a print book, and the fact that this is not so results in a poor user experience.

2.2 Threats to patron privacy

What most patrons who use OverDrive do not know ahead of time is that in order to download a title to their Kindle, they must log in through Amazon's servers, not their library's, allowing Amazon access to their private data, including their reading habits [5]. Sarah Houghton, Director for the San Rafael Public Library, warns that with patron information in the hands of a corporation, all the government has to do is subpoena Amazon to find out what someone has been reading, and there will not be an impassioned ALA librarian standing in the way to prevent it from happening [2]. Furthermore, this may be in direct violation of some states' laws, including California's Reader Privacy Act, which protects records of patron library and bookstore transactions [2]. So not only is

Amazon holding on to private data that it legally is not allowed to, but it is also making librarians complicit in its guilt whenever they direct patrons to use OverDrive's Kindle lending system.

3. FUTURE WORK

Improving the user experience for patrons requires several steps. The most immediate improvement would be to fix the design of the search experience, followed by eliminating formatting challenges, with the ultimate goal of protecting patron privacy.

3.1 Improving the search experience

Ideally, patrons should be able to remain within the digital ecosystem of their own libraries as they search for and borrow ebooks [3]. Libraries should work with distributors to integrate entries for ebooks into their existing catalogs. That way, ebooks could be treated as just another format patrons could specify in their search, just the same as if they were searching for a large-print book or a DVD.

3.2 Determining formatting standards

The best way to escape the walled gardens of various distributors' digital ecosystems would be to agree upon on a single, universally accepted format that all devices would be capable of viewing. If the various competing interests in the ebook market cannot agree on one, then publishers and distributors should make their titles available in a wider variety of formats. This would eliminate the artificial restrictions that require users to jump through hoops just to view the ebook they want on the device they have.

3.3 Protecting patron privacy

Integrating distributors' systems with libraries' own systems and adopting a universal formatting standard would go a long way toward protecting patron privacy. Together these steps would keep patrons within the library's digital ecosystem and remove the necessity of going through, say, Amazon's environment just to load an ebook onto a device.

References

[1] Marx, A. W. (2013, April 25). E-Books and Democracy. *New York Times*, sec. A, p. 25

[2] Houghton, S. (2011, October 18). Libraries got screwed by Amazon and OverDrive [Blog post]. Retrieved from Librarian in Black website: http://librarianinblack.net/librarianinblack/2011/10/wegotscrewed.html

[3] *Libraries, e-Lending and the future of public access to digital content* (Civic Agenda, Comp.). (n.d.). Retrieved from The International Federation of Library Associations and Institutions website: http://www.ifla.org/node/7447

[4] A primer on ebooks for libraries just starting with downloadable media. (2012, April 18). Retrieved March 22, 2013, from The Digital Shift website: http://www.thedigitalshift.com/2012/04/ebooks/an-ebook-primer-many-small-libraries-are-still-just-getting-started-with-ebooks-heres-a-helpful-guide-on-those-first-steps/

[5] Zickuhr, K., Rainie, L., Purcell, K., Madden, M., & Brenner, J. (2012, July 22). *Libraries, patrons, and e-books*. Retrieved March 24, 2013, from Pew Internet & American Life Project website: http://libraries.pewinternet.org/files/legacy-pdf/PIP_Libraries_and_Ebook_Patrons%206.22.12.pdf

Making Complex Simple

Kent Eisenhuth
keisenhuth@electronicink.com

Jeanne Adamson
jadamson@electronicink.com

Justin Wear
jwear@electronicink.com

Electronic Ink
1 South Broad St. 19th Floor
Philadelphia, PA 19107

ABSTRACT

This poster illustrates our process for transforming an error-inducing, bewildering application into an intuitive workflow designed around user needs.

Categories and Subject Descriptors

H.5.3, H.1.2

General Terms

Design, Documentation, Human Factors, Verification

Keywords

Business System Design, Web Design, User Experience Design, Aesthetics, Content Strategy

1. INTRODUCTION

Why are complicated systems and processes left tangled? Because the unraveling is anything but simple. In large organizations, system redesign typically requires buy-in across rank, discipline and locale. It's a daunting task to get that many people in the same room, let alone on the same page. To help our client meet such a challenge, we developed a diagram and iconography inspired by Harry Beck's iconic London Underground network map [1].

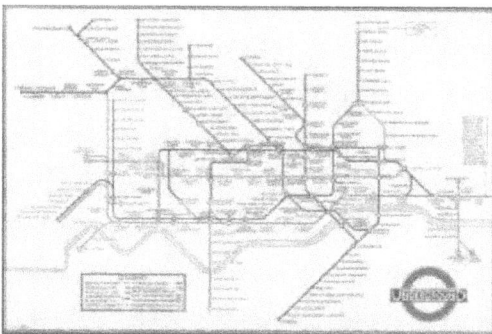

Figure 1. Harry Beck's 1933 Tube Map

SIGDOC'13, September 30–October 1, 2013, Greenville, North Carolina, USA.
ACM 978-1-4503-2131-0/13/09.
http://dx.doi.org/10.1145/2507065.2507091

By communicating a complex workflow visually, we were able to share ideas across language barriers and appeal to those who lacked the time or interest to read findings and recommendations reports.

Although we have not collected measurable results at this juncture, user reaction has been uniformly positive. Our success in adopting the subway map metaphor is consistent with the results reported by Nesbitt in his work diagramming complex theses ideas [3].

2. PARTICIPATORY DESIGN PROCESS

To get a full understanding of an overly wrought system prior to its redesign, we held multiple working sessions with users. Through these sessions, we uncovered users' mental models of the system and their pain points within them. As we worked, we mapped the current-state workflow. During these sessions, we also were able to capture and define some of the terminology that was adding confusion to the system workflow.

We then used workflow diagramming to illustrate an ideal system as imagined by the participants. Seeing their collaboration result in a diagram was inspiring to the participants and fostered a sense of teamwork among them.

Armed with a set of requirements derived from the workshops, we held card sorting and affinity diagramming sessions to uncover repetitive or unnecessary steps and confusing language. Discoveries here allowed us to distill each user type's workflow to its essential steps.

3. HOW DO WE TURN THIS INTO A DESIGN?

Our research took us to a crossroads. We understood where the redundancy was, which fields were critical and why the users were frustrated. Diagramming processes and connecting workflows begot a decision tree that represented the application flow for each user type.

However, we needed buy-in before beginning the wire-framing phase of the system redesign. To elicit feedback and build consensus, we needed a fast way to capture and communicate our findings first. Rejecting off-the-shelf products with cryptic workflow language, we made a decision to create a new tool that our client would experience as both friendly and trustworthy. The tool had to be intuitive to our audience and invite candid, focused feedback that would prompt meaningful adjustments.

4. SUBWAY DIAGRAM CONCEPT

As our client was in an urban environment, we were confident our audience could read a subway map and would understand a subway diagram as an abstraction [2]. The subway line metaphor visually represented the different paths in our client's workflow. Processes within the flow were broken into sections with "stops" indicating data entry points. To further the analogy, we represented user decisions as junctions where the path splits based upon their response.

The clarity provided by our map allowed us to work across business areas and groups to create a-one-size-fits-all workflow that was still customized for and relevant to each distinct user group. The map facilitated conversation without minimizing the complex decisions or nuanced relationships between data points.

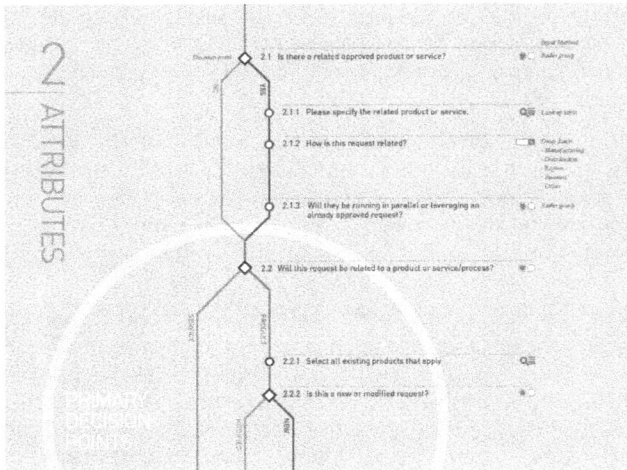

Figure 2. Decision-Tree Diagram as Subway Map (detail)

To capitalize further on the subway metaphor and give the diagram a customized feel, we retitled the map depending on who we were presenting to. Stakeholders in Chicago received the "L" map, and those in New York City were presented with a subway map. This localization added a bit of fun and helped stakeholders embrace the methodology.

Partitioning the decision points allowed us to suggest a wizard-like design for the workflow, and we layered other features into each step. For example, much like subway maps use iconography to show amenities like handicap accessibility, we used iconography to illustrate our recommended methods for data entry and contextual help.

Throughout the redesign process, our clients used the map with ease – both as a means for understanding the workflow and as the requirements document of record. One diagram was vetted internationally, including in China, and won support for the planned redesign. Later in the project, sections of this diagram were paired with wire-framed screens to help the development team contextualize their current work in the larger system workflow.

5. CONCLUSION

In closing, the subway diagram:

- Provides comprehensive transition from research to design
- Promotes understanding across disciplines
- Can be understood regardless of language/culture
- Is easy to read, which improves quality of feedback, client collaboration and buy-in
- Can be used as workflow/requirements guide by development team

In this case, it also reassured a client nervous about our design process and our ability to deliver value in a high-profile project.

6. ACKNOWLEDGMENTS

The authors wish to thank Electronic Ink, our project sponsor.

7. REFERENCES

[1] Garland, K., & Beck, H. C. 1994. *Mr Beck's Underground Map*. Capital Transport.

[2] Kramer, J. 2007. *Is abstraction the key to computing?*. Communications of the ACM, 50(4), 36-42.

[3] Nesbitt, K. V. 2004. *Getting to more Abstract Places using the Metro Map Metaphor*.

Evaluating a Workflow for Authoring Multimodal DITA

Carlos Evia
Virginia Tech
Blacksburg, VA
carlos.evia@vt.edu

Sean Healy
Healy Consulting Services
Walla Walla, WA
sjh@seanhealy.com

Tim Lockridge
Saint Joseph's University
Philadelphia, PA
tlockrid@sju.edu

ABSTRACT

This poster presentation reports on preliminary evaluation of OVID (Online Video), an open source DITA Open Toolkit plug-in that allows insertion of HTML5 video tags in web help topics. OVID converts DITA inline links into multimedia HTML5 tags (video, audio, and canvas). Students in an advanced undergraduate technical communication course participated in a quasi-empirical evaluation of the authoring workflow needed to create OVID-enhanced DITA topics and maps. Findings suggest that the process of identifying, tagging, and coding video elements does not represent a serious burden to authors, and participants described it as being easier and faster than writing DITA topics and maps.

Categories and Subject Descriptors

H.5.2 [**User Interfaces**]: Training, help, and documentation; I.7.2 [**Document Preparation**]: Markup languages

Keywords

DITA, XML, HTML5, multimodal help, video.

1. INTRODUCTION

OVID (Online Video) is an open source plug-in that allows insertion of HTML5 multimodal elements in web help topics created with the Darwin Information Typing Architecture (DITA). OVID transforms DITA inline links, "cross-references that you insert in the topic rather than create the link by using a DITA map or relationship table" [1], into HTML5 *video*, *audio*, and *canvas* tags without requiring DITA specialization. The main anticipated result is an alternative to text-based topics for users' diverse information needs and preferences.

Previous attempts to create multimodal input and output in DITA topics "transform DITA material to SSML (Speech Synthesis Markup Language) to enable auditory access" [2]. OVID takes advantage of HTML5's native multimedia tags to deliver audio and video inside web help topics produced with DITA. Creating multimodal DITA deliverables with OVID involves separate processes to a) build a playlist in XML Shareable Playlist Format (XSPF) to identify topic-equivalent segments in an instructional video file, and b) author topics and map(s) in DITA to host the video segments. The purpose of this study is to evaluate the feasibility and easiness of having a technical writer conduct both processes in a timely and efficient manner.

2. RAPID EVALUATION

We conducted quasi-empirical evaluation of the OVID workflow with students in an advanced technical communication course at Virginia Tech. The test's objective was to make users perform the tasks needed to create an OVID project. The course's syllabus included two DITA projects and one instructional video. Therefore, the students were familiar with both processes. The evaluation involved five participants (four female and one male) with ages ranging from 19 to 22 years old. All participants said they were very or somewhat interested in pursuing a career in technical writing, somewhat to very comfortable authoring DITA topics, and from not at all to very comfortable working with video files.

Tasks assigned during the test included creating the XSPF file identifying the main topics in the video developed for the course. Participants then had to create DITA topics to convert the tracks identified in the video. Using the OVID admin interface, participants selected references to specific sections in the video and pasted them as inline links in the corresponding sections of the DITA topics. The last task was to create a DITA map and generate a video-enhanced web help deliverable.

All participants said the process of creating the playlist and identifying topic-equivalent segments in a video was easy and did not represent a serious burden from a writer's perspective. Students pointed out that creating the playlist and working with the video file was easier and faster than authoring DITA topics and maps. Minor problems were related to the original video's long introduction and plot lines.

3. CONCLUSIONS

With limitations because of the informal evaluation and small number of participants, creating multimodal DITA topics with OVID was easy and feasible for novice technical writers. These conclusions open the possibility for future studies evaluating DITA deliverables for users with information needs that text-based deliverables would not satisfy (low-literacy or illiterate, non-native English speakers, visual learners). Recommendations include developing simple videos based on principles of structured authoring to facilitate track-to-topic conversion.

4. REFERENCES

[1] L. Bellamy, M. Carey, and J. Schlotfeldt. DITA Best Practices: A Roadmap for Writing, Editing, and Architecting in DITA. IBM Press, 2012.

[2] A. Kehoe and I. Pitt. Implementing a multimodal interface to a DITA user assistance repository. *In Proceedings of the 5th international conference on Adaptive Hypermedia and Adaptive Web-Based Systems,* Springer-Verlag Berlin, Heidelberg, 308–311, 2008.

Building a Better Conference Experience through User-Centered Design

Rachael Hodder
North Carolina State University
rachael.hodder@gmail.com

Michael McLeod
University of Washington
mikemcleod@gmail.com

Donnie Johnson Sackey
Wayne State University
donniejsackey@gmail.com

ABSTRACT

In this poster, we present user experience research demonstrating that current tools designed to facilitate conference communication and organization fail to support the needs of attendees and the goals of academia in general. Current conference technologies have failed to support the scholarly exchange of ideas at conferences, both in effectively facilitating dialogue at conferences and preserving those exchanges for later scholarly purposes. We recommend new information models and interfaces that can better support how conferences actually work that, when utilized, can better facilitate the exchange of ideas and can prevent that exchange from being lost in the ether.

Categories and Subject Descriptors

H.5.2 [**Information Interfaces and Presentation**]: User Interfaces – *Evaluation/methodology, User-centered design, Prototyping.*

Keywords

Twitter, conferences, community-centered design, accessibility, information architecture, user experience research, archive design

1. INTRODUCTION

As conference discourse in industry and academic contexts alike is proliferated increasingly by digital, networked technologies, it has become more urgent to reconcile traditional conference genres with the possibilities offered by new technologies. While new technologies such as archival, recording, writing, and storage tools have been adapted by with relative ease by presenters and attendees of conferences, the genre of the conference has remained largely unchanged.

2. ABOUT CONFERENCE COMMUNICATION

2.1 The Problem

2.1.1 Conferences

Conference meetings are designed to be places where ideas are exchanged. Participants present their work and ideas, while attendees react to those ideas, offering constructive criticism and making connections with other work. This idea exchange is almost universally ethereal, lost in the vapor once attendees depart, with no way of tracking connections that were made or ideas that developed, outside of individual memory. A conference that publishes proceedings leaves a record, but there's no way to trace how attendees engaged with those ideas. In recent years, ad hoc social networks have provided space to continue these conversations, but they still do not leave an enduring record or reliable means of tracking the evolution of ideas.

For example, Twitter.com is widely seen as a platform for "backchannel" discourse, or online communication that runs concurrent to conference events. Such activities have become commonplace at conference meetings and are discussed in terms of etiquette and best practices [1, 2] and inclusion and privilege [3, 4, 5, 6]. Proliferation of new communication technology has indeed impacted conference discourse, but there is no adequate solution for archiving the exchange of ideas that happen at conferences, connecting it to presenters and attendees, or tracking the evolution of an idea as it evolves across conferences, disciplines, and individuals.

2.1.2 Web-based conference applications

Existing social networking sites and conference applications fail because they are constructed with a flawed understanding of conferences. Conference applications are designed to support specific tasks such as event discovery, professional networking, and attendance, but they do so by constructing each meeting of a conference as an isolated silo with no connection to other fields or even to other meetings of the same conference, making any sort of research across time or tracking of speakers and conversations impossible *by design*.

These applications seem to be designed based on overly simplistic Use Cases (Find an Event, Network with Peers, Attend/Experience an Event) such as those found in Unified Modeling Language (UML) [7]. Likewise, they provide simple solutions that do not enhance conference experiences, but add additional steps or tasks to conference experiences under the guise of enriched interaction.

2.2 The Opportunity

Interfaces of present applications demonstrate misunderstanding of conferences as isolated events, rather than as complex ecosystems of activity. We believe that the theory, methods, and research of rhetoric and technical communication illuminate a more richly considered understanding of conferences both as reoccurring rhetorical action, or genre [8], and intricate actor-networks [7]. Following Hart-Davidson's [9] call for technical communicators to take an active role in the invention of tools, we aim to build a better conference application and affect the development of more meaningful, more accessible conferences.

2.3 Challenges

Our primary challenge will be to preserve autonomy for conference meeting organizers and presenters. We do not wish to compete with organizers or presenters, but to be their partners. We hope to accomplish this by conducting user experience (UX) research on conferences and applications (rather than conference applications alone) and enacting user-centered design methods.

Our second challenge will be to develop a shared metadata schema across conferences in industry or corporate settings, academia, and among hobbyists or enthusiasts. Employing variant methods of UX research will help us trace the complex ecosystem of conference activity in order to model an appropriately complex information architecture to support conferences of any topic, field, or breadth of reoccurring instances.

3. PRACTICING USER-CENTERED DESIGN

3.1 Research Questions

Our research will be guided by the following questions: What is a conference? What makes a conference different from an event or meeting? How do conference attendees and organizers (stakeholders) experience conferences? What tools or methods do stakeholders use to create more accessible conference experiences for themselves or their colleagues? These questions, along with our desire to involve stakeholders in the design process, have driven our research and resulting designs to date.

3.2 Research Methods

Through the implementation of a variety of research methods, we are afforded a prismatic perspective on conferences and their activity networks. To date, we have conducted survey research on conference communication practices within an academic conference stakeholder community in spring 2013. Based on survey responses, we created a basic heuristic for analyzing web services used in conference communication.

Thus far, we have utilized this heuristic to analyze three tools our survey participants identified as having been used at conferences: Twitter for ad-hoc communication as well as Lanyrd.com and Conferize.com for conference facilitation. Our findings reveal that while some conferences have become proactive in assigning hashtags to sessions to better aggregate conference communication, Twitter makes researching past events exceptionally difficult and fails as a long-term solution for archiving conference dialogue. Lanyrd and Conferize aim to help conference organizers publicize sessions, facilitate attendance, and have recently begun to archive materials, but by constructing events as content silos that don't speak to one another, these tools fail to enable users to research the history of a conference, let alone the development of an idea across scholars and disciplines.

We have also carried out some early iterative user-centered design work based on survey participant responses as well as our perceived need. We developed a complex object model and information architecture that address the structural failures of current tools, compiled a set of desired features, and constructed initial wireframe interfaces. Most recently, we held a focus group with stakeholders to review our design work. This poster displays findings from our research and some mock-ups of our early designs.

3.3 Future Work

A new conference communication tool has the potential to change the experience of conference attendance, research methods and development activities, and the nature of field-specific discourse. We have demonstrated that current tools fail because of their focus on tasks associated with conferences, rather than the complexity of conferences themselves.

The next steps for this project will be to improve our designs based on further research and stakeholder feedback. We also plan to seek resources that will support the construction of a new conference communication tool.

4. REFERENCES

[1] Bruff, D. 2011. Encouraging a conference backchannel on Twitter. http://chronicle.com/blogs/profhacker/encouraging-a-conference-backchannel-on-twitter/30612

[2] Sample, M. 2011. Building a better backchannel: THATCamp report. http://chronicle.com/blogs/profhacker/building-a-better-backchannel-thatcamp-report/33932

[3] Williams, G. 2011. Academics and social media: #mla11, free wi-ii, and the question of inclusion. http://chronicle.com/blogs/profhacker/academics-and-social-media-mla11-free-wifi-and-the-question-of-inclusion/29945

[4] Nowviskie, B. 2012. uninvited guests: regarding twitter at invitation-only academic events. http://nowviskie.org/2010/uninvited-guests/

[5] Jurgenson, N. 2012. Twitter isn't a backchannel (#ASA2012). http://thesocietypages.org/cyborgology/2012/08/17/twitter-isnt-a-backchannel-asa2012/

[6] Boesel, W. E. 2012. Toward a more inclusive backchannel: an unusual call to action. http://thesocietypages.org/cyborgology/2012/08/15/toward-a-more-inclusive-backchannel-an-unusual-call-to-action/

[7] Potts, L. 2008. Diagramming with Actor Network Theory: A method for modeling holistic experience. *IEEE International Professional Communication Conference.*

[8] Miller, C. R. 1984. Genre as social action. *Quarterly Journal of Speech 70*, 2, 151-167.

[9] Hart-Davidson, W. 2001. On writing, technical communication, and information technology: The core competencies of technical communication. *Technical Communication* (May 2001), 145-155.

[10] Garrett, J. J. 2011. *The Elements of User Experience: User-Centered Design for the Web and Beyond.* Berkley, CA: New Riders.

[11] Krug, S. 2006. *Don't Make Me Think! A Common Sense Approach to Web Usability.* Berkley, CA: New Riders.

[12] Morville, P., & Rosenfeld, L. 2008. *Information Architecture for the World Wide Web.* O'Reilly Media, Inc.

Determining Optimal Caption Placement Using Eye Tracking

Andrew D. Ouzts
School of Computing
Clemson University
aouzts@cs.clemson.edu

Nicole E. Snell
Information Design and
Corporate
Communication
Bentley University
nsnell@bentley.edu

Prabudh Maini
School of Computing
Clemson University
pmaini@clemson.edu

Andrew T. Duchowski
School of Computing
Clemson University
andrewd@cs.clemson.edu

ABSTRACT

In this study, the effect of caption placement on information intake is examined. Eye movement data is used to quantitatively analyze the effect of four different captioning methods. Information intake (i.e. Information Assimilation (IA)) is measured via a 4-category comprehension quiz, developed by S.R Gulliver and G. Ghinea, which measures key differing aspects of captioned videos. Results indicate that caption placement can have significant effects on reading time, number of saccadic crossovers, and ratio of fixations on captions.

Categories and Subject Descriptors

D.3.2. C++ [**Programming Language**]. H2.3. SDL [**Simple DirectMedia Layer**]: *a cross-platform multimedia library*. D.4.0 Linux [**Computer Operating System**].C.2.2 TCP/IP [**Transmission Control Protocol/Internet Protocol**].

Keywords:

Closed Captioning, Information Assimilation, Eyetracking

1. INTRODUCTION

Closed captioning is a technology, as defined by US law, which ensures the civil right of an individual to have equal access to emergency information, national and local news, and public entertainment regardless of their ability to hear. In order to ensure that users of captions gain a comparable amount of information to that of viewers who have access to both the audio and video action, it is necessary to determine the most efficient and effective presentation of captions. To do so, one must determine how variables such as caption placement affect the viewer's comprehension of captioned media. We therefore investigate the impact that caption placement has on the amount of information assimilated by viewers. We hypothesize that depending on the caption placement method used, a viewer's information assimilation (IA) is either enhanced or diminished.[1]

2. METHODOLOGY

To quantitatively assess the validity of our hypothesis and each of our captioning methods, we performed a validation study. We sought to determine the captioning method(s) that minimize reading time and maximize information intake. In order to quantitatively measure these factors, we designed an eye tracking study in which four different captioning methods were examined using eye movement data, in addition to the qualitative measurements of IA.

2.1 Apparatus

Eye movements were captured by a Tobii ET-1750 eye tracker, a 17 inch (1280 x 1024) flat panel with built-in eye tracking optics. The eye tracker is binocular, sampling at 50 Hz with $0.5°$ accuracy. A PC with dual AMD Opteron 64 processors running Microsoft Windows XP and software provided by Tobii streams eye gaze data via TCP/IP. The display and data collection program was run on a PC with an AMD Opteron processor running Fedora Core Linux. The Linux client used TCP/IP to collect the data from the Windows server.

2.2 Software

The (previously created) display and data collection application was developed with C++, OpenGL, SDL (Simple DirectMedia Layer, a cross-platform multimedia library). The ffmpeg library was used to render video so that the data collection application also served as the video player. Andrew Duchowski's Linux Tobii library[2] was used to interact with the eye tracker.

This program was further extended with the capacity to interpret and display SRT (SubRip Text - a popular file format used for storing subtitle timings and text). An additional parameter was added to the SRT files specifying the placement strategy to be used by each individual caption. Captions were displayed on an 80% transparent black box whose length is adapted to the length of the caption, using sans-serif font.

Using this program, each viewing by each participant results in a text file containing (x, y, t) data for each raw gazepoint recorded by the eye tracker. A separate text file records video events such as pauses and timestamps for each frame, and both text files are used to match gazepoints to frame numbers.

2.3 Stimulus

The video used as stimulus was a 2m34s long clip BBC News clip that aired February 16 2009 about the replacement of checks and cash with electronic payment. The clip was subtitled verbatim. The video was played in full screen on a 1280 x 1024 resolution monitor and encoded using the MPEG-1 standard, which provides VHS-quality compression.

2.4 Participants

20 participants (7 male, 13 female) took part in the study. Participants were volunteers recruited from Clemson University's Human Participation in Research student pool. Participants ages

SIGDOC'13, September 30–October 1, 2013, Greenville, North Carolina, USA.
ACM 978-1-4503-2131-0/13/09.
TTP://DX.DOI.ORG/10.1145/2507065.2507100

[1] Available at http://andrewd.ces.clemson.edu/tobii/

ranged from 17 to 51 (mean 20.85, median 19). Four participants were excluded from the final analysis due to data collection issues, bringing the total to 16 participants (6 male, 10 female).

2.5 Experimental Design

The experimental design took the form of a single factor (captioning method) with four levels. The four captioning methods examined were:

- Method A: All subtitles displayed 64 pixels from bottom

- Method B: All subtitles displayed 64 pixels from top

- Method C: Constant alternation between 64 pixels from top and 64 pixels from bottom. That is, if the nth frame is displayed at the top, then the $(n+1)^{th}$ frame will be displayed at the bottom, and vice versa.

- Method D: A method in which captions were placed above a speaker to identify him/her as the source of the closed captions, and at the bottom when no speaker was visible or the visual speaker was not the source of the captions. This is similar in many respects to the methods used in [2].

All participants viewed the video using each method. Order of presentation was counterbalanced using a 4 x 4 Latin square so that approximately a quarter of all subjects saw the videos in order {A, B, C, D}, {B, C, D, A}, {C, D, A, B}, or {D, A, B, C}.

As an extension of our general hypothesis that depending on the caption placement method used, a viewer's IA is either enhanced or diminished, we in particular hypothesized the following:

1. Method A will minimize reading time. Viewers typically expect to see the captions at the bottom, and due to the unchanging nature of this method, no time is needed to search for the location of the captions.

2. Method D will maximize information intake. Due to the additional information encoded in the location of the captions, viewers should have increased scene comprehension.

2.6 Procedure

Participants were seated in front of the eye tracker at a distance of about 60 cm. The eye tracker was calibrated to the participant before each video clip was shown; that is, four times total per person. Calibration required a participant to track a moving circle with their eyes to 9 points.

Following calibration, participants were instructed to watch the video clip normally as they would at home - that is, an unguided viewing. They were informed that they would be given a quiz after playback to gauge their comprehension, but given no other specific information.

After the first video clip, participants were given a quiz based on (IA) information assimilation categories.

After the participant had viewed all 4 captioning methods, they were asked to answer some final preference-based and qualitative questions about the study. We also asked if the participant had been aware of the different captioning.

3. RESULTS

Within subjects analysis was performed for each of the three eye tracking metrics. A between subjects analysis was performed for quiz data.

A significant difference was found in the number of saccadic crossovers between each captioning method using a within-subjects ANOVA ($F(3, 45) = 4.43$, $p < 0.01$). Pairwise t-tests (no correction) showed a marginally significant difference between captioning methods C and A ($p < 0.05$).

Analysis of the reading time data also shows significance. A significant difference was found in the amount of reading time spent ($F(3,45) = 19.11$, $p < 0.01$). Pairwise t-tests (no correction) show significance between methods A and C ($p < 0.01$), B and C ($p < 0.01$), C and D ($p < 0.01$), and marginal significance between A and D ($p < 0.05$).

Differences were also found for the fixation ratio metric. Within-subjects ANOVA shows a significant difference ($F(3, 4) = 22.36$, $p < 0.01$) in the mean ratio of fixations, and pairwise t-tests (no correction) reveal significance between methods A and C ($p < 0.01$), B and C ($p < 0.01$), and D and C ($p < 0.01$).

Between subjects analysis was performed on the quiz data (based on the video the participant first saw). No significant differences were found for any of the quiz results or preferences, and the mean correct answers for methods A, B, C, and D were 52.5%, 50%, 55%, and 47%, respectively.

4. CONCLUSION

An eye tracking study was presented in which several different captioning styles were examined. Significant differences were found between eye movement metrics depending on the captioning style used, suggesting that captioning styles play an important role in viewing strategies. Participants underwent large amounts of saccadic crossovers and spent much less time reading the captions when captions changed position frequently. Future work is needed to fully examine the implications of these differences.

5. REFERENCES

1. Gulliver, S. R., and Ghinea, G. How level and type of deafness affect user perception of multimedia videoclips. *Universal Access Information Society*, 2 (2003), 374-386.
2. Vy, Q.V. and Fels, D.I. Using placement and name for speaker identification. ICCHP 2010 Conference Proceedings.

Social Media Infrastructure: Supporting Communication Practices from Behind the Scenes

Laura A. Palmer
Southern Polytechnic State University
1100 South Marietta Parkway
Marietta, GA 30060
01-678-915-7202
lpalmer2@spsu.edu

ABSTRACT
In this poster, I propose a design for a communication infrastructure to support social media practices in businesses and organizations. Many professional social media efforts are poorly conceived and executed due to a limited understanding of how social media should function for professional purposes. Yet, through a simple model that begins with the development of policies and strategic plans, and includes audit, legal considerations, and style, many of the risks and uncertainties of social media can be mitigated. The poster presented here outlines key areas for this communication infrastructure and seeks input as to how the model could be expanded.

Categories and Subject Descriptors
H.5.3 **[Information Interfaces and Presentation]**: Group and Organization Interfaces; H.3.4 **[Information Storage and Retrieval]**: Systems and Software

Keywords
Social media, communication infrastructure.

1. INTRODUCTION
Effective professional communication with social media requires a social business model and a solid social communication infrastructure; yet, for most companies, this communication model is non-existent. Rather, in the rush to become a social business and engage with the online community and dynamic conversations, many organizations jumped on the social media bandwagon with little thought as to the critical connections social media must make to not only business goals, but also the overall corporate communication ecosystem. Because of this lack of connectivity, it is often the case that social media practices of communication become an improvisation rather than part of a strategic plan that reduces risk, capitalizes on opportunity, and aligns to business goals and objectives [2, 4, 5, 6].

The dangers of an unstructured social media presence are many. The number of users on any social network site (SNS) and the virality of their communications are powerful. The social clout of this digital *vox populi* is not to be discounted—corporate reputations today are made or broken via the Enter key. As a result, this necessitates that companies have a model to support their communication efforts with social media rather than relying on an ad hoc adaptation of personal, informal social media use. By designing a substantive model for social media communication, an organization can not only mitigate risk, manage reputation, and maximize brand messages; it can provide a way to harness unexpected and unbridled successes in social media campaigns [3, 5].

2. UNDERSTANDING SOCIAL MEDIA
Scholarly studies of social media are growing, yet the identification and development of an effective corporate social media infrastructure remains elusive in the research. Most current academic work centers on the myriad technologies available or studies of social ties and interactions within a social media ecosphere.

However, research on determining what the design of an effective social media infrastructure could look like, how it could support communication, and how it could manage what Jacka and Scott call the "reputational, strategic, and governance risks" in social media requires investigation [5]. Thus, it is the goal of this poster to propose an early idea of what an effective social media infrastructure should include and how this infrastructure could support research related to the design of communication.

3. MODELLING AN INFRASTUCTURE
In order for social media communication to be effective—whether in a business-to-customer (B2C) or business-to-business (B2B) capacity—it must be supported by an infrastructure that forms a dynamic and iterative feedback loop as shown in Figure 1. Below are topics the poster will explore as starting points for building a comprehensive social media infrastructure.

3.1 Policies
Social media policy documents perform multiple roles in an organization. Typically, these are single charters that guide employees on their personal use of social media in the workplace. This charter may include policies on workplace access to personal accounts and circumscribe what employees can say about their employer. However, such a document is insufficient when employees become part of the social sphere on behalf of their employer. Thorough social media policies guide communication conventions on corporate any SNS; as well, these policies define workflow processes and approvals. Such policies govern how/when/if new social tools will be selected and incorporated. Crisis communication plans and risk management form a significant part of this expanded document set [4, 5].

SIGDOC'13, September 30–October 1, 2013, Greenville, North Carolina, USA.
ACM 978-1-4503-2131-0/13/09.

Figure 1: Social media communication infrastructure informing social media practices

3.2 Strategic Planning

According to Jacka and Scott, most organizations are at risk due to lack of a strategy or inadequate strategy for social media [5]. Strategic documents make the critical alignments between social media efforts and business objectives and goals; they also form a linkage to measuring return-on-investment [2, 6]. Therefore, developing a comprehensive social media plan must include adequate strategy and define how it will be implemented.

3.3 Audit and Compliance

Even with communication policies and strategic plans in place, many organizations skip the important step of audit and compliance. The question of social media activities complying with the outlined policies and strategic plans is critical for success. Audits can help identify areas of risk/opportunity and close gaps; additionally, as the poster will convey, audits can help iteratively shape policies for the communicative situation [5].

3.4 Legal/Regulatory

Accidental disclosures, Federal Trade Commission requirements, and labor law violations are only some of the pressing legal issues surrounding social media. Unless the communication infrastructure has been designed with these in mind, social media activities can result in a maelstrom of lawsuits and court cases [4, 7].

3.5 Style

Communication policies ensure consistent messaging aligned with corporate philosophies and goals; however, style guides rarely consider how to reflect how the "voice" of a company in social media. Thus, the role of voice and how it informs the design of communication can be viewed as a significant component of an overall social media presence [1].

4. CONCLUSIONS

For social media to be effective, it requires a significant infrastructure. This poster presents a model for the infrastructure an organization should implement if it wishes to capitalize on the benefits social media can offer while reducing many of the risks. As an exploratory piece, the poster is designed to start a conversation about professional social media practices and the design of communication in this arena.

5. REFERENCES

[1] J. Belosic, "8 Tips for Training Social Media Marketers," Social Media Examiner, 2012. [Online]. Available: http://www.socialmediaexaminer.com/tag/social-style-guide/. [Accessed: 29-May-2013].

[2] O. Blanchard, Social Media ROI. Indianapolis: Que, 2011.

[3] A. Cain, "The Social Media Scene," *Internal Auditor*, pp. 45–49, Aug-2012.

[4] N. Flynn, The Social Media Handbook. San Francisco: Pfeiffer, 2012.

[5] J. M. Jacka and P. R. Scott, "The Whole World's Talking," *Internal Auditor*, June, pp. 52–56, 2011.

[6] N. Kelly, How to Measure Social Media. Indianapolis: Que, 2013.

[7] R. McHale, Navigating Social Media Legal Risks. Indianapolis: Que, 2012.

Participatory Documentation: A Case Study & Rationale

Elizabeth A. Pitts
Communication, Rhetoric & Digital Media Program
North Carolina State University
Raleigh, NC
eapitts@ncsu.edu

ABSTRACT

This poster focuses on how consumers learn to use marketing automation software, what types of documentation they prefer, and why. Interviews with U.S. and U.K. marketers demonstrate that implementing marketing automation software requires users to re-learn their jobs, and requires companies to reconfigure organizational structures and workflows. Accordingly, users are interested in knowing how counterparts apply the software, despite raising concerns about privacy. Based on these findings, the poster illustrates the advantages that software companies— especially those operating on a Waterfall development model— can gain by allowing users to participate in creating and refining documentation. In addition to reducing the learning curve for users, participatory documentation enables companies to gather feedback that is critical to making documentation and software more usable.

Categories and Subject Descriptors

H.5.2 User Interfaces

Keywords

Documentation, instructional design, marketing automation software, participatory culture, technical communication.

1. INTRODUCTION

Digital media are facilitating the development of a "participatory culture." Unlike consumers of print media, users of digital media can annotate, appropriate and share content, playing a more active role in shaping and distributing information. As media scholar Henry Jenkins notes, "Rather than talking about media producers and consumers as occupying separate roles, we might now see them as participants who interact with each other according to a new set of rules that none of us fully understands" [1]. He counsels corporate leaders to reconsider the ways in which they relate to these more demanding, fickle, and socially connected customers.

Studying how consumers learn to use complex software offers an opportunity to explore the relevance of this advice. For instance, citing cybertheorist Pierre Levy, Jenkins argues that "the dynamic, collective and reciprocal nature of [digital] exchanges undermines traditional forms of expertise," including "static forms of writing" [2]. Print documentation exemplifies such a static form. Rather than allowing readers to define a task or

SIGDOC'13, September 30–October 1, 2013, Greenville, North Carolina, USA.
ACM 978-1-4503-2131-0/13/09.
http://dx.doi.org/10.1145/2507065.2507092

decide how to execute it, print documentation predetermines their course of action.

2. DOCUMENTATION USABILITY

This poster presents the initial results of a nine-month research project concluding in August 2013. The study addressed how customers learn to use marketing automation software, including the contexts in which such learning takes place. It also explored the types of documentation that users found more or less helpful, and why. Data were gathered through interviews with U.S. and U.K. marketers in multiple industries, all using the same type of software. Interview transcripts were coded using a grounded theory approach [3]. Key findings include:

- Implementing marketing automation software requires marketers to do more than learn how to use a tool. Like other complex software [4], it requires individuals to re-learn their jobs, and requires companies to reconfigure organizational structures and workflows.

- Accordingly, users are interested in learning how counterparts in their own and other industries work with the software, despite also raising concerns about the privacy of data sets.

3. TYPESET TEXT

Based on the above findings, the poster illustrates the advantages that software companies can gain by allowing users to participate in developing task-oriented documentation. Participatory documentation is especially well-suited to organizations operating on a Waterfall development model. Compared to the iterative Agile software development lifecycle, the Waterfall lifecycle offer clients fewer opportunities to learn firsthand from developers. Participatory documentation offers one way of compensating for this relative lack of interaction. For users, it offers a way of gaining insights into best practices, as well as an increased likelihood of getting the help they need quickly and in an easily negotiable format. For companies, it offers an inexpensive means of gathering frequently updated feedback that can improve the usability of both documentation and the software itself. Essentially, participatory documentation enables companies using the Waterfall model to garner some of the benefits that Agile development provides, without having to reconfigure their organizational structures or profit models substantially.

4. REFERENCES

[1] Jenkins, H. 2006. *Convergence Culture: Where Old and New Media Collide*. NYU, New York, NY. Kindle location 198.

[2] Jenkins, H. 2006. *Fans, Bloggers and Gamers: Exploring Participatory Culture*. NYU, New York, NY. 140.

[3] Lindlof, T. and Taylor, B. 2002. *Qualitative Communication Research Methods*. Sage, Thousand Oaks, CA. 218-222.

[4] See Scott, J. 2008. Technology acceptance and ERP documentation usability. *Communications of the ACM.* 51, 11 (Nov. 2008), 121-124. DOI= http://dl.acm.org/citation.cfm?doid=1400214.1400239

Remediation in Data Visualization: Two Examples of Learning in Real-Time Data Processing Environments

Charlie Potter
Eastern Washington University
Cheney WA 99004
1-509-359-7021
cpotter@ewu.edu

Justin Young
Eastern Washington University
Cheney WA 99004
1-509-359-7062
jayoung@ewu.edu

ABSTRACT
Our poster is an exploration of the effects of quantifying physical experiences and refashioning them into new, interactive, live experiences through data visualization; in other words, we are exploring how data visualizations are designed to teach and effect change.

Categories and Subject Descriptors
J.1 [**Administrative Data Processing**]: Education; J.7 [**Computers in Other Systems**]: Real time; K.3.0 [**Computers in Education**]: General

Keywords
teacher education, sports, data visualization, real-time computing

1. INTRODUCTION
Our poster is an exploration of the effects of quantifying physical experiences and refashioning them into new, interactive, live experiences through data visualization; in other words, we are investigating how data visualizations are designed to teach and effect change. Specifically, we examine two topics: athletic training and teacher training. Both of these fields have been inundated by data analysis tactics; sports data visualizations are highly developed and hypermediate while teacher training data are still largely immediate and static Through an analysis related to theories of phenomenography and remediation, we discuss how the use of real-time data analysis and data visualization common in sports training might inform other fields, such as teaching.

2. LITERATURE REVIEW
Several recent studies explore the relationship between learning and phenomenography, a qualitative research method that attempts to explore how people interpret various lived old) experiences of [a] skill or concept to their new experience of the skill or concept" [1]. Teaching principles derived from experiences. When used in relation to learning outcomes,

SIGDOC'13, Sep 30 - Oct 01 2013, Greenville, NC, USA
ACM 978-1-4503-2131-0/13/09.
http://dx.doi.org/10.1145/2507065.2507094

phenomenography allows people "to compare their original (or phenomenographic methods seek to change and/or investigate the ways that students view an aspect of their world [2]. When applied to teachers themselves, phenomenographic studies suggest that teachers have radically different understandings of student engagement and learning [3].

Each of the aforementioned studies uses a type of data visualization and real-time process to reach conclusions about human perception. The reverse is also true; phenomenography can help researchers understand the ways people interpret data visualizations [4]. Specifically, phenomenography can help teachers understand the ways their data visualization tools are received by students [5]. Our research project imagines the opportunities offered by information visualization for changing practice in educational processes like teaching, coaching, and learning through a theoretical interpretation of the power of real-time data analysis and phenomenography.

3. THEORY AND METHODS
This poster specifically reports on a theoretical inquiry into current practices of data analysis and visualization in sports and education. The researchers will use the theory of remediation, described by Jay David Bolter and David Grusin, to conduct an analysis of current practices of data analysis and visualization in athletic training and teacher training [6]. The authors hypothesize that the practice of real-time data collection and analysis in professional sports training is largely hypermediate, while teacher education and assessment continues to rely on data that are immediate and static. These contrasting approaches will be evaluated. Theoretical implications for current data visualization theory, as well as current practices in phenomenography and teacher training will be addressed.

A clear connection exists between the prominence of data visualization and the new media concepts of hypermediacy, immediacy, and remediation [6]. Interactive or artistic remediations of numeric symbols attempt to improve upon raw data while reminding users of the original, immediate symbols; in this way, visualizations of data are hypermediate, interactive, and immersive. Bolter and Grusin explore the influence of this interactivity on mediated human experiences, arguing that "[i]f the logic of immediacy leads one either to erase or to render automatic the act of representation, the logic of hypermediacy acknowledges multiple acts of representation and makes them visible" [6]. Data imagery is hypermediate, acknowledging and making visible acts of remediation. Conversely, raw data is much more immediate or transparent. The numeric symbol, however, is not a window to the real. Kenneth Burke argues that "naïve verbal realism" relies on the immediacy of language; similarly, a certain "naïve numeric realism" is present in interactions with raw numeric data [7]. If the concept of immediacy is the perfection of the gap between signifier and signified, it should not be surprising that quantitative data feel so "real" and "meaningful"; yet, they are still remediations.

Efforts to promote improvement and change should be based on the analysis and visualization of real-time, hypermediated data, rather than static, immediate data. Such efforts should enable individuals to interpret lived experience in light of hypermediated data in order to improve future practice and outcomes.

4. CONCLUSIONS

Sports data visualizations are highly developed and hypermediate, as in the case of SportVU, a service that provides 25-frames-per-second optical tracking data, quantifying video of player performance for visualization and analysis [8]. At least 15 NBA teams now employ this SportVU system for data capture, which includes cameras originally developed for tracking missiles [9]. SportVU provides the hardware system, tracks the movement of each player in every game played at the given arena, and then provides the derived raw data in the form of spreadsheets to each participating team [10]. The teams themselves are responsible for analyzing and then visually presenting that data so that it can be applied to training as well as game time situations [10]. Data analysts and programmers are currently developing strategies and tools that enable interactive, rapid analysis of SportVU data so that it can be collected and applied in real-time [11, 12, 13]. The collection of data from the physical, lived experience of the players (and hypermediation of that data via visualizations that can be presented back to participants in real-time) has the potential to dramatically impact how players are coached and the game played. An example that illustrates the contrast between the usefulness of immediate raw data and hypermediated data is seen in the current sports analytics discussion of three point shooting [10]. Analysis of optical tracking data suggests that teams should shoot more three pointers, challenging the naïve numeric realism of coaches who rely on conventional statistical benchmarks to determine who should be taking three point shots, and when.

Teacher training data are still largely immediate and static, as evidenced in the numerical evaluations of the edTPA test, created by Stanford University and administered by Pearson, and the Teacher/Principal Evaluation Project. For example, in the case of the edTPA test, which has been adopted by several states for use as a formative and/or summative assessment of P-12 teacher candidates, feedback on the test is *only* provided in the form of a set of autonomous scores. At the time of this research, neither the test taker nor the institution that has administered the test is provided with any explanatory feedback tied to this raw data. In another example, under programs such as No Child Left Behind and The Race to the Top, teachers are fired, and schools are shut down on the basis of immediate, static test scores. Major decisions, in an effort to promote change, are made on the basis of data that has not been derived from lived practice, nor has this data been collected and then hypermediated in an effort to inform and shift practice in real-time.

Training teachers using the hypermediated, data visualization strategies deployed in sports could move the discussion of teacher accountability away from the analysis of (raw, autonomous) student test data and towards the real-time analysis and visualization of data derived from the "lived experience" of a teacher in the midst of training. Finally, we suggest that the use of data in this way may move us away from a naïve numerical realism—the trust that raw data will tell the truth of a situation—towards a more insightful analysis and application of data, which are derived from lived experience, represented visually, analyzed in real-time, and used to alter behavior and decision-making.

5. ACKNOWLEDGEMENTS

The authors would like to thank Eastern Washington University for its support of this study.

6. ADDITIONAL AUTHORS

There are no additional authors of this paper.

7. REFERENCES

[1] Yates, C., Partridge, H. and Bruce, C. 2012. Exploring information experiences through phenomenography. *Library and Information Research* 36, 112, 96-119.

[2] Booth, S. 1997. On phenomenography, learning, and teaching. *Higher Education Research & Development* 16, 2, 135-158.

[3] Harris, L. R. 2008. A phenomenographic investigation of teacher conceptions of student engagement in learning. *The Australian Educational Researcher*, 35, 1, 57-79

[4] Isenberg, P., Zuk, T., Collins, C., and Carpendale, S. 2008. Grounded evaluation of information visualizations. In *Proceedings of the 2008 Workshop on Beyond Time and Errors: Novel Evaluation Methods for Information Visualization*. BELIV'08. ACM: Florence, Italy, 9.

[5] Levy, R. B. B., & Ben-Ari, M. 2007. We work so hard and they don't use it: Acceptance of software tools by teachers. *ACM SIGCSE Bulletin*, 39, 3, 246-250.

[6] Grusin, R., & Bolter, J. D. 2000. *Remediation: Understanding New Media*. MIT Press, Cambridge, MA.

[7] Burke, K. 1966. *Language as Symbolic Action: Essays on Life, Literature and Method*. University of California Press, Berkeley, CA.

[8] Maymin, P. 2013, March. Acceleration in the NBA: Towards an Algorithmic Taxonomy of Basketball Plays. MIT Sloan Sports Analytics Conference.

[9] Goldsberry, K., Kopp, B., Pavildis, H., & Zander, R. XY Panel: The Revolution in Visual Tracking. MIT Sloan Sports Analytics Conference.

[10] Lowe, Z. Lights, camera, revolution. 2013, March. *Grantland*. Retrieved from http://www.grantland.com/story/_/id/9068903/the-toronto-raptors-sportvu-cameras-nba-analytical-revolution

[11] Maheswaran, R., Chang, Y. H., Henehan, A., & Danesis, S. 2012, February. Deconstructing the rebound with optical tracking data. MIT Sloan Sports Analytics Conference.

[12] Goldsberry, K. & Weiss, E. 2013, March. The Dwight effect: A new ensemble of interior defense analytics for the NBA. MIT Sloan Sports Analytics Conference.

[13] Maheswaran, R. 2013, March. DataMorphing: Dynamic interaction with basketball big data. MIT Sloan Sports Analytics Conference.

Browsing as a Learning Practice in the Information Management Work of Technical Communicators

Stewart Whittemore
9030 Haley Center
Auburn University
Auburn, AL 36801
1-334-844-9028

whittemore@auburn.edu

ABSTRACT

This poster reports data from a case study of the information management practices technical communicators at a software company in the U.S. Midwest. The study found that the technical communicators preferred location-based file folder browsing for their information finding and retrieval activities. Building on situated cognition theories of learning, the researcher speculates that file folder browsing may serve a learning purpose for the technical communicators by helping them internalize technical information about their products and social information about their work teams and processes.

Categories and Subject Descriptors
Documentation

Keywords
information management, technical communication, file browsing, searching

1. POSTER DESCRIPTION

Jones and Teevan (2007) define information management activities as "activities people perform to acquire, organize, maintain, retrieve, use, and control the distribution of information items" [1, p. 3]. Examples of these activities include: a) Finding and re-finding activities like searching for a document in a file cabinet or a computer file or performing a keyword search using Google; b) Keeping activities like saving a downloaded PDF to a local computer; and c) Meta-level activities like setting up folder structures on a computer disk drive; cleaning out an email inbox.

During the first decade of the 21st century, new communication technologies and work arrangements greatly increased the need for effective information management in the workplace. These developments include flattened organizational hierarchies, which led to more team-based collaborative work environments in which information must be shared vertically and horizontally [2]; new communication technologies (e.g., wikis, blogs, Campfire) enabled distributed work arrangements like telecommuting, remote teams, and flexible work hours, which resulted in a much larger information stream to maintain team awareness and enable joint cognition [3]; and the introduction of new work methodologies (e.g., content management, Agile software development) greatly expanded the need for speedy, secure, and accurate information transfer among work teams [4].

Because of their expertise in communication, technical communicators are often perceived as the best members of their work teams to handle the new information management tasks enabled by new technologies and methodologies. To better prepare future graduates for these types of work, we need to better understand the information management preferences and needs of technical communicators.

This poster reports an intriguing finding from a case study of a group of technical communicators at a software firm. This finding was that the technical communicators displayed a definite preference for file folder browsing over searching when engaging in re-finding activities. While this is not an entirely unusual finding, it did appear out-of-place given the exigencies of the particular research site and participants. That is, given that browsing has been shown to be generally less efficient and more time-consuming than searching, why did a group of well-trained and tech-savvy technical communicators in a fast-paced and dynamic workplace rely so heavily on antiquated file folder browsing to keep and re-find their information? Turning to social theories of cognition and learning, including especially situated cognition theory [6], I speculate that navigating these structures served important social and technical learning functions.

2. REFERENCES

[1] Jones, W., and Teevan, J. 2007. Introduction. In *Personal Information Management*, W. Jones & J. Teevan, Eds. Seattle: University of Washington Press, Seattle, 3-20.

[2] Amidon, S., and Blythe, S. 2008. Wrestling with proteus: Tales of communication managers in a changing economy. *Journal of Business and Technical Comm.* 22, 1 (Jan. 2008), 5-37.

[3] Slattery, S. 2007. Un-distributing work through writing: How technical writers manage texts in complex information environments. *Technical Communication Qtrly.* 16, 3 (July-Sept. 2007), 311-325.

[4] Mott, R. K., and Ford, J. D. 2007. The convergence of technical communication and information architecture: Managing single source objects for contemporary media. *Technical Comm.* 54, 1 (Feb. 2007), 27-45.

[5] Brown, J. S., Collins, A., and Duguid, P. 1989. Situated cognition and the culture of learning. *Educational Researcher.* 18, 1 (Jan. 1989), 32-42.

SIGDOC'13, September 30–October 1, 2013, Greenville, North Carolina, USA.
ACM 978-1-4503-2131-0/13/09.

Building Better Help Before We Build It: User Characteristics' Effect on Library Help Design

Tao Zhang
Purdue University Libraries
504 W. State Street
West Lafayette, IN 47907, USA
(+1) 765-496-3869
zhan1022@purdue.edu

Ilana R. Barnes
Purdue University Libraries
504 W. State Street
West Lafayette, IN 47907, USA
(+1) 765-494-6243
ibarnes@purdue.edu

ABSTRACT
The goal of this study is to examine the effect of user help seeking characteristics on their perceptions of library help design principles, formats and tools. Structural equation modeling (SEM) of a questionnaire survey results showed a number of significant regression relationships. Analysis of open-end survey questions revealed existing user behaviors such as preferred help formats and likelihood of using a help system.

Categories and Subject Descriptors
H.5.2 [**Information Interfaces and Presentation**]: User Interfaces – *Training, help, and documentation.*

Keywords
User Characteristics, Help, Library.

1. INTRODUCTION
Online user help has become an important part of a library's service for effective information access. There are help design principles and various help formats and tools available [1]; however, they are not linked with user characteristics and help seeking preferences [2], especially in the library context. In this study, we have identified characteristics influencing users' help seeking and thus the effectiveness of library help design. Those characteristics include: library familiarity, perceived competence, work avoidance, and task orientations (learning- vs. performance-oriented). There is a need to examine how user characteristics could affect perception of library help design, in order to create library help tailored to individual characteristics and needs.

2. METHOD
Thirty-six student participants (15 females and 21 males, mean age = 21.5 years and SD = 3.5 years) were recruited for a 30-minutes questionnaire survey about user characteristics and library help. Participants provided five-point Likert scale ratings for questions regarding familiarity of libraries, perceived competence, work avoidance, and task orientations. They ranked help design principles, formats of help documentation (e.g., index, videos, and screenshots), and tools available in help systems (e.g.,

search, top questions, and expert chat). Participants also answered open-ended questions regarding their experience, preferences, and expectations of library help.

3. RESULTS
3.1 Structural Equation Modeling
We developed a structural equation model between user characteristics and rankings of general help design principles, help formats and help tools. The modeling results showed significant relationships between user characteristics and rankings, including perceived competence and Design Principle #3 (help should be conceptual; regression coefficient b = 0.358), and library familiarity and screenshots (b = -0.377). We will present the complete modeling results in the poster.

3.2 Open-Ended Questions
Open-ended questions were coded into groups of responses and revealed aspects of user help seeking habits not fully explored in the SEM that are valuable for library help design. For example, 11% of respondents (n = 4) said they would still not use any help system even if the help is much improved, explaining they liked to experiment, never used help systems, or preferred in-person help.

4. DISCUSSION & CONCLUSION
The modeling and qualitative results provide empirical guidance for prioritizing help design principles, formats, and tools in library help implementation and evaluation for users with different help seeking characteristics and preferences. The user characteristics measured in this study could be useful for user segmentation and personas creation as part of user-centered design process for library help systems. The SEM methodology complemented by open-ended questions could be extended to similar efforts of linking user characteristics to help design.

5. REFERENCES
[1] Purchase, H.C. and Worrill, J. 2002. An empirical study of on-line help design: features and principles. *International Journal of Human-Computer Studies.* 56, 5, 539–566.

[2] Bartholomé, T. et al. 2006. What matters in help-seeking? A study of help effectiveness and learner-related factors. *Computers in Human Behavior.* 22, 1, 113–129.

SIGDOC'13, September 30–October 1, 2013, Greenville, North Carolina, USA.
ACM 978-1-4503-2131-0/13/09.
http://dx.doi.org/10.1145/2507065.2507093

Author Index

www.ingramcontent.com/pod-product-compliance
Lightning Source LLC
Chambersburg PA
CBHW061420210326
41598CB00035B/6279